SAINT AUGUSTINE

THE CITY OF GOD AGAINST THE PAGANS

III

BOOKS VIII—XI

THE LOEB CLASSICAL LIBRARY

FOUNDED BY JAMES LOEB

EDITED BY
T. E. PAGE, C.H., LITT.D.

PREVIOUS EDITORS
† E. CAPPS, PH.D., LL.D.   † W. H. D. ROUSE, LITT.D.
L. A. POST, L.H.D.   E. H. WARMINGTON, M.A., F.R.HIST.SOC.

SAINT AUGUSTINE

THE CITY OF GOD AGAINST THE PAGANS

III

BOOKS VIII–XI

SAINT AUGUSTINE

THE CITY OF GOD AGAINST THE PAGANS

IN SEVEN VOLUMES

III

BOOKS VIII–XI

WITH AN ENGLISH TRANSLATION BY

DAVID S. WIESEN

ASSOCIATE PROFESSOR OF CLASSICS
BRANDEIS UNIVERSITY

CAMBRIDGE, MASSACHUSETTS
HARVARD UNIVERSITY PRESS
LONDON
WILLIAM HEINEMANN LTD
MCMLXVIII

Printed in Great Britain

CONTENTS

INTRODUCTION

THE task of St. Augustine's life and work, it has been well said, was " to kindle the light of things eternal in human hearts no longer supported by temporal institutions which had seemed eternal but which were crashing on all sides." [1] The *City of God* was the central work by which Augustine hoped to turn men's eyes from a collapsing commonwealth to one built to last for ever. On this masterpiece Augustine spent thirteen years of his life, from 413 to 426.[2] However, at no time during this period could he hope to concentrate all his energies on the book which was to prove his greatest and most influential contribution to Christian thought. The Bishop of Hippo was primarily occupied during these years, of course, with the onerous duties arising directly from his episcopal office. These had to be performed at a time when the Donatist schismatics, although condemned by the imperial commissioner Marcellinus in 411, continued to rage over North Africa and when the Pelagian heresy was rending the Church. " The sea storms that rock the Church shake up its helmsman," remarks Augustine in his *Enarrationes in Psalmos*.[3] Small wonder that to Augustine the

[1] Marthinus Versfeld, *A Guide to the City of God* (London and New York 1958), p. 2.
[2] See vol. 1 of this series, pp. lxxviii–lxxxii.
[3] 106. 7.

term "episcopate" suggested labour, rather than honour.[1] In addition to his regular pastoral tasks, Augustine's literary activity was ceaseless; many of his exegetical, doctrinal and polemical works were begun, many others were completed in these years.[2] These varied undertakings and distractions prevented Augustine from ever devoting his single-minded attention to fulfilling the promise made to Count Marcellinus, "to defend the City of God against those who esteem their own gods above her Founder."[3] Lack of time and the immensity of the task itself, as well, perhaps, as an innate *amor flexuosarum viarum*, account for the confusing structure of the *City of God* and for many digressions, or seeming digressions, that have made the progress of St. Augustine's thought hard for readers to follow.

The four books of Augustine's masterpiece contained in this volume (Books 8–11) occupy a central place in the organization of the work as a whole. To show this, let us refer briefly to the author's own remarks on the basic plan that he followed as he wrote. Such remarks are to be found, if we exclude passing allusions, in three places: the *City of God* itself, the *Retractations*,[4] and in a letter written by

[1] *City of God* 19.19. Cf. *Letter* 48.1.
[2] See the convenient list of the works of Augustine and their dates of composition in Henri Marrou, *Saint Augustine and his Influence through the Ages*, "Men of Wisdom Series" (London and New York, no date), pp. 183–186.
[3] *City of God* Book 1, preface.
[4] *City of God* 1.35–36, 10.32 and 18.1. *Retractations* 2.43 [70]. For a list of other passages where the plan of the work is mentioned and for a detailed outline of the whole *City of*

Augustine to accompany a complete, revised copy
of the *City of God* that he sent to his friend, the
African priest Firmus. This letter is particularly
useful, since it outlines very briefly and clearly the
design of the whole monumental work. It was
discovered attached as a preface to two manuscripts
of the *City of God*, one of the twelfth or thirteenth
century and one of the fourteenth, and has been
published by C. Lambot in the *Revue Bénédictine*,
Volume 51, 1939.[1] Augustine here gives instruc-
tions for distributing the twenty-two books of the
City of God into smaller groups, since, as he recognizes, they are too bulky to be bound together under
one cover. If a division into two volumes is wanted
the break should occur at the end of Book 10, where
it naturally belongs, for it is at this point, says
Augustine, that he has finished his attack on the
vain opinions of godless men and turns now to the
defence and demonstration of the true religion. But
if a division into smaller units is preferred, he continues, the twenty-two books should be arranged in
five codices as follows: Books 1–5 (against those who
argue that the worship of gods and demons contributes to the felicity of this life); Books 6–10 (against
those who support polytheism for the sake of the life

God, see R. J. Deferrari and M. J. Keeler, "St. Augustine's
City of God: Its Plan and Development," *American Journal of
Philology*, 50 (1929), 109–137. See also J.-C. Guy, *Unité et
structure logique de la "Cité de Dieu*," (Paris, 1961).

[1] Pp. 109–121. Dom Lambot suggests, p. 118, that Firmus
himself was the first to attach the letter, because of its use-
fulness, to the manuscript of the *City of God*. From this copy,
then, the earlier of the two manuscripts in which the letter was
found may have descended.

to come); Books 11–14 (the origin of the City of God); Books 15–18 (its progress and development); Books 19–22 (its appointed ends).

We see, then, that the four books included in the present volume span the two divisions of the *City of God*, forming a transition from the destructive first part, directed against the earthly city, to the second, more important, constructive part that describes the divine plan of salvation. Furthermore, Books 8–10 not only complete Augustine's reply to the enemies of the City of God but mark an important turning-point in his whole argument as well, for hitherto his opponents have fallen rather easily. Augustine must now face his most formidable adversaries, the pagan thinkers who stand highest in reputation, the Platonic philosophers. In Book 1 (Chapter 36) Augustine refers forward to the questions that are to be treated in Books 8–10 [1] and declares that these will furnish much more difficult matter for discussion and more deserving of closer-knit argumentation than the problems handled up to that point, inasmuch as he will then be holding discussion with philosophers— and not with just any philosophers, but with such as are most renowned among the pagans, and who, indeed, agree with the Christians on many points. Books 8–10, then, complete the refutations of the pagan philosophers, and Augustine passes on in Book 11 to the construction of a Christian philosophy, beginning with an account of the differences that

---

[1] Augustine appears at first to be referring here to the subject-matter of Books 6–10. However, the mention of the most renowned philosophers suggests that his remarks apply in fact only to the material that he later treated in Books 8–10.

brought about the original separation of the heavenly
and earthly cities.

The present translation is based, as are the other
volumes in this series embracing St. Augustine's *City
of God*, on the fourth edition of B. Dombart's Teubner
text, revised by A. Kalb, 1928–29. The punctuation
and division into paragraphs have been changed
throughout to conform to current English usage.
Manuscript variants of special importance are noted
in the apparatus. In rendering biblical quotations
into English, the Revised Standard Version is followed, in so far as the Latin text that Augustine
had before him allows this.

The work on the present volume was originally
undertaken by Professor Robert J. Getty of the
University of North Carolina. Professor Getty had
completed a first draft of Books 8–11 before the
burden of his many other duties forced him to pass
his manuscript into other hands. The present
translator profited greatly from his labour and learning and acknowledges with much appreciation the
valuable assistance provided by his manuscript.
Professor Getty stipulated that his name should not
appear on the title-page.

Although this version is throughout based directly
on the Latin, other renderings into English and
French have been consulted for the clarification of
difficult points. The best previous English translation of the *City of God* is that of Marcus Dods, assisted
by G. Wilson and J. J. Smith, published originally in
1872 and now reprinted in the Modern Library (New
York, 1950). Another translation that proved useful is that of D. B. Zema, G. G. Walsh, G. Monahan,

and D. J. Honan printed in the series "Fathers of the Church", volumes 8, 14, and 24 (New York, 1950–54). Especially excellent and helpful was the French version of G. Combès, with introduction and notes by G. Bardy, in "Bibliothèque Augustinienne, Œuvres de Saint Augustin", 5ᵉ série, volumes 33–37 (Paris–Bruges 1959–60), which is notable for the lucidity of its language and the erudition of its notes.

The notes in the present volume attempt only to ease the reader's journey over some particularly rough spots. The translator is indebted from time to time to the commentary of J. E. C. Welldon (London, 1924), but every student of Saint Augustine must feel the great need for a full theological and philological commentary on the *City of God*. Meanwhile let us approach this vast, rich, and complex work with the attitude expressed by the words of St. Augustine, *Sic ergo quaeramus tamquam inventuri, et sic inveniamus tamquam quaesituri*, " Let us search, then, with the assurance of finding, and let us find with the assurance of continuing the search." ¹

---

¹ *De Trinitate* 9.1 (1).

SAINT AUGUSTINE

THE CITY OF GOD AGAINST THE PAGANS

S. AURELII AUGUSTINI

DE CIVITATE DEI CONTRA PAGANOS

LIBER VIII

I

De quaestione naturalis theologiae cum philosophis
excellentioris scientiae discutienda.

Nunc intentiore nobis opus est animo multo quam
erat in superiorum solutione quaestionum et ex-
plicatione librorum. De theologia quippe quam
naturalem vocant non cum quibuslibet hominibus
—non enim fabulosa est vel civilis, hoc est vel
theatrica vel urbana; quarum altera iactitat deorum
crimina, altera indicat deorum desideria criminosiora
ac per hoc malignorum potius daemonum quam
deorum—sed cum philosophis est habenda conlatio;
quorum ipsum nomen si Latine interpretemur,
amorem sapientiae profitetur.

Porro si sapientia Deus est, per quem facta sunt
omnia, sicut divina auctoritas veritasque monstravit,

---

[1] Cf. below, Chapter II and Cicero, *De Oratore* 1.49.212,
Tusc. Disp. 5.3.8–9.

[2] Wisdom 7.24–27.

SAINT AURELIUS AUGUSTINE

THE CITY OF GOD AGAINST THE PAGANS

BOOK VIII

I

*On the necessity of discussing the question of natural
theology with those philosophers whose knowledge is
superior.*

AT this point we must make a far greater mental
effort than was involved in solving and explaining the
questions raised in our earlier books. Natural
theology, so-called, of course should not be discussed
with the man in the street, for it is not concerned
either with mythology or with politics. In other
words it belongs neither to the theatre nor to the
city, for the one parades the crimes of the gods, while
the other reveals the even greater criminality of their
desires and so exposes them as malevolent demons
rather than gods. Instead we must hold a conference
about it with the philosophers, whose very name,
when interpreted in our own language, proclaims
their love of wisdom.[1]

Furthermore if God, the maker of all things, is
wisdom, as Divine Authority and Truth have shown,[2]

verus philosophus est amator Dei. Sed quia res ipsa cuius hoc nomen est non est in omnibus qui hoc nomine gloriantur—neque enim continuo verae sapientiae sunt amatores quicumque appellantur philosophi—profecto ex omnibus quorum sententias litteris nosse potuimus eligendi sunt cum quibus non indigne quaestio ista tractetur. Neque enim hoc opere omnes omnium philosophorum vanas opiniones refutare suscepi, sed eas tantum quae ad theologian pertinent, quo verbo Graeco significari intellegimus de divinitate rationem sive sermonem; nec eas omnium, sed eorum tantum qui cum et esse divintatem et humana curare consentiant, non tamen sufficere unius incommutabilis Dei cultum ad vitam adipiscendam etiam post mortem beatam, sed multos ab illo sane uno conditos atque institutos ob eam causam colendos putant.

Hi iam etiam Varronis opinionem veritatis propinquitate transcendunt; si quidem ille totam theologian naturalem usque ad mundum istum vel animam eius extendere potuit, isti vero supra omnem animae naturam confitentur Deum, qui non solum mundum istum visibilem, qui saepe caeli et terrae nomine nuncupatur, sed etiam omnem omnino animam fecerit, et qui rationalem et intellectualem, cuius generis anima humana est, participatione sui luminis incommutabilis et incorporei beatam facit. Hos philosophos Platonicos appellatos a Platone

---

[1] See *City of God*, 7.6.

the true philosopher is one who loves God. But philosophy in the real sense of the word does not always exist in those who boast of it, for those who are called philosophers are not necessarily lovers of true wisdom. Assuredly, then, we must select, from all those whose recorded opinions we have been able to ascertain, exponents with whom this question may appropriately be argued. I have certainly not undertaken in this work to rebut all the futile tenets of every one of the philosophers, but only those opinions that concern theology, a Greek word which we understand to mean thought or speech explaining the divine essence, nor even those in the case of all philosophers. I consider only such thinkers as, though they agree with us that the divine exists and takes an interest in the affairs of men, yet do not believe it sufficient to worship one unchangeable God in order to secure a life of bliss even after death, but hold that, to attain this end, we must worship a number of deities whose creation and establishment are due to that one true God.

These philosophers attain a higher degree of truth even than Varro, inasmuch as he was able to extend the entire scope of natural theology only to the aforesaid universe or the soul that animates it,[1] while they admit that, transcending all animate nature, there is a God who made not only this visible universe which is often called heaven and earth, but also every living soul whatever, and who blesses such as are rational and intellectual—and the human soul is in this class—by giving them a share of his own immutable and incorporeal light. Everybody with even meagre information about such subjects knows of

doctore vocabulo derivato nullus qui haec vel tenuiter audivit ignorat. De hoc igitur Platone quae necessaria praesenti quaestioni existimo breviter adtingam, prius illos commemorans qui eum in eodem genere litterarum tempore praecesserunt.

II

De duobus philosophorum generibus, id est Italico et Ionico, eorumque auctoribus.

QUANTUM enim adtinet ad litteras Graecas, quae lingua inter ceteras gentium clarior habetur, duo philosophorum genera traduntur: unum Italicum ex ea parte Italiae quae quondam magna Graecia nuncupata est, alterum Ionicum in eis terris ubi et nunc Graecia nominatur. Italicum genus auctorem habuit Pythagoram Samium, a quo etiam ferunt ipsum philosophiae nomen exortum. Nam cum antea sapientes appellarentur qui modo quodam laudabilis vitae aliis praestare videbantur, iste interrogatus quid profiteretur, philosophum se esse respondit, id est studiosum vel amatorem sapientiae; quoniam sapientem profiteri arrogantissimum videbatur.

Ionici vero generis princeps fuit Thales Milesius, unus illorum septem qui sunt appellati sapientes. Sed illi sex vitae genere distinguebantur et quibusdam praeceptis ad bene vivendum accommodatis;

---

[1] See Cicero, *Tusc. Disp.* 5.3.8–9.

these philosophers, who were called Platonists, the name being derived from their master Plato. With respect to Plato, then, I shall briefly touch upon the points I consider essential for the question before us, first mentioning those who preceded him chronologically in the same branch of letters.

II

Of the two schools of philosophy, the Italian and the Ionian, and their founders

In connection with the literature of the Greeks, whose language is held in higher esteem than any other in the gentile world, there are two traditional schools of philosophy. One, the Italian, originated in that part of Italy which was formerly called Magna Graecia; and the other, the Ionian, flourished in the lands where the name " Greece " still holds good. The Italian school considered its founder to be Pythagoras of Samos, who, they also say, originally gave philosophy its name. Before his day those who appeared to be pre-eminent among their fellows for their praiseworthy mode of life were called " wise men." When Pythagoras was asked what his profession was, he replied that he was a philosopher, that is to say a seeker after or lover of wisdom; for he thought it the height of presumption to claim that he was a wise man.[1]

The Ionian school, however, began with Thales of Miletus, one of the so-called Seven Sages. The remaining six were distinguished for their manner of life and the enunciation of certain principles which

iste autem Thales ut successores etiam propagaret rerum naturam scrutatus suasque disputationes litteris mandans eminuit maximeque admirabilis extitit quod astrologiae numeris conprehensis defectus solis et lunae etiam praedicere potuit. Aquam tamen putavit rerum esse principium et hinc omnia elementa mundi ipsumque mundum et quae in eo gignuntur existere. Nihil autem huic operi, quod mundo considerato tam mirabile aspicimus, ex divina mente praeposuit.

Huic successit Anaximander eius auditor mutavitque de rerum natura opinionem. Non enim ex una re, sicut Thales ex umore, sed ex suis propriis principiis quasque res nasci putavit. Quae rerum principia singularum esse credidit infinita, et innumerabiles mundos gignere et quaecumque in eis oriuntur; eosque mundos modo dissolvi, modo iterum gigni existimavit, quanta quisque aetate sua manere potuerit; nec ipse aliquid divinae menti in his rerum operibus tribuens. Iste Anaximenen discipulum et successorem reliquit, qui omnes rerum causas aeri infinito dedit, nec deos negavit aut tacuit; non tamen ab ipsis aerem factum, sed ipsos ex aere ortos credidit.

---

[1] Augustine seems to be confused here, for Anaximander taught that the origin of all things was τὸ ἄπειρον, the Infinite or Non-Limited, from which the four substances, Hot and Cold, Wet and Dry, were derived and paired off as opposites. Anaxagoras (see below) appears to have held that all things have their origin in infinitely small particles or 'seeds' (σπέρματα or, as Aristotle called them, ὁμοιομερῆ).

were designed to promote a good life. Thales, on the other hand, investigated the nature of things and, in order to establish a school that would survive him, recorded his findings in works which made him famous. His most wonderful achievement lay in his ability to foretell solar and lunar eclipses through his grasp of astronomical calculation. He did hold, however, that water is the primary substance and that from it originate all the elements of the universe, the universe itself, and everything that comes into being therein. Yet he set over this great work, the universe which seems so marvellous when we contemplate it, no regulation by divine intelligence.

Anaximander, who was his pupil, succeeded him, but held a different view about nature. He did not postulate any single original substance, as Thales did in choosing moisture, but thought that individual substances are engendered in each case by their own proper primordial elements. He believed in an infinite number of these primordial elements for each kind of substance,[1] and held that they bring into being countless universes along with whatever is produced in them. These universes, he thought, are subjected continually to alternate dissolution and regeneration, with as long a period of existence as is possible in each case. He likewise granted no rôle in these workings of nature to a divine intelligence. Anaximander was succeeded by his disciple Anaximenes, who ascribed the origin of everything to infinite air. He did not deny the existence of the gods or ignore the question, but he believed that they were not the creators of air, but were themselves derived from air.

Anaxagoras vero eius auditor harum rerum omnium quas videmus effectorem divinum animum sensit et dixit ex infinita materia, quae constaret similibus inter se particulis rerum omnium; quibus suis et propriis singula fieri, sed animo faciente divino. Diogenes quoque Anaximenis alter auditor aerem quidem dixit rerum esse materiam de qua omnia fierent; sed eum esse compotem divinae rationis, sine qua nihil ex eo fieri posset. Anaxagorae successit auditor eius Archelaus. Etiam ipse de particulis inter se similibus, quibus singula quaeque fierent, ita putavit constare omnia ut inesse etiam mentem diceret, quae corpora aeterna, id est illas particulas, coniungendo et dissipando ageret omnia. Socrates huius discipulus fuisse perhibetur, magister Platonis propter quem breviter cuncta ista recolui.[1]

III

De Socratica disciplina.

SOCRATES ergo primus universam philosophiam ad corrigendos componendosque mores flexisse memoratur, cum ante illum omnes magis physicis, id est naturalibus, rebus perscrutandis operam maximam inpenderent. Non mihi autem videtur posse ad

---

[1] Augustine here agrees with the statement of Cicero, *Academics* 2.37.118. But some scholars wish to emend Augustine's text because in the philosophy of Anaxagoras the elements of the universe are infinitely various rather than " similar to one another." Yet Augustine is here emphasizing not the original variety of the particles but rather the action of divine mind in bringing together similar particles to form the separate substances of the world. See J. S. Reid in *Harv. Stud. Class. Phil.* 22 (1911), 13–14.

However, his pupil Anaxagoras adopted the view
and stated that everything we see is the work of a
divine mind using infinite matter, which consists of
particles, similar to one another, of every substance.[1]
According to him, each substance is made out of its
own kind of particles, but a divine mind is the maker.
Diogenes, who was another pupil of Anaximenes, also
declared that air is indeed the primary substance
from which all things are made, but adds that it partakes of divine reason, without which nothing can be
produced from it. Anaxagoras was succeeded by his
pupil Archelaüs. He too held that everything is
composed of similar particles out of which each
individual substance is made, but he qualified his
theory by saying that there is an indwelling mind
which brings everything to pass by combining and
dispersing eternal bodies, namely the aforesaid particles. Socrates is said to have been the disciple of
Archaelaüs. He was the teacher of Plato, on whose
account I have given a brief summary of all these
details.

III

On the teaching of Socrates.

SOCRATES, then, is remembered as having been the
first to divert the whole of philosophy towards the
improvement and regulation of morals,[2] when all
his predecessors preferred to devote their efforts
mainly to research in ' physical ' or natural science.
But I do not think that we can clearly decide whether

[2] Cf. Cicero, *Tusc. Disp.* 5.4.10.

liquidum colligi utrum Socrates, ut hoc faceret,
taedio rerum obscurarum et incertarum ad aliquid
apertum et certum reperiendum animum intenderit
quod esset beatae vitae necessarium, propter quam
unam omnium philosophorum invigilasse ac laborasse videtur industria, an vero, sicut de illo quidam
benevolentius suspicantur, nolebat inmundos terrenis
cupiditatibus animos se extendere in divina conari.
Quando quidem ab eis causas rerum videbat inquiri,
quas primas atque summas non nisi in unius ac summi Dei voluntate esse credebat; unde non eas putabat nisi mundata mente posse conprehendi; et ideo
purgandae bonis moribus vitae censebat instandum,
ut deprimentibus libidinibus exoneratus animus
naturali vigore in aeterna se adtolleret naturamque
incorporei et incommutabilis luminis, ubi causae omnium factarum naturarum stabiliter vivunt, intellegentiae puritate conspiceret.

Constat eum tamen inperitorum stultitiam scire se
aliquid opinantium etiam in ipsis moralibus quaestionibus quo totum animum intendisse videbatur
vel confessa ignorantia sua vel dissimulata scientia
lepore mirabili disserendi et acutissima urbanitate
agitasse atque versasse. Unde et concitatis inimi-
citiis calumniosa criminatione damnatus morte mul-
tatus est. Sed eum postea illa ipsa quae publice

Socrates was led to this course because he became impatient with problems to which no clear and definite answer can be found, and so applied his mind to discovering something plain and definite that was essential to a happy life, which appears to have been the sole object of the sleepless and laborious efforts of all philosophers. Or, as some more generously surmise about him, perhaps he was unwilling to see minds contaminated by earthly desires attempting to reach the level of the divine. For he observed them inquiring into the causes of things, but he believed that the first and highest causes lie solely within the will of the one and supreme God. Hence he thought that they could not be comprehended, save by a mind that has been cleansed; and therefore he held that men ought to devote their efforts to the purification of life by sound morals, so that the mind, thus freed from the oppressive weight of lower appetites, might rise by its natural impulse to the realm of eternal things and behold with unmixed intelligence the essence of incorporeal and unchangeable light, in which the causes of all created things have their firm abode.

At any rate it is certain that he used to mock and assail the folly of the uninstructed who thought that they possessed some knowledge, even in those very moral questions to which it was apparent he had devoted his whole mind. His practice was either to confess his ignorance or to conceal his knowledge, employing a marvellous grace of discourse and a most refined wit. In fact this is how it came that he stirred up enemies, was condemned on a false charge and incurred the death penalty. Some time after-

damnaverat Atheniensium civitas publice luxit, in duos accusatores eius usque adeo populi indignatione conversa ut unus eorum oppressus vi multitudinis interiret, exilio autem voluntario atque perpetuo poenam similem alter evaderet.

Tam praeclara igitur vitae mortisque fama Socrates reliquit plurimos suae philosophiae sectatores, quorum certatim studium fuit in quaestionum moralium disceptatione versari, ubi agitur de summo bono, quo fieri homo beatus potest. Quod in Socratis disputationibus, dum omnia movet asserit destruit, quoniam non evidenter apparuit, quod cuique placuit inde sumpserunt et ubi cuique visum est constituerunt finem boni. Finis autem boni appellatur quo quisque cum pervenerit beatus est. Sic autem diversas inter se Socratici de isto fine sententias habuerunt ut—quod vix credibile est unius magistri potuisse facere sectatores—quidam summum bonum esse dicerent voluptatem, sicut Aristippus; quidam virtutem, sicut Antisthenes. Sic alii atque alii aliud atque aliud opinati sunt, quos commemorare longum est.

---

[1] Such tales of a reaction in favour of Socrates, recorded also by Diodorus Siculus 14.37 and Diogenes Laertius 2.43, are poorly attested and in themselves unlikely. Good evidence suggests rather that Socrates' memory was long unpopular at Athens.

wards, however, that same city of Athens which had officially condemned him actually went into official mourning for him; and public indignation turned against his two prosecutors to such a degree that one of them was set upon and killed by the violence of the multitude, while the other escaped a similar fate only by going voluntarily into permanent exile.[1]

The story of his life and death accordingly made so strong an impression that he left behind him large numbers who adhered to his philosophy. These vied with one another in arguing about moral questions, where the problem debated is the highest good by virtue of which men are made happy. This supreme good was not clearly defined in the discussions of Socrates, for he was in the habit of starting every possible argument and maintaining or demolishing all possible positions. So each of his followers took one of his positions dogmatically and set up his own standard of the good wherever he thought best. Now the term " standard of the good " means the goal at which a man must arrive in order to be happy. But so contradictory were the opinions maintained among the Socratics about this goal that, incredible as it seems for adherents of a single master, some, such as Aristippus, asserted that pleasure is the supreme good, while others, such as Antisthenes, said that it is virtue. Thus there was a wide variety among the views held, and it would be tedious to report them all.

IV

*De praecipuo inter Socratis discipulos Platone, qui
omnem philosophiam triplici partitione
distinxit.*

SED inter discipulos Socratis, non quidem inmerito,
excellentissima gloria claruit qua omnino ceteros
obscuraret Plato.

Qui cum esset Atheniensis honesto apud suos loco
natus et ingenio mirabili longe suos condiscipulos
anteiret, parum tamen putans perficiendae philosophiae sufficere se ipsum ac Socraticam disciplinam,
quam longe ac late potuit peregrinatus est, quaqua-
versum eum alicuius nobilitatae scientiae percipiendae fama rapiebat. Itaque et in Aegypto didicit
quaecumque magna illic habebantur atque doce-
bantur, et inde in eas Italiae partes veniens ubi
Pythagoreorum fama celebrabatur, quidquid Italicae
philosophiae tunc florebat, auditis eminentioribus in
ea doctoribus facillime conprehendit. Et quia
magistrum Socratem singulariter diligebat, eum
loquentem faciens fere in omnibus sermonibus suis
etiam illa quae vel ab aliis didicerat, vel ipse quanta
potuerat intellegentia viderat cum illius lepore et
moralibus disputationibus temperavit.

Itaque cum studium sapientiae in actione et contemplatione versetur, unde una pars eius activa,

IV

On Plato, the most important disciple of Socrates, and his threefold division of the whole of philosophy.

But among the disciples of Socrates, the one who certainly achieved—and indeed deserved—such a brilliant reputation that he completely eclipsed all the others, was Plato.

He was an Athenian, born in a good station of society; and he far surpassed his fellow-students by his amazing powers of intellect. But believing that, if he was to complete his study of philosophy, his own understanding and the training of Socrates were not enough, he travelled as far and wide as he could, whithersoever rumour of loftier knowledge to be attained transported him. In this way he learned in Egypt too whatever theories were held important and were taught there. From Egypt he came to the district of Italy where the Pythagoreans enjoyed a great reputation, and grasped with the greatest ease any Italian philosophy then in vogue, when he had heard the teaching of its more distinguished exponents. And because he was uniquely devoted to his master Socrates, he made him a participant in practically all his dialogues. Thus he blended his instruction, whether it was something learned from others or what he had seen for himself through using the full power of his own understanding, with the charming style and interest in moral discussions that belonged to Socrates.

Now the pursuit of wisdom is concerned both with action and with speculation, so that it can be divided

altera contemplativa dici potest—quarum activa ad
agendam vitam, id est ad mores instituendos pertinet, contemplativa autem ad conspiciendas naturae
causas et sincerissimam veritatem—, Socrates in activa
excelluisse memoratur; Pythagoras vero magis
contemplativae quibus potuit intellegentiae viribus institisse. Proinde Plato utrumque iungendo
philosophiam perfecisse laudatur, quam in tres partes
distribuit: unam moralem, quae maxime in actione
versatur; alteram naturalem, quae contemplationi
deputata est; tertiam rationalem, qua verum dister-
minatur a falso. Quae licet utrique, id est actioni et
contemplationi, sit necessaria, maxime tamen con-
templatio perspectionem sibi vindicat veritatis.
Ideo haec tripertitio non est contraria illi distinctioni
qua intellegitur omne studium sapientiae in actione
et contemplatione consistere.

Quid autem in his vel de his singulis partibus
Plato senserit, id est, ubi finem omnium actionum,
ubi causam omnium naturarum, ubi lumen omnium
rationum esse cognoverit vel crediderit, disserendo
explicare et longum esse arbitror et temere adfirman-
dum esse non arbitror. Cum enim magistri sui
Socratis, quem facit in suis voluminibus disputantem,
notissimum morem dissimulandae scientiae vel
opinionis suae servare adfectat, quia et illi ipse mos

into two branches, one being called *practical* and the other *theoretical*. The first is concerned with the conduct of life, that is to say with the shaping of morals; the second with the discovery of natural principles and truth in its purest form. Socrates is said to have excelled in the former, while Pythagoras on the other hand bent all his intellectual strength rather to the theoretical side. Hence Plato is extolled because he united the two branches and so perfected philosophy, which he divided into three parts: *moral*, which is chiefly concerned with practice; *natural*, which is devoted to theory; and *logical*, which distinguishes truth from falsehood.[1] This last is of course indispensable for both practice and theory, but it is theoretical philosophy that especially claims as its object insight into truth. So this threefold division does not upset the previous classification, which gives us to understand that the pursuit of wisdom in the widest sense is made up of practice and theory.

However, I consider it too tedious to expound in detail what conclusion Plato reached within or concerning each of these fields of study, or, in other words, what he discovered or believed to be the goal of all actions, the cause of all natural objects and the light of every act of reason; nor do I consider it right to make statements that may be rash. For Plato makes a point of perpetuating the notorious habit of his master Socrates, whom he represents in his books as leading the discussions but concealing any knowledge or any opinion of his own; and because he too chose to adopt this same habit, the

[1] Cf. Cicero, *Academics* 1.5.19–21.

placuit, factum est ut etiam ipsius Platonis de rebus magnis sententiae non facile perspici possint.

Ex his tamen quae apud eum leguntur, sive quae dixit, sive quae ab aliis dicta esse narravit atque conscripsit, quae sibi placita viderentur, quaedam commemorari et operi huic inseri oportet a nobis, vel ubi suffragatur religioni verae, quam fides nostra suscepit ac defendit, vel ubi ei videtur esse contrarius, quantum ad istam de uno Deo et pluribus pertinet quaestionem, propter vitam quae post mortem futura est veraciter beatam. Fortassis enim qui Platonem ceteris philosophis gentium longe recteque praelatum acutius atque veracius intellexisse ac secuti esse fama celebriore laudantur, aliquid tale de Deo sentiunt ut in illo inveniatur et causa subsistendi et ratio intellegendi et ordo vivendi; quorum trium unum ad naturalem, alterum ad rationalem, tertium ad moralem partem intellegitur pertinere. Si enim homo ita creatus est ut per id quod in eo praecellit adtingat illud quod cuncta praecellit, id est unum verum optimum Deum, sine quo nulla natura subsistit, nulla doctrina instruit, nullus usus expedit, ipse quaeratur ubi nobis serta[1] sunt omnia, ipse cernatur ubi nobis certa sunt omnia, ipse diligatur ubi nobis recta sunt omnia.

---

[1] serta *some MSS:* certa *corrected to* diserta *codex Corbeiensis (saec. VII):* secura *some MSS. and Migne:* seria *Dombart[3] and Hoffmann:* sita *one MS. and Welldon.*

result is that Plato's own views on important subjects are also far from easy to decipher.

At the same time, I ought to note and record in this work certain tenets that appear in his writings, either pronounced by himself or recounted and written down by him as having been expressed by others and presumably approved by him. I shall do so, whether he supports the true religion which is adopted and vindicated by our faith, or appears to be opposed to it, as in the question whether there is one God or many and how this is related to the true happiness which we expect from life after death. Perhaps indeed those who with good reason prefer Plato greatly to other pagan philosophers and possess a higher reputation for more than ordinary subtlety and comprehension of the truth in following his teaching, have a theory of God which would discover in him the cause of physical existence, the ground of rational thought, and the pattern of life. Of these three, the first is assumed to belong to the natural, the second to the logical and the third to the moral subdivision of philosophy. Man has been so created that, through what is excellent in him, he attains what transcends all else, namely the one true and supremely good God, without whom nothing in nature exists, no doctrine instructs and no employment is profitable. And so let him alone be sought in whom we find all reality interwoven, let our eyes be on him alone who has the certainty of all things for us, let him alone be loved in whom all things for us are right.

V

Quod de theologia cum Platonicis potissimum dis-
ceptandum sit, quorum opinioni omnium philoso-
phorum postponenda sint dogmata.

SI ergo Plato Dei huius imitatorem cognitorem
amatorem dixit esse sapientem, cuius participatione
sit beatus, quid opus est excutere ceteros? Nulli
nobis quam isti propius accesserunt.

Cedat eis igitur non solum theologia illa fabulosa
deorum criminibus oblectans animos impiorum, nec
solum etiam illa civilis ubi inpuri daemones terrestribus gaudiis deditos populos deorum nomine
seducentes humanos errores tamquam suos divinos
honores habere voluerunt, ad spectandos suorum
criminum ludos cultores suos tamquam ad suum
cultum studiis inmundissimis excitantes et sibi
delectabiliores ludos de ipsis spectatoribus exhibentes—ubi si qua velut honesta geruntur in templis,
coniuncta sibi theatrorum obscenitate turpantur, et
quaecumque turpia geruntur in theatris, comparata
sibi templorum foeditate laudantur—, et ea quae
Varro ex his sacris quasi ad caelum et terram rerum-
que mortalium semina et actus interpretatus est
—quia nec ipsa illis ritibus significantur quae ipse

---

[1] For this view, see also Minucius Felix, *Octavius* 19.14–15
and Augustine, *De Vera Religione* 4.7.

V

That theology must be discussed above all with the Platonists, for their opinion is preferable to the creeds of all other philosophers.

IF Plato, therefore, has declared that the wise man imitates, knows and loves this God and is blessed through fellowship with him, why should we have to examine other philosophers? No school has come closer to us than the Platonists.[1]

Let them triumph then not only over the mythical theology, which delights the minds of the irreligious by showing them the crimes of the gods, nor only over political theology, in which foul demons under the name of gods lead astray communities that are devoted to earthly delights, and have chosen to appropriate men's errors as gods' honours. By exciting the filthiest appetites in their worshippers, they stimulate them to be spectators at stage shows in which their own crimes are enacted, while the same spectators provide even better entertainment as a spectacle for the demons. Any ostensibly honourable ceremonies which are performed in the temples are defiled by the addition of obscene shows in the theatres; and, no matter what disgraceful performances are enacted in the theatres, they are commended in comparison with the abominations in the temples. Let the Platonists triumph also over Varro's interpretations in which he explained these rites with reference to heaven and earth, and to the seeds and operations of perishable things. For one thing the rites do not have the hidden meaning that

23

insinuare conatur, et ideo veritas conantem non
sequitur; et si ipsa essent, tamen animae rationali ea
quae infra illam naturae ordine constituta sunt, pro
deo suo colenda non essent, nec sibi debuit praeferre
tamquam deos eas res quibus ipsam praetulit verus
Deus—, et ea quae Numa Pompilius re vera ad sacra
eius modi pertinentia secum sepeliendo curavit
abscondi et aratro eruta senatus iussit incendi.

In eo genere sunt etiam illa, ut aliquid de Numa
mitius suspicemur, quae Alexander Macedo scribit
ad matrem sibi a magno antistite sacrorum Aegyptiorum quodam Leone patefacta, ubi non Picus et
Faunus et Aeneas et Romulus vel etiam Hercules et
Aesculapius et Liber Semela natus et Tyndaridae
fratres et si quos alios ex mortalibus pro diis habent,
sed ipsi etiam maiorum gentium dii, quos Cicero in
Tusculanis tacitis nominibus videtur adtingere,
Iuppiter, Iuno, Saturnus, Vulcanus, Vesta et alii
plurimi, quos Varro conatur ad mundi partes sive
elementa transferre, homines fuisse produntur.
Timens enim et ille quasi revelata mysteria petens
admonet Alexandrum ut, cum ea matri conscripta
insinuaverit, flammis iubeat concremari.

Non solum ergo ista quae duae theologiae fabulosa

---

[1] See *City of God*, 7.34.

[2] See below, Book 8.27 and Book 12.11. Also Plutarch,
Alexander 27.5; Cyprian, *De Idol. Vanit.* 3; Minucius Felix,
Octavius 21.3. This apocryphal letter of Alexander the
Great to his mother Olympias was really the composition of
Leon of Pella, who lived at the end of the fourth and beginning
of the third century BC. Leon is confused by Augustine with
the Egyptian priest who was supposed to have informed
Alexander about the history of the gods of Egypt and told
him that they were originally kings.

he suggests, so that truth does not give her sanction to his attempt. Nor even if the rites had this significance, should the rational soul worship as its god things which in the pattern of nature are subordinated to it, nor ought it to exalt as gods the very things over which the true God has exalted it. The same must be said of the writings that surely concerned ceremonies of this kind, writings which Numa Pompilius took pains to conceal when he had them buried along with himself, and which when unearthed by a plough were burned by order of the Senate.[1]

We may regard Numa somewhat more charitably, since in this same class of writings belongs a letter of Alexander of Macedon to his mother reporting what a certain Egyptian high priest called Leo divulged to him.[2] In it, apart from Picus, Faunus, Aeneas and Romulus, or, for that matter, Hercules, Aesculapius, Liber the son of Semele, the twin sons of Tyndareus and any other mortals who have been deified, even the gods of higher lineage, to whom Cicero in his *Tusculans* [3] seems to allude without mentioning their names, Jupiter, Juno, Saturn, Vulcan, Vesta and many others, whom Varro attempts to interpret figuratively as the parts or elements of the universe, are exposed as having been men. Fearful, like Numa, of any revelation of the mysteries, the priest begged and urged Alexander, when he had put in writing and imparted this secret to his mother, to order that the letter be consigned to the flames.

Thus not only the doctrines of both theologies,

[3] Cicero, *Tusc. Disp.* 1.13.29.

continet et civilis Platonicis philosophis cedant, qui
verum Deum et rerum auctorem et veritatis inlustra-
torem et beatitudinis largitorem esse dixerunt; sed
alii quoque philosophi, qui corporalia naturae principia corpori deditis mentibus opinati sunt, cedant
his tantis et tanti Dei cognitoribus viris, ut Thales in
umore, Anaximenes in aere, Stoici in igne, Epicurus
in atomis, hoc est minutissimis corpusculis quae nec
dividi nec sentiri queunt, et quicumque alii, quorum
enumeratione inmorari non est necesse, sive simplicia sive coniuncta corpora, sive vita carentia sive
viventia, sed tamen corpora, causam principiumque
rerum esse dixerunt. Nam quidam eorum a rebus
non vivis res vivas fieri posse crediderunt, sicut
Epicurei; quidam vero a vivente quidem et viventia
et non viventia, sed tamen a corpore corpora. Nam
Stoici ignem, id est corpus unum ex his quattuor
elementis quibus visibilis mundus hic constat et
viventem et sapientem et ipsius mundi fabricatorem
atque omnium quae in eo sunt, eumque omnino
ignem deum esse putaverunt.

Hi et ceteri similes eorum id solum cogitare
potuerunt, quod cum eis corda eorum obstricta
carnis sensibus fabulata sunt. In se quippe habe-
bant quod non videbant, et apud se imaginabantur
quod foris viderant, etiam quando non videbant sed
tantummodo cogitabant. Hoc autem in conspectu

26

mythical and political alike, must give way to the
philosophy of the Platonists, for they have said
that the true God is the author of all things, the
illuminator of truth, and the bestower of happiness,
but so must the other philosophers too who have
adopted a belief in the material elements of nature
because their own minds are subservient to the body
give way to these great men who recognize so great
a God. Such were Thales with his moisture, Anaximenes with his air, the Stoics with their fire, Epicurus
with his atoms, that is, very minute bodies which are
indivisible and imperceptible, and any others that
there are whom we need not stop to enumerate,
whether they named bodies simple or compound,
animate or inanimate, as the cause and primary substance of everything, as long as they named bodies.
For some of them, like the Epicureans, have believed
that living things could originate from things without
life, while others have held that both living and life-
less objects come from what is living, yet still that
these are bodies produced from bodily matter. For
instance, the Stoics have held that fire, one of the
four material elements of which the visible universe
is composed, is endowed with life and wisdom and is
the creator both of the universe and of everything
within it, and that such fire is in the fullest sense god.

They and the others like them have not been able
to imagine anything more than the fabrications of
their own wit, confined as it is in the bonds of their
fleshly senses. Note that they had within themselves what they did not see, and they pictured inwardly what they had seen externally, even when
they did not see it but only had it in their mind.

talis cogitationis iam non est corpus, sed similitudo
corporis; illud autem unde videtur in animo haec
similitudo corporis, nec corpus est nec similitudo
corporis; et unde videtur atque utrum pulchra an
deformis sit iudicatur, profecto est melius quam
ipsa quae iudicatur.   Haec mens hominis et rationalis
animae natura est, quae utique corpus non est, si
iam illa corporis similitudo, cum in animo cogitantis
aspicitur atque iudicatur, nec ipsa corpus est.   Non
est ergo nec terra nec aqua, nec aer nec ignis, quibus quattuor corporibus, quae dicuntur quattuor
elementa, mundum corporeum videmus esse com-
pactum.   Porro si noster animus corpus non est,
quo modo Deus creator animi corpus est?

Cedant ergo et isti, ut dictum est, Platonicis;
cedant et illi quos quidem puduit dicere Deum corpus
esse, verum tamen eiusdem naturae cuius ille est
animos nostros esse putaverunt; ita non eos movit
tanta mutabilitas animae, quam Dei naturae tri-
buere nefas est. Sed dicunt: Corpore mutatur
animae natura, nam per se ipsa incommutabilis est.
Poterant isti dicere: Corpore aliquo vulneratur caro,
nam per se ipsa invulnerabilis est. Prorsus quod
mutari non potest, nulla re potest, ac per hoc quod
corpore mutari potest, aliqua re potest et ideo incommutabile recte dici non potest.

---

[1] Augustine probably refers to the Pythagoreans.

Now the representation that appears to that sort of mental scrutiny is no longer a body but only the likeness of a body, and the faculty by which this likeness of a body is seen within the soul is neither a body nor the likeness of a body. Moreover, the faculty that sees and judges whether the likeness is beautiful or ugly is assuredly superior to the actual likeness on which such a judgement is passed. Now that faculty is the human mind and the substance of a rational soul, and it is certainly not material, if even the likeness of a body, when seen and judged in the mind of one who is engaged in thinking, is not itself material. It is, then, neither earth nor water nor air nor fire, of which four materials, or elements as they are called, we see the material universe to have been composed. Furthermore, if our mind is not material, how can God, the mind's creator, be material?

So, as we have said, these philosophers must make way for the Platonists, and so must those who blushed to say that God is material, yet nevertheless held that our minds are of the same substance as God.[1] So blind were they to the soul's great variability, which it is impious to attribute to the divine nature. But they say that it is the body that changes the substance of the soul, which in itself is unchangeable. They might as well say that it is some body that wounds the flesh, which in itself is invulnerable. In fact what is unchangeable can be altered by nothing, and in so far as a thing can be altered by a body, it can be altered by something, and therefore cannot properly be described as unchangeable.

VI

*De Platonicorum sensu in ea parte philosophiae
quae physica nominatur.*

VIDERUNT ergo isti philosophi quos ceteris non
inmerito fama atque gloria praelatos videmus nullum corpus esse Deum, et ideo cuncta corpora
transcenderunt quaerentes Deum. Viderunt quidquid mutabile est non esse summum Deum, et ideo
animam omnem mutabilesque omnes spiritus transcenderunt quaerentes summum Deum. Deinde
viderunt omnem speciem in re quacumque mutabili,
qua est quidquid illud est, quoquo modo et qualiscumque natura est, non esse posse nisi ab illo qui vere
est quia incommutabiliter est, ac per hoc sive uni-
versi mundi corpus figuras qualitates ordinatumque
motum et elementa disposita a caelo usque ad terram
et quaecumque corpora in eis sunt, sive omnem vitam,
vel quae nutrit et continet, qualis est in arboribus,
vel quae et hoc habet et sentit, qualis est in pecoribus, vel quae et haec habet et intellegit, qualis est
in hominibus, vel quae nutritorio subsidio non
indiget, sed tantum continet sentit intellegit, qualis
est in angelis, nisi ab illo esse non posse qui simpliciter
est; quia non aliud illi est esse, aliud vivere, quasi

---

[1] Plato expounds the immutability of God in *Republic* 2.
380 D–381 B.

VI

On the views of the Platonists in the branch of philosophy that is called physical.

So these philosophers who, as we see, have not undeservedly achieved a glorious reputation beyond all others, perceived that no material body is God; and therefore in seeking God they have gone above and beyond all material bodies. They perceived that anything susceptible to change is not the Most High God; and that is why in seeking the Most High God they have gone above and beyond every living soul and all disembodied spirits that are susceptible to change.[1] Next they saw that every ideal form in any changeable thing whatever, whereby the thing is whatever it is, no matter how the thing exists or of what nature it may be, can have no existence except from him whose being is real because unchangeable. Nor, consequently, can the matter of the whole universe with its shapes, qualities and regulated movement, nor can the elements that are severally disposed from heaven to earth with whatever bodies exist in them, nor again can any life, either the nutritive and conservative, such as is found in trees, or the life that in addition possesses feeling, such as is found in animals, or that which in addition to these two has intelligence, such as is found in man, or that which has no need of food to sustain it, but conserves, perceives and reasons, such as is found in angels, have any existence except as it comes from him who is absolute being. For his being and living are not separate, as if he could

31

possit esse non vivens; nec aliud illi est vivere, aliud intellegere, quasi possit vivere non intellegens; nec aliud illi est intellegere, aliud beatum esse, quasi possit intellegere non beatus; sed quod est illi vivere, intellegere, beatum esse, hoc est illi esse.

Propter hanc incommutabilitatem et simplicitatem intellexerunt eum et omnia ista fecisse et ipsum a nullo fieri potuisse. Consideraverunt enim quidquid est vel corpus esse vel vitam, meliusque aliquid vitam esse quam corpus, speciemque corporis esse sensibilem, intellegibilem vitae. Proinde intellegibilem speciem sensibili praetulerunt. Sensibilia dicimus quae visu tactuque corporis sentiri queunt; intellegibilia, quae conspectu mentis intellegi. Nulla est enim pulchritudo corporalis sive in statu corporis, sicut est figura, sive in motu, sicut est cantilena, de qua non animus iudicet. Quod profecto non posset, nisi melior in illo esset haec species, sine tumore molis, sine strepitu vocis, sine spatio vel loci vel temporis. Sed ibi quoque nisi mutabilis esset, non alius alio melius de specie sensibili iudicaret; melius ingeniosior quam tardior, melius peritior quam inperitior, melius exercitatior quam minus exercitatus, et idem ipse unus, cum proficit,

exist without living; nor are his living and exercise
of reason separate, as if he could live without exercise
of reason; nor are his exercise of reason and happiness separate, as if he could reason without being
happy; but for him to be means to live, to reason and
to be happy.

Because he is unchanging and uniform, they have
reasoned both that he created all these things and
that he himself could have been created from none
of them. They have reflected that whatever is, is
either bodily matter or life, that life is something
better than bodily matter, and that the form of
bodily matter is apparent to the senses while that of
life is to be grasped by the intelligence. So they
have proceeded to give a higher place to the form
which is intelligible than to that which is sensible.
We mean by sensible those things which can be
perceived by the bodily sensations of sight and
touch, and by intelligible those things which can be
grasped by mental vision. There is no physical
beauty, whether in the structure of a body, for instance its shape, or in its movement, as in a song,
that is not judged by the mind. This would assuredly be impossible unless a more ideal form of
these things existed in the mind, with no accumula-
tion of mass, with no vocal din, and with no extension
either of space or of time. But within the mind too
the ideal form is variable, or else one man would have
no better judgement of a sensible form than another
man. The more intelligent will be better than the
slower of wit, the skilled better than the unskilled,
the expert better than the less experienced, and the
individual too, as he progresses, will certainly be

melius utique postea quam prius. Quod autem recipit magis et minus, sine dubitatione mutabile est.

Unde ingeniosi et docti et in his exercitati homines facile collegerunt non esse in eis rebus primam speciem, ubi mutabilis esse convincitur. Cum igitur in eorum conspectu et corpus et animus magis minusque speciosa essent, si autem omni specie carere possent, omnino nulla essent, viderunt esse aliquid ubi prima esset incommutabilis et ideo nec comparabilis; atque ibi esse rerum principium rectissime crediderunt quod factum non esset et ex quo facta cuncta essent.

Ita quod notum est Dei, manifestavit eis ipse, cum ab eis invisibilia eius per ea quae facta sunt, intellecta conspecta sunt; sempiterna quoque virtus eius et divinitas; a quo etiam visibilia et temporalia cuncta creata sunt.

Haec de illa parte quam physicam, id est naturalem nuncupant, dicta sint.

VII

Quanto excellentiores ceteris in logica, id est rationali philosophia, Platonici sint habendi.

Quod autem adtinet ad doctrinam ubi versatur pars altera, quae ab eis logica, id est rationalis, vocatur, absit ut his comparandi videantur qui

---

[1] Romans 1.19–20.

better than he was earlier. But what admits of
greater or less is unquestionably variable.

So the Platonists, who were talented, instructed
and well practised in these studies, found it easy to
deduce that the fundamental form is not found in
those cases where the form is convincingly shown to
be variable. According to their view, both body and
mind have form with variation of much and little.
Moreover, if they could have no form at all, they
would then be nothing at all. Thus they saw that
something exists wherein the fundamental form is
unchangeable and for that reason incomparable; and
they were absolutely right in believing that there the
primary reality resides that was not created but was
the source of all creation.

Accordingly, that which is known of God he himself made plain to them, when his invisible attributes
as well as his eternal power and godhead were clearly
seen and understood by them through created
things.[1] For by him were all things visible and
temporal also created.

Let this serve as a discussion of what the Platonists
call the physical or natural branch of philosophy.

VII

*How far superior the Platonists are to all others
in logic, that is, rational philosophy.*

As for their teaching in the second department of
philosophy, which they call logic or rational philosophy, far be it from me to think of comparing with

35

posuerunt iudicium veritatis in sensibus corporis
eorumque infidis et fallacibus regulis omnia quae
discuntur metienda esse censuerunt, ut Epicurei et
quicumque alii tales, ut etiam ipsi Stoici, qui cum
vehementer amaverint sollertiam disputandi, quam
dialecticam nominant, a corporis sensibus eam
ducendam putarunt, hinc asseverantes animum
concipere notiones, quas appellant ἐννοίας, earum
rerum scilicet quas definiendo explicant; hinc pro-
pagari atque conecti totam discendi docendique
rationem.

Ubi ego multum mirari soleo, cum pulchros dicant
non esse nisi sapientes, quibus sensibus corporis
istam pulchritudinem viderint, qualibus oculis carnis
formam sapientiae decusque conspexerint.

Hi vero, quos merito ceteris anteponimus, dis-
creverunt ea quae mente conspiciuntur ab his quae
sensibus adtinguntur, nec sensibus adimentes quod
possunt, nec eis dantes ultra quam possunt. Lumen
autem mentium esse dixerunt ad discenda omnia
eundem ipsum Deum, a quo facta sunt omnia.

them those who have placed the criterion of truth in the bodily senses and decreed that all learning should be measured by such unreliable and deceptive standards. I mean the Epicureans and others like them, and even the Stoics, who, though mightily enamoured of skill in debate, which they call dialectic, still held that it must derive by induction from the bodily senses, affirming that these are the source from which the mind conceives the ideas or *ennoiai*, as they call them, of those things which, if you please, they explain by means of definitions, and that these senses are the source from which their whole system of learning and instruction is developed and strung together.

Here I never cease to wonder, when the Stoics assert that only the wise are beautiful, with what physical senses they have seen that particular beauty, and with what eyes of the flesh they have beheld the form and the loveliness of wisdom.

On the other hand, the philosophers whom, on their merits, we put before all the rest, have distinguished those things that are observed by the mind from those which make contact with the senses, neither denying to the senses those powers that they have, nor attributing to them more than they possess. Moreover, they have declared that the light which illumines the intellects of men in all things that may be learned is this selfsame God by whom all things were made.

VIII

Quod etiam in morali philosophia Platonici obtineant principatum.

RELIQUA est pars moralis, quam Graeco vocabulo dicunt ethicam, ubi quaeritur de summo bono, quo referentes omnia quae agimus, et quod non propter aliud, sed propter se ipsum adpetentes idque adipiscentes nihil quo beati simus ulterius requiramus. Ideo quippe et finis est dictus quia propter hunc cetera volumus, ipsum autem non nisi propter ipsum.

Hoc ergo beatificum bonum alii a corpore, alii ab animo, alii ab utroque homini esse dixerunt. Videbant quippe ipsum hominem constare ex animo et corpore et ideo ab alterutro istorum duorum aut ab utroque bene sibi esse posse credebant, finali quodam bono, quo beati essent, quo cuncta quae agebant referrent atque id quo referendum esset non ultra quaererent. Unde illi qui dicuntur addidisse tertium genus bonorum, quod appellatur extrinsecus, sicuti est honor gloria pecunia et si quid huius modi, non sic addiderunt ut finale esset, id est propter se ipsum adpetendum, sed propter aliud; bonumque esse hoc genus bonis, malum autem malis. Ita bonum hominis qui vel ab animo vel a corpore vel

38

VIII

That the Platonists hold the primacy in moral philosophy too.

THERE remains moral philosophy, for which the Greek term is ethics (*ēthicē*), where the object of investigation is the supreme good. By this we measure all our actions, and this we strive after for no ulterior motive, but simply for its own sake; and if we attain it, we need seek no further source of happiness. That is why, of course, it is called the end, since we make all other choices for its sake, but never choose it except for its own sake.

Now this good that confers happiness on man is said by some to come from the body, by others from the mind, and by others again from both. They saw, of course, that man himself is composed of both mind and body, and so they believed that they could derive well-being from one or the other of these two sources, or from both together. Thus they might achieve a kind of final good, whereby they might be happy, and which they might make their standard, without having to seek anything further that could serve as a standard for it. So those who are said to have added a third class of good things called extrinsic, such as honour, glory, money and similar things, did not admit things of this class as a final good or, in other words, as a good that is desirable for its own sake, but as a good to be sought for the sake of some other good. This class of good, they hold, is good for good men, but bad for bad men. So whether they sought to derive the good of man from the mind or

ab utroque expetiverunt, nihil aliud quam ab homine
expetendum esse putaverunt; sed qui id adpetive-
runt a corpore, a parte hominis deteriore; qui vero ab
animo, a parte meliore; qui autem ab utroque, a toto
homine. Sive ergo a parte qualibet sive a toto, non
nisi ab homine. Nec istae differentiae, quoniam tres
sunt, ideo tres, sed multas dissensiones philosophorum sectasque fecerunt, quia et de bono corporis
et de bono animi et de bono utriusque diversi diversa
opinati sunt.

Cedant igitur omnes illis philosophis qui non
dixerunt beatum esse hominem fruentem corpore
vel fruentem animo, sed fruentem Deo; non sicut
corpore vel se ipso animus aut sicut amico amicus,
sed sicut luce oculus, si aliquid ab his ad illa similitudinis adferendum est, quod quale sit, si Deus ipse
adiuverit, alio loco, quantum per nos fieri poterit,
apparebit. Nunc satis sit commemorare Platonem
determinasse finem boni esse secundum virtutem
vivere et ei soli evenire posse qui notitiam Dei
habeat et imitationem nec esse aliam ob causam
beatum; ideoque non dubitat hoc esse philosophari,
amare Deum, cuius natura sit incorporalis. Unde
utique colligitur tunc fore beatum studiosum sapientiae—id enim est philosophus— cum frui Deo coe-

from the body, or from both together, they held that no other good was to be sought except what derives from man. But those who sought to derive the good from the body took it from the baser part of man, while those who derived it from the mind took it from the higher part. Those who took it from both derived it from the whole man. So whether it came from some one part or from the whole man, in any case it came from man. Although these differences of opinion are three in number, they gave rise not to three but to many dissenting schools of philosophy, because various groups have held various opinions about the good of the body, the good of the mind and the good of both together.

So let them all yield place to those philosophers who asserted that a man cannot be happy in the enjoyment of his body or of his mind, but only in the enjoyment of God, enjoying him not as the mind enjoys the body or itself, or as one friend enjoys another friend, but as the eye enjoys light, if it is possible to draw any analogy between such things and the divine. The nature of this analogy I shall explain elsewhere with God's help, as far as in me lies. For the moment let me content myself with recalling that Plato defined the ultimate good as living in conformity with virtue, that he held this possible only for the man who comes to know God and to copy him, and that he believed happiness to be due to this cause alone. For this reason he has no doubt that philosophy is the love of God, whose nature is incorporeal. From this it certainly follows that the man who pursues wisdom—for that is the meaning of philosopher—will be happy only when he begins to

perit. Quamvis enim non continuo beatus sit qui eo fruitur quod amat—multi enim amando ea quae amanda non sunt miseri sunt et miseriores cum fruuntur—, nemo tamen beatus est qui eo quod amat non fruitur. Nam et ipsi qui res non amandas amant non se beatos putant amando, sed fruendo. Quisquis ergo fruitur eo quod amat verumque et summum bonum amat, quis eum beatum nisi miserrimus negat? Ipsum autem verum ac summum bonum Plato dicit Deum, unde vult esse philosophum amatorem Dei ut, quoniam philosophia ad beatam vitam tendit, fruens Deo sit beatus qui Deum amaverit.

IX

De ea philosophia, quae ad veritatem fidei Christianae propius accessit.

Quicumque igitur philosophi de Deo summo et vero ista senserunt, quod et rerum creatarum sit effector et lumen cognoscendarum et bonum agendarum, quod ab illo nobis sit et principium naturae et veritas doctrinae et felicitas vitae, sive Platonici accommodatius nuncupentur, sive quodlibet aliud sectae suae nomen inponant; sive tantummodo

enjoy God. For although a man who enjoys what he loves is not happy without qualification, since many are unhappy because they love what they should not love and are still more unhappy when they come to enjoy it, yet no one is happy who does not come to enjoy what he loves. Even those who love things that they should not love do not think themselves happy merely in loving them, but in coming to enjoy them. So who but the unhappiest of men denies that a man who comes to enjoy what he loves is happy, when the object of his love is the true and supreme good? Now this true and supreme good, according to Plato, is God; and so he requires his philosopher to be a lover of God in order that, since philosophy aims at a happy life, he who has set his affection on God may be happy in the enjoyment of him.

IX

On the philosophy that has come nearest to the true Christian faith.

So those philosophers, whoever they may be, who have come to the above conclusions about the true and most high God, namely that he is the author of created things, the light by which things become known, and the good for which things are done and who believe that we derive from him the origin of our substance, the truth of our instruction and the happiness of our life, whether these philosophers are more appropriately termed Platonists or else attach some other name to their school, or whether it was

Ionici generis, qui in eis praecipui fuerunt, ista senserint, sicut idem Plato et qui eum bene intellexerunt; sive etiam Italici, propter Pythagoram et Pythagoreos et si qui forte alii eiusdem sententiae indidem fuerunt; sive aliarum quoque gentium qui sapientes vel philosophi habiti sunt, Atlantici Libyes, Aegyptii, Indi, Persae, Chaldaei, Scythae, Galli, Hispani, aliqui reperiuntur qui hoc viderint ac docuerint, eos omnes ceteris anteponimus eosque nobis propinquiores fatemur.

X

Quae sit inter philosophicas artes religiosi excellentia Christiani.

Quamvis enim homo Christianus litteris tantum ecclesiasticis eruditus Platonicorum forte nomen ignoret, nec utrum duo genera philosophorum extiterint in Graeca lingua, Ionicorum et Italicorum, sciat, non tamen ita surdus est in rebus humanis ut nesciat philosophos vel studium sapientiae vel ipsam sapientiam profiteri. Cavet eos tamen qui secundum elementa huius mundi philosophantur, non secundum Deum, a quo ipse factus est mundus. Admonetur enim praecepto apostolico fideliterque audit quod dictum est: *Cavete ne quis vos decipiat per philosophiam et inanem seductionem secundum elementa mundi.* Deinde ne omnes tales esse arbitretur,

---

[1] The epithet " Libyan " of Mt. Atlas probably gave rise to the misnomer of " Atlantic Libyans." Cf. Diogenes Laertius 1.1, where a similar passage, which enumerates a list of races who practised philosophy in former days, includes Λίβυν Ἄτλαντα.   [2] Colossians 2.8.

only the leaders of the Ionian school who held these opinions, for example Plato himself and those who understand him best, or whether the Italian school did so too thanks to Pytharogas and the Pythagoreans and any others from the same region who may have held the same view, or whether some men of other nations who were considered wise men and philosophers are found to have discovered and taught this doctrine, Atlantic Libyans,[1] Egyptians, Indians, Persians, Chaldaeans, Scythians, Gauls and Spaniards —all of these we set above any others and avow that they are closer to us.

X

The superiority of a practising Christian over the attainments of philosophers.

Although a Christian whose education has been in ecclesiastical literature alone is perhaps ignorant of the name of Platonists and may not know that two schools of Greek-speaking philosophers, the Ionian and the Italian, existed, yet he is not so naïve regarding human affairs as to be unaware that philosophers profess either the study of wisdom or else wisdom itself. Yet he distrusts those who philosophize with reference to the elements of this universe and not with reference to God, by whom the universe itself was made; for he is warned by the injunction of the Apostle and faithfully heeds his words: " See to it that no one man trap you through philosophy and empty delusions about the cosmic elements."[2] Then, lest he think all philosophers

45

audit ab eodem apostoli dici de quibusdam: *Quia
quod notum est Dei, manifestum est in illis; Deus enim
illis manifestavit. Invisibilia enim eius a constitutione
mundi per ea quae facta sunt intellecta conspiciuntur,
sempiterna quoque virtus eius et divinitas,* et ubi Athen-
iensibus loquens, cum rem magnam de Deo dixisset
et quae a paucis possit intellegi, quod *in illo vivimus
et movemur et sumus,* adiecit et ait, *Sicut et vestri quidam
dixerunt.* Novit sane etiam ipsos, in quibus errant,
cavere; ubi enim dictum est quod per ea quae facta
sunt Deus illis manifestavit intellectu conspicienda
invisibilia sua, ibi etiam dictum est non illos ipsum
Deum recte coluisse, quia et aliis rebus, quibus non
oportebat, divinos honores illi uni tantum debitos
detulerunt: *Quoniam cognoscentes Deum non sicut
Deum glorificaverunt aut gratias egerunt, sed evanuerunt
in cogitationibus suis et obscuratum est insipiens cor
eorum. Dicentes enim se esse sapientes stulti facti sunt
et inmutaverunt gloriam incorruptibilis Dei in similitudinem imaginis corruptibilis hominis et volucrum et
quadrupedum et serpentium;* ubi et Romanos et
Graecos et Aegyptios, qui de sapientiae nomine
gloriati sunt, fecit intellegi. Sed de hoc cum istis
post modum disputabimus. In quo autem nobis
consentiunt de uno Deo huius universitatis auctore,
qui non solum super omnia corpora est incorporeus,
verum etiam super omnes animas incorruptibilis,

[1] Romans 1.19 f. [2] Acts 17.28
[3] Romans 1.21–23. [4] See below, Book 8.23 ff.

are like that, he hears the same Apostle saying of some: " Because that which is known of God is plain among them, for God has shown it to them. For his invisible attributes from the creation of the world as well as his eternal power and godhead are clearly seen and understood through created things." [1] And, speaking to the Athenians, after stating a great truth about God, one that only a few can understand, namely: "In him we live, and move, and have our being," he added: "as certain also of your own number have said." [2] The Apostle, to be sure, recognizes that he must shun even those philosophers when they are in error. For the passage which states that through the things which were created God revealed his invisible attributes to be seen by their understanding also says that they did not worship God himself aright, because they paid to other undeserving objects the divine honours due to him alone: " For although they knew God, they did not honour him as God or give thanks to him, but became futile in their thinking, and their senseless minds were darkened. Claiming to be wise, they became fools, and exchanged the glory of the incorruptible God for an image resembling corruptible man, or birds, or four-footed animals, or reptiles." [3] Here the Apostle meant us to understand the Romans, the Greeks and the Egyptians, who have prided themselves on their reputation for wisdom. But we shall discuss this point with these philosophers later on. [4] However, in so far as they agree with us about one God, the author of this universe, who, in being incorporeal, is above all that is corporeal, and also, in being incorruptible, is above all souls, and is our

47

principium nostrum, lumen nostrum, bonum nostrum, in hoc eos ceteris anteponimus.

Nec, si litteras eorum Christianus ignorans verbis quae non didicit in disputatione non utitur, ut vel naturalem Latine vel physicam Graece appellet eam partem in qua de naturae inquisitione tractatur, et rationalem sive logicam, in qua quaeritur quonam modo veritas percipi possit, et moralem vel ethicam, in qua de moribus agitur bonorumque finibus adpetendis malorumque vitandis, ideo nescit ab uno vero Deo atque optimo et naturam nobis esse, qua facti ad eius imaginem sumus, et doctrinam, qua eum nosque noverimus, et gratiam, qua illi cohaerendo beati simus.

Haec itaque causa est cur istos ceteris praeferamus, quia, cum alii philosophi ingenia sua studiaque contriverint in requirendis rerum causis, et quinam esset modus discendi atque vivendi, isti Deo cognito reppererunt ubi esset et causa constitutae universitatis et lux percipiendae veritatis et fons bibendae felicitatis. Sive ergo isti Platonici sive quicumque alii quarumlibet gentium philosophi de Deo ista sentiunt, nobiscum sentiunt. Sed ideo cum Platonicis magis agere placuit hanc causam, quia eorum sunt litterae notiores. Nam et Graeci, quorum lingua in gentibus praeminet, eas magna praedicatione celebrarunt, et Latini permoti earum vel

---

[1] Genesis 1.26–27.

origin, our light and our good, in that respect we rate them above all others.

And if a Christian who does not know their writings fails in discussion to make use of words that he has not learned, with the result that he does not use the respective Latin or Greek terms, such as natural or physical for that part of philosophy which deals with the investigation of nature, and rational or logical for that which discusses the question by what means truth can be discovered, and moral or ethical for that which concerns morals, the final good to be sought and the supreme evil to be avoided, he is not therefore ignorant that it is from the one true and infinitely good God that we have the substance with which we were created in his image,¹ the teachings by which we have come to know him and ourselves, and the grace with which, through cleaving to him, we are blessed.

This, then, is the reason why we prefer the Platonists to all the others. Other philosophers have worn out their talents and their zeal in seeking the causes of things and the right way to learn and to live; but they, because they knew God, have discovered where to find the cause by which the universe was established, the light whereby truth may be apprehended and the spring where happiness may be imbibed. So if Platonists or any other philosophers of any nation hold such opinions about God, they agree with us. My reason for preferring to debate with the Platonists is that their writings are better known. The Greeks, whose language is pre-eminent among the gentiles, have honoured their books with great acclaim; and the Latins, influenced either by their

excellentia vel gloria, ipsas libentius didicerunt atque
in nostrum eloquium transferendo nobiliores clario-
esque fecerunt.

XI

Unde Plato eam intellegentiam potuerit adquirere,
qua Christianae scientiae propinquavit.

MIRANTUR autem quidam nobis in Christi gratia
sociati, cum audiunt vel legunt Platonem de Deo ista
sensisse quae multum congruere veritati nostrae
religionis agnoscunt. Unde nonnulli putaverunt
eum, quando perrexit in Aegyptum, Hieremiam
audisse prophetam vel scripturas propheticas in
eadem peregrinatione legisse; quorum quidem
opinionem in quibusdam libris meis posui. Sed
diligenter supputata temporum ratio, quae chronica
historia continetur, Platonem indicat a tempore quo
prophetavit Hieremias centum ferme annos postea
natum fuisse; qui cum octoginta et unum vixisset,
ab anno mortis eius usque ad id tempus quo Ptolomaeus rex Aegypti scripturas propheticas gentis
Hebraeorum de Iudaea poposcit et per septuaginta
viros Hebraeos, qui etiam Graecam linguam noverant, interpretandas habendasque curavit, anni
reperiuntur ferme sexaginta. Quapropter in illa
peregrinatione sua Plato nec Hieremiam videre

---

[1] *De Doctrina Christiana* 2.28.43. In *Retractationes* 2.4.2,
Augustine notes his mistake here as due to a slip of memory.

superiority or their renown, have been more eager to
study them and have made them more widely known
and famous by translating them into our language.

XI

*Where Plato was able to acquire the understanding by
which he came near to Christian knowledge.*

MOREOVER some of those who are our fellows in the
grace of Christ are astonished when they hear or read
that Plato had views about God which they can see
are in close agreement with the truth of our religion.
For this reason some have thought that, when he
went to Egypt, he heard the prophet Jeremiah speak
or read the books of the prophets in the course of
this same journey; and I have recorded their
opinion in some of my books.[1] But a careful calculation of dates according to chronology shows that
Plato was born about one hundred years after the
time when Jeremiah uttered his prophecies.[2] Plato
lived eighty-one years; and from the year of his death
until the time when Ptolemy, king of Egypt, sent for
the prophetic Scriptures of the Hebrew people from
Judea and had them translated and safeguarded by
seventy Hebrew scholars who also knew Greek, we
find that about sixty years elapsed. Therefore in
the course of that journey of his Plato could not have
seen Jeremiah, who died so long before, nor could he
have read the Scriptures, which had not yet been

---

[2] Augustine's chronology is inexact. Jeremiah's prophetic
activity can be dated between 627 and 586. Plato was born
about 429 B.C.

potuit tanto ante defunctum, nec easdem scripturas legere, quae nondum fuerant in Graecam linguam translatae qua ille pollebat; nisi forte, quia fuit acerrimi studii, sicut Aegyptias, ita et istas per interpretem didicit, non ut scribendo transferret—quod Ptolomaeus pro ingenti beneficio, qui a regia potestate etiam timeri poterat, meruisse perhibetur —, sed ut conloquendo quid continerent, quantum capere posset, addisceret.

Hoc ut existimetur, illa suadere videntur indicia, quod liber geneseos sic incipit: *In principio fecit Deus caelum et terram. Terra autem erat invisibilis et incomposita, et tenebrae erant super abyssum, et spiritus Dei superferebatur super aquam*; in Timaeo autem Plato, quem librum de mundi constitutione conscripsit, Deum dicit in illo opere terram primo ignemque iunxisse. Manifestum est autem quod igni tribuat caeli locum: habet ergo haec sententia quandam illius similitudinem qua dictum est: *In principio fecit Deus caelum et terram.* Deinde ille duo media, quibus interpositis sibimet haec extrema copularentur, aquam dicit et aerem; unde putatur sic intellexisse quod scriptum est: *spiritus Dei superferebatur super aquam.* Parum quippe adtendens quo more soleat illa scriptura appellare spiritum Dei, quoniam et aer spiritus dicitur, quattuor opinatus elementa loco illo commemorata videri potest. Deinde quod Plato

---

[1] The reference is to the freeing by Ptolemy Philadelphus of a large number of Jewish slaves (110,000 according to Josephus) and his sending gifts to the temple. See Josephus, *Antiquities* 12.11 ff.

[2] Genesis 1.1–2.   [3] *Timaeus* 31 B.

translated into Greek, the language in which he was competent. Unless perhaps, because he was an eager student, he studied them by means of an interpreter, as he did Egyptian books, not with a view to writing a scriptural translation—this privilege, we are told, Ptolemy obtained only in return for a great exercise of kindness [1] and because he also could inspire awe by virtue of his royal power—, but in order to assimilate as much as he could understand by discussing their content.

Certain indications seem to support this supposition. For example, the book of Genesis begins with the words: " In the beginning God created the heaven and the earth. And the earth was invisible and without form, and darkness was over the abyss, and the spirit of God moved over the waters." [2] Moreover, in the *Timaeus*, his treatise on the formation of the universe, Plato says that God in this operation first united earth and fire.[3] But it is clear that he assigns to fire the region of heaven. So this opinion bears a certain resemblance to the statement: "In the beginning God created the heaven and the earth." Next Plato speaks of the two elements, water and air, which by their intermediate position form a bond between the two extremes.[4] This prompts the thought that he so understood the scriptural words: " The spirit of God moved over the waters." I mean that he did not note accurately what term Scripture usually employs for the Spirit of God and, because air too is called spirit, it may be thought that he supposed that the four elements are mentioned in this text. Then we have Plato's

[4] Earth and fire: *Timaeus* 32 B.

SAINT AUGUSTINE

dicit amatorem Dei esse philosophum, nihil sic illis
sacris litteris flagrat; et maxime illud—quod et me
plurimum adducit ut paene assentiar Platonem illorum librorum expertem non fuisse—, quod, cum ad
sanctum Moysen ita verba Dei per angelum per-
ferantur, ut quaerenti quod sit nomen eius qui eum
pergere praecipiebat ad populum Hebraeum ex
Aegypto liberandum, respondeatur, *Ego sum qui
sum, et dices filiis Israel: Qui est, misit me ad vos*, tamquam in eius comparatione qui vere est quia incommutabilis est, ea quae mutabilia facta sunt non sint,
vehementer hoc Plato tenuit et diligentissime com-
mendavit. Et nescio utrum hoc uspiam reperiatur
in libris eorum qui ante Platonem fuerunt, nisi ubi
dictum est, *Ego sum qui sum, et dices eis: Qui est,
misit me ad vos*.

XII

*Quod etiam Platonici, licet de uno vero Deo bene
senserint, multis tamen diis sacra facienda
censuerint.*

Sed undecumque ille ista didicerit, sive praeceden-
tibus eum veterum libris sive potius, quo modo dicit
apostolus, *quia quod notum est Dei manifestum est in
illis; Deus enim illis manifestavit; invisibilia enim*

---

[1] Exodus 3.14. In this biblical passage the Hebrew name
of God, *YHWH*, is etymologically connected with the verb
hayah, to be.

54

saying that the philosopher is one who loves God, and nothing is put with more burning eloquence than that in those sacred scriptures. But above all— and this especially brings me virtually to an admission that Plato was not without knowledge of those books—there is the fact that, when the angel brought the words of God to Moses, and the holy man asked the name of the one who charged him to go and deliver the Hebrew people out of Egypt, the answer was given: "I am he who is, and you are to say to the children of Israel: 'He-who-is has sent me to you,'"[1]—signifying that, in comparison with him who really is because he is unchangeable, things which have been created subject to change have no being. This tenet Plato strenuously upheld and most earnestly urged upon others. Yet I do not know whether this statement can be found anywhere in the writings of those who preceded Plato, except where it is said: "I am he who is, and you are to say to them: 'He-who-is has sent me to you.'"

XII

That even the Platonists, although they did well to hold that there is one true God, nevertheless took the position that many gods should be worshipped.

BUT from whatever source Plato learned these things, whether from books of ancient writers who came before him or, as is more likely, to quote the Apostle: "Because that which is known of God is plain among them, for God has showed it to them.

eius a constitutione mundi per ea, quae facta sunt,
intellecta conspiciuntur, sempiterna quoque virtus eius et
divinitas, nunc non inmerito me Platonicos philosophos elegisse cum quibus agam quod in ista quaestione, quam modo suscepimus, agitur de naturali
theologia, utrum propter felicitatem quae post mortem futura est uni Deo an pluribus sacra facere
oporteat, satis, ut existimo, exposui.

Ideo quippe hos potissimum elegi, quoniam de uno
Deo qui fecit caelum et terram, quanto melius
senserunt, tanto ceteris gloriosiores et inlustriores
habentur, in tantum aliis praelati iudicio posterorum
ut, cum Aristoteles Platonis discipulus, vir excellentis
ingenii et eloquio Platoni quidem impar, sed multos
facile superans, cum sectam Peripateticam condi-
disset, quod deambulans disputare consueverat,
plurimosque discipulos praeclara fama excellens vivo
adhuc praeceptore in suam haeresim congregasset,
post mortem vero Platonis Speusippus, sororis eius
filius, et Xenocrates, dilectus eius discipulus, in
scholam eius, quae Academia vocabatur, eidem suc-
cessissent atque ob hoc et ipsi et eorum successores
Academici appellarentur, recentiores tamen philosophi nobilissimi, quibus Plato sectandus placuit,
noluerint se dici Peripateticos aut Academicos, sed
Platonicos.

Ex quibus sunt valde nobilitati Graeci Plotinus,
Iamblichus, Porphyrius; in utraque autem lingua, id

---

[1] Romans 1.19–20.
[2] These philosophers, who flourished in the third and early
fourth centuries of our era, are today termed Neoplatonists.

For his invisible attributes from the creation of the world as well as his eternal power and godhead are clearly seen and understood through created things,"[1] in either case I think I have sufficiently demonstrated that I had good reason to select the Platonic philosophers in order to debate with them a point of natural theology that needs to be settled in connection with the topic just now taken up, namely whether for the sake of happiness after death we must worship one God or many.

The reason why I have given them special preference is of course that their glory and lustre surpass that of all other philosophers as greatly as does their doctrine of the one God who made heaven and earth. They have been preferred to others by the verdict of posterity to such an extent that, although Aristotle, a disciple of Plato, a man of outstanding ability, and in literary style easily the superior of many, although certainly no match for Plato, founded the Peripatetic school (so called because his habit was to walk about as he lectured) and by his brilliant reputation and eminence gathered to his own sect a very large number of pupils during his master's lifetime, while after Plato's death Speusippus, his sister's son, and Xenocrates, his beloved disciple, succeeded him in his school which was called the Academy, for which reason they and their successors were called Academics, none the less the best known philosophers of more modern times who have chosen to follow Plato have refused to be spoken of as Peripatetics or Academics, but call themselves Platonists.

The best known of them are Plotinus, Iamblichus and Porphyry, who were Greeks;[2] moreover,

est et Graeca et Latina, Apuleius Afer extitit Platonicus nobilis. Sed hi omnes et ceteri eius modi et ipse Plato diis plurimis esse sacra facienda putaverunt.

XIII

De sententia Platonis, qua definivit deos non esse
nisi bonos amicosque virtutum.

QUAMQUAM ergo a nobis et in aliis multis rebus magnisque dissentiant, in hoc tamen quod modo posui, quia neque parva res est et inde nunc quaestio est, primum ab eis quaero, quibus diis istum cultum exhibendum arbitrentur, utrum bonis an malis an et bonis et malis. Sed habemus sententiam Platonis dicentis omnes deos bonos esse nec esse omnino ullum deorum malum. Consequens est igitur ut bonis haec exhibenda intellegantur; tunc enim diis exhibentur, quoniam nec dii erunt, si boni non erunt.

Hoc si ita est—nam de diis quid aliud decet credere?—illa profecto vacuatur opinio qua nonnulli putant deos malos sacris placandos esse, ne laedant, bonos autem, ut adiuvent, invocandos. Mali enim nulli sunt dii; bonis porro debitus, ut dicunt, honor sacrorum est deferendus.

Qui sunt ergo illi qui ludos scaenicos amant eosque

---

[1] Born *circa* A.D. 125. See *City of God*, 4. 2.
[2] *Republic* 2.379.

writing in both languages, Greek and Latin, the
African Apuleius gained fame as a Platonist.[1] But
all these and others of the same persuasion, as well as
Plato himself, believed in polytheistic worship.

XIII

*On Plato's opinion, according to which he defined as
gods only such as were good and friends of
virtuous conduct.*

THEREFORE, although they differ from us in many
other important respects, my first question to them
concerns the matter which I have just mentioned, inasmuch as, being of no small importance, it is the
starting-point of our present investigation. It is:
To which gods do they think worship should be
offered—to the good, or the evil, or to good and evil
alike? But we have Plato's opinion, for he said that
all gods are good and that there is absolutely no evil
god.[2] It follows, then, that we are to understand
that this worship is to be paid to the good. For in
that case it is paid to gods, since they will not be gods
if they are not good.

If this is so—indeed what else can we decently
believe of gods?—it immediately cancels the view
held by some who believe that evil gods must be
appeased by sacrifice to prevent them from doing us
injury, while the good ones are to be called upon to
help us. For there are no evil gods; so it is to good
gods that what they call the due tribute of worship
should be paid.

Who, then, are the gods who love stage plays,

divinis rebus adiungi et suis honoribus flagitant exhiberi? Quorum vis non eos indicat nullos, sed iste affectus nimirum indicat malos.

Quid enim de ludis scaenicis Plato senserit notum est, cum poetas ipsos, quod tam indigna deorum maiestate atque bonitate carmina composuerint, censet civitate pellendos. Qui sunt igitur isti dii qui de scaenicis ludis cum ipso Platone contendunt? Ille quippe non patitur deos falsis criminibus infamari; isti eisdem criminibus suos honores celebrari iubent. Denique isti cum eosdem ludos instaurari praeciperent, poscentes turpia etiam maligna gesserunt, Tito Latinio auferentes filium et inmittentes morbum, quod eorum abnuisset imperium, eumque morbum retrahentes cum iussa complesset; iste autem illos nec tam malos timendos putat, sed suae sententiae robur constantissime retinens omnes poetarum sacrilegas nugas, quibus illi inmunditiae societate oblectantur, a populo bene instituto removere non dubitat. Hunc autem Platonem, quod iam in secundo libro commemoravi, inter semideos Labeo ponit. Qui Labeo numina mala victimis cruentis atque huius modi supplicationibus placari

---

[1] *Republic*, Book 3. Cf. *City of God*, Book 2.14.

[2] See *City of God*, Book 4.26. The story is told by Cicero, *De Divinatione* 1.26.55, Livy 2.36, Valerius Maximus 1.7.4.

[3] *City of God*, Book 2.11 and 14.

demand that they should be a part of divine ritual
and insist on such performances at ceremonies in
their honour? Their power shows that they are not
non-existent, but their passion for such things certainly shows that they are evil.

The verdict of Plato regarding stage plays is not in
doubt, since he rules that the poets themselves
should be expelled from the state for composing
poems so unworthy of the majesty and goodness of
the gods.[1] What then must we call the gods who
are at variance with Plato himself about stage plays?
Here is the point: he will not suffer the gods to be
dishonoured by fictional crimes, but they demand
that honour be done to themselves by representation
of these same crimes. In fact when they enjoined
the renewal of these same plays, they did not merely
make shameful demands, but even acted viciously,
when they took away the son of Titus Latinius and
sent a disease upon Titus himself because he had dis-
obeyed their orders, which disease they withdrew
when he had complied entirely with their bidding.[2]
Plato, however, does not consider them proper
objects of fear, evil as they are, but on the contrary
he maintains with the greatest firmness his own
stoutly held opinion and does not hesitate to remove
from a well constituted state all the sacrilegious
frivolities of the poets, in which those gods who
belong to the fellowship of filth take delight. Now
this same Plato, as I have already mentioned in my
second book, is listed by Labeo among the demigods.[3]
And this same Labeo thinks that evil deities are
appeased by the blood of sacrificial victims and that
sort of rites, and the good deities by plays and other

existimat, bona vero ludis et talibus quasi ad laetitiam pertinentibus rebus. Quid est ergo quod semideus Plato non semideis, sed deis, et hoc bonis, illa oblectamenta, quia iudicat turpia, tam constanter audet auferre? Qui sane dii refellunt sententiam Labeonis; nam se in Latinio non lascivos tantum atque ludibundos, sed etiam saevos terribilesque monstrarunt.

Exponant ergo nobis ista Platonici, qui omnes deos secundum auctoris sui sententiam bonos et honestos et virtutibus sapientium socios esse arbitrantur aliterque de ullo deorum sentiri nefas habent. Exponimus, inquiunt. Adtente igitur audiamus.

XIV

De opinione eorum qui rationales animas trium generum esse dixerunt, id est in diis caelestibus, in daemonibus aeriis et in hominibus terrenis.

OMNIUM, inquiunt, animalium in quibus est anima rationalis tripertita divisio est, in deos, homines, daemones. Dii excelsissimum locum tenent, homines infimum, daemones medium. Nam deorum sedes in caelo est, hominum in terra, in aere daemonum. Sicut eis diversa dignitas est locorum, ita etiam naturarum. Proinde dii sunt hominibus daemonibusque potiores; homines vero infra deos et dae-

entertainments which he classifies among joyful
ceremonies. How is it, then, that the demigod
Plato dares so stoutly to deprive not demigods, but
gods, yes and good gods too, of those entertainments,
because he thinks them vile? The gods certainly
give the lie to Labeo's opinion, for, in the case of
Latinius, they showed themselves not merely playful
and festive, but cruel and formidable as well.

Let the Platonists, then, explain this situation to
us, for, according to the opinion of their founder, they
think that all gods are good, honourable and allied
with the wise in a fellowship of virtue, and they hold
it sacrilege to have any other opinion of any god.
Here, they say, is our explanation. Let us then
listen attentively.

XIV

*On the view of those who have said that rational souls
belong to three categories, namely gods in
heaven, demons of the air and men
on earth.*

ALL living beings, they say, in whom dwells a
rational soul, are divided into three categories,
namely, gods, men and demons. The gods occupy
the most exalted region, men the lowest, and
demons a region between the two. The gods dwell
in heaven, men on earth, and demons in the air.
With the gradation of the elements in which they
live goes a gradation of rank in nature. Accordingly
gods are superior to men and to demons, but men are
inferior to gods and demons in the system, both

mones constituti sunt, ut elementorum ordine, sic
differentia meritorum. Daemones igitur medii,
quem ad modum diis, quibus inferius habitant, post-
ponendi, ita hominibus, quibus superius, praeferendi
sunt. Habent enim cum diis communem inmortalitatem corporum, animorum autem cum hominibus
passiones. Quapropter non est mirum, inquiunt, si
etiam ludorum obscenitatibus et poetarum figmentis
delectantur, quando quidem humanis capiuntur
affectibus, a quibus dii longe absunt et modis omnibus alieni sunt. Ex quo colligitur Platonem poetica
detestando et prohibendo figmenta non deos, qui
omnes boni et excelsi sunt, privasse ludorum
scaenicorum voluptate, sed daemones.

Haec si ita sunt—quae licet apud alios quoque repe-
riantur, Apuleius tamen Platonicus Madaurensis de
hac re sola unum scripsit librum, cuius esse titulum
voluit "De Deo Socratis," ubi disserit et exponit ex
quo genere numinum Socrates habebat adiunctum et
amicitia quadam conciliatum, a quo perhibetur soli-
tus admoneri ut desisteret ab agendo, quando id
quod agere volebat non prospere fuerat eventurum;
dicit enim apertissime et copiosissime asserit non
illum deum fuisse, sed daemonem, diligenti disputatione pertractans istam Platonis de deorum sublimitate et hominum humilitate et daemonum medietate
sententiam—haec ergo si ita sunt, quonam modo
ausus est Plato, etiamsi non diis, quos ab omni

---

[1] This extravagant discourse, still extant, is available in the
edition of P. Thomas (Leipzig, 1908).

when ranked by elements and when judged on their merits. Therefore just as the demons, midway between the two, are to be held inferior to the gods because their dwelling is lower, so they are to be ranked as superior to men because their dwelling is higher. For they share bodily immortality with the gods, but mental variations with men. Therefore it is not surprising, they say, if they also take pleasure in obscene plays and the fictions of the poets, since they are subject to human emotions from which the gods are far removed and to which they are in every respect strangers. From this we conclude that Plato, in denouncing poetry and banning works of fiction, cut off from their pleasure in stage plays, not the gods, who are all good and sublime, but the demons.

Although these beliefs can be found in the works of other writers too, the Platonist Apuleius of Madaura wrote a single book about this subject alone, choosing to call it *On the God of Socrates*.[1] In it he discusses and explains to which category of divinities belonged the familiar spirit that Socrates had attached and bound to himself by a kind of friendship, and which, as is generally believed, was accustomed to warn him against a meditated action, when such an action would not have had a happy conclusion. Apuleius declares in the clearest manner and offers abundant argument for his assertion that this was no god, but a demon; and he takes pains to support by argument the theory of Plato concerning the sublimity of the gods, the lowly situation of men and the position of the demons midway between the two. Since this is so, how did Plato dare, in driving poets from the city, to deprive,

65

humana contagione semovit, certe ipsis daemonibus poetas urbe pellendo auferre theatricas voluptates, nisi quia hoc pacto admonuit animum humanum, quamvis adhuc in his moribundis membris positum, pro splendore honestatis impura daemonum iussa contemnere eorumque inmunditiam detestari? Nam si Plato haec honestissime arguit et prohibuit, profecto daemones turpissime poposcerunt atque iusserunt. Aut ergo fallitur Apuleius et non ex isto genere numinum habuit amicum Socrates aut contaria inter se sentit Plato modo daemones honorando, modo eorum delicias a civitate bene morata removendo, aut non est Socrati amicitia daemonis gratulanda, de qua usque adeo et ipse Apuleius erubuit ut de deo Socratis praenotaret librum, quem secundum suam disputationem qua deos a daemonibus tam diligenter copioseque discernit non appellare de deo, sed de daemone Socratis debuit. Maluit autem hoc in ipsa disputatione quam in titulo libri ponere. Ita enim per sanam doctrinam, quae humanis rebus inluxit, omnes vel paene omnes daemonum nomen exhorrent ut, quisquis ante disputationem Apulei qua daemonum dignitas commendatur titulum libri de daemone Socratis legeret, nequaquam illum hominem sanum fuisse sentiret.

Quid autem etiam ipse Apuleius quod in daemonibus laudaret invenit praeter subtilitatem et firmi-

if not the gods, whom he removed far from all human contamination, at any rate the demons of the pleasures of the theatre, unless by this means he meant to urge the mind of man, even though still confined in these mortal members, to spurn, in the name of glorious honour, the impure commands of the demons and to detest their filth? For if it was highly honourable for Plato to attack and forbid these pleasures, surely it was utterly ignoble of the demons to demand and commend them. So either Apuleius is mistaken and it is not to this class of supernatural beings that Socrates' familiar spirit belongs; or Plato is inconsistent in honouring demons at one time and banishing their pleasure at another from a virtuous state; or else Socrates is not to be congratulated on his friendship with a demon, which so embarrassed even Apuleius that he gave his book the title *On the God of Socrates*, although to conform with his discussion, in which he so painstakingly and thoroughly distinguishes gods from demons, he should have called it not *On the God*, but *On the Demon of Socrates*. But he preferred to use this expression in the body of his argument rather than in the title of the book. For, thanks to the wholesome doctrine which has shed its light on the world, all men, or nearly all, have such a horror of the name of demons that anyone at all, before the treatise of Apuleius upholding the dignity of demons was published, on reading the title *On the Demon of Socrates* would have concluded that this Socrates was certainly no healthy specimen.

But what could even Apuleius himself find to praise in demons apart from the combination of fine struc-

tatem corporum et habitationis altiorem locum?
Nam de moribus eorum, cum de omnibus generaliter
loqueretur, non solum nihil boni dixit, sed etiam
plurimum mali. Denique lecto illo libro prorsus
nemo miratur eos etiam scaenicam turpitudinem in
rebus divinis habere voluisse, et cum deos se putari
velint, deorum criminibus oblectari potuisse, et
quidquid in eorum sacris obscena sollemnitate seu
turpi crudelitate vel ridetur vel horretur, eorum
affectibus convenire.

XV

*Quod neque propter aeria corpora neque propter
superiora habitacula daemones hominibus
antecellant.*

QUAM ob rem absit ut ista considerans animus veraciter religiosus et vero Deo subditus ideo arbitretur
daemones se ipso esse meliores, quod habeant corpora meliora. Alioquin multas sibi et bestias prae-
laturus est, quae nos et acrimonia sensuum et motu
facillimo atque celerrimo et valentia virium et anno-
sissima firmitate corporum vincunt. Quis hominum
videndo aequabitur aquilis et vulturibus? Quis
odorando canibus? Quis velocitate leporibus, cervis,
omnibus avibus? Quis multum valendo leonibus et
elephantis? Quis diu vivendo serpentibus, qui
etiam deposita tunica senectutem deponere atque

ture and firmness in their bodies and the loftier region they inhabit? For concerning their behaviour, when he was discussing them all in general terms, not only had he no good to say but, on the contrary, he said a great deal that was to their discredit. In fact no one who has read his book can wonder any more that the demons wanted to include even these shameful stage displays among their sacred rites, and that, wishing as they did to pass themselves off as gods, they could have found pleasure in the crimes of the gods, or that whatever in their worship arouses laughter or revulsion, by lewd ceremony or shameful cruelty, is attuned to their emotions.

XV

Neither their aerial bodies nor their loftier habitation confer on demons a superiority over men.

THEREFORE, when a man who is genuinely religious and a servant of the true God considers this, far be it from him to suppose that demons are better than himself merely because, according to Apuleius, their bodies are superior. If that is so, he will have to consider many animals better than himself, because they surpass us in the keenness of their senses, their agility and speed, their vigorous strength and their preservation of bodily soundness to extreme old age. What man can equal the eagle or the vulture in vision, or the dog in scent, or the hare, the stag or any bird in speed? Who can equal in strength the lion or the elephant, or in length of life the serpent, which, they say, sloughs off old age with

in iuventam redire perhibentur? Sed sicut his
omnibus ratiocinando et intellegendo meliores sumus,
ita etiam daemonibus bene atque honeste vivendo
meliores esse debemus. Ob hoc enim et providentia
divina eis quibus nos constat esse potiores data sunt
quaedam potiora corporum munera, ut illud quo eis
praeponimur etiam isto modo nobis commendaretur
multo maiore cura excolendum esse quam corpus,
ipsamque excellentiam corporalem, quam daemones
habere nossemus, prae bonitate vitae, qua illis ante-
ponimur, contemnere disceremus, habituri et nos
inmortalitatem corporum, non quam suppliciorum
aeternitas torqueat, sed quam puritas praecedat
animorum.

Iam vero de loci altitudine, quod daemones in
aere, nos autem habitamus in terra, ita permoveri ut
hinc eos nobis esse praeponendos existimemus,
omnino ridiculum est. Hoc enim pacto nobis et
omnia volatilia praeponimus. At enim volatilia cum
volando fatigantur vel reficiendum alimentis corpus
habent, terram repetunt vel ad requiem vel ad
pastum, quod daemones, inquiunt, non faciunt.
Numquid ergo placet eis ut volatilia nobis, daemones
autem etiam volatilibus antecellant? Quod si
dementissimum est opinari, nihil est quod de habita-
tione superioris elementi dignos esse daemones
existimemus quibus nos religionis affectu subdere
debeamus. Sicut enim fieri potuit ut aeriae
volucres terrestribus nobis non solum non praeferantur, verum etiam subiciantur propter rationalis

its skin and become young again? But just as we are superior to all of them in reasoning and understanding, so by a good and honourable life we ought to prove our superiority to the demons as well. The reason why Divine Providence has bestowed on those beings, to whom we are manifestly superior, certain superior bodily gifts is in order to stimulate us in this way too to cherish with much greater care than we devote to our bodies our one advantage, and to learn to despise bodily excellence, which we know the demons possess, in comparison with a good life, in which we take precedence over them, knowing as we do that we too shall have bodily immortality, not an immortality eternally tortured with punishment, but one which purity of heart prepares us for.

Now to be so struck by the demons' lofty situation, I mean the fact that they have their dwelling in the air and we on the earth, as to conclude from this that they are to be regarded as superior to us, is completely ridiculous. For on this principle we should consider ourselves inferior to all the birds. But, our opponents remark, when birds become tired with flying or want to restore their bodies with food, they make for the earth for rest or for nourishment, which demons, they say, do not. Do they mean, then, that, as birds are superior to us, demons are also superior to birds? And if this view is completely foolish, there is no reason either why, simply because they inhabit a superior element, we should allow the demons any just claim to be worshipped with feelings of devotion. For, just as it might and does happen that the birds of the air are not only not superior to us who dwell on the earth, but are even subordinated

animae quae in nobis est dignitatem, ita fieri potuit ut daemones, quamvis magis aerii sint, terrestribus nobis non ideo meliores sint quia est aer quam terra superior; sed ideo eis homines praeferendi sint quoniam spei piorum hominum nequaquam illorum desperatio comparanda est.

Nam et illa ratio Platonis qua elementa quattuor proportione contexit atque ordinat, ita duobus extremis, igni mobilissimo et terrae inmobili, media duo, aerem et aquam, interserens ut, quanto est aer aquis et aere ignis, tanto et aquae superiores sint terris, satis nos admonet animalium merita non pro elementorum gradibus aestimare. Et ipse quippe Apuleius cum ceteris terrestre animal hominem dicit, qui tamen longe praeponitur animalibus aquatilibus, cum ipsas aquas terris praeponat Plato, ut intellegamus non eundem ordinem tenendum, cum agitur de meritis animarum, qui videtur esse ordo in gradibus corporum; sed fieri posse ut inferius corpus anima melior inhabitet deteriorque superius.

XVI

Quid de moribus atque actionibus daemonum Apuleius Platonicus senserit.

DE moribus ergo daemonum cum idem Platonicus loqueretur, dixit eos eisdem quibus homines animi

---

[1] *Timaeus* 32 B.
[2] *De Deo Socratis* 3.

to us because of the high value set on the rational soul which resides in us, so the demons, although their dwelling is in a higher region of the air, are not better than we who live on the earth, merely because the air is higher than the earth. On the contrary, men are to be preferred to them, because their hopelessness is by no means to be compared with the hope of men who believe.

Indeed even Plato's system [1] of intertwining and arranging the four elements according to a ratio which inserts the two intermediate elements, air and water, between the two extremes, namely fire which is so volatile and earth which is immovable, so that, in proportion as air is above water and fire above air, so water is above earth, is sufficient warning to us not to judge the merits of living beings according to the high or low rank of the elements they inhabit. Even Apuleius himself is a case in point, for he like all the rest calls man a terrestrial animal,[2] but places him far above aquatic animals, although Plato ranks water itself above earth. This gives us to understand that, when it is a question of assigning to souls their proper degree, we must not maintain the same order as appears right when bodies are graded, for it may happen that an inferior body may house a finer soul, while an inferior soul may occupy a better body.

XVI

What view the Platonist Apuleius adopted about the characters and actions of the demons.

So when this same Platonist came to speak of the characters of the demons, he said that they are subject

73

perturbationibus agitari, inritari iniuriis, obsequiis donisque placari, gaudere honoribus, diversis sacrorum ritibus oblectari et in eis si quid neglectum fuerit conmoveri. Inter cetera etiam dicit ad eos pertinere divinationes augurum, aruspicum, vatum atque somniorum; ab his quoque esse miracula magorum. Breviter autem eos definiens ait daemones esse genere animalia, animo passiva, mente rationalia,[1] corpore aeria, tempore aeterna; horum vero quinque tria priora illis esse quae nobis, quartum proprium, quintum eos cum diis habere commune. Sed video trium superiorum, quae nobiscum habent, duo etiam cum diis habere. Animalia quippe esse dicit et deos, suaque cuique elementa distribuens in terrestribus animalibus nos posuit cum ceteris quae in terra vivunt et sentiunt, in aquatilibus pisces et alia natatilia, in aeriis daemones, in aetheriis deos. Ac per hoc quod daemones genere sunt animalia, non solum eis cum hominibus verum etiam cum diis pecoribusque commune est; quod mente rationalia, cum diis et hominibus; quod tempore aeterna, cum diis solis; quod animo passiva, cum hominibus solis; quod corpore aeria, ipsi sunt soli.

Proinde quod genere sunt animalia, non est magnum, quia hoc sunt et pecora; quod mente rationalia,

---

[1] ingenio rationabilia *Apuleius.*

---

[1] *De Deo Socratis* 12 and 14.
[2] *De Deo Socratis* 6.
[3] *De Deo Socratis* 13.
[4] *De Deo Socratis* 7 and 8.

to the same mental disturbances as men, irritated by slights, mollified by homage and presents, pleased with honours, delighted by a variety of sacred rites and disturbed by the omission of any one of them.[1] Among other things too he mentions as under their jurisdiction the predictions of augury, soothsaying, prophecies and dreams, and says that they are also the source of the miracles performed by magicians.[2] He briefly defines them by remarking that demons are animal in genus, affected by emotions, rational in intelligence, aerial in body and eternal in time. Of these five qualities he points out that they have the first three in common with us, the fourth is peculiar to them, while the fifth they share with the gods.[3] But I observe that, of the first three characteristics which they share with us, they share two also with the gods. In fact Apuleius says that the gods are also animal, and, when he was assigning to each category its appropriate element, he placed us among the terrestrial animals along with everything that has life and sensation on the earth. Among the aquatic animals he put fish and other creatures that swim, and he classified the demons as aerial and the gods as ethereal.[4] And inasmuch as demons are in the class of 'animal' beings, they have this in common, not only with men, but also with gods and beasts. They resemble gods and men in that they are rational in intelligence, but the gods alone in that they are eternal in time, and men alone in that they are affected by emotions; and in that they are aerial in body, they are unique.

Hence, the fact that they are animal in genus is no great matter, for so are the beasts; that they are

75

non est supra nos, quia sumus et nos; quod tempore
aeterna, quid boni est, si non beata? Melior est
enim temporalis felicitas quam misera aeternitas.
Quod animo passiva, quo modo supra nos est, quando
et nos hoc sumus, nec ita esset nisi miseri essemus?
Quod corpore aeria, quanti aestimandum est, cum
omni corpori praeferatur animae qualiscumque
natura, et ideo religionis cultus, qui debetur ex
animo, nequaquam debeatur ei rei quae inferior est
animo? Porro si inter illa quae daemonum esse
dicit, adnumeraret virtutem, sapientiam, felicitatem
et haec eos diceret habere cum diis aeterna atque
communia, profecto aliquid diceret exoptandum
magnique pendendum; nec sic eos tamen propter
haec tamquam Deum colere deberemus, sed potius
ipsum a quo haec illos accepisse nossemus. Quanto
minus nunc honore divino aeria digna sunt animalia,
ad hoc rationalia ut misera esse possint, ad hoc
passiva ut misera sint, ad hoc aeterna ut miseriam
finire non possint!

rational in intelligence does not make them superior to us, for so are we; that they are eternal in time, what does that profit them, if they are not blessed? Better temporary felicity than everlasting misery. In that they are affected by emotion, how is that a proof of their superiority to us, since we too are so affected, but would not be were we not unhappy? In that they are aerial in body, of what account is that, since a soul of whatever kind is to be preferred to any body? And therefore religious worship, which ought to come from the mind, can never be due to what is inferior to the mind. Moreover if, among the qualities he attributes to demons, Apuleius had included virtue, wisdom and felicity, and had added that they share these qualities for ever with the gods, then certainly he would be telling us of something desirable and highly valuable. But, even so, this would still be no reason why we ought to worship them as we worship God. Rather we ought to worship God himself, from whom we should know that they had received these gifts. How much less worthy, in fact, of divine honour are these aerial creatures, whose reason merely enables them to be unhappy, whose minds, by being subject to emotion, actually make them unhappy, whose immortality means only that they will never be able to put an end to their unhappiness!

XVII

An dignum sit eos spiritus ab homine coli, a quorum vitiis eum oporteat liberari.

QUAPROPTER, ut omittam cetera et hoc solum pertractem, quod nobiscum daemones dixit habere commune, id est animi passiones, si omnia quattuor elementa suis animalibus plena sunt, inmortalibus ignis et aer, mortalibus aqua et terra, quaero cur animi daemonum passionum turbelis et tempestatibus agitentur. Perturbatio est enim quae Graece πάθος dicitur; unde illa voluit vocare animo passiva, quia verbum de verbo πάθος passio diceretur motus animi contra rationem. Cur ergo sunt ista in animis daemonum quae in pecoribus non sunt? Quoniam si quid in pecore simile apparet, non est perturbatio, quia non est contra rationem, qua pecora carent. In hominibus autem ut sint istae perturbationes, facit hoc stultitia vel miseria; nondum enim sumus in illa perfectione sapientiae beati quae nobis ab hac mortalitate liberatis in fine promittitur. Deos vero ideo dicunt istas perturbationes non perpeti, quia

---

[1] For this equation cf. below, Book 9.4 and see Cicero, *Tusc. Disp.* 3.4.7; 4.5.10; *De Finibus* 3.10.35.

XVII

*Whether it is fitting that man should worship those
spirits from whose vices he ought to be freed.*

In view of all this, to omit every other consideration
and deal with this point alone, namely, Apuleius'
statement that demons have in common with us a
mind subject to emotion, I ask why, if all four elements are full of living beings, each element having
its own kind, and fire and air are populated with
immortal, and water and earth with mortal beings,
it should happen that the minds of demons are tossed
by the whirlwinds and tempests of emotion. For
perturbatio (disturbance) is what the Greeks call
pathos,[1] and this is why he chose to call the demons
passiva or subject to emotion, because the word
passio (emotion) for the Greek word *pathos* means a
mental agitation which is contrary to reason. Why
then do such emotions exist in the minds of demons,
although they are not found in beasts? For if anything of the kind can be seen in beasts, it is not a
disturbance, because it is not contrary to reason,
which is lacking in beasts. In men, however, the
occasion of these disturbances is folly or unhappiness,
for we are not yet blessed by that perfect wisdom
which is promised us at the end, when we are freed
from our present mortality. But the gods, they say,
do not suffer these disturbances, because they are
not only eternal but also blessed. This is because
they are believed to have the same kind of rational
souls, but perfectly free from every stain and uncleanness. If, then, the gods are free from disturbances because they are animal beings who are

non solum aeterni, verum etiam beati sunt. Easdem
quippe animas rationales etiam ipsos habere perhibent, sed ab omni labe ac peste purissimas. Quam
ob rem si propterea dii non perturbantur quod animalia sunt beata, non misera, et propterea pecora non
perturbantur quod animalia sunt quae nec beata
possunt esse nec misera, restat ut daemones sicut
homines ideo perturbentur quod animalia sunt non
beata, sed misera.

Qua igitur insipientia vel potius amentia per aliquam religionem daemonibus subdimur, cum per
veram religionem ab ea vitiositate in qua illis sumus
similes liberemur? Cum enim daemones, quod et
iste Apuleius, quamvis eis plurimum parcat et divinis
honoribus dignos censeat, tamen cogitur confiteri,
ira instigentur, nobis vera religio praecipit ne ira
instigemur, sed ei potius resistamus. Cum daemones
donis invitentur, nobis vera religio praecipit ne
cuiquam donorum acceptione faveamus. Cum daemones honoribus mulceantur, nobis vera religio
praecipit ut talibus nullo modo moveamur. Cum
daemones quorundam hominum osores, quorundam
amatores sint, non prudenti tranquilloque iudicio,
sed animo ut appellat ipse passivo, nobis vera religio
praecipit ut nostros etiam diligamus inimicos.
Postremo omnem motum cordis et salum mentis
omnesque turbelas et tempestates animi, quibus
daemones aestuare atque fluctuare asserit, nos vera
religio deponere iubet. Quae igitur causa est nisi

---

[1] *De Deo Socratis* 13.
[2] Matthew 5.22, James 1.19.
[3] Luke 6.34–35, James 2.1.

happy and not miserable, and if beasts are not troubled because they are animal beings that have no capacity for happiness or unhappiness, we are left with the conclusion that demons, like men, are disturbed because they are animal beings who are not happy but miserable.

What kind of folly, then, or rather madness is it to subject ourselves to the demons under the name of some religion, when true religion frees us from the vicious inclinations in which we resemble them? For the demons, as even Apuleius is forced to admit, although he allows them the greatest possible indulgence and deems them worthy of divine honours, are the prey of anger,[1] while we are enjoined by true religion not to yield to anger, but rather to resist it.[2] Demons are enticed by gifts, but true religion prescribes that we should favour no man on account of gifts received.[3] Demons are mollified by honours, but true religion teaches us on no account to be moved by such considerations Demons hate some men and love others, not after they have judged men calmly and dispassionately, but as they are influenced by minds subject to emotion—to use the term employed by Apuleius himself—[4] whereas true religion bids us love even our enemies.[5] Finally we are commanded by true religion to put aside all restlessness of heart and turbulence of spirit and all the hurricanes and tempests of passion, with which he declares the souls of demons seethe and boil. What reason, then, is there except folly and a wretched mistake for you to humble yourself in worship before a being whom you wish to avoid re-

[4] *De Deo Socratis* 12.   [5] Matthew 5.44.

stultitia errorque miserabilis ut ei te facias venerando
humilem cui te cupias vivendo dissimilem; et
religione colas quem imitari nolis, cum religionis
summa sit imitari quem colis?

XVIII

*Qualis religio sit, in qua docetur quod homines, ut
commendentur diis bonis, daemonibus uti debeant
advocatis.*

FRUSTRA igitur eis Apuleius, et quicumque ita sentiunt, hunc detulit honorem, sic eos in aere medios
inter aetherium caelum terramque constituens ut,
quoniam nullus deus miscetur homini, quod Platonem
dixisse perhibent, isti ad deos perferant preces
hominum et inde ad homines inpetrata quae poscunt.
Indignum enim putaverunt qui ista crediderunt
misceri homines diis et deos hominibus; dignum
autem misceri daemones et diis et hominibus, hinc
petita qui allegent, inde concessa qui apportent;
ut videlicet homo castus et ab artium magicarum
sceleribus alienus eos patronos adhibeat per quos
illum dii exaudiant, qui haec amant quae ille non
amando fit dignior quem facilius et libentius exaudire
debeant. Amant quippe illi scaenicas turpitudines,
quas non amat pudicitia; amant in maleficiis magorum mille nocendi artes, quas non amat innocentia.

---

[1] *Symposium* 203 A; cf. Apuleius, *De Deo Socratis* 4 and 6.

sembling in your way of life; and why should you pay religious honours to one whom you do not wish to imitate, when the essence of religion is to imitate the one whom you worship?

XVIII

What kind of religion can that be which teaches that men should use demons as intermediaries between themselves and good gods?

IT was useless, then, for Apuleius and those who agree with him to confer an honourable position on the demons, when he established them in the air, midway between the ethereal heaven and the earth, so that, as "no god has any dealings with men" according to the reported statement of Plato,[1] they may convey to the gods the prayers of men and then bring back to men favourable answers to their requests. Those who held this theory thought it improper that men should associate with gods and gods with men, but they saw nothing improper in the association of demons with both gods and men for the purpose of presenting petitions from men and of bringing to men anything granted by the gods. So we are to suppose that an upright man, quite unpractised in the criminal arts of magic, in order to obtain a hearing from the gods, is to invite the aid of those who cherish the very practices by not cherishing which he better deserves a hearing that should be more easily and cheerfully granted. The point is that the demons do cherish those shameful stage displays which modesty detests; they cherish " the thousand

Ergo et pudicitia et innocentia si quid ab diis in-
petrare voluerit, non poterit suis meritis nisi suis
intervenientibus inimicis. Non est quod iste poetica
figmenta et theatrica ludibria iustificare conetur.
Habemus contra ista magistrum eorum et tantae
apud eos auctoritatis Platonem, si pudor humanus ita
de se male meretur ut non solum diligat turpia verum
etiam divinitati existimet grata.

XIX

*De impietate artis magicae, quae patrocinio nititur
spirituum malignorum.*

PORRO adversus magicas artes, de quibus quosdam
nimis infelices et nimis impios etiam gloriari libet,
nonne ipsam publicam lucem testem citabo? Cur
enim tam graviter ista plectuntur severitate legum,
si opera sunt numinum colendorum? An forte istas
leges Christiani instituerunt quibus artes magicae
puniuntur? Secundum quem alium sensum, nisi
quod haec maleficia generi humano perniciosa esse
non dubium est, ait poeta clarissimus:

Testor, cara, deos et te, germana, tuumque
Dulce caput, magicas invitam accingier artes?

---

[1] Virgil, *Aeneid* 7.338.
[2] Virgil, *Aeneid* 4.492–493.

arts of injuring "[1] that the magicians practise in their sorceries and that innocence detests. So modesty and innocence will not be able by their own deserts to obtain any favourable answer from the gods to their prayers, but must rely on the intervention of their enemies. Apuleius gains nothing by his attempt to justify these poetic fictions and theatrical entertainments. We have on our own side against such things the master of their school, Plato, whose authority they rate so high—if human decency does itself such poor service as not only to like what is foul but actually to suppose that divinity relishes such stuff.

XIX

On the impiety of the art of magic, which depends on the support of evil spirits.

FURTHERMORE, against the magic arts, in which certain people who are excessively unfortunate and excessively irreligious are actually pleased to take pride, shall I not cite in evidence public opinion itself? Why are such practices so severely castigated by the law, if they are the work of deities who deserve worship? Or was it perhaps the Christians who introduced these laws under which the magic arts are punished? What other meaning, save that these magic practices without question do deadly harm to mankind, can we attach to these words of the illustrious poet: " I swear, dear sister, by the gods, by you, and by your beloved head, that I am using magic arts as a weapon unwillingly?"[2]

85

Illud etiam, quod alio loco de his artibus dicit:

Atque satas alio vidi traducere messes,

eo quod hac pestifera scelerataque doctrina fructus
alieni in alias terras transferri perhibentur, nonne in
duodecim tabulis, id est Romanorum antiquissimis
legibus, Cicero commemorat esse conscriptum et ei
qui hoc fecerit supplicium constitutum?

Postremo Apuleius ipse numquid apud Christianos
iudices de magicis artibus accusatus est? Quas
utique sibi obiectas si divinas et pias esse noverat et
divinarum potestatum operibus congruas, non solum
eas confiteri debuit, sed etiam profiteri, leges culpans
potius, quibus haec prohiberentur et damnanda
putarentur, quae haberi miranda et veneranda
oporteret. Ita enim vel sententiam suam persua-
deret iudicibus, vel, si illi secundum iniquas leges
saperent eumque talia praedicantem atque laudan-
tem morte multarent, digna animae illius daemones
dona rependerent, pro quorum divinis operibus prae-
dicandis humanam vitam sibi adimi non timeret;
sicut martyres nostri, cum eis pro crimine obiceretur
Christiana religio, qua noverant se fieri salvos et
gloriosissimos in aeternum, non eam negando tem-

---

[1] *Eclogue* 8.99.
[2] The passage of Cicero here referred to has not been found.
But see Pliny, *Natural History* 28.4.
[3] Apuleius married the wealthy widow Pudentilla, whose
affections he was accused of having won through magic

86

So with his other reference to witchcraft, which occurs in another poem: " And I have seen him charm the sown crops to another field " [1]—a reference to the story that, by means of the arts taught in this criminal and pestilential school, one man's harvest could be transferred to another's land. Does not Cicero record the fact that in the Twelve Tables, I mean in the most ancient laws of Rome, the practice was noted and a penalty prescribed for anyone who did so? [2]

Finally, as for Apuleius himself, was it before Christian judges that he was accused of practising magic arts? [3] Assuredly, when these practices were actually charged to him, if he had known that they were divine, free from impiety and in accord with the play of divine forces, he should not only have made confession but have made open profession of them to boot, indicting rather the laws which forbade them and held them worthy of condemnation, when they should have been considered admirable and suitable objects of veneration. For by this course he would either have won the judges over to his own way of thinking or, if they were guided by unjust laws and sentenced him to death for his commendation and praise of such practices, the demons would have recompensed him with gifts befitting so great a soul, who did not fear losing his human life for the sake of preaching their divine works; just as our martyrs, when the Christian religion, which they knew would assure them salvation and eternal glory,

practices. He was tried on this charge before Claudius Maximus, the pagan proconsul of Africa, about A.D. 157 and was acquitted.

porales poenas evadere delegerunt, sed potius confitendo profitendo praedicando et pro hac omnia fideliter fortiterque tolerando et cum pia securitate moriendo leges quibus prohibebatur erubescere compulerunt mutarique fecerunt.

Huius autem philosophi Platonici copiosissima et disertissima extat oratio, qua crimen artium magicarum a se alienum esse defendit seque aliter non vult innocentem videri nisi ea negando quae non possunt ab innocente committi. At omnia miracula magorum, quos recte sentit esse damnandos, doctrinis fiunt et operibus daemonum, quos viderit cur censeat honorandos, eos necessarios asserens perferendis ad deos precibus nostris, quorum debemus opera devitare, si ad Deum verum preces nostras volumus pervenire.

Deinde quaero, quales preces hominum diis bonis per daemones allegari putat, magicas an licitas? Si magicas, nolunt tales; si licitas, nolunt per tales. Si autem peccator paenitens preces fundit, maxime si aliquid magicum admisit, itane tandem illis intercedentibus accipit veniam quibus inpellentibus aut faventibus se cecidisse plangit in culpam? An et ipsi daemones, ut possint paenitentibus mereri indulgentiam, priores agunt, quod eos deceperint,

---

[1] The *Apologia* or *Pro se de magia*, still extant. In this speech, Apuleius, while denying that he had won his wife through magic arts, does not reject magic altogether, claiming that all natural philosophers are to some extent magicians. Indeed, Apuleius himself was a magician of high repute among the pagans. See Augustine, *Letters* 136.1 and 138.18–19.

was charged to them as a crime, chose not to escape temporal punishment by denying it; but rather by confessing, proclaiming and preaching it, and in its name enduring all things with faith and fortitude, and by meeting death with devout composure, they put to shame the laws that sought to forbid it, and caused them to be changed.

But of this Platonist philosopher, Apuleius, there survives a very full and elegant speech,[1] in which he defends himself against the charge of practising the arts of magic and shows no desire to appear innocent except by denying actions which cannot be performed by an innocent man. But all the miracles performed by magicians, whom he rightly judges to be worthy of condemnation, are accomplished by the teachings and the actions of the demons. Let him find some reason to explain why he thinks that they should receive honour, why he maintains that they are necessary for conveying our prayers to the gods, when in fact we ought to shun their works, if we wish our prayers to reach the true God.

Now, I ask, what kind of prayers of men does he suppose are carried to the good gods by demons—magical prayers or legitimate? If they are magical, the gods want none of them, if legitimate, they want no such messengers to deliver them. Suppose, for example, a penitent sinner pours out prayers, especially if the sin he has committed has something to do with magic, is it really only after the intercession of those through whose prompting or influence he laments having fallen into sin that he obtains pardon? Or is it the demons themselves who, in order to win some indulgence for the penitent, show

paenitentiam? Hoc nemo umquam de daemonibus dixit, quia, si ita esset, nequaquam sibi auderent divinos honores expetere qui paenitendo desiderarent ad gratiam veniae pertinere. Ibi enim est detestanda superbia, hic humilitas miseranda.

XX

An credendum sit quod dii boni libentius daemonibus quam hominibus misceantur.

AT enim urgens causa et artissima cogit daemones medios inter deos et homines agere, ut ab hominibus adferant desiderata, et a diis referant inpetrata. Quaenam tandem ista causa est et quanta necessitas? Quia nullus, inquiunt, Deus misceatur homini.

Praeclara igitur sanctitas Dei, qui non miscetur homini supplicanti, et miscetur daemoni arroganti; non miscetur homini paenitenti, et miscetur daemoni decipienti; non miscetur homini confugienti ad divinitatem, et miscetur daemoni fingenti divinitatem; non miscetur homini petenti indulgentiam, et miscetur daemoni suadenti nequitiam; non miscetur homini per philosophicos libros poetas de bene instituta civitate pellenti, et miscetur daemoni a principibus et pontificibus civitatis per scaenicos

---

[1] Plato is meant.

penitence first for having led them astray? Nobody
has ever said this of demons, because, if it were so, it
would be vain for them to dare to seek divine honours
for themselves while they felt the need of repentance
to obtain the grace of pardon. For in the former case
they would display abominable arrogance, in the
latter a humility deserving of pity.

XX

Are we to believe that good gods are more willing to
associate with demons than with men?

But we shall be told that there is a pressing and
compelling reason why the demons must act as intermediaries between gods and men, to carry prayers
from men and to fetch back favourable answers from
the gods. Then what, pray, is this reason, this important necessity? Because no God, they say, deals
directly with man.

A fine thing, then, is the sanctity of God! He has
no communication with a man who entreats him, but
he has with a demon who acts insolently. He has
no communication with a man full of repentance, but
he has with a demon full of cheats. He has no communication with a man who takes refuge in his
divinity, but he has with a demon who counterfeits
divinity. He has no communication with a man who
craves mercy, but he has with a demon who prompts
men to vice. He has no communication with a man [1]
who by means of philosophical writings seeks to expel
poets from a well regulated state, but he has with a
demon who demands from the chiefs and pontiffs of

ludos poetarum ludibria requirenti; non miscetur
homini deorum crimina fingere prohibenti, et miscetur daemoni se falsis deorum criminibus oblectanti;
non miscetur homini magorum scelera iustis legibus
punienti, et miscetur daemoni magicas artes do-
centi et implenti; non miscetur homini imitationem
daemonis fugienti, et miscetur daemoni deceptionem
hominis aucupanti.

XXI

An daemonibus nuntiis et interpretibus dii
utantur fallique se ab eis aut ignorent
aut velint.

SED nimirum tantae huius absurditatis et indigni-
tatis est magna necessitas, quod scilicet deos aetherios humana curantes quid terrestres homines agerent
utique lateret, nisi daemones aerii nuntiarent;
quoniam aether longe a terra est alteque suspensus,
aer vero aetheri terraeque contiguus.

O mirabilem sapientiam! Quid aliud de diis isti
sentiunt, quos omnes optimos volunt, nisi eos et
humana curare, ne cultu videantur indigni, et propter
elementorum distantiam humana nescire, ut cre-

the state the stage representation of the ribald compositions of the poets. He has no communication with a man who forbids writers of fiction to attribute crimes to the gods, but he has with a demon who takes delight in fictitious crimes of the gods. He has no communication with a man who punishes the evil acts of the magicians by just laws, but he has with a demon who teaches and executes magic arts. He has no communication with a man who will not follow the example of a demon, but he has with a demon who lies in wait to ensnare a man.

XXI

Do the gods employ demons as messengers and inter-
mediaries, and are they unaware that they are
being deceived by them, or do they choose
to be deceived?

But surely there is an overpowering necessity for this absurd and disgraceful situation, for obviously the gods dwelling in the ether and solicitous about human affairs would have no actual means of knowing what men on earth were doing, if the demons who live in the air did not bring them news; for the ether is remote from the earth and suspended far above it, while air adjoins both ether and earth.

What wonderful wisdom! Do these authorities hold any other opinion about the gods, all of whom they presume to be perfect, than that they both have regard for human affairs—otherwise they would not seem worthy of worship—and, because of the distance separating the elements, have no knowledge of

dantur daemones necessarii et ob hoc etiam ipsi
putentur colendi per quos dii possint et quid in
rebus humanis agatur addiscere et ubi oportet
hominibus subvenire? Hoc si ita est, diis istis bonis
magis notus est daemon per corpus vicinum quam
homo per animum bonum. O multum dolenda
necessitas, an potius inridenda vel detestanda vani-
tas, ne sit vana divinitas! Si enim animo ab ob-
staculo corporis libero animum nostrum videre dii
possunt, non ad hoc indigent daemonibus nuntiis;
si autem animorum indicia corporalia, qualia sunt
locutio vultus motus, per corpus suum aetherii dii
sentiunt et inde colligunt quid etiam daemones
nuntient, possunt et mendaciis daemonum decipi.
Porro si deorum divinitas a daemonibus non potest
falli, eadem divinitate quod agimus non potest
ignorari.

Vellem autem mihi isti dicerent, utrum diis daemones nuntiaverint de criminibus deorum poetica
Platoni displicere figmenta et sibi ea placere cela-
verint, an utrumque occultaverint deosque esse
maluerint totius rei huius ignaros, an utrumque
indicaverint, et religiosam erga deos Platonis prudentiam et in deos iniuriosam libidinem suam, an

---

[1] That is, if the gods are dependent on the demons for their
information, they are impotent without demonic help.

human affairs—otherwise it could not be held that the demons are indispensable and are therefore themselves duly bound to receive worship, because it is only through them that the gods can both gain additional knowledge about what is happening in the course of human events and can help men where their help is needed. If this is so, then a demon is better known to these good gods because of bodily proximity than a man is because of goodness of mind. What a very deplorable necessity! Or is this not rather a piece of futility that must be ridiculed and denounced, lest divinity itself should be futile?[1] For if the gods, with minds free from corporeal hindrances, can see into our minds, they have no need of demons as messengers for this purpose; but if the gods who dwell in the ether perceive through their own bodies the physical manifestations of the mind, such as speech, facial expression and gesture, and from these physical manifestations gather the sense of whatever the demons report to them, it is possible for them also be misled by any falsehoods which the demons dispense. Moreover, if the divinity of the gods cannot be deceived by the demons, this same divinity makes it impossible for them to be unaware of our actions.

But I should like the Platonists to tell me whether the demons have reported to the gods Plato's displeasure at the fictions of the poets concerning the gods' crimes, while at the same time concealing their own approval of them. Or have they concealed both facts, preferring the gods to be kept in ignorance of the whole subject, or have they reported both the religious concern of Plato for the gods and their own

sententiam quidem Platonis, qua noluit deos per impiam licentiam poetarum falsis criminibus infamari,
ignotam diis esse voluerint, suam vero nequitiam,
qua ludos scaenicos amant quibus illa deorum dede-
cora celebrantur prodere non erubuerint vel ti-
muerint.

Horum quattuor quae interrogando proposui,
quodlibet eligant et in quolibet eorum quantum mali
de diis bonis opinentur adtendant.

Si enim primum elegerint, confessuri sunt non
licuisse diis bonis habitare cum bono Platone, quando
eorum iniurias prohibebat, et habitasse cum daemonibus malis, quando eorum iniuriis exultabant,
cum dii boni hominem bonum longe a se positum
non nisi per malos daemones nossent, quos vicinos
nosse non possent.

Si autem secundum elegerint et utrumque occul-
tatum a daemonibus dixerint, ut dii omnino nescirent
et Platonis religiosissimam legem et daemonum
sacrilegam delectationem, quid in rebus humanis
per internuntios daemones dii nosse utiliter possunt,
quando illa nesciunt quae in honorem bonorum
deorum religione bonorum hominum contra libidinem malorum daemonum decernuntur?

appetite for fables that insult the gods? Or did they want Plato's verdict, whereby he refused to allow the gods to be libelled by the impious licence of poets as guilty of imaginary crimes, to remain unknown to the gods, while they themselves were neither ashamed nor afraid to reveal their own depraved taste which makes them relish stage plays wherein these shameful actions of the gods are depicted?

Of these four alternatives which I have put forward under the form of questions, let them choose which they please; but, whichever they choose, let them mark well how evil is their opinion of the good gods.

If they choose the first, they will have to admit that the good gods were not permitted to associate with Plato, who was good, since he strove to prevent their being insulted, and that they associated with demons who were evil, since they rejoiced to see them insulted; the reason was that the good gods did not get to know a good man who was situated so far from them, except through evil demons, whom, in spite of their proximity, they could not know either.

But if they choose the second alternative and admit that the demons have kept the gods in ignorance of both the law of Plato which displays a high sense of religion and the demons' own sacrilegious pleasure, what is there in human affairs that the gods can usefully learn through demons as intermediaries, when they do not know what measures are taken by the religious scruples of honourable men to protect the honour of the good gods against the licence of the evil demons?

Si vero tertium elegerint et non solum sententiam Platonis deorum iniurias prohibentem, sed etiam daemonum nequitiam deorum iniuriis exultantem per eosdem daemones nuntios diis innotuisse responderint, hoc nuntiare est an insultare? Et dii utrumque sic audiunt, sic utrumque cognoscunt ut non solum malignos daemones deorum dignitati et Platonis religioni contraria cupientes atque facientes a suo accessu non arceant, verum etiam per illos malos propinquos Platoni bono longinquo dona transmittant? Sic enim eos elementorum quasi catenata series conligavit ut illis a quibus criminantur coniungi possint, huic a quo defenduntur non possint, utrumque scientes, sed aeris et terrae transmutare pondera non valentes.

Iam, quod reliquum est, si quartum elegerint, peius est ceteris. Quis enim ferat, si poetarum de diis inmortalibus criminosa figmenta et theatrorum indigna ludibria suamque in his omnibus ardentissimam cupiditatem et suavissimam voluptatem diis daemones nuntiaverunt, et quod Plato philosophica gravitate de optima re publica haec omnia censuit removenda tacuerunt; ut iam dii boni per tales nuntios nosse cogantur mala pessimorum, nec aliena, sed eorundem nuntiorum, atque his contraria non

If they choose the third alternative and reply that not only the verdict of Plato, who forbade insults to the gods, but also the wickedness of the demons, who exult when the gods are wronged, have been reported to the gods by these same demons, is this a report or an insult? And do the gods hear both sides and recognize both sides, and yet not only fail to exclude from their presence these malign demons whose desires and actions are in direct contradiction to the dignity of the gods and the religious feeling of Plato, but actually use those evil neighbours to convey their gifts to the good Plato who is far away from them? They are so tied down by the chain, so to speak, of a gradation of elements that they can join hands with those who attack them, but are unable to do so with one who defends them. They know the truth on both sides but are powerless to interchange the gravity of earth and air.

The remaining alternative, if they choose the fourth, is the worst of all. For who could endure the thought that the scandalous fictions of the poets about the immortal gods and the base entertainments in the theatres have been reported to the gods by the demons along with their own ardent desire for all these spectacles and the delicious pleasure thus aroused in them, while these same demons have kept it to themselves that Plato, being a serious-minded philosopher, enacted that all these things should be abolished in his ideal state? The result of this would be that the good gods are now forced to learn from such messengers the misdeeds, not of others, but of these very same most wicked messengers, but are not permitted to know the good deeds of the philosophers in oppo-

sinantur nosse bona philosophorum, cum illa sint in
iniuriam, ista in honorem ipsorum deorum?

XXII

De abiciendo cultu daemonum contra
Apuleium.

QUIA igitur nihil istorum quattuor eligendum est,
ne in quolibet eorum de diis tam male sentiatur,
restat ut nullo modo credendum sit quod Apuleius
persuadere nititur et quicumque alii sunt eiusdem
sententiae philosophi, ita esse medios daemones inter
deos et homines tamquam internuntios et interpretes, qui hinc ferant petitiones nostras, inde referant deorum suppetias; sed esse spiritus nocendi
cupidissimos, a iustitia penitus alienos, superbia
tumidos, invidentia lividos, fallacia callidos, qui in
hoc quidem aere habitant, quia de caeli superioris
sublimitate deiecti merito inregressibilis transgres-
sionis in hoc sibi congruo velut carcere praedamnati
sunt; nec tamen, quia supra terras et aquas aeri
locus est, ideo et ipsi sunt meritis superiores homini-

---

[1] There appears to be a conflation here of the Hebrew idea
of fallen angels with the pagan doctrine of demons.

sition to the messengers, although the former do despite and the latter do honour to the gods themselves.

XXII

In refutation of Apuleius on the matter of demon-worship, which must be abolished.

So none of these four alternatives is to be chosen, since we must avoid thinking so badly of the gods, as we should have to whichever one we adopted. We are reduced, then, to the conclusion that we can by no means accept the theory which Apuleius does his best to prove, not to mention other philosophers of the same persuasion, whoever they may be, namely, that demons are situated midway between gods and men to serve as intermediaries and interpreters, that is to carry our petitions from earth, and to bring back help from the gods. On the contrary we should believe that they are spirits fanatically bent on doing harm, completely at odds with justice, swollen with pride, green with envy and well practised in deceit, who live, it is true, in our air, but do so because they were cast out from the lofty regions of the higher heavens and were condemned in the beginning to dwell in this region, which is, as it were, a prison appropriate to their nature, in just punishment for a transgression from which there is no retreat.[1] Nor, on the other hand, does it follow from the location of their dwelling, the air, above earth and water, that they are themselves on that account superior in merits to men, for we easily surpass them, not by

bus, qui eos non terreno corpore, sed electo in auxilium Deo vero pia mente facillime superant.

Sed multis plane participatione verae religionis indignis tamquam captis subditisque dominantur, quorum maximae parti mirabilibus et fallacibus signis sive factorum sive praedictorum deos se esse persuaserunt. Quibusdam vero vitia eorum aliquanto adtentius et diligentius intuentibus non potuerunt persuadere quod dii sint, atque inter deos et homines internuntios ac beneficiorum inpetratores se esse finxerunt; si tamen non istum saltem honorem homines eis deferendum putarunt qui illos nec deos esse credebant, quia malos videbant, deos autem omnes bonos volebant, nec audebant tamen omnino indignos dicere honore divino, maxime ne offenderent populos a quibus eis cernebant inveterata superstitione per tot sacra et templa serviri.

XXIII

Quid Hermes Trismegistus de idolatria senserit et unde scire potuerit superstitiones Aegyptias auferendas.

NAM diversa de illis Hermes Aegyptius, quem Trismegiston vocant, sensit et scripsit.

---

[1] Hermes Trismegistus, Milton's "thrice-great Hermes," was identified with the Egyptian god Thoth by popular belief, but the *Hermetica* and other works which were ascribed to him were late compositions by Hellenized Egyptians or by Greeks living in Egypt. One of these, the *Asclepius* which is quoted below, was in the form of a dialogue between Hermes and Asclepius. On the vexed question of the date and authorship of this work and on the historical circumstances sur-

reason of our earthly body, but by our devout choice of the true God to be our help.

Admittedly the demons hold sway over many men who are clearly not fit to partake in true religion, and these men are their prisoners and subjects, the greater part of whom they have persuaded of their divinity by miraculous but fraudulent signs in the form of either deeds or prophecies. There are, however, some who have observed their vices with somewhat closer and more careful attention and whom they have not been able to persuade of their divinity; and so they have invented a rôle for themselves as intermediaries between gods and men and as agents in securing benefits. Perhaps there were some men who still thought them unworthy even of the deference to be gained by this rôle, yet, though they did not believe them to be gods because they realized that they were evil and would have none but good gods, at the same time they did not dare to say that they were altogether unworthy of divine honour, chiefly for fear of giving offence to the multitude who, as they saw, maintained so many rites and temples for the service of the gods through their long tradition of false religion.

XXIII

The verdict of Hermes Trismegistus on idolatry and the source which enabled him to know that the superstitions of Egypt were to be abolished.

A DIFFERENT opinion of the demons was adopted and expressed in his writings by the Egyptian Hermes, who is called Trismegistus.[1]

Apuleius enim deos quidem illos negat; sed cum dicit ita inter deos et homines quadam medietate versari ut hominibus apud ipsos deos necessarii videantur, cultum eorum a supernorum deorum religione non separat. Ille autem Aegyptius alios deos esse dicit a summo Deo factos, alios ab hominibus.

Hoc qui audit, sicut a me positum est, putat dici de simulacris, quia opera sunt manuum hominum; at ille visibilia et contrectabilia simulacra velut corpora deorum esse asserit; inesse autem his quosdam spiritus invitatos, qui valeant alquid sive ad nocendum sive ad desideria nonnulla complenda eorum a quibus eis divini honores et cultus obsequia deferuntur.

Hos ergo spiritus invisibiles per artem quandam visibilibus rebus corporalis materiae copulare, ut sint quasi animata corpora illis spiritibus dicata et subdita simulacra, hoc esse dicit deos facere eamque

---

rounding its composition, see W. Scott, *Hermetica*, Vol. I (Oxford, 1924), pp. 51–81. Scott argues that Hermes' prediction of the impending doom of the Egyptian religion, quoted below by Augustine, must have been written in the years A.D. 268–273, a time of great political and religious unrest in Egypt. Queen Zenobia of Palmyra had invaded the land, bringing with her foreign troops whose hostility or indifference to the traditional Egyptian cults served to promote the spread of already powerful Christianity. A. S. Ferguson, however, maintains that " The prophecy fits the conditions of the last great uprising of the Jews [A.D. 115], which was heralded by ominous natural disasters and wrought immense havoc in Egypt and Libya." It is also possible that the author of the prophecy develops commonplaces of apocalyptic literature without reference to any specific historical event. If so, the date of the *Asclepius* cannot be exactly ascertained, except

Apuleius, it is true, denies that demons are gods, but when he says that they perform a kind of intermediate function between gods and men, so that they seem indispensable to men in their relations with the gods, he makes no religious distinction between their worship and that of the gods on high. But this Egyptian says that there are two classes of gods, one created by the supreme God and the other by men.

Anyone who hears this stated just as I have put it down will naturally suppose that Hermes is speaking of idols, because they are the handiwork of men. But he maintains that visible and tangible images are in a sense only bodies of the gods, and that there reside in them by invitation certain spirits which have the power either to injure or to fulfill some desires of those who pay them divine honours and religious worship.

To unite, therefore, these invisible spirits to visible objects of bodily substance by some strange technique, so that the result is something like animated bodies, idols dedicated and subject to these spirits, this, Hermes says, is "making gods," and this great

that it must be earlier than Lactantius (c. A.D. 240–320), who quotes from it extensively in his *Divinae Institutiones*. See A. S. Ferguson in Scott's *Hermetica*, Vol. IV (Oxford, 1936), pp. x–xvi, and also A. D. Nock and A. J. Festugière, *Corpus Hermeticum* (Paris, 1945), Vol. II, p. 288 ff.

The Latin translation of the *Asclepius* used by Augustine has come down to us among the works of Apuleius, who was born about A.D. 125. But the style and general ineptitude of the translation make it certain that this is not the work of Apuleius. Lactantius did not know the translation used by Augustine; his Latin version of the Greek is his own.

magnam et mirabilem deos faciendi accepisse homines potestatem.

Huius Aegyptii verba, sicut in nostram linguam interpretata sunt, ponam. " Et quoniam de cognatione," inquit, " et consortio hominum deorumque nobis indicitur sermo, potestatem hominis, o Asclepi, vimque cognosce. Dominus," inquit, " et Pater vel quod est summum Deus ut effector est deorum caelestium, ita homo fictor est deorum qui in templis sunt humana proximitate contenti." Et paulo post: " Ita humanitas," inquit, " semper memor naturae et originis suae in illa divinitatis imitatione perseverat ut, sicuti Pater ac Dominus, ut sui similes essent, deos fecit aeternos, ita humanitas deos suos ex sui vultus similitudine figuraret."

Hic cum Asclepius, ad quem maxime loquebatur, ei respondisset atque dixisset: " Statuas dicis, o Trismegiste?" tum ille: " Statuas," inquit. " O Asclepi, vides quatenus tu ipse diffidas; statuas animatas sensu et spiritu plenas tantaque facientes et talia, statuas futurorum praescias eaque sorte vate somniis multisque aliis rebus praedicentes, inbecillitates hominibus facientes easque curantes, tristitiam laetitiamque pro meritis. An ignoras, o Asclepi,

---

[1] Plainly, Augustine himself did not suppose the Latin translation of the *Asclepius* to be by Apuleius, since he names no translator, even though he has just been speaking about Apuleius and contrasting Apuleius' views with those of Hermes. Of the Greek original, only fragments survive,

and miraculous power, he adds, of making gods has been given to men.

I shall quote the words of this Egyptian, as they have been translated into our language.[1] " Since our discussion is concerned with the relationship and fellowship of men with gods, learn, Asclepius, of the power and the capacity of man. As the Lord and Father or, highest title of all, God is the creator of the celestial gods, so is man the artificer of those gods who in their temples are content to live in the midst of men.[2] " A little later he says: " So humanity, ever mindful of its nature and origin, perseveres in this imitation of the divine, so that, just as the Lord and Father, in order that others like himself might exist, made everlasting gods, in the same way humanity fashioned its own gods after the likeness of its own countenance.[3] "

Here Asclepius, his principal interlocutor, answered and said: "Is it of statues you speak, Trismegistus ? " " Yes," he replied, " I am speaking of statues. You see how even you lack faith, Asclepius, for I mean statues endowed with life, pregnant with sensation and inspiration, and performing so many wonderful things, statues that have foreknowledge of the future and can predict it by sortition, by prophecy, by dreams, and by many other methods, statues that can bring maladies upon men and heal them again, allotting them sadness or joy according to their deserts. Do you not know, Asclepius, that Egypt is

However, in 1948 a complete Coptic translation of the *Asclepius* was found in Egypt, together with a large number of Gnostic texts.

[2] *Asclepius* 23. [3] *Asclepius* 23.

quod Aegyptus imago sit caeli, aut, quod est verius, translatio aut descensio omnium quae gubernantur atque exercentur in caelo. Ac si dicendum est verius, terra nostra mundi totius est templum. Et tamen quoniam praescire cuncta prudentem decet, istud vos ignorare fas non est: Futurum tempus est cum [1] appareat Aegyptios incassum pia mente divinitatem sedula religione servasse."

Deinde multis verbis Hermes hunc locum exequitur, in quo videtur hoc tempus praedicere quo Christiana religio, quanto est veracior atque sanctior, tanto vehementius et liberius cuncta fallacia figmenta subvertit, ut gratia verissimi Salvatoris liberet hominem ab eis diis quos facit homo, et ei Deo subdat a quo factus est homo. Sed Hermes cum ista praedicit, velut amicus eisdem ludificationibus daemonum loquitur, nec Christianum nomen evidenter exprimit, sed tamquam ea tollerentur atque delerentur quorum observatione caelestis similitudo

---

[1] cum *Asclepius and most Augustine MSS.:* quo *codex Corbeiensis (saec. VII) Migne Hoffmann Dombart* [3] *Welldon.*

---

[1] In *Asclepius* 10, the Latin translator of the dialogue explains the word *mundus* as a translation of the Greek κόσμος, the whole ordered universe. However, in *Asclepius* 14 b, we are told that *mundus* is the Greek ὕλη, or ' matter,' for which the usual Latin words are *materia* or *silva.* Cf. Asclepius 7 b, where *mundanum* is used to translate ὑλικόν, ' material '. Such inconsistencies in the Latin translation of the Greek *Asclepius* have made an obscure treatise even more so.

[2] *Asclepius* 24.

[3] Scott argues that Augustine is correct in his belief that

an image of heaven or, more exactly, that all the administrative and executive activities of heaven have left their place and come down to Egypt. In fact, if the truth must be told, our land is a temple where the whole cosmos [1] is enshrined. And yet, since a wise man ought to have foreknowledge at every point, it is not lawful that you should remain in ignorance of this other fact: a time will come when it will become clear that the Egyptians have in vain worshipped the gods with religious devotion and constant service." [2]

Then Hermes expands this subject at great length and seems to predict our own time when the Christian religion, with an energy and freedom corresponding to its higher truth and superior holiness, is overthrowing all these fraudulent artifacts, so that the grace of the true Saviour may release man from the gods made by man and deliver him to the God by whom man was made.[3] But, while making these predictions, Hermes speaks as if he looked kindly upon those same delusive contrivances of the demons and does not expressly mention Christianity by name, but as if he were deploring the future abolition and destruction of the rites by whose observance the

the author of the *Asclepius* foretells the coming victory of Christianity over the pagan cults. As Scott notes, however, Augustine supposes that Hermes speaks many centuries before the birth of Christianity and that his foreknowledge was provided by evil spirits. See Scott, *Hermetica*, Vol. IV., p. 181. It is possible that when the Christian persecution of paganism had begun in the fourth century, Hermes' prophecy was elaborated in the light of contemporary events. For a different view see A. S. Ferguson in Scott, *Hermetica*, Vol. IV, pp. xii–xiii.

custodiretur in Aegypto, ita haec futura deplorans luctuosa quodam modo praedicatione testatur. Erat enim de his de quibus dicit apostolus, quod *cognoscentes Deum non sicut Deum glorificaverunt aut gratias egerunt, sed evanuerunt in cogitationibus suis, et obscuratum est insipiens cor eorum; dicentes enim se esse sapientes stulti facti sunt et inmutaverunt gloriam incorrupti Dei in similitudinem imaginis corruptibilis hominis* et cetera, quae commemorare longum est.

Multa quippe talia dicit de uno vero Deo fabricatore mundi qualia veritas habet; et nescio quo modo illa obscuratione cordis ad ista delabitur ut diis quos confitetur ab hominibus fieri semper velit homines subdi et haec futuro tempore plangat auferri quasi quicquam sit infelicius homine cui sua figmenta dominantur; cum sit facilius ut tamquam deos colendo quos fecit nec ipse sit homo, quam ut per eius cultum dii possint esse quos fecit homo. Citius enim fit ut homo in honore positus pecoribus non intellegens comparetur quam ut operi Dei ad eius imaginem facto, id est ipsi homini, opus hominis praeferatur. Quapropter merito homo deficit ab illo qui eum fecit, cum sibi praeficit ipse quod fecit.

Haec vana deceptoria, perniciosa sacrilega Hermes Aegyptius, quia tempus quo auferrentur venturum sciebat, dolebat; sed tam inpudenter dolebat, quam

---

[1] Romans 1.21–23.   [2] Cf. Psalm 49.20.

replica of heaven was safeguarded in Egypt, his predictions take on a certain mournful tone. He was, in fact, one of those of whom the Apostle says: "Although they knew God, they did not honour him as God or give thanks to him, but they became futile in their thinking and their senseless minds were darkened. Claiming to be wise, they became fools and exchanged the glory of the immortal God for an image resembling mortal men,"[1] and all the rest, which is too long to quote.

In fact he makes many statements about the one true God, the artificer of the universe, which closely resemble the assertions of Truth; and it is puzzling how by that "darkening of the mind" he falls so low as to require men always to be in subjection to gods who he admits are made by men, and so low as to bewail the future abolition of such things. As if anything could be more hapless than a man who is a slave to his own artifacts. It is easier for man to become less than man by worshipping, as if they were gods, the works of his own hands, than it is for those works to become divine by man's worshipping them. For it can more readily happen that a man of position but without understanding become comparable to the beasts[2] than that the work of man should be preferred to the work of God made after his own image, that is, to man himself. And so man deserves his alienation from his Maker, when he makes more of what he makes than of himself.

So the Egyptian Hermes grieved for these foolish snares, deadly and damnable as they are, because he knew the time would come when these would be swept away; but his grief was as impudent as his

inprudenter sciebat. Non enim haec ei revelaverat
sanctus Spiritus, sicut prophetis sanctis, qui haec
praevidentes cum exultatione dicebant: *Si faciet*
homo deos, et ecce ipsi non sunt dii; et alio loco: *Erit*
in illo die, dicit Dominus, exterminabo nomina simulacro-
rum a terra, et non iam erit eorum memoria; proprie vero
de Aegypto, quod ad hanc rem adtinet, ita sanctus
Esaias prophetat: *Et movebuntur manufacta Aegypti*
a facie eius, et cor eorum vincetur in eis, et cetera huius
modi.

Ex quo genere et illi erant qui venturum quod
sciebant venisse gaudebant; qualis Symeon, qualis
Anna, qui mox natum Iesum; qualis Elisabeth, quae
etiam conceptum in Spiritu agnovit; qualis Petrus
revelante Patre dicens: *Tu es Christus, filius Dei vivi.*
Huic autem Aegyptio illi spiritus indicaverant futura
tempora perditionis suae, qui etiam praesenti in
carne Domino trementes dixerunt: *Quid venisti ante*
tempus perdere nos? sive quia subitum illis fuit, quod
futurum quidem, sed tardius opinabantur, sive quia
perditionem suam hanc ipsam dicebant, qua fiebat
ut cogniti spernerentur, et hoc erat *ante tempus,* id
est ante tempus iudicii, quo aeterna damnatione

---

[1] Jeremiah 16.20. The Latin version of the Old Testament
used by Augustine, a translation of the Greek Septuagint,
differed considerably from the Hebrew text, on which our own
Authorized Version is based.
[2] Zechariah 13.2.   [3] Isaiah 19.1.
[4] Cf. Luke 2.25 ff.; 1.41 ff.   [5] Matthew 16.16.
[6] Matthew 8.29; cf. below *City of God,* 9. 21.

knowledge was imprudent. For it was not the Holy Spirit who had revealed this knowledge to Hermes, as he had to the holy prophets, who when they saw what was to come cried exultantly: " If a man shall make gods, lo and behold they are no gods." [1] And in another passage: " And it shall happen on that day, says the Lord, that I will cut off the names of the idols out of the land, and they shall be remembered no more." [2] Specifically with regard to Egypt, in connection with this matter, the holy Isaiah thus prophesies: " And the idols of Egypt made by hand shall be upheaved from before him, and the heart of Egypt shall· be overcome within them," [3] and so on to the same effect.

In the same class as the prophets were those who, knowing what was to come, rejoiced when it had come to pass. Such were Simeon and Anna who recognized Jesus when in due time he was born, such was Elisabeth who recognized him by the Spirit even at the time of his conception,[4] such was Peter who, when the Father revealed it to him, said: " You are the Christ, the Son of the living God." [5] But to this Egyptian the same spirits predicted the time of their own ruin as they had said trembling to the Lord, when he was still before them in the flesh: " Why have you come to destroy us before the time?" [6] They asked this either because what they knew must indeed come came upon them suddenly when they expected it to be delayed, or because they meant by destruction their being recognized for what they were, and so despised. And this happened " before the time," that is before the day of judgement, on which they are to be punished by eternal damnation along

puniendi sunt cum omnibus etiam hominibus qui
eorum societate detinentur, sicut religio loquitur
quae nec fallit nec fallitur, non sicut iste quasi omni
vento doctrinae hinc atque inde perflatus et falsis
vera permiscens dolet quasi perituram religionem,
quem postea confitetur errorem.

XXIV

*Quo modo Hermes parentum suorum sit confessus
errorem, quem tamen doluerit destruendum.*

Post multa enim ad hoc ipsum redit ut iterum dicat de diis quos homines fecerunt, ita loquens: "Sed
iam de talibus sint satis dicta talia. Iterum," inquit,
"ad hominem rationemque redeamus, ex quo divino
dono homo animal dictum est rationale. Minus
enim miranda, etsi miranda sunt, quae de homine
dicta sunt. Omnium enim mirabilium vicit admira-
tionem quod homo divinam potuit invenire naturam
eamque efficere. Quoniam ergo proavi nostri multum errabant circa deorum rationem increduli et
non animadvertentes ad cultum religionemque

---

[1] Ephesians 4.14.
[2] As Scott points out (*Hermetica*, Vol. IV, p. 183), in the
Greek original the word here translated "since" was probably ἐπειδή, meaning "when" or "after." Hermes is saying, then, that *after* a time when men were in error and did
not worship the gods, the art of making gods was discovered
and religion thus established. Augustine, however, has been
misled by the translation of ἐπειδή as *quoniam* and supposes

with all men also who are involved in fellowship with them. Such is the teaching of a religion that never deceives nor is deceived, unlike Hermes who is, as it were, "tossed to and fro with every wind of doctrine," [1] and, intermingling some truth with his falsehoods, sorrows over the future destruction of a religion which he later admits to be erroneous.

XXIV

How Hermes admitted the error of his own fore-fathers, while lamenting that it must be wiped out.

AFTER a long digression Hermes returns to his main point and again discusses the gods made by men in the following words: "But now let what I have said on this subject suffice. Let us return once more to man and to reason, that divine gift thanks to which man has been termed a rational animal. For admirable as are all the things that have been said of man, they are not the most admirable. For arousing greater wonder than all other marvels is the fact that man has been able to discover and manufacture the divine nature. Therefore, since [2] our ancestors erred gravely in their concept of the gods through their unbelief and because they did not give any

Hermes to mean that the art of making gods was discovered *because* men were in error. Augustine is puzzled to find Hermes making so damaging an admission and is forced to explain it by the supposition that Hermes was inspired at times by God and at times by an evil spirit, by God when he admits that the art of god-making was the result of error, by an evil spirit when he speaks of god-making with approval.

divinam, invenerunt artem qua efficerent deos. Cui
inventae adiunxerunt virtutem de mundi natura
convenientem, eamque miscentes, quoniam animas
facere non poterant, evocantes animas daemonum
vel angelorum eas indiderunt imaginibus sanctis
divinisque mysteriis, per quas idola et bene faciendi
et male vires habere potuissent."

Nescio utrum sic confiterentur ipsi daemones
adiurati, quo modo iste confessus est. "Quoniam,"
inquit, "proavi nostri multum errabant circa deorum
rationem increduli et non animadvertentes ad cultum religionemque divinam, invenerunt artem qua
efficerent deos." Numquidnam saltem mediocriter
eos dixit errasse, ut hanc artem invenirent faciendi
deos, aut contentus fuit dicere: Errabant, nisi ad-
deret et diceret: Multum errabant? Iste ergo
multus error et incredulitas non animadvertentium
ad cultum religionemque divinam invenit artem qua
efficeret deos. Et tamen quod multus error et
incredulitas et a cultu ac religione divina aversio
animi invenit, ut homo arte faceret deos, hoc dolet vir
sapiens tamquam religionem divinam venturo certo

---

[1] Scott (Vol. I, p. 358) seeks to clarify this passage by trans-
posing the phrase *de mundi natura convenientem* so that it
follows *qua efficerent deos* and by reading *conveniente* for *convenientem*. He then translates, "they invented the art of
making gods out of some material substance suited for the
purpose." He understands *mundi natura* to mean ὑλική τις
φύσις as suggested in *Asclepius* 7 and 14. Scott's interpretation may be correct: the statues are made of natural substances into which a supernatural efficacy (*virtus*) is introduced
by the evocation of souls.

heed to worship and divine religion, they invented
the art of making gods.[1] When they had invented
it, they added to it the appropriate natural force [2]
belonging to the substance of the universe and combined the two, and, since they were unable to create
souls, they called upon the souls of demons or angels
and introduced them into holy images and divine
mysteries so that, with their assistance, idols might
have the power of doing both good and harm." [3]

I do not know whether the demons themselves, if
called upon to testify, would admit as much as does
Hermes. He says: "Since our ancestors erred
gravely in their concept of the gods through their unbelief and because they did not give any heed to
worship and divine religion, they invented the art of
making gods." Did he say that at least they erred
in a moderate sort of way and so were led to invent
the art of making gods, or was he content to say:
"They erred" without adding "gravely"? No, it
was this *grave* error and unbelief on the part of men
who did not pay due attention to worship and divine
religion that invented the art of making gods. And
yet it is the loss of what was invented by grave error,
unbelief and an aversion from worship and divine
religion, namely the art whereby man could make
gods, that the sage deplores, as if he mourned the
loss, at a definite time to come, of a religion of
divine origin. Consider whether it is not under the

[2] After *virtutem* Scott omits *de . . . convenientem* and inserts *per quam (quas MSS.) idola et bene faciendi et male vires
habere potuissent* from below. He then translates, "they added
a supernatural force whereby the images might have power to
work good or hurt . . ." See *Hermetica*, Vol. I, p. 358 and
Vol. III, p. 222.   [3] Asclepius 37.

tempore auferri. Vide si non et vi divina maiorum
suorum errorem praeteritum prodere, et vi diabolica
poenam daemonum futuram dolere compellitur. Si
enim proavi eorum multum errando circa deorum
rationem incredulitate et aversione animi a cultu ac
religione divina invenerunt artem qua efficerent deos,
quid mirum si haec ars detestanda quidquid fecit
aversa a religione divina aufertur religione divina,
cum veritas emendat errorem, fides redarguit incredulitatem, conversio corrigit aversionem?

Si enim tacitis causis dixisset proavos suos invenisse artem qua facerent deos, nostrum fuit utique,
si quid rectum piumque saperemus, adtendere et
videre nequaquam illos ad hanc artem perventuros
fuisse qua homo deos facit si a vertitate non aberrarent, si ea quae Deo digna sunt crederent, si animum
adverterent ad cultum religionemque divinam; et
tamen si causas artis huius nos diceremus multum
errorem hominum et incredulitatem et animi errantis
atque infidelis a divina religione aversionem, utcumque ferenda esset inpudentia resistentium veritati.
Cum vero idem ipse qui potestatem huius artis super
omnia cetera miratur in homine, qua illi deos facere
concessum est, et dolet venturum esse tempus quo
haec omnia deorum figmenta ab hominibus instituta

---

[1] If this is a reference to laws prohibiting pagan worship, it
must have been inserted into the Hermetic prophecy some
time during the fourth century, after the Christian persecution
of paganism had begun. However, the reference may be a

influence of divine power that he is driven to reveal the error committed in the past by his ancestors, while it is a diabolical influence that makes him bewail the future punishment of the demons. For if men's ancestors discovered the art of making gods only by grave error in their concept of the gods, by unbelief, and by an aversion from worship and divine religion, what wonder is it if whatever this detestable art has achieved in its aversion from divine religion is swept away by divine religion, at a time when truth rectifies error, faith refutes unbelief, and conversion remedies aversion?

Now if Hermes had said simply that his ancestors invented the art of making gods without mentioning the reasons, it would still have been our duty, if we had any sense of right and piety, to take note of his statement and to reflect that they would never have arrived at this art which enables men to make gods, if they had not strayed from the truth, if they had held beliefs worthy of God and if they had directed their thoughts to worship and divine religion. On the other hand, if it had been we who alleged that the origins of this art were grave human error, unbelief and the aversion of an erring and faithless mind from divine religion, the impudence of those who resist the truth would be in some measure endurable. But when Hermes himself, who admires above all else in man his mastery of the art which empowers him to make gods, and who grieves that a time will come when all the images of deities set up by man will be swept away by order of the laws themselves,[1]

mere apocalyptic commonplace, a prediction of the total dissolution of all cosmic and human order.

etiam legibus iubeantur auferri, confitetur tamen
atque exprimit causas quare ad ista perventum sit,
dicens proavos suos multo errore et incredulitate et
animum non advertendo ad cultum religionemque
divinam invenisse hanc artem, qua facerent deos,
nos quid oportet dicere, vel potius quid agere nisi
quantas possumus gratias Domino Deo nostro, qui
haec contrariis causis quam instituta sunt abstulit?
Nam quod instituit multitudo erroris, abstulit via
veritatis; quod instituit incredulitas, abstulit fides;
quod instituit a cultu divinae religionis aversio,
abstulit ad unum verum Deum sanctumque conversio.

Nec in sola Aegypto, quam solam in isto plangit
daemonum spiritus, sed in omni terra, quae cantat
Domino canticum novum, sicut vere sacrae et vere
propheticae litterae praenuntiarunt, ubi scriptum
est: *Cantate Domino canticum novum, cantate Domino
omnis terra.* Titulus quippe psalmi huius est: *Quando domus aedificabatur post captivitatem.* Aedificatur
enim domus Domino civitas Dei, quae est sancta
ecclesia, in omni terra post eam captivitatem qua
illos homines, de quibus credentibus in Deum tamquam lapidibus vivis domus aedificatur, captos daemonia possidebant. Neque enim, quia deos homo
faciebat, ideo non ab eis possidebatur ipse qui fecerat,

---

[1] Psalm 96.1.

[2] This title, found in the Septuagint version of the Psalter,
indicates that the psalm in question was written after the return from the Babylonian captivity for services in the second
temple.

[3] I Peter 2.5.

when Hermes himself nevertheless admits and
emphasizes the reasons that led men into this kind
of worship, namely the grave error, unbelief and
aversion from worship and divine religion on the part
of his ancestors whereby they were led to their discovery of the art of making gods, what ought we to
say or rather what ought we to do but offer the most
fervent thanks possible to the Lord our God, who has
abolished these practices for reasons opposite to
those for which they were established? For what
was established by a multiplicity of errors has been
abolished by the one way of truth, what was established by unbelief has been abolished by faith, and
what was established by turning away from the
worship that is part of divine religion has been
abolished by turning back to the one true and holy
God.

And it is not only in Egypt, for which alone the
spirit of the demons wept in Hermes' lament, that this
change has taken place, but in all the earth, which
sings to the Lord a new song, as the truly sacred and
truly prophetic Scriptures predicted, where it was
written: " Sing unto the Lord a new song, sing unto
the Lord, all the earth." [1] Now the title of this
psalm is: " When the house was a-building after the
captivity." [2] For a house is being built for the Lord
in all the earth, the City of God, which is the holy
Church, after that captivity in which the demonic
powers held prisoner those men who now believe in
God and of whom " as living stones a house is being
built." [3] For although man was the creator of his
gods, he was not, their very maker, any the less
possessed by them when he was delivered by his

quando in eorum societatem colendo traducebatur;
societatem dico, non idolorum stolidorum, sed
versutorum daemoniorum. Nam quid sunt idola,
nisi quod eadem scriptura dicit: *Oculos habent, et*
non videbunt, et quidquid tale de materiis licet affabre
effigiatis, tamen vita sensuque carentibus dicendum
fuit? Sed inmundi spiritus eisdem simulacris arte
illa nefaria conligati cultorum suorum animas in suam
societatem redigendo miserabiliter captivaverant.
Unde dicit apostolus: *Scimus quia nihil est idolum;*
sed quae immolant gentes, daemoniis immolant, et non
Deo; nolo vos socios fieri daemoniorum. Post hanc
ergo captivitatem qua homines a malignis daemonibus
tenebantur, Dei domus aedificatur in omni terra;
unde titulum ille psalmus accepit, ubi dicitur: *Can-*
tate Domino canticum novum, cantate Domino omnis
terra. Cantate Domino, benedicite nomen eius, bene
nuntiate diem ex die salutare eius. Adnuntiate in genti-
bus gloriam eius, in omnibus populis mirabilia eius;
quoniam magnus Dominus et laudabilis nimis, terribilis
est super omnes deos. Quia omnes dii gentium daemonia,
dominus autem caelos fecit.

Qui ergo doluit venturum fuisse tempus quo aufer-
retur cultus idolorum et in eos qui colerent dominatio
daemoniorum, malo spiritu instigatus semper volebat
istam captivitatem manere, qua transacta psalmus
canit aedificari domum in omni terra. Praenuntia-

---

[1] Psalm 115.5.   [2] I Corinthians 10.19–20.
[3] Psalm 96.1–5.

worship into their fellowship; a fellowship, I mean, not with stupid idols, but with wily demons. For what are idols but what the same Scripture describes in these words: " Eyes have they, and they shall not see," [1] and whatever else may be said of substances however skilfully carved into shape, but withal lacking life and sense? But unclean spirits, bound to these same images by that wicked art, had miserably enslaved the souls of their devotees by bringing them into fellowship with themselves. Hence the words of the Apostle: " We know that the idol is not any thing, but the things which the Gentiles sacrifice, they sacrifice to demons, and not to God; I do not want you to enter into fellowship with demons." [2] So after this captivity in which men were held prisoner by malicious demons, the house of God is a-building in every land; and from this the psalm takes its title, where it is said: " Sing to the Lord a new song, sing to the Lord, all the earth. Sing to the Lord, bless his name; tell of his salvation from day to day. Declare his glory among the nations, his marvelous works among all the peoples. For the Lord is great, and greatly to be praised; he is to be feared above all gods. For all the gods of the nations are demons; but the Lord made the heavens." [3]

So then, when Hermes lamented that the time would come when the worship of idols would be abolished along with the tyranny of the demonic powers over their worshippers, it was an evil spirit that prompted him to wish for the everlasting continuance of this captivity, of which the Psalmist sings that once it is finished, a house of the Lord is

bat illa Hermes dolendo; praenuntiabat haec propheta gaudendo. Et quia Spiritus victor est qui
haec per sanctos prophetas canebat, etiam Hermes
ipse ea quae nolebat et dolebat auferri, non a prudentibus et fidelibus et religiosis, sed ab errantibus et
incredulis et a cultu divinae religionis aversis esse
instituta miris modis coactus est confiteri. Qui
quamvis eos appellet deos, tamen cum dicit a talibus
hominibus factos quales esse utique non debemus,
velit nolit, ostendit colendos non esse ab eis qui tales
non sunt quales fuerunt a quibus facti sunt, hoc est a
prudentibus, fidelibus, religiosis; simul etiam de-
monstrans ipsos homines qui eos fecerunt sibimet
inportasse, ut eos haberent deos, qui non erant dii.
Verum est quippe illud propheticum: *Si faciet
homo deos, et ecce ipsi non sunt dii.*

Deos ergo tales, talium deos, arte factos a talibus,[1]
id est idolis daemones per artem nescio quam cupiditatum suarum vinculis inligatos cum appellaret factos
ab hominibus deos, non tamen eis dedit, quod
Platonicus Apuleius—unde iam satis diximus et
quam sit inconveniens absurdumque monstravimus—
ut ipsi essent interpretes et intercessores inter deos
quos fecit Deus et homines quos idem fecit Deus;
hinc adferentes vota, inde munera referentes. Nimis

---

[1] cum appellasset Hermes *deleted by Dombart after* talibus.

[1] Jeremiah 16.20.

being built in all the earth. Hermes predicted these
things, grieving as he did so; the prophet too predicted them, but with rejoicing. And because the
Spirit who made these predictions through the holy
prophets is victorious, even Hermes himself was by a
miracle obliged to admit that what was abolished
against his will and to his grief had been established,
not by the prudent, the faithful or the religious, but
by the erring, the unbelieving and those who were
opposed to the worship that is a part of divine
religion. And although he calls them gods, nevertheless when he says that they were created by such
men as we certainly ought not to be, he shows willy
nilly that they should not be worshipped by men who
do not resemble those who created them, but who are
instead prudent, believing and religious. At the
same time too he shows that the very men who made
them had introduced as gods for their own worship
those who were no gods. So the saying of the prophet is proved true: " If a man shall make gods, lo
and behold they are no gods." [1]

Such gods then, the gods worshipped by such men
and by such men artfully fabricated, gods that are in
fact demons bound by the chains of their desires
through some strange technique to idols, when they
were described by Hermes as gods made by men,
were nevertheless not endowed by him, as they were
by the Platonist Apuleius (with whom we have
already dealt adequately and shown how illogical
and absurd are his opinions), with the office of being
interpreters and intercessors between gods made by
God and men whom God also made, carrying prayers
to heaven and fetching back gifts as answers to

enim stultum est credere deos quos fecerunt homines
plus valere apud deos quos fecit Deus quam valent
ipsi homines, quos idem ipse fecit Deus.

Daemon quippe simulacro arte impia conligatus
ab homine factus est deus, sed tali homini, non
omni homini. Qualis est ergo iste deus quem non
faceret homo nisi errans et incredulus et aversus a
vero Deo? Porro si daemones, qui coluntur in
templis, per artem nescio quam imaginibus inditi,
hoc est visibilibus simulacris, ab eis hominibus qui
hac arte fecerunt deos, cum aberrarent aversique
essent a cultu et religione divina, non sunt internun-
tii nec interpretes inter homines et deos, et propter
suos pessimos ac turpissimos mores, et quod homines,
quamvis errantes et increduli et aversi a cultu ac
religione divina, tamen eis sine dubio meliores
sunt quos deos ipsi arte fecerunt, restat ut quod possunt tamquam daemones possint, vel quasi beneficia
praestando magis nocentes, quia magis decipientes,
vel aperte malefaciendo—nec tamen quodlibet
horum, nisi quando permittuntur alta et secreta Dei
providentia— non autem tamquam medii inter
homines et deos per amicitiam deorum multum apud
homines valeant. Hi enim diis bonis, quos sanctos
angelos nos vocamus rationalesque creaturas sanctae

prayers. For it is extremely foolish to suppose that gods made by men have more influence with gods made by God than have men themselves, who were also made by the same God.

A demon presumably is bound to an idol by impious art and is a god made by man, but for a man of that kind, not for every man. What kind of god, then, is this whom man would not make unless he were mistaken, unbelieving and opposed to the true God? Moreover if demons, who are worshipped in temples and introduced by some strange art into images, that is to say visible representations, by the men who by this art made them gods when these men had strayed away from and become opposed to worship and divine religion, if demons, I say, are not messengers and interpreters between gods and men, both because of their utterly vile and depraved characters and because men, however mistaken, unbelieving and opposed to worship and divine religion they may be, are still undoubtedly superior to those whom they themselves have fashioned as gods, we must conclude that what power they have is merely their demonic power, either when in pretending to confer kindnesses they do the more harm as their fraud is greater, or when they openly do us hurt, although anything hurtful that they do and the time when they do it are only as permitted by the deep and mysterious will of God. In any case, they have no function as intermediaries between gods and men so as to exercise great power over men through their friendly relations with the gods. They certainly cannot be friends at all of the good gods whom we call holy angels and rational

caelestis habitationis sive sedes sive dominationes
sive principatus sive potestates, amici esse omnino
non possunt, a quibus tam longe absunt animi
affectione quam longe absunt a virtutibus vitia et a
bonitate malitia.

XXV

*De his quae sanctis angelis et hominibus bonis possunt
esse communia.*

Nullo modo igitur per daemonum quasi medietatem ambiendum est ad benevolentiam seu bene-
ficentiam deorum vel potius angelorum bonorum,
sed per bonae voluntatis similitudinem, qua cum illis
sumus et cum illis vivimus et cum illis Deum quem
colunt colimus, etsi eos carnalibus oculis videre non
possumus; in quantum autem dissimilitudine voluntatis et fragilitate infirmitatis miseri sumus, in tantum ab eis longe sumus vitae merito, non corporis
loco. Non enim quia in terra condicione carnis
habitamus, sed si inmunditia cordis terrena sapimus,
non eis iungimur. Cum vero sanamur, ut quales ipsi
sunt simus, fide illis interim propinquamus, si ab illo
nos fieri beatos a quo et ipsi facti sunt etiam ipsis
faventibus credimus.

---

[1] Colossians 1.16.
[2] Cf. Philippians 3.19; Colossians 3.2.

creatures dwelling in the holy precincts of heaven, " whether they be thrones, or dominions, or principalities, or powers," [1] from whom they are as far removed in the feelings that rule their heart as is vice from virtue and malice from goodwill.

XXV

Concerning what holy angels and good men can have in common.

So there is no need at all to take a roundabout route through the fancied mediation of demons in order to secure the good will or the good offices of gods, or rather of good angels; the right way is through resembling them in good will, which enables us to be with them, to live with them, and to worship with them the God they worship, even if we cannot see them with the eyes of the flesh. But in as far as we are wretched because we are unlike them in our will, and our weakness makes us frail, in so far are we much inferior to them in our standard of life, rather than in the spatial position of our bodies. For our failure to be united to them is not due to our dwelling on earth through the limitations of our flesh, but is due rather to the uncleanness of our hearts with which we mind earthly things.[2] But while we are being healed, so that we may be as they themselves are, during this period we come close to them through our faith, if, with the help that they themselves also provide, we believe that we are receiving the blessing of happiness from him who had already conferred it upon them.

XXVI

*Quod omnis religio paganorum circa homines mor-
tuos fuerit implicata.*

SANE advertendum est quo modo iste Aegyptius,
cum doleret tempus esse venturum quo illa auferrentur ex Aegypto quae fatetur a multum errantibus et
incredulis et a cultu divinae religionis aversis esse
instituta, ait inter cetera: " Tunc terra ista, sanctissima sedes delubrorum atque templorum, sepulcrorum erit mortuorumque plenissima "; quasi vero,
si illa non auferrentur, non essent homines mori-
turi, aut alibi essent mortui ponendi quam in terra;
et utique, quanto plus volveretur temporis et dierum,
tanto maior esset numerus sepulcrorum propter
maiorem numerum mortuorum.

Sed hoc videtur dolere, quod memoriae martyrum
nostrorum templis eorum delubrisque succederent,
ut videlicet qui haec legunt animo a nobis averso
atque perverso putent a paganis cultos fuisse deos in
templis, a nobis autem coli mortuos in sepulcris.
Tanta enim homines impii caecitate in montes quodam modo offendunt resque oculos suos ferientes

---

[1] *Asclepius* 24. Augustine understands *mortuorum* and
sepulcrorum as references to Christian martyrs and their
shrines. He supposes Hermes to be bewailing a time when the
worship of pagan gods will be replaced by the worship of
Christian martyrs, a rite which will pollute the land. Augustine can then make much of Hermes' own admission (*Asclepius*
37) that the pagan religion that he himself advocates is a
worship of dead men. However, Hermes is probably referring
not to a time when Egypt will be covered with Christian shrines
but rather to a time when the land will be filled with slaughter

XXVI

That all pagan religion was connected with dead men.

WE must certainly take note how this Egyptian, pained to think that the time would arrive when abolition would come in Egypt of all that worship which by his own admission was set up by men who were gravely in error, unbelievers and indifferent to the observance of divine religion, said among other things: " Then this land, this holy seat of shrines and temples, will be covered with sepulchres and with dead men," [1] as if, were it not for the removal of such worship, men would not be subject to death, or as if the dead were to be laid somewhere else and not in the earth. And in any case, the greater the sum of revolving days and years, the greater the number of sepulchres must be because of the greater number of the dead.

But what seems to grieve him is the thought that the memorials of our martyrs were taking the place of their temples and shrines. Evidently he wants those who read his writings in a spirit of obstinacy and hostility to us to suppose that, while the pagans worshipped gods in temples, we worship dead men in tombs. For so blindly do impious men, as it were, stumble over mountains and refuse to see things which hit them in the eye that they do not

and death resulting from the collapse of cosmic and human order. The pagan worship of deities who were believed to have once lived as men on earth was so widespread and deeply rooted, especially in Egypt, that it would hardly be possible for the Hermetic writer to refer with detestation to the cult of the martyrs.

nolunt videre ut non adtendant in omnibus litteris
paganorum aut non inveniri aut vix inveniri deos qui
non homines fuerint mortuisque divini honores delati
sint. Omitto quod Varro dicit omnes ab eis mortuos existimari manes deos et probat per ea sacra
quae omnibus fere mortuis exhibentur, ubi et ludos
commemorat funebres, tamquam hoc sit maximum
divinitatis indicium, quod non soleant ludi nisi
numinibus celebrari.

Hermes ipse, de quo nunc agitur, in eodem ipso
libro, ubi quasi futura praenuntiando deplorans ait:
" Tunc terra ista, sanctissima sedes delubrorum atque
templorum, sepulcrorum erit mortuorumque plenissima," deos Aegypti homines mortuos esse testatur.
Cum enim dixisset proavos suos multum errantes
circa deorum rationem, incredulos et non animadvertentes ad cultum religionemque divinam, invenisse artem qua efficerent deos: " Cui inventae,"
inquit, " adiunxerunt virtutem de mundi natura convenientem eamque miscentes, quoniam animas facere
non poterant, evocantes animas daemonum vel
angelorum eas indiderunt imaginibus sanctis divinisque mysteriis, per quas idola et bene faciendi et
male vires habere potuissent." Deinde sequitur
tamquam hoc exemplis probaturus et dicit: " Avus
enim tuus, o Asclepi, medicinae primus inventor, cui
templum consecratum est in monte Libyae circa

---

[1] i.e. the Egyptian god Imhotep, with whom the Greeks
identified their own god of healing Asclepius (the Roman
Aesculapius), son of Apollo.

observe that in all pagan literature we either do not find at all, or scarcely find, any instances of gods who were not originally men to whom divine honours were paid after their death. I pass over Varro's statement that *all* the dead were regarded by the pagans as divine spirits or *manes* and his proving it by citing the rites paid to practically all the dead, among which rites he mentions funeral games, implying that this is an outstanding proof of divinity, because games are usually celebrated only in honour of divine beings.

Hermes himself, whom we are now discussing, says dolefully as if he were foretelling the future: " Then this land, this holy seat of shrines and temples, will be covered with sepulchres and with dead men." Then in this same book he bears witness that the gods of Egypt are men who have died. For after saying that his ancestors had erred gravely in their concept of the gods through their unbelief and because they did not give any heed to worship and divine religion, and that they accordingly invented the art of making gods, he remarks: " When they had invented it, they added to it the appropriate natural force belonging to the substance of the universe and combined the two, and, since they were unable to create souls, they called upon the souls of demons or angels and introduced them into holy images and divine mysteries so that, with their assistance, idols might have the power of doing both good and harm." Then he continues as if to prove this by examples, saying: " Your grandfather, for instance, Asclepius, the first inventor of medicine,[1] to whom was consecrated on a mountain in Libya near the shore of the

litus crocodilorum, in quo eius iacet mundanus
homo, id est corpus; reliquus enim, vel potius totus,
si est homo totus in sensu vitae, melior remeavit in
caelum, omnia etiam nunc hominibus adiumenta
praestans infirmis numine nunc suo quae solebat
medicinae arte praebere." Ecce dixit mortuum coli
pro deo in eo loco ubi habebat sepulcrum, falsus ac
fallens quod remeavit in caelum.

Adiungens deinde aliud : " Hermes," inquit, " cuius
avitum mihi nomen est, nonne in sibi cognomine
patria consistens omnes mortales undique venientes
adiuvat atque conservat ? " Hic enim Hermes maior,
id est Mercurius, quem dicit avum suum fuisse, in
Hermopoli, hoc est in sui nominis civitate, esse
perhibetur. Ecce duos deos dicit homines fuisse,
Aesculapium et Mercurium. Sed de Aesculapio
et Graeci et Latini hoc idem sentiunt; Mercurium
autem multi non putant fuisse mortalem, quem
tamen iste avum suum fuisse testatur. At enim
alius est ille, alius iste, quamvis eodem nomine nuncupentur. Non multum pugno, alius ille sit, alius
iste; verum et iste, sicut Aesculapius, ex homine
deus secundum testimonium tanti apud suos viri,
huius Trismegisti, nepotis sui.

---

[1] Probably at Crocodilopolis, also called Arsinoe, in the
Fayum.   [2] *Asclepius* 37.

[3] Two Egyptian cities of this name are known, but it is
uncertain to which of the two reference is here made.

[4] The Academic interlocutor in Cicero's *De Natura Deorum*
(3.22) refers derisively to five different Mercuries, one of whom,
having killed the monster Argus, fled in exile to Egypt, where
he bestowed upon the Egyptians their laws and letters. This
Mercury was identified by the Egyptians with their god Thoth.
Cf. Lactantius, *Divinae Institutiones* 1.6.

crocodiles[1] a temple in which is laid his earthly
person, that is to say his body,—for what remains of
him, or rather the whole of his person, if the whole
person consists of sentient life, has gone back in
more exalted form to heaven, supplying even now,
by his divine power, to men who are sick all the
ministrations that he once provided by the art of
medicine." [2] Here we have Hermes declaring that a
dead man receives worship as a god in the place where
he had his tomb, and we find him deceiving others as
he deceived himself in supposing that he returned to
heaven.

Then he goes on to say: " Does not Hermes, my
ancestor whose name I bear, have his dwelling in the
city to which he has given his name, and does he not
help and protect all men who come from every
place?" For this elder Hermes, that is to say,
Mercury, whom he calls his ancestor, is said to have
his dwelling in Hermopolis, that is, in the town that
bears his name.[3] So there we have two gods whom
he declares to have been men, Aesculapius and
Mercury. But Greeks and Latins hold the same
opinion of Aesculapius; as for Mercury, however,
many do not believe that he was a mortal, and yet
Hermes asserts that he was his ancestor. We shall
be told: " But Hermes the god is a different person
from the ancestor of Hermes, although both bear
the same name." [4] I shall not make a great issue
of the contention that the two are different. But I
do note that one Hermes, like Aesculapius, is a god
who was once a man according to the testimony of
his descendant Trismegistus, whose prestige is so
great among his followers.

Adhuc addit et dicit: " Isin vero Osiris quam multa bona praestare propitiam, quantis obesse scimus iratam! " Deinde ut ostenderet ex hoc genere esse deos quos illa arte homines faciunt (unde dat intellegi daemones se opinari ex hominum mortuorum animis extitisse, quos per artem quam invenerunt homines multum errantes, increduli et inreligiosi, ait inditos simulacris, quia hi qui tales deos faciebant animas facere non utique poterant), cum de Iside dixisset quod commemoravi, " quantis obesse scimus iratam," secutus adiunxit : " Terrenis etenim diis atque mundanis facile est irasci, utpote qui sint ab hominibus ex utraque natura facti atque composti." "Ex utraque natura " dicit ex anima et corpore, ut pro anima sit daemon, pro corpore simulacrum. "Unde contigit," inquit, " ab Aegyptiis haec sancta animalia nuncupari colique per singulas civitates eorum animas, quorum sunt consecratae viventes, ita ut eorum legibus incolantur et eorum nominibus nuncupentur."

---

[1] Scott (I, p. 361) takes *quantis* as dative masculine (Greek ὅσοις) and translates " how many men she harms." In this case *quantis* would be the equivalent of *quot hominibus*. But Festugière (II, p. 348) translates " quels maux elle envoie," understanding *quantis* as ablative and neuter. The preceding neuter *quam multa bona* would seem to support the second interpretation. But see Nock-Festugière, Vol. II, p. 395, note 322.

[2] *Mundani* represents the Greek ὑλικοί, " material." Cf. Asclepius 7.

Hermes goes on to say: " We know how many benefits Isis, the wife of Osiris, bestows on us when she is in kindly mood, and how great are the evils she sends when she is angry." [1]   Then he shows that to this same class of gods belong the deities whom men make by the art I have described (in showing which he lets it be understood that in his opinion demons had their origin in the souls of the dead and, by the art invented by men who were gravely in error and were unbelievers and irreligious, have been introduced into images, because those who made gods of this kind could not by any means make souls). To demonstrate his point, after speaking about Isis and saying " how great are the evils she sends when she is angry," which I quoted, he added: " To be sure earthly and material [2] gods get angry easily, made and put together as they are by men out of both kinds of substance." By " both kinds of substance " he means soul and body, the demon serving as soul and the image as body. " Whence," he says, " it has come to pass that certain animals, as we know, are officially recognized [3] as sacred by the Egyptians, and that the various cities of Egypt worship the souls of those who, while still living, were consecrated as their gods, honouring them to such an extent that their populations live according to their laws and the cities are known by their names." [4]

[3] Scott (I. p. 361) suggests that *nuncupari* translates Greek ὀνομάζεσθαι, (" to be named "), which was wrongly substituted for νομίζεσθαι (" to be recognized ").

[4] *Asclepius* 37. On this difficult passage, see Nock-Festugière, *Corpus Hermeticum*, II, p. 348 and p 395, notes 323 and 324.

Ubi est illa velut querela luctuosa quod terra Aegypti, sanctissima sedes delubrorum atque templorum, sepulcrorum futura esset mortuorumque plenissima? Nempe spiritus fallax, cuius instinctu Hermes ista dicebat, per eum ipsum coactus est confiteri iam tunc illam terram sepulcrorum et mortuorum quos pro diis colebant fuisse plenissimam. Sed dolor daemonum per eum loquebatur, qui suas futuras poenas apud sanctorum martyrum memorias inminere maerebant. In multis enim talibus locis torquentur et confitentur et de possessis hominum corporibus eiciuntur.

XXVII

De modo honoris quem Christiani martyribus inpendunt.

Nec tamen nos eisdem martyribus templa, sacerdotia, sacra et sacrificia constituimus, quoniam non ipsi, sed Deus eorum nobis est Deus. Honoramus sane memorias eorum tamquam sanctorum hominum Dei, qui usque ad mortem corporum suorum pro veritate certarunt, ut innotesceret vera religio falsis fictisque convictis; quod etiam si qui antea sentiebant, timendo reprimebant.

Quis autem audivit aliquando fidelium stantem sacerdotem ad altare, etiam super sanctum corpus

---

[1] Possession of the human body by demons and the efficacy of holy relics in exorcizing such demons were regarded as established facts in the time of St. Augustine. See H. Delehaye, *Les origines du culte des martyrs* (2nd ed., Brussels, 1933), 142–146.

What becomes of the mournful complaint, if we may so describe it, that the land of Egypt, that most holy seat of shrines and temples, was destined to become covered with tombs and with dead men? Surely the fraudulent spirit that inspired Hermes to utter these words was compelled through his mouth to admit that the land was even then already covered with tombs and dead men, whom they worshipped as gods. But it was the agony of the demons that found utterance by his lips, as they grieved for the imminent punishment that would be theirs at the memorials of the holy martyrs. For there are many such places where demons are tormented and made to confess and are cast out from the bodies of men whom they have possessed.[1]

XXVII

How Christians ascribe honour to their martyrs.

But in fact we do not set up for these same martyrs temples, priesthoods, rites and sacrifices, for they themselves are not gods, but their God is our God. We honour their memorials,[2] of course, because we regard them as holy men of God who have fought for the truth even to the death of their bodies, in order to win renown for true religion by the defeat of falsehood and fiction. There were perhaps men who held such opinions before them, but they kept them hidden through fear.

But who of the faithful ever heard a priest standing at an altar, even if it was built over the holy body of a

---

[2] Or 'memories.'

martyris ad Dei honorem cultumque constructum,
dicere in precibus: Offero tibi sacrificium Petre vel
Paule vel Cypriane, cum apud eorum memorias
offeratur Deo, qui eos et homines et martyres fecit et
sanctis suis angelis caelesti honore sociavit, ut ea
celebritate et Deo vero de illorum victoriis gratias
agamus et nos ad imitationem talium coronarum
atque palmarum eodem invocato in auxilium ex
illorum memoriae renovatione adhortemur? Quaecumque igitur adhibentur religiosorum obsequia in
martyrum locis, ornamenta sunt memoriarum, non
sacra vel sacrificia mortuorum tamquam deorum.

Quicumque etiam epulas suas eo deferunt—quod
quidem a Christianis melioribus non fit, et in plerisque
terrarum nulla talis est consuetudo—, tamen quicumque id faciunt, quas cum apposuerint, orant et
auferunt, ut vescantur vel ex eis etiam indigentibus
largiantur, sanctificari sibi eas volunt per merita
martyrum in nomine domini martyrum. Non autem
esse ista sacrificia martyrum novit qui novit unum,
quod etiam illic offertur, sacrificium Christianorum.

Nos itaque martyres nostros nec divinis honoribus
nec humanis criminibus colimus, sicut colunt illi deos
suos, nec sacrificia illis offerimus, nec eorum probra
in eorum sacra convertimus.

---

[1] Cyprian, bishop of Carthage A.D. 248–258, martyred in
the persecution under the Emperor Valerian.

[2] This custom was derived from the pagan *parentalia*, a
rite intended to appease the souls of dead parents. The
Christians of Africa in particular practised it. When Augustine's mother Monica first came to Milan, she brought food to
the martyrs' shrines, unaware that St. Ambrose had already
forbidden this practice. See *Confessions* 6. 2. 2.

martyr for the honour and the worship of God, say when he prayed: " I offer sacrifice to thee, Peter, or to thee, Paul, or to thee, Cyprian "? [1] No one, for at their memorials sacrifice is offered to God, who made them both men and martyrs and united them in heavenly honour with his holy angels. This is a ceremony of thanksgiving to the true God for the victories of the martyrs, and at the same time we encourage ourselves to imitate them in winning like crowns and palms, as we call upon the same God to aid us and as we renew our memory of them. So whatever offerings are brought by the faithful to the shrines of the martyrs are intended as decorations of their memorials, and are not sacred objects or sacrificial offerings made to the dead as if they were gods.

Some even bring their food to the shrines—this is not done by Christians of the better sort, and in most countries the custom is unknown—but in any case those who do so say a prayer when they have laid the food down by the shrine, and then take it away to eat it or to bestow some of it also upon the needy.[2] Their desire is that the food should be made holy for them through the merits of the martyrs in the name of the Lord of the martyrs. But that this is no sacrifice offered to the martyrs is well known to anybody who knows the one sacrifice of the Christians, which is offered there as well as elsewhere.

So we honour our martyrs neither with divine honours nor with human crimes, as do the pagans when they worship their gods, nor do we offer them sacrifices, nor do we convert their evil doings into religious celebrations in their honour.

Nam de Iside, uxore Osiris, Aegyptia dea, et de parentibus eorum, qui omnes reges fuisse scribuntur —quibus parentibus suis illa cum sacrificaret, invenit hordei segetem atque inde spicas marito regi et eius consiliario Mercurio demonstravit, unde eandem et Cererem volunt—, quae et quanta mala non a poetis, sed mysticis eorum litteris memoriae mandata sint, sicut Leone sacerdote prodente ad Olympiadem matrem scribit Alexander, legant qui volunt vel possunt, et recolant qui legerunt, et videant quibus hominibus mortuis vel de quibus eorum factis tamquam diis sacra fuerint instituta. Absit ut eos, quamvis deos habeant, sanctis martyribus nostris, quos tamen deos non habemus, ulla ex parte audeant comparare. Sic enim non constituimus sacerdotes nec offerimus sacrificia martyribus nostris, quia incongruum indebitum inlicitum est atque uni Deo tantummodo debitum, ut nec criminibus suis nec ludis eos turpissimis oblectemus, ubi vel flagitia isti celebrant deorum suorum, si cum homines essent talia commiserunt, vel conficta delectamenta daemonum noxiorum, si homines non fuerunt.

Ex isto genere daemonum Socrates non haberet deum, si haberet deum; sed fortasse homini ab illa arte faciendi deos alieno et innocenti illi inport-

---

[1] Cf. *City of God*, Book 8.5 and 12.11.

Let us take, for example, Isis, the Egyptian goddess and wife of Osiris, and their ancestors, all of whom, according to written tradition, were kings.— This Isis, when offering sacrifice to her ancestors, found a crop of barley, from which she showed ears to her husband the King and his counsellor Mercury. That is why people choose to identify her with Ceres.—All the great evils she wrought were recorded, not by the poets, but in the Egyptian mystic writings, as Alexander writes to his mother Olympias. The secret was betrayed to him by the priest Leo.[1] Let those who will, or who can, read, and let those who have read them reflect upon them and see who were the men for whom, or what were their deeds for which rites were established after their death as if for gods. Let them never, however much they may regard them as gods, dare in any sense to compare them with our holy martyrs, whom nevertheless we do not regard as gods. This is why we have not set up priests for their worship, nor do we offer sacrifice to our martyrs, because such a rite is neither appropriate nor required nor permitted, for it is a rite that belongs to the service of one God alone. Neither do we entertain them with their own crimes nor with shameful exhibitions, as the pagans do when they exhibit the disgraceful actions of their gods, whether committed by them when they were men or, if they were not men before, mere inventions cooked up to titillate baneful demons.

It cannot be that the god of Socrates belonged to this class of demons, if he had a god; but perhaps an honest man like Socrates, to whom the art of making gods was quite foreign, may have had foisted on him

averint talem deum qui eadem arte excellere
voluerunt.

Quid ergo plura? Non esse spiritus istos colendos
propter vitam beatam quae post mortem futura est,
nullus vel mediocriter prudens ambigit. Sed fortasse dicturi sunt deos quidem esse omnes bonos,
daemones autem alios malos, alios bonos, et eos per
quos ad vitam in aeternum beatam perveniamus
colendos esse censebunt, quos bonos opinantur.
Quod quale sit iam in volumine sequenti videndum
est.

a god of this kind by those who chose to excel in this art.

What more shall I say? No man of even moderate intelligence doubts that these spirits need not be worshipped for the sake of the life of blessedness that is to come after death. But perhaps we shall be told that all the gods are good, while of the demons some are bad and some good; and we shall be advised to worship those who are thought good that we may by their agency attain to a life of eternal bliss. The value of this theory must now be examined in the following book.

BOOK IX

LIBER IX

I

*Ad quem articulum disputatio praemissa pervenerit et
quid discutiendum sit de residua quaestione.*

ET bonos et malos deos esse quidam opinati sunt;
quidam vero de diis meliora sentientes tantum eis
honoris laudisque tribuerunt ut nullum deorum
malum credere auderent. Sed illi qui deos quosdam
bonos, quosdam malos esse dixerunt, daemones
quoque appellaverunt nomine deorum, quamquam
et deos, sed rarius, nomine daemonum, ita ut ipsum
Iovem, quem volunt esse regem ac principem
ceterorum, ab Homero fateantur daemonem nuncu-
patum.

Hi autem qui omnes deos non nisi bonos esse
adserunt et longe praestantiores eis hominibus qui
perhibentur boni, merito moventur daemonum factis,
quae negare non possunt, eaque nullo modo a diis,
quos omnes bonos volunt, committi posse existi-
mantes differentiam inter deos et daemones adhibere
coguntur, ut quidquid eis merito displicet in operibus
vel affectibus pravis quibus vim suam manifestant
occulti spiritus, id credant esse daemonum, non

---

[1] Cf. Lactantius, *Divinae Institutiones* 2.14.6, 4.27.14 f.
[2] *Iliad* 1.222.

BOOK IX

I

*The point reached in the foregoing argument and
what remains of the inquiry to be discussed.*

SOME men have held the view that there are both
good and bad gods; others again, with a higher
opinion of their deities, have ascribed to them so
much honour and glory that they did not venture to
believe that any god is bad. But those who have
declared that some gods are good and some bad
have spoken of demons as gods [1]; however, they have
also spoken of gods as demons, though less frequently. Indeed, they admit that Jupiter himself,
who in their system is king and foremost of all the
gods, was entitled a demon by Homer. [2]

Those, however, who maintain that there are no
gods who are not good and far superior to such men
as are generally known as good, are, with excellent
cause, perturbed by the acts of demons, which they
are unable to deny. Believing that such acts could
not possibly be the work of gods, who according to
them are without exception good, they are compelled
to make a distinction between gods and demons.
Accordingly, whatever rightly displeases them in the
ignoble actions and passions whereby occult spirits
manifest their power, is attributed by them to
demons and not to gods. But holding as they do that

149

deorum. Sed quia eosdem daemones inter homines
et deos ita medios constitutos putant, tamquam
nullus deus homini misceatur, ut hinc perferant desiderata, inde referant inpetrata, atque hoc Platonici, praecipui philosophorum ac nobilissimi, sentiunt,
cum quibus velut cum excellentioribus placuit istam
examinare quaestionem utrum cultus plurimorum
deorum prosit ad consequendam vitam beatam quae
post mortem futura est, libro superiore quaesivimus
quo pacto daemones, qui talibus gaudent qualia
boni et prudentes homines aversantur et damnant,
id est sacrilega flagitiosa facinerosa non de
quolibet homine, sed de ipsis diis figmenta poetarum et magicarum artium sceleratam puniendamque
violentiam, possint quasi propinquiores et amiciores
diis bonis conciliare homines bonos, et hoc nulla
ratione posse compertum est.

II

*An inter daemones, quibus dii superiores sunt, sit
aliqua pars bonorum, quorum praesidio ad
veram beatitudinem possit humana anima
pervenire.*

PROINDE hic liber, sicut in illius fine promisimus,
disputationem continere debebit de differentia—si
quam volunt esse—non deorum inter se, quos omnes

---

[1] See above, Book 8.5 and 8.12.

no god has any dealings with man, they also believe that these same demons have been placed midway between gods and men in order to carry prayers to heaven and to fetch back favourable answers to earth. This is the opinion of the Platonists, the most outstanding and renowned of philosophers, with whom, because of their eminence, we chose to discuss the question whether the worship of many gods contributes anything to the attainment of the blessed life that is to come after death.[1] In the preceding book we inquired how demons can possibly, as being nearer neighbours and better friends to the good gods, serve as a connecting link between them and good men. For we saw that demons take pleasure not only in things that good and prudent men loathe and condemn—namely impious, shameful and wicked stories concocted by poets, not about some human being or other but about the gods themselves—but also in the criminal and punishable violation of the law by magic arts. Hence the conclusion was reached that it is utterly impossible for the demons to serve as such a connecting link.

II

Is there among the demons, who are inferior to the gods, any class of good demons by whose aid the human soul can attain true blessedness?

ACCORDINGLY, as I promised at the end of the preceding book, this one will not properly include any discussion of possible distinctions between god and god, for all of them are said to be good, nor of the

bonos dicunt, nec de differentia deorum et daemonum, quorum illos ab hominibus longe alteque seiungunt, istos inter deos et homines conlocant; sed de differentia ipsorum daemonum, quod ad praesentem pertinet quaestionem. Apud plerosque enim usitatum est dici alios bonos alios malos daemones; quae sive sit etiam Platonicorum, sive quorumlibet sententia, nequaquam eius est neglegenda discussio, ne quisquam velut daemones bonos sequendos sibi esse arbitretur, per quos tamquam medios diis, quos omnes bonos credit, dum conciliari adfectat et studet, ut quasi cum eis possit esse post mortem, inretitus malignorum spirituum deceptusque fallacia longe aberret a vero Deo, cum quo solo et in quo solo et de quo solo anima humana, id est rationalis et intellectualis, beata est.

III

Quae daemonibus Apuleius ascribat, quibus cum rationem non subtrahat, nihil virtutis assignat.

QUAE igitur est differentia daemonum bonorum et malorum? Quando quidem Platonicus Apuleius de his universaliter disserens et tam multa loquens de aeriis eorum corporibus de virtutibus tacuit animorum, quibus essent praediti, si essent boni. Tacuit

distinction between gods and demons, for the Platonists put a great height and distance between gods and men, but assign demons a place between them. Rather it must deal with the question, in so far as it pertains to the present inquiry, whether a distinction is to be made among the demons themselves. For in most circles it has become the custom to say that some demons are good and some bad. No matter which school maintains this theory, whether the Platonists or any other at all, we must on no account fail to discuss it, lest any man be led to think that he should follow the supposedly good demons, and while seeking and striving through their mediation to become reconciled with the gods, all of whom he believes to be good, so that he may join them, as he supposes, after death, he should find himself ensnared and entrapped by the guile of malicious spirits and far indeed from the path that leads to the true God, with whom alone, in whom alone, and by whom alone the human soul, by which I mean the rational and intellectual soul, can enjoy a state of bliss.

III

The qualities attributed by Apuleius to the demons, to whom he ascribes no degree of goodness, though not denying them reason.

WHAT then is the distinction between good and evil demons? Certainly the Platonist Apuleius, in discussing demons generally and discoursing at such length about their aerial bodies, said nothing about any good qualities of mind, with which they would

ergo beatitudinis causam, indicium vero miseriae
tacere non potuit, confitens eorum mentem, qua
rationales esse perhibuit, non saltem inbutam
munitamque virtute passionibus animi inrationabili-
bus nequaquam cedere, sed ipsam quoque, sicut
stultarum mentium mos est, procellosis quodam modo
perturbationibus agitari. Verba namque eius de hac
re ista sunt: " Ex hoc ferme daemonum numero,"
inquit," poetae solent haudquaquam procul a veritate
osores et amatores quorundam hominum deos
fingere; hos prosperare et evehere, illos contra
adversari et adfligere; igitur et misereri et indignari,
et angi et laetari omnemque humani animi faciem
pati, simili motu cordis et salo mentis per omnes
cogitationum aestus fluctuare. Quae omnes turbe-
lae tempestatesque procul a deorum caelestium
tranquillitate exulant."

Num est in his verbis ulla dubitatio quod non
animorum aliquas inferiores partes, sed ipsas daemonum mentes, quibus rationalia sunt animalia, velut
procellosum salum dixit passionum tempestate tur-
bari? Ut ne hominibus quidem sapientibus comparandi sint, qui huius modi perturbationibus animorum, a quibus humana non est inmunis infirmitas,

---

[1] Apuleius, *De Deo Socratis* 12. Augustine does not cite
Apuleius' words with complete accuracy.

be endowed if they were good. Of that which is the source of blessedness he said nothing, but to say nothing of one clear proof of their misery was not in his power. For he admitted that their minds, by virtue of which he affirmed that they were rational, were not even permeated and fortified by sufficient moral strength to resist to any extent the irrational passions of the soul, but were themselves, after the usual fashion of stupid minds, subject to stormy tempests, so to speak, of emotional turmoil. Here are his own words on this subject. " It is generally of this category of demons that the poets are accustomed to write—and here they are not far from telling the truth—when they describe the fictional gods as hating or loving some particular mortal. They are presented as furthering the hopes and careers of those whom they love, and correspondingly thwarting and plaguing the others. Thus they have feelings of pity and wrath, anguish and joy, in fact every manifestation of human emotion. Their hearts are stirred by impulses resembling men's, and their minds are rocked upon the surge of a restless imagination. But all such shocks and tempests are banished far from the serene existence of the heavenly gods." [1]

Surely these words allow no doubt that the very minds of the demons which make them rational beings, and not some lower parts of their souls, were said by Apuleius to be agitated, like a stormy sea, by a tempest of passions. It follows that demons cannot stand comparison even with wise men who, whenever they are assailed, as part of their lot in life, by storms of emotion of the sort that human

etiam cum eas huius vitae condicione patiuntur,
mente inperturbata resistunt, non eis cedentes ad
aliquid adprobandum vel perpetrandum quod exor-
bitet ab itinere sapientiae et lege iustitiae; sed stultis
mortalibus et iniustis non corporibus, sed moribus
similes—ut non dicam deteriores, eo quo vetustiores
et debita poena insanabiles—ipsius quoque mentis,
ut iste appellavit, salo fluctuant, nec in veritate atque
virtute, qua turbulentis et pravis affectionibus
repugnatur, ex ulla animi parte consistunt.

IV

De perturbationibus quae animo accidunt, quae sit
Peripateticorum Stoicorumque sententia.

DUAE sunt sententiae philosophorum de his animi
motibus, quae Graeci πάθη, nostri autem quidam,
sicut Cicero, perturbationes, quidam affectiones vel
affectus, quidam vero, sicut iste, de Graeco expressius passiones vocant. Has ergo perturbationes sive
affectiones sive passiones quidam philosophi dicunt
etiam in sapientem cadere, sed moderatas rationique
subiectas, ut eis leges quodam modo quibus ad
necessarium redigantur modum dominatio mentis

---

[1] Cf. Book 8.17.

weakness is not immune from, stand firm against them with mind unswayed; they do not yield so far as to consent to or engage in any action that would divert them from the straight path of wisdom and the law of righteousness. Demons, on the contary, resemble foolish and unrighteous men; their bodies are different, but morally they are the same. I might well have said they are worse, in that they are more inveterate sinners, and incapable of being cured even when punished as they deserve to be. So they are tossed about on a surge that affects the mind itself, to use Apuleius' own word, nor have they in any portion of the soul a solid core of truth and moral strength wherewith to do battle against riotous and base emotions.

IV

The opinions of the Peripatetics and Stoics on the disturbances that assail the mind.

THERE are two opinions among the philosophers concerning the mental emotions, which the Greeks call *pathē*, while certain of our fellow countrymen, like Cicero, describe them as disturbances,[1] others as affections or affects, and others again, like Apuleius, as passions, which renders the Greek word more explicitly. Now these disturbances, affections or passions are said by certain philosophers to assail even the wise man, but in him they are governed by subjection to reason, so that his mind as master lays down, as it were, laws for them, whereby they may be held to a minimum. Those who hold this view

inponat. Hoc qui sentiunt Platonici sunt sive
Aristotelici, cum Aristoteles discipulus Platonis
fuerit, qui sectam Peripateticam condidit. Aliis
autem sicut Stoicis, cadere ullas omnino huiusce
modi passiones in sapientem non placet. Hos autem,
id est Stoicos, Cicero in libris de finibus bonorum et
malorum verbis magis quam rebus adversus Platonicos seu Peripateticos certare convincit; quando
quidem Stoici nolunt bona appellare, sed commoda
corporis et externa, eo quod nullum bonum volunt
esse hominis praeter virtutem, tamquam artem bene
vivendi, quae non nisi in animo est. Haec autem isti
simpliciter et ex communi loquendi consuetudine
appellant bona; sed in comparatione virtutis qua
recte vivitur parva et exigua. Ex quo fit ut ab
utrisque quodlibet vocentur, seu bona seu commoda,
pari tamen aestimatione pensentur, nec in hac
quaestione Stoici delectentur nisi novitate verborum.
Videtur ergo mihi etiam in hoc, ubi quaeritur utrum
accidant sapienti passiones animi, an ab eis sit
prorsus alienus, de verbis eos potius quam de rebus
facere controversiam. Nam et ipsos nihil hinc aliud
quam Platonicos et Peripateticos sentire existimo,
quantum ad vim rerum adtinet, non ad vocabulorum
sonum.

Ut enim alia omittam quibus id ostendam, ne
longum faciam, aliquid unum quod sit evidentissi-

---

[1] For this disagreement between Stoics and Peripatetics see
Cicero, *Tusc. Disp.* 4.17.38–4.20.46.
[2] *De Finibus*, Books 3 and 4.

may be either Platonists or Aristotelians, since Aristotle, who founded the Peripatetic school, was the pupil of Plato. Others, however, like the Stoics, hold that passions of this kind do not affect the wise man at all.[1] But Cicero in his treatise *On the Supreme Good and Evil* [2] shows convincingly that the latter, namely the Stoics, disagree with the Platonists and Peripatetics verbally rather than essentially. He points out that the Stoics refuse to speak of bodily and external things as goods, but employ the term " advantages " on the ground that, according to them, there is no good for man save virtue, which is defined as the art of right living, and exists only as a state of mind. The other philosophers use the straightforward language of customary speech and call these advantages goods, but hold that in comparison with the virtue that is the norm of right living, they are slight and trivial. The result is that, no matter what they are called by the two parties, good or advantageous, still their value is the same for both ; and in debating this point the Stoics are merely pluming themselves on a new fashion in words. Hence it seems to me that here too, when the question is asked whether mental passions affect the wise man, or whether he is a complete stranger to them, they are again basing an argument on words rather than on facts. For I judge that the Stoics themselves hold exactly the same view as the Platonists and Peripatetics, in so far as the gist of the matter is concerned and not the mere jingle of the words.

To avoid a tedious explanation of this point, I shall omit other illustrations and content myself with one instance that brings it out very clearly. In his work

mum dicam. In libris quibus titulus est Noctium
Atticarum, scribit A. Gellius, vir elegantissimi
eloquii et multae undecumque scientiae, se navigasse
aliquando cum quodam philosopho nobili Stoico. Is
philosophus—sicut latius et uberius, quod ego
breviter adtingam, narrat A. Gellius—cum illud navi-
gium horribili caelo et mari periculosissime iactaretur,
vi timoris expalluit. Id animadversum est ab eis
qui aderant, quamvis in mortis vicinia curiosissime
adtentis, utrum necne philosophus animo turbaretur.
Deinde tempestate transacta mox ut securitas
praebuit conloquendi vel etiam garriendi locum,
quidam ex his quos navis illa portabat, dives luxuri-
osus Asiaticus philosophum compellat inludens quod
extimuisset atque palluisset, cum ipse mansisset
intrepidus in eo quod inpendebat exitio. At ille
Aristippi Socratici responsum rettulit, qui cum in re
simili eadem verba ab homine simili audisset, respondit illum pro anima nequissimi nebulonis merito
non fuisse sollicitum, se autem pro Aristippi anima
timere debuisse. Hac illo divite responsione de-
pulso postea quaesivit A. Gellius a philosopho
non exagitandi animo, sed discendi, quaenam illa
ratio esset pavoris sui. Qui ut doceret hominem
sciendi studio naviter accensum, protulit statim de
sarcinula sua Stoici Epicteti librum, in quo ea scripta

---

[1] *Noctes Atticae* 19.1.

entitled *Attic Nights* Aulus Gellius, a distinguished stylist who acquired a great store of knowledge from every kind of source, tells how one day he was on shipboard in company with a well-known Stoic philosopher.[1]—I shall sketch briefly the story that Gellius tells at length and in rich detail.—This philosopher turned ghastly pale with fear when sky and sea became threatening and the ship began to be tossed about in a very dangerous manner. Those on board noticed this and, in spite of the near approach of death, watched with the greatest curiosity to see whether the philosopher's mind would be disturbed. When in due course the storm subsided and a sense of security opened the way for conversation and even for idle chatter, one of the passengers, a wealthy and self-indulgent man from Asia, derisively taxed the philosopher with having turned pale and shown fear, while he himself had remained undismayed in the face of impending death. But the philosopher replied in the words of Aristippus, the pupil of Socrates, who on a similar occasion was addressed by a man of the same kind in the same terms and replied: " You were quite right to feel no anxiety for the life of a depraved scoundrel, but I was bound to fear for the life of Aristippus." [2] This reply disposed of the rich man; but afterwards Aulus Gellius asked the philosopher with no desire to hound him, but simply in a spirit of inquiry, what was the reason for his panic. Willing to instruct a man really fired with a desire for knowledge, the philosopher at once brought out from his little bag a work of the Stoic Epictetus, which contained doctrines

[2] Cf. Diogenes Laertius 2.8.7.

essent quae congruerent decretis Zenonis et Chrysippi, quos fuisse Stoicorum principes novimus.

In eo libro se legisse dicit A. Gellius hoc Stoicis placuisse, quod animi visa, quas appellant phantasias nec in potestate est utrum et quando incidant animo, cum veniunt ex terribilibus et formidabilibus rebus, necesse est etiam sapientis animum moveant, ita ut paulisper vel pavescat metu, vel tristitia contrahatur, tamquam his passionibus praevenientibus mentis et rationis officium; nec ideo tamen in mente fieri opinionem mali, nec adprobari ista eisque consentiri. Hoc enim esse volunt in potestate idque interesse censent inter animum sapientis et stulti, quod stulti animus eisdem passionibus cedit atque adcommodat mentis adsensum; sapientis autem, quamvis eas necessitate patiatur, retinet tamen de his quae adpetere vel fugere rationabiliter debet veram et stabilem inconcussa mente sententiam. Haec ut potui non quidem commodius A. Gellio, sed certe brevius et, ut puto, planius exposui, quae ille se in Epicteti libro legisse commemorat eum ex decretis Stoicorum dixisse atque sensisse.

Quae si ita sunt, aut nihil aut paene nihil distat inter Stoicorum aliorumque philosophorum opinionem

---

[1] Aulus Gellius states that this passage of Epictetus which he translates into Latin comes from the fifth book of the *Discourses*, as arranged by Arrian. There were probably eight books of *Discourses* originally, of which only four survive.

that agreed with the pronouncements of Zeno and Chrysippus, who were, as we know, the founders of the Stoic school.

Aulus Gellius says that he read in this work that the Stoics believed in mental visions which they call phantasies, and no man can prevent their impact on the mind or choose the time thereof. When these sensations arise from terrifying and awe-inspiring circumstances, the mind of even the wise man must unavoidably be disturbed, so that for a little while he either becomes pale with fear or is depressed by gloom, inasmuch as these passions inhibit the proper activity of mind and reason. Yet this does not cause the mind to fear any evil, nor to give assent to the emotions nor to yield to them. For this assent, they maintain, is within the power of man to grant or withhold, and they think the difference between the mind of the wise and that of the foolish man is just this, that the mind of the foolish man yields to these same passions and subordinates his mental judgement to them, while the wise man, though obliged to experience them, preserves with mind unshaken a true and steadfast opinion regarding the things that he ought rationally to pursue or avoid. I have described as well as I could, not, it is true, more attractively than Aulus Gellius, but certainly more briefly and, to my mind, more clearly, what he relates that he read, in a book by Epictetus, of that philosopher's utterances and opinions, which follow the tenets of the Stoics.[1]

This being so, there is no disagreement, or practically none, between the opinion of the Stoics and that of other philosophers about the passions and per-

de passionibus et perturbationibus animorum; utrique enim mentem rationemque sapientis ab earum dominatione defendunt. Et ideo fortasse dicunt eas in sapientem non cadere Stoici, quia nequaquam eius sapientiam, qua utique sapiens est, ullo errore obnubilant aut labe subvertunt. Accidunt autem animo sapientis salva serenitate sapientiae propter illa quae commoda vel incommoda appellant, quamvis ea nolint dicere bona vel mala. Nam profecto si nihili penderet eas res ille philosophus quas amissurum se naufragio sentiebat, sicuti est vita ista salusque corporis, non ita illud periculum perhorrresceret ut palloris etiam testimonio proderetur. Verum tamen et illam poterat permotionem pati, et fixam tenere mente sententiam vitam illam salutemque corporis, quorum amissionem minabatur tempestatis inmanitas, non esse bona quae illos quibus inessent facerent bonos, sicut facit iustitia.

Quod autem aiunt ea nec bona appellanda esse, sed commoda, verborum certamini, non rerum examini deputandum est. Quid enim interest utrum aptius bona vocentur an commoda, dum tamen ne his privetur non minus Stoicus quam Peripateticus pavescat et palleat, ea non aequaliter appellando, sed aequaliter aestimando? Ambo sane, si bonorum istorum seu commodorum periculis ad flagitium vel facinus urgeantur, ut aliter ea retinere non

turbations of the mind, for both parties defend the
wise man's intellect and reason against enslavement
to the passions. And perhaps the reason why the
Stoics declare that passions do not affect the wise man
is that the passions achieve no success at all in
obscuring by any mist of error, or in overthrowing by
any blow, that wisdom which a man certainly has if
he is wise. But when passions do assail the mind of
the wise man without affecting the serenity of his
wisdom, it is because of such things as the Stoics call
advantages or disadvantages, although they refuse to
speak of them as good or evil. For surely if the
philosopher set no store by the things he expected
to lose if the ship were wrecked, namely his life or
his bodily welfare, he would not have been so intimidated by the danger as to betray his terror by the
evidence of his pallor. Nevertheless, he was both
able to endure the emotional shock and to hold
firmly by his conviction that life and bodily welfare,
the loss of which was threatened by the raging storm,
are not goods that can make their possessors good, as
does righteousness.

As for their saying that these are not to be called
good things but advantages, this is to be rated as the
arraying of words, not the assaying of facts. For
what does it matter whether it is more suitable to
call them good things or advantages, so long as Stoic,
no less than Peripatetic, trembles and grows pale at
the thought of being deprived of them? If they do
not use the same words for them, they nevertheless
put the same value on them. Both, it will be agreed,
if pressed to commit some shameful or criminal
action on pain of forfeiting these good things or

possint, malle se dicunt haec amittere quibus natura corporis salva et incolumis habetur, quam illa committere quibus iustitia violatur. Ita mens ubi fixa est ista sententia nullas perturbationes, etiamsi accidunt inferioribus animi partibus, in se contra rationem praevalere permittit; quin immo eis ipsa dominatur eisque non consentiendo et potius resistendo regnum virtutis exercet. Talem describit etiam Vergilius Aenean, ubi ait:

Mens inmota manet, lacrimae volvuntur inanes.

V

Quod passiones quae Christianos animos afficiunt non in vitium trahant, sed virtutem exerceant.

Non est nunc necesse copiose ac diligenter ostendere quid de istis passionibus doceat scriptura divina, qua Christiana eruditio continetur. Deo quippe illa ipsam mentem subicit regendam et iuvandam mentique passiones ita moderandas atque frenandas ut in usum iustitiae convertantur. Denique in disciplina nostra non tam quaeritur utrum pius animus irascatur, sed quare irascatur; nec utrum sit tristis, sed unde sit tristis; nec utrum timeat, sed quid timeat.

---

[1] *Aeneid* 4.449. Most modern commentators believe that Augustine has either misread this line or has simply forced it to bear a meaning not intended by Virgil. In the original, according to this view, the mind is Aeneas', but the tears Dido's. Augustine would refer both to Aeneas. However, Servius interprets the passage in the same way as Augustine, and V. Pöschl maintains that Servius and Augustine have understood the passage correctly. See Pöschl, *The Art of Vergil*, trans. by Gerda Seligson (Ann Arbor, 1962), p. 46.

advantages, say that they would rather give up what is necessary for the safety and welfare of the body than give in and be guilty of acts that do violence to righteousness. So the mind in which this principle is firmly rooted permits no perturbations, however they may affect the lower levels of the soul, to prevail in it over reason. No, on the contrary, the mind itself is their master and, when it will not consent but rather stands firm against them, upholds the sovereign rule of virtue. Such a one is Aeneas, as described by Virgil in the words:

" His mind remains unshaken; in vain flow forth the tears." [1]

V

That the passions which affect the minds of Christians do not drag them into vice but exercise their virtue.

THERE is no need at the moment to point out at length and in detail what lessons divine Scripture, which is our store of Christian learning, teaches concerning these passions. The point is that Scripture subordinates the higher mind itself to God, to be governed and succoured by him, and puts the passions into keeping of the mind, to be so regulated and restrained as to be converted into servants of righteousness. Consequently, in our system we do not so much ask whether a religious mind will become angry, but rather what should make it angry, nor whether it will be sad, but what should make it sad, nor whether it will be afraid, but what should make it afraid.

Irasci enim peccanti ut corrigatur, contristari pro adflicto ut liberetur, timere periclitanti ne pereat nescio utrum quisquam sana consideratione reprehendat. Nam et misericordiam Stoicorum est solere culpare; sed quanto honestius ille Stoicus misericordia perturbaretur hominis liberandi quam timore naufragii. Longe melius et humanius et piorum sensibus accommodatius Cicero in Caesaris laude locutus est, ubi ait: " Nulla de virtutibus tuis nec admirabilior nec gratior misericordia est." Quid est autem misericordia nisi alienae miseriae quaedam in nostro corde compassio qua utique si possumus subvenire compellimur? Servit autem motus iste rationi quando ita praebetur misericordia ut iustitia conservetur, sive cum indigenti tribuitur, sive cum ignoscitur paenitenti. Hanc Cicero locutor egregius non dubitavit appellare virtutem, quam Stoicos inter vitia numerare non pudet, qui tamen, ut docuit liber Epicteti, nobilissimi Stoici, ex decretis Zenonis et Chrysippi, qui huius sectae primas habuerunt, huiusce modi passiones in animum sapientis admittunt quem vitiis omnibus liberum volunt. Unde fit consequens ut haec ipsa non putent vitia quando sapienti sic accidunt ut contra virtutem mentis rationemque nihil possint, et una sit eademque

---

[1] The Stoic distinction between mercy and pity is seen in Seneca, *De Clementia* 2.5., where the latter quality is condemned as the failing of a weak nature, whereas mercy and gentleness are qualities of all good men. Cf. Cicero, *Tusc. Disp.* 3.9.20. [2] *Pro Ligario* 12.37.

For instance, anger with a sinner in order to reform him, or sadness on behalf of one who is distressed in order to relieve him, or fear for one in danger, to save him from death—with such feelings I hardly suppose that anyone of sane and thoughtful mind would find fault. No doubt the Stoic practice is to condemn even pity,[1] but how much more honourable it would have been for the Stoic described by Aulus Gellius to be deeply moved by pity for a fellow-creature in order to save him than by fear of being shipwrecked. Far better and more humane, and more in keeping with the feeling of religious men, were the words of Cicero in praise of Caesar: "None of your virtues is more admirable or more welcome than pity."[2] But what is pity except a kind of fellow-feeling in our own hearts for the sufferings of others that in fact impels us to come to their aid as far as our ability allows? This impulse is loyal to reason when pity is shown in such a way that justice suffers no encroachment, whether we show it by giving alms to the needy or by forgiving the penitent. Cicero, a man so distinguished for his use of language, did not hesitate to call pity a virtue, although the Stoics brazenly list it among the vices. Yet we learn from the book of that eminent Stoic Epictetus, following the principles of Zeno and Chrysippus, who were leaders of the school, that the Stoics allow passions of this sort to visit the mind of the wise man, although in their system such a mind is free of every vice. The conclusion to be drawn from this is that they do not consider these same passions to be vices when they affect the wise man without undermining at all his strength of character and his gift of reason. It

sententia Peripateticorum vel etiam Platonicorum et ipsorum Stoicorum, sed, ut ait Tullius, verbi controversia iam diu torqueat homines Graeculos contentionis cupidiores quam veritatis.[1]

Sed adhuc merito quaeri potest utrum ad vitae praesentis pertineat infirmitatem etiam in quibusque bonis officiis huiusce modi perpeti affectus, sancti vero angeli et sine ira puniant quos accipiunt aeterna Dei lege puniendos, et miseris sine miseriae compassione subveniant, et periclitantibus eis quos diligunt, sine timore opitulentur; et tamen istarum nomina passionum consuetudine locutionis humanae etiam in eos usurpentur propter quandam operum similitudinem, non propter affectionum infirmitatem, sicut ipse Deus secundum scripturas irascitur,[2] nec tamen ulla passione turbatur. Hoc enim verbum vindictae usurpavit effectus, non illius turbulentus affectus.

---

[1] *De Oratore* 1.11.47.
[2] The meaning of biblical references to God's anger was frequently discussed by the Church Fathers. Such references were usually explained away as allegorical. Lactantius

follows, moreover, that Peripatetics, Platonists and the Stoics themselves hold but one and the same tenet. But, as Cicero said, it's an old story now, the agony suffered by the poor Greeks in the strife of words, because they are more enamoured of rivalry than of truth.[1]

But at this point we may justifiably ask whether it is one of the afflictions of our present life that we are subject to emotions of this kind even while we are performing our several good actions, though the holy angels may certainly punish without anger those handed over to them for punishment under the eternal law of God and may minister to the sorrowing without themselves sharing a feeling of sorrow, and when those they love are in danger, may bring succour, unmoved by fear. Nevertheless the words denoting these passions are employed in ordinary usage of angels as well; but this is due to a generic likeness between their behaviour and ours, and not to their being afflicted by our emotions. In the same way God himself, according to the Scriptures, becomes angry, and yet he is never moved by any passions. For this word is used to indicate the consequences of his vengeance and not any violent emotion on his part.[2]

devoted a special treatise, *De Ira Dei*, to the problem, and Augustine returns to the question frequently. See *Contra Adversarium Legis et Prophetarum*, 1.40.

VI

*Quibus passionibus daemones confitente Apuleio
exagitentur, quorum ope homines apud deos
asserit adiuvari.*

Qua interim de sanctis angelis quaestione dilata
videamus quem ad modum dicant Platonici medios
daemones inter deos et homines constitutos istis
passionum aestibus fluctuare. Si enim mente ab his
libera eisque dominante motus huiusce modi pate-
rentur, non eos diceret Apuleius simili motu cordis
et salo mentis per omnes cogitationum aestus
fluctuare. Ipsa igitur mens eorum, id est pars animi
superior qua rationales sunt, in qua virtus et sapientia, si ulla eis esset, passionibus turbulentis
inferiorum animi partium regendis moderandisque
dominaretur,—ipsa, inquam, mens eorum, sicut iste
Platonicus confitetur, salo perturbationum fluctuat.
Subiecta est ergo mens daemonum passionibus libi-
dinum formidinum irarum atque huiusmodi ceteris.
Quae igitur pars in eis libera est composque sapientiae qua placeant diis et ad bonorum morum
similitudinem hominibus consulant, cum eorum
mens passionum vitiis subiugata et oppressa, quidquid rationis naturaliter habet, ad fallendum et
decipiendum tanto acrius intendat, quanto eam
magis possidet nocendi cupiditas?

---

[1] Cf. above, Book 9.3.

VI

*The passions which, according to Apuleius, agitate
the demons by whose means, he maintains, men
secure the support of the gods.*

LET us postpone for the moment the question of the
holy angels and consider the meaning of the Platonists' view that the demons, situated midway between
gods and man, are tossed upon these swelling waves
of passion. The point is that if their minds remained
free and in command of these emotions which they
experience, Apuleius would not have said of them,
"their hearts are stirred by impulses resembling
men's, and their minds are rocked upon the surge of
a restless imagination." [1] So then, it is their mind
itself—that higher element in their personality which
makes them rational beings and in which would
reside the virtue and wisdom, if they possessed any,
that would rule the stormy passions belonging to the
lower parts of the personality so as to govern and
control them—it is their mind itself, I repeat, as this
Platonist admits, that is tossed on the furious sea of
the passions. And so the mind of the demons is a
prey to the passions of lust, fear, anger and every
other passion of that sort. What part of them, then,
is free and in possession of the wisdom whereby they
may find favour with the gods and encourage men to
follow a pattern of higher morals, when their own
mind, enslaved and oppressed by vicious passions,
employs whatever reason nature has bestowed upon
it to cheat and ensnare us so much the more fiercely
the more it is held in the grip of its lust to do harm?

VII

Quod Platonici figmentis poetarum infamatos asserant
deos de contrariorum studiorum certamine,
cum hae partes daemonum,
non deorum sint.

Quod si quisquam dicit non ex omnium, sed ex malorum daemonum numero esse quos poetae quorundam hominum osores et amatores deos non procul
a veritate confingunt—hos enim dixit Apuleius salo
mentis per omnes cogitationum aestus fluctuare—,
quo modo istud intellegere poterimus, quando, cum
hoc diceret, non quorundam, id est malorum, sed
omnium daemonum medietatem propter aeria
corpora inter deos et homines describebat?

Hoc enim ait fingere poetas, quod ex istorum daemonum numero deos faciunt et eis deorum nomina
inponunt et quibus voluerint hominibus ex his amicos
inimicosque distribuunt ficti carminis inpunita
licentia, cum deos ab his daemonum moribus et
caelesti loco et beatitudinis opulentia remotos esse
perhibeat. Haec est ergo fictio poetarum, deos
dicere qui dii non sunt, eosque sub deorum nominibus
inter se decertare propter homines quos pro studio
partium diligunt vel oderunt. Non procul autem a
174

VII

The assertions of the Platonists that the gods have been slandered by the poetic accounts of rivalry between opposing interests, since, as they maintain, such division into factions is characteristic, not of the gods, but of the demons.

BUT if anyone says that not all demons but only evil demons are meant when poets invent stories that are not far from the truth about their hatred or love for certain men—for these are the ones of whom Apuleius is thinking when he speaks of minds "rocked upon the surge of a restless imagination"— how shall we be able to understand this, when his description of the demons' position midway between gods and men because of their aerial bodies applies not to one class, namely those who are evil, but to all?

The fictitious element in the poets consists, according to Apuleius, in their depicting some of the demons as gods, in giving them the names of gods, and in assigning certain gods of this kind as friends or enemies to mortals of the poets' own choosing— since the indulgence accorded to poetic fiction gives them impunity—whereas in reality, Apuleius maintains, the gods are raised far above such practices of demons by their higher place in heaven and by the abundance of their felicity. This, then, is the fiction of the poets, to describe as gods those who are not gods and to represent them, under the name of gods, as quarrelling among themselves because of men whom they love or hate with partisan zeal. Still,

veritate dicit hanc esse fictionem, quoniam deorum appellati vocabulis qui dii non sunt, tales tamen describuntur daemones quales sunt. Denique hinc esse dicit Homericam illam Minervam, " quae mediis coetibus Graium cohibendo Achilli intervenit." Quod ergo Minerva illa fuerit poeticum vult esse figmentum, eo quod Minervam deam putat eamque inter deos, quos omnes bonos beatosque credit, in alta aetheria sede conlocat, procul a conversatione mortalium; quod autem aliquis daemon fuerit Graecis favens Troianisque contrarius, sicut alius adversus Graecos Troianorum opitulator, quem Veneris seu Martis nomine idem poeta commemorat, quos deos iste talia non agentes in habitationibus caelestibus ponit, et hi daemones pro eis quos amabant, contra eos quos oderant, inter se decertaverint, hoc non procul a veritate poetas dixisse confessus est.

De his quippe ista dixerunt quos hominibus simili motu cordis et salo mentis per omnes cogitationum aestus fluctuare testatur, ut possint amores et odia non pro iustitia, sed sicut populus similis eorum in venatoribus et aurigis secundum suarum studia partium pro aliis adversus alios exercere. Id enim videtur philosophus curasse Platonicus, ne, cum haec

---

[1] *De Deo Socratis* 11. Cf. *Iliad*, I, 193 ff. Minerva is, of course, Homer's Athena.

[2] Aphrodite and Ares in Homer.

[3] Elaborate contests, called *venationes*, that pitted men against wild beasts of every kind were among the favourite amusements of the Roman populace. Circus races retained their traditional popularity well into the sixth century. Four teams, distinguished by their red, white, green or blue liveries, competed, and the inhabitants of Christian Rome followed the

Apuleius says, this fiction is not so far from the truth, for although the demons are called by the name of gods without being gods, yet they are described as they really are. In fact he places in this category Homer's Minerva, "who in the midst of the assembled Greeks intervened to restrain Achilles." [1] To call her Minerva is, he says, a poetic fiction, because he believes Minerva to be a goddess and gives her a place among the gods, all of whom he considers good and blessed, in a lofty region of the upper air, far from intercourse with mortals. But that there was some demon who favoured the Greeks and opposed the Trojans, just as the Trojans were helped against the Greeks by another demon, whom the same poet mentions under the name of Venus or Mars,[2] although Venus and Mars are, according to Apuleius, gods dwelling in heavenly homes and not behaving in such a way; and that these demons fought among themselves for those they liked against those they hated, this, he acknowledges, is, in the poets' description, not far from the truth.

The poets of course in their account were dealing with those " whose hearts," so his statement runs, " are stirred by impulses resembling man's, and their minds are rocked upon the surge of a restless imagination." This makes it possible for them to indulge their loves and their hates with no regard for justice, just as the mob, which resembles them, indulges its own passionate feelings towards beast-baiters in the arena and charioteers, zealously supporting one favourite faction against the others.[3] Our Platonic

fortunes of their chosen factions with a passionate enthusiasm which at times incited civil disturbances.

a poetis canerentur, non a daemonibus mediis, sed
ab ipsis diis, quorum nomina poetae fingendo ponunt,
fieri crederentur.

VIII

*De diis caelestibus et daemonibus aeriis hominibusque
terrenis Apulei Platonici definitio.*

Quid? Illa ipsa definitio daemonum parumne
intuenda est—ubi certe omnes determinando complexus est—, q 10d ait daemones esse genere animalia,
animo passiva, mente rationalia,[1] corpore aeria,
tempore aeterna? In quibus quinque commemoratis nihil dixit omnino quo daemones cum bonis
saltem hominibus id viderentur habere commune
quod non esset in malis. Nam ipsos homines cum
aliquanto latius describendo complecteretur, suo
loco de illis dicens tamquam de infimis atque terrenis, cum prius dixisset de caelestibus diis, ut commendatis duabus partibus ex summo et infimo ultimis tertio loco de mediis daemonibus loqueretur:
"Igitur homines," inquit, "ratione gaudentes,[2]
oratione pollentes, inmortalibus animis, moribundis
membris, levibus et anxiis mentibus, brutis et ob-

---

[1] ingenio rationabilia *Apuleius.*
[2] gaudentes *codex Corbeiensis:* plaudentes *Apuleius and
some MSS: other MSS. read* claudentes: cluentes *Migne.*

---

[1] Cf. *De Deo Socratis* 12: "A god ought to experience no
temporal emotion either of love or of hate. And so he ought
not to be affected either by anger or by pity, nor gripped by
fear nor elated by joy. Free, rather, from all passions of the

philosopher seems, then, to have taken pains to see that when these stories were treated by poets, they should not be believed of the gods themselves, whose names the poets use in their fiction, but rather of the demons who dwell in the middle region.[1]

VIII

Apuleius' classification of gods dwelling in heaven, demons in the air and men on earth.

WELL then, are we to take little or no account of his own definition of the demons, which certainly includes all of them in one category? He says that demons are animal in genus, affected by emotions, rational in intelligence, airy in body and eternal in time.[2] In this list of five characteristics he has mentioned absolutely nothing that demons appear to have in common with good men in particular that is not found also in those who are bad. For when he broadened his description somewhat to include men themselves, he described them in their turn as at the bottom and earthly. He had already spoken of the gods in heaven so that, having described the two extremes, the highest and the lowest, he might speak in the third place of the demons who hold the middle rank. " So men," he says, " dwell upon the earth, proud of their reasoning faculty, gifted with speech, with immortal spirits but mortal members, their minds fickle and worried, their bodies stupid and

soul, a god ought never to grieve nor rejoice nor feel any sudden likes or dislikes."

[2] *De Deo Socratis* 13.

SAINT AUGUSTINE

noxiis corporibus, dissimilibus moribus, similibus
erroribus, pervicaci audacia, pertinaci spe, casso
labore, fortuna caduca, singillatim mortales, cuncti
tamen universo genere perpetui, vicissim sufficienda
prole mutabiles, volucri tempore, tarda sapientia,
cita morte, querula vita terras incolunt.''

Cum hic tam multa diceret quae ad plurimos
homines pertinent, numquid etiam illud tacuit quod
noverat esse paucorum, ubi ait " tarda sapientia "?
Quod si praetermisisset, nullo modo recte genus
humanum descriptionis huius tam intenta diligentia
terminasset. Cum vero deorum excellentiam com-
mendaret, ipsam beatitudinem quo volunt homines
per sapientiam pervenire in eis adfirmavit excellere.
Proinde si aliquos daemones bonos vellet intellegi,
aliquid etiam in ipsorum descriptione poneret unde
vel cum diis aliquam beatitudinis partem, vel cum
hominibus qualemcumque sapientiam putarentur
habere communem. Nunc vero nullum bonum
eorum commemoravit quo boni discernuntur a malis.

Quamvis et eorum malitiae liberius exprimendae
pepercerit, non tam ne ipsos, quam ne cultores eorum
apud quos loquebatur, offenderet. Significavit tamen prudentibus quid de illis sentire deberent,

---

[1] *De Deo Socratis* 4.

vulnerable, unlike in their ways, alike in their failures, irrepressible in their audacity, unyielding in their hope, their toil unavailing, their fortune precarious, mortal as individuals, yet collectively persisting as a race, successively moving on as new generations replace the old, their time winging swiftly by, their wisdom arriving late, their death speedy, their life a lamentation." [1]

In mentioning so many features that apply to most men's lives did he omit even that attainment which he was well aware belongs to but few? I mean when he said " their wisdom comes late." But if he had left this out, he would by no means, for all the taut industry of his description, have made an accurate map of man's limits. Certainly when he expatiated on the superiority of the gods, he declared that they possess in an outstanding degree the very felicity that men have as their goal in their pursuit of wisdom. It follows that if he had meant it to be understood that some demons are good, he would have inserted something in his description of them too from which it might be supposed that they either had in common with the gods some measure of felicity, or with men a kind of wisdom, however poor. But as it is, he has recorded among their qualities none whereby the good may be distinguished from the bad.

Yet he was careful also not to speak too freely of their malice, in order to avoid giving offence, not so much to the demons themselves, as to their worshippers to whom his words were addressed. Nevertheless he suggested to the intelligent what they ought to think about the demons when in speaking

quando quidem deos, quos omnes bonos beatosque
credi voluit, ab eorum passionibus atque, ut ait ipse,
turbelis omni modo separavit, sola illos corporum
aeternitate coniungens, animo autem non diis, sed
hominibus similes daemones apertissime inculcans; et
hoc non sapientiae bono, cuius et homines possunt
esse participes, sed perturbatione passionum, quae
stultis malisque dominatur, a sapientibus vero et
bonis ita regitur ut malint eam non habere quam
vincere. Nam si non corporum, sed animorum
aeternitatem cum diis habere daemones vellet
intellegi, non utique homines ab huius rei consortio
separaret, quia et hominibus aeternos esse animos
procul dubio sicut Platonicus sentit. Ideo cum hoc
genus animantum describeret, inmortalibus animis,
moribundis membris dixit esse homines. Ac per
hoc si propterea communem cum diis aeternitatem
non habent homines, quia corpore sunt mortales,
propterea ergo daemones habent, quia corpore sunt
inmortales.

IX

An amicitia caelestium deorum per intercessionem
daemonum possit homini provideri.

QUALES igitur mediatores sunt inter homines et
deos, per quos ad deorum amicitias homines ambiant,

of the gods—all of whom, he would have us believe, are good and happy—he dissociated them entirely from the passions and shocks, to use his word, to which the demons are subject. He puts gods and demons in the same category only by virtue of the immortality of their bodies, while he most explicitly maintains that in mind the demons resemble not gods but men, this resemblance consisting not in the demons' possessing wisdom, to which even men can in part attain, but in their susceptibility to those emotional disturbances that enslave stupid and bad men but are kept under by wise and good men, even though they would prefer not to feel them at all rather than to subdue them. For if Apuleius had wished it to be understood that the immortality that the demons have in common with the gods is of the mind and not of the body, he would clearly not have excluded men from this privileged fellowship, since as a Platonist he undoubtedly holds that the minds of men too are immortal. This is the reason why he said, when he was describing this class of living beings, that men have immortal minds and mortal members. And from this we deduce that, if men do not share immortality with the gods precisely because their bodies are mortal, then the demons share it precisely because their bodies are immortal.

IX

Whether the friendship of the celestial gods can be won for man by the intercession of the demons.

What is the nature then of these mediators between gods and men, through whose agency men are

qui hoc cum hominibus habent deterius quod est in
animante melius, id est animum; hoc autem habent
cum diis melius quod est in animante deterius, id est
corpus? Cum enim animans, id est animal, ex
anima constet et corpore, quorum duorum anima est
utique corpore melior, etsi vitiosa et infirma, melior
certe corpore etiam sanissimo atque firmissimo,
quoniam natura eius excellentior nec labe vitiorum
postponitur corpori, sicut aurum etiam sordidum
argento seu plumbo, licet purissimo, carius aestimatur,
isti mediatores deorum et hominum, per quos inter-
positos divinis humana iunguntur, cum diis habent
corpus aeternum, vitiosum autem cum hominibus
animum; quasi religio, qua volunt diis homines per
daemones iungi, in corpore sit, non in animo
constituta.

Quaenam tandem istos mediatores falsos atque
fallaces quasi capite deorsum nequitia vel poena
suspendit, ut inferiorem animalis partem, id est
corpus, cum superioribus, superiorem vero, id est
animum, cum inferioribus habeant, et cum diis
caelestibus in parte serviente coniuncti, cum hominibus autem terrestribus in parte dominante sint
miseri? Corpus quippe servum est, sicut etiam
Sallustius ait: " Animi imperio, corporis servitio

---

[1] Augustine appears here to connect the word *religio* etymologically with the verb *religare*, " bind," although in Book
10.3 he derives it from *religere* " to choose."

to sue for the friendship of the gods? They have in common with men an inferior quality of what is the higher part in a living creature, namely the mind, while they share with the gods a higher quality of what is the inferior part, namely the body. For since every living creature, that is every animal, consists of soul and body, of which two elements the soul is clearly superior to the body—even when it is vicious and weak the soul still unquestionably surpasses the body at its healthiest and most vigorous, since the soul's essential nature is superior and, even when blemished by vice, yields no precedence to the body, just as gold, even when impure, is esteemed as being more valuable than silver and lead, though these be perfectly pure—these mediators, then, between gods and men, whose location between the two is a bond between the human sphere and the divine, possess like the gods an eternal body but like men a vicious mind, as if the essence of religion, which in their system binds men to the gods through the agency of demons, lay in the body and not in the mind.[1]

What wickedness, pray, or what punishment suspends these false and fallacious mediators head downwards as it were, so that they share the inferior part of a living being, namely the body, with superior beings, but the superior part, namely the mind, with inferior beings? So they are united with the gods of heaven in the part that serves, but are one in misery with the men of earth in the part that rules. The body of course is a slave, as Sallust too remarks: "We employ our minds chiefly to govern, our bodies to serve." He added: "We share the one with the

magis utimur." Adiunxit autem ille: "Alterum
nobis cum diis, alterum cum beluis commune est,"
quoniam de hominibus loquebatur, quibus sicut
beluis mortale corpus est. Isti autem, quos inter nos
et deos mediatores nobis philosophi providerunt,
possunt quidem dicere de animo et corpore: Alterum
nobis cum diis, alterum cum hominibus commune
est; sed, sicut dixi, tamquam in perversum ligati
atque suspensi, servum corpus cum diis beatis,
dominum animum cum hominibus miseris, parte
inferiore exaltati, superiore deiecti. Unde etiamsi
quisquam propter hoc eos putaverit aeternitatem
habere cum diis, quia nulla morte, sicut animalium
terrestrium, animi eorum solvuntur a corpore, nec
sic existimandum est eorum corpus tamquam
honoratorum aeternum vehiculum, sed aeternum
vinculum damnatorum.

X

*Quod secundum Plotini sententiam minus miseri sint
homines in corpore mortali quam daemones in
aeterno.*

PLOTINUS certe nostrae memoriae vicinis temporibus Platonem ceteris excellentius intellexisse laudatur. Is cum de humanis animis ageret: "Pater,"
inquit, "misericors mortalia illis vincla faciebat."
Ita hoc ipsum, quod mortales sunt homines corpore,

---

[1] *Catiline* 1.
[2] Plotinus, the great Neoplatonist, died about A.D. 270.
[3] *Enneads* 4.3.12.

gods and the other with the beasts,"[1] for he was speaking of men, whose bodies are mortal like those of beasts. But these demons, whom the philosophers have provided for us as mediators between us and the gods, can certainly say of mind and body: "The one we share with the gods, the other with men." But, as I have said, they are, as it were, bound and suspended upside down, having their subservient bodies like those of the blessed gods and their sovereign minds like those of wretched men, being exalted in their inferior and cast down in their superior part. Hence, even if one were to suppose that they have eternal life like that of the gods because, unlike living beings on earth, their minds are never separated from their bodies by death, still we must think of their bodies not as an eternal chariot bearing them high in honour, but as an eternal prison cell in which they are condemned to dishonour.

X

According to the view of Plotinus, men are less miserable in their mortal than demons in their eternal bodies.

PLOTINUS is certainly praised as surpassing, in the period just preceding our own recollections, the rest of Plato's followers in his understanding of the master.[2] Now he said when discussing human minds: "The Father in his mercy made for them bonds that are mortal."[3] So he gave it as his judgement that even the fact that men have mortal bodies derives from the

ad misericordiam Dei patris pertinere arbitratus est,
ne semper huius vitae miseria tenerentur. Hac
misericordia indigna iudicata est iniquitas daemonum, quae in animi passivi miseria non mortale sicut
homines, sed aeternum corpus accepit. Essent
quippe feliciores hominibus, si mortale cum eis
haberent corpus et cum diis animum beatum.
Essent autem pares hominibus, si cum animo misero
corpus saltem mortale cum eis habere meruissent;
si tamen adquirerent aliquid pietatis, ut ab aerumnis
vel in morte requiescerent. Nunc vero non solum
feliciores hominibus non sunt animo misero, sed
etiam miseriores sunt perpetuo corporis vinculo.
Non enim aliqua pietatis et sapientiae disciplina
proficientes intellegi voluit ex daemonibus fieri
deos, cum apertissime dixerit daemones aeternos.

XI

De opinione Platonicorum qua putant animas
hominum daemones esse post corpora.

Dicit quidem et animas hominum daemones esse
et ex hominibus fieri lares, si boni meriti sunt; lemures, si mali, seu larvas; manes autem deos dici,
si incertum est bonorum eos seu malorum esse

mercy of God our Father who would not have men always held in bondage to the misery of this life. But the wickedness of the demons was judged unworthy of his mercy, and so along with the misery of a mind subject to passions they received a body, not mortal like that of men, but immortal. They would of course be happier than men, if they shared with them a mortal body and with the gods a mind blest and happy. Moreover, they would be the equals of men, if along with an unhappy mind they had won the privilege of having like them at least a mortal body, but only if at the same time they achieved enough religion to enable them to find rest from woe, albeit in death. As it is, not only are they no happier than men inasmuch as their minds are unhappy, but they are even more unhappy than men because their bodies are an everlasting prison. For Apuleius did not mean us to understand that demons could become gods through schooling in religion and wisdom, since he spoke very explicitly of demons as eternal.

XI

On the belief of the Platonists that the souls of men are demons after leaving their bodies.

APULEIUS indeed also says that the souls of men are demons and that, on ceasing to be men, they become *lares*, if they have deserved this reward for their good conduct, and *lemures* or *larvae* if they have been bad, while they are called *di manes* if it is uncertain

meritorum. In qua opinione quantam voraginem
aperiant sectandis perditis moribus quis non videat,
si vel paululum adtendat? Quando quidem quamlibet nequam homines fuerint, vel larvas se fieri dum
opinantur, vel dum manes deos, tanto peiores fiunt
quanto sunt nocendi cupidiores, ut etiam quibusdam
sacrificiis tamquam divinis honoribus post mortem se
invitari opinentur ut noceant. Larvas quippe dicit
esse noxios daemones ex hominibus factos. Sed hinc
alia quaestio est. Inde autem perhibet appellari
Graece beatos εὐδαίμονας quod boni sint animi, hoc
est boni daemones, animos quoque hominum daemones esse confirmans.

XII

*De ternis contrariis quibus secundum Platonicos
daemonum hominumque natura distinguitur.*

SED nunc de his agimus quos in natura propria
descripsit inter deos et homines genere animalia,
mente rationalia, animo passiva, corpore aeria,

---

[1] *De Deo Socratis* 15. The Latin terms refer to various
categories of disembodied spirits feared or honoured by the
Romans. In spite of Apuleius' subtle distinctions, the
Romans frequently confused the character and functions of
the several types of beings named. In origin the *Lares* were
probably farm-land deities who became tutelary spirits of the
household. Later they were identified with the protecting
souls of deceased ancestors. *Lemures* and *larvae* were dreadful
wandering ghosts of the unquiet dead who haunted the air
at night. (But Apuleius actually uses *lemures* as a general

whether they have behaved well or ill.[1] What an abysmal pit of profligacy is opened up before men's feet by those who hold this belief, as anyone can see if he gives the matter even the slightest attention! For, however wicked men may have been, let them but believe that they may become *larvae* or *di manes*, and they become just so much worse as their interest in doing harm is increased, even to the point where they suppose themselves encouraged to do hurt by the promise of certain sacrifices, divine honours, you might say, after death. This is implied in Apuleius' statement that *larvae* are harmful demons who once were men. But this leads to another question. He furthermore asserts that men who are blessed are called *eudaimones* in Greek because they are good souls, that is they are good demons; thus he supports his view that the souls of men are also demons.[2]

XII

On the three opposites by which the Platonists distinguish between the nature of demons and of men.

But now we are dealing with the demons whose peculiar nature has been described by Apuleius as animal in genus, affected by emotions, rational in

term for all disembodied souls. Augustine is wrong in asserting that he confines this term exclusively to the evil spirits). In contrast the *di manes* were probably the duly honoured dead whom their descendants did not have to fear so long as they honoured them with banquets at the proper festivals. See A. Grenier, *Les Religions Etrusque et Romaine*, pp. 156–157, and Ward Fowler, *Roman Festivals*, pp. 107–109.

[2] *De Deo Socratis* 14.

tempore aeterna. Nempe cum prius deos in sublimi caelo, homines autem in terra infima disiunctos locis et naturae dignitate secerneret, ita conclusit: " Habetis," inquit, " interim bina animalia: deos ab hominibus plurimum differentes loci sublimitate, vitae perpetuitate, naturae perfectione, nullo inter se propinquo communicatu, cum et habitacula summa ab infimis tanta intercapedo fastigii dispescat, et vivacitas illic aeterna et indefecta sit, hic caduca et subsiciva, et ingenia illa ad beatitudinem sublimata, haec ad miserias infimata."

Hic terna video commemorata contraria de duabus naturae partibus ultimis, id est summis atque infimis. Nam tria quae proposuit de diis laudabilia, eadem repetivit, aliis quidem verbis, ut eis adversa alia tria ex hominibus redderet. Tria deorum haec sunt: loci sublimitas, vitae perpetuitas, perfectio naturae. Haec aliis verbis ita repetivit, ut eis tria contraria humanae condicionis opponeret. " Cum et habitacula," inquit, " summa ab infimis tanta intercapedo fastigii dispescat," quia dixerat loci sublimitatem; " et vivacitas," inquit, " illic aeterna et indefecta sit,

---

[1] Cf. above, Book 9.8.
[2] *De Deo Socratis* 4.

intelligence, airy in body and eternal in time.[1] As will be remembered, after placing the gods as high as possible—in heaven—and men as low as possible—on earth—and distinguishing them by their situations and the unequal rank of their natures, he thus concluded: "You have at this point two kinds of animated beings, gods differing in the highest degree from men by the loftiness of their situation, the everlasting continuity of their life and the perfection of their nature, with no immediate communication between them; for not only are the highest dwelling places separated from the lowest by so vast a gap, but the vital impulse is also eternal there and unfailing, while here it is precarious and intermittent, and furthermore their natural endowments are raised to the highest of blessedness, while ours are sunk into the depths of wretchedness."[2]

Here I see recorded three pairs of opposites belonging to the two opposite extremes of nature, the highest and the lowest. For he repeated, in different words, it is true, the three traits that he put forward as notably superior in the existence of the gods, in order to match them with three opposites drawn from the human world. The three characteristics of the gods are the loftiness of their situation, the everlasting continuity of their life, and the perfection of their nature. He repeated these in different words, so as to contrast with them three opposites belonging to man's condition. "Since the highest dwelling places," he says, "are separated from the lowest by so vast a gap"—for he had spoken of the loftiness of their situation—"since the vital impulse there is eternal and unfailing, while here it is precarious and

hic caduca et subsiciva," quia dixerat vitae per-
petuitatem; " et ingenia illa," inquit, " ad beatitudinem sublimata, haec ad miserias infimata,"
quia dixerat naturae perfectionem. Tria igitur ab
eo posita sunt deorum, id est locus sublimis, aeternitas, beatitudo; et his contraria tria hominum,
id est locus infimus, mortalitas, miseria.

XIII

*Quo modo daemones, si nec cum diis beati nec cum
hominibus sunt miseri, inter utramque partem
sine utriusque communione sint medii.*

INTER haec terna deorum et hominum quoniam
daemones medios posuit, de loco nulla est controversia; inter sublimem quippe et infimum medius
locus aptissime habetur et dicitur. Cetera bina
restant, quibus cura adtentior adhibenda est, quem
ad modum vel aliena esse a daemonibus ostendantur,
vel sic eis distribuantur ut medietas videtur ex-
poscere. Sed ab eis aliena esse non possunt. Non
enim sicut dicimus locum medium nec summum
esse nec infimum, ita daemones, cum sint animalia
rationalia, nec beatos esse nec miseros, sicuti sunt
arbusta vel pecora, quae sunt sensus vel rationis

intermittent "—for he had spoken of the everlasting continuity of their life—" and since their natural endowments are raised to the height of blessedness, while ours are sunk into the depths of wretchedness " —for he had spoken of the perfection of their nature. Thus we see that he postulated three attributes of the gods, loftiness of situation, eternity and blessedness, and as opposites to these three attributes of men, lowliness of situation, mortality and wretchedness.

XIII

How the demons, if they share neither blessedness with the gods nor misery with men, can be midway between the two and have nothing in common with either.

SINCE Apuleius assigned to the demons a middle state between the extremes of the three opposite attributes that distinguish gods and men, there is no dispute about their place in the universe. For the place that exists between highest and lowest is quite appropriately held and stated to be the middle or mean. That leaves the other two pairs of opposites, which require our closer attention. How are we either to show that these are not relevant to demons or to assign the demons such participation in them as is consistent with the stipulation of their middle state? Well, we cannot say that they are not relevant. Though in speaking of place, we may say that the middle position is neither the highest nor the lowest, we cannot in the same way correctly assert that demons are neither blessed nor miserable, like plants or beasts which lack sensation and reason,

expertia, recte possumus dicere. Quorum ergo
ratio mentibus inest, aut miseros esse aut beatos
necesse est. Item non possumus recte dicere nec
mortales esse daemones nec aeternos. Omnia
namque viventia aut in aeternum vivunt, aut finiunt
morte quod vivunt. Iam vero iste tempore aeternos
daemones dixit. Quid igitur restat nisi ut hi
medii de duobus summis unum habeant et de duobus
infimis alterum? Nam si utraque de imis habebunt
aut utraque de summis, medii non erunt, sed in
alterutram partem vel resiliunt vel recumbunt.
Quia ergo his binis, sicut demonstratum est, carere
utrisque non possunt, acceptis ex utraque parte
singulis mediabuntur. Ac per hoc quia de infimis
habere non possunt aeternitatem, quae ibi non est,
unum hoc de summis habent; et ideo non est alterum
ad complendam medietatem suam quod de infimis
habeant nisi miseriam.

Est itaque secundum Platonicos sublimium deorum
vel beata aeternitas vel aeterna beatitudo; hominum vero infimorum vel miseria mortalis vel mortalitas misera; daemonum autem mediorum vel
misera aeternitas vel aeterna miseria. Nam et
quinque illis quae in definitione daemonum posuit,
196

for demons are rational animals. We know that where capacity to reason exists in a mind, its possessor must necessarily be either miserable or blessed. In the same way we cannot rightly say that the demons are neither mortal nor everlasting. For all living beings either live for ever or make an end of life by dying. But Apuleius has already said that the demons are everlasting in time. What recourse is there but to conclude that these intermediate beings possess the highest extreme of one of the two opposite attributes and the lower extreme of the other? For if they are to possess the higher of both pairs of opposites or the lower of both, they will not be in the middle but must either go bounding up or fall to the bottom, whichever it is. Therefore since, as we have proved, they cannot lack either one of the two kinds of opposites, they will find their middle place between zenith and nadir by receiving one property from above and the other from below. Moreover, since everlasting life is not to be obtained from the lowest level, where it does not exist, this one attribute of theirs they must receive from the highest level. Accordingly, there is nothing but misery left for them to receive from the lowest level, in order to complete their position midway between gods and men.

So, according to the Platonists, the gods who dwell on high have what we may call either a blissful eternity or eternal bliss, while men who dwell in the lowest region have either mortal misery or miserable mortality, but demons who dwell in the middle position have either a miserable eternity or an eternal misery. Now in citing those five attributes that

non eos medios, sicut promittebat, ostendit; quoniam tria dixit eos habere nobiscum, quod genere animalia, quod mente rationalia, quod animo passiva sunt; cum diis autem unum, quod tempore aeterna; et unum proprium, quod corpore aeria. Quo modo ergo medii, quando unum habent cum summis, tria cum infimis? Quis non videat relicta medietate quantum inclinentur et deprimantur ad infima? Sed plane etiam ibi medii possunt ita inveniri, ut unum habeant proprium, quod est corpus aerium, sicut et illi de summis atque infimis singula propria, dii corpus aetherium hominesque terrenum; duo vero communia sint omnibus, quod genere sunt animalia et mente rationalia. Nam et ipse cum de diis et hominibus loqueretur: " Habetis," inquit, " bina animalia," et non solent isti deos nisi rationales mente perhibere. Duo sunt residua, quod sunt animo passiva et tempore aeterna; quorum habent unum cum infimis, cum summis alterum, ut proportionali ratione librata medietas neque sustollatur in summa, neque in infima deprimatur. Ipsa est autem illa daemonum misera aeternitas vel aeterna

---

[1] Cf. above, Book 9.8.

he used to define the demons,[1] Apuleius did not
prove, as he promised, that they have an intermediate position. For he said that they have three
qualities in common with us: they are animal in
genus, rational in intelligence and affected by emotions, while they have one quality in common with
the gods, their everlasting existence and also one
quality peculiar to themselves, that they are airy in
body. How then can their position be a mean when
they have one characteristic in common with the
highest and three with the lowest? Who can fail
to see that they have deserted the mean and are
reduced and depressed towards the lower extreme.
But obviously we can find evidence even in that
passage that they are a mean, in the following way.
The demons possess one attribute peculiar to themselves, namely an airy body, just as the dwellers on
high and on earth also have each a special characteristic: the gods have an ethereal and men an earthly
body. But two attributes are common to all, being
animal in genus and rational in intelligence. For
Apuleius himself in fact said, when speaking of gods
and men: " You have two kinds of animals or living
beings," and your Platonists never teach that the
gods are other than rational in mind. Two traits
remain, their susceptibility to emotion and their
eternity in time, of which they have one in common
with the lowest and the other with the highest. In
this way they are maintained in their intermediate
position by an exact equilibrium which prevents
their deviating either by rising to the top or sinking
to the bottom. But this is in itself the essence of the
demons' miserable eternity or eternal misery, as you

miseria. Qui enim ait " animo passiva," etiam
" misera " dixisset, nisi eorum cultoribus erubuisset.
Porro quia providentia summi Dei, sicut etiam ipsi
fatentur, non fortuita temeritate regitur mundus,
numquam esset istorum aeterna miseria nisi esset
magna malitia.

Si igitur beati recte dicuntur eudaemones, non sunt
eudaemones daemones, quos inter homines et deos
isti in medio locaverunt. Quis ergo est locus bonorum daemonum, qui supra homines, infra deos istis
praebeant adiutorium, illis ministerium? Si enim
boni aeternique sunt, profecto et beati sunt. Aeterna autem beatitudo medios eos esse non sinit,
quia multum cum diis comparat multumque ab
hominibus separat. Unde frustra isti conabuntur
ostendere quo modo daemones boni, si et inmortales
sunt et beati, recte medii constituantur inter deos
inmortales ac beatos et homines mortales ac miseros.
Cum enim utrumque habeant cum diis, et beatitudinem scilicet et inmortalitatem, nihil autem horum
cum hominibus et miseris et mortalibus, quo modo
non potius remoti sunt ab hominibus diisque coniuncti quam inter utrosque medii constituti?

Tunc enim medii essent, si haberent et ipsi duo
quaedam sua, non cum binis alterutrorum, sed cum

---

[1] Cf. above, Book 9.11.

please. For the philosopher who described them as
" affected by emotion " would also have called them
" miserable, " had he not blushed for their worshippers. We may add that, inasmuch as the universe is governed by the providence of a supreme
God, as even the Platonists themselves admit, and
not by purposeless chance, the demons would never
suffer eternal misery, were it not for their great
wickedness.

So then, if it is right to call *eudaimones* those who
are blessed,[1] we cannot describe demons as *eudaimones*, for these philosophers have placed them midway between men and gods. What room is there
then for good demons who, being above men and
below the gods, would provide help for humanity,
service for divinity? For if they are good and
eternal, assuredly they are blessed as well. But
eternal bliss bars them from an intermediate position;
it puts them much nearer to the gods and much
farther from men. This leads to the conclusion that
the Platonists will endeavour in vain to explain how
good demons, if they are both immortal and blessed,
can rightly be placed midway between the gods who
are immortal and blessed and men who are mortal
and miserable. For since they share both attributes,
namely bliss and immortality, with the gods, but
have neither of these in common with men who are
both miserable and mortal, how can they escape
being remote from men and closely joined with the
gods rather than midway between the two?

The condition under which the demons would be a
mean is this: they must possess two attributes one
of which they share with each of the extremes while

singulis utrorumque communia; sicut homo medium
quiddam est, sed inter pecora et angelos, ut, quia
pecus est animal inrationale atque mortale, angelus
autem rationale et inmortale, medius homo est, sed
inferior angelis, superior pecoribus, habens cum
pecoribus mortalitatem, rationem cum angelis,
animal rationale mortale. Ita ergo cum quaerimus
medium inter beatos inmortales miserosque mortales,
hoc invenire debemus, quod aut mortale sit beatum,
aut inmortale sit miserum.

XIV

An homines, cum sint mortales, possint vera beatitudine esse felices.

Utrum et beatus et mortalis homo esse possit,
magna est inter homines quaestio. Quidam enim
condicionem suam humilius inspexerunt negave-
runtque hominem capacem esse posse beatitudinis
quamdiu mortaliter vivit. Quidam vero extulerunt
se et ausi sunt dicere sapientiae compotes beatos
esse posse mortales. Quod si ita est, cur non ipsi
potius medii constituuntur inter mortales miseros et
inmortales beatos, beatitudinem habentes cum
inmortalibus beatis, mortalitatem cum mortalibus
miseris? Profecto enim, si beati sunt, invident

---

[1] This view is common to both Stoics and Epicureans.

not holding both attributes in common with one or the other extreme. For instance, man is a kind of mean; but a mean between beasts and angels. Granted that a beast is an irrational and mortal animal and an angel a rational and immortal one, man is intermediate between them, lower than the angels and higher than the beasts, possessing mortality in common with the beasts and reason in common with the angels, a living being, rational and mortal. Just so, when we are trying to find a being intermediate between the blessed immortals and the miserable mortals we can solve the problem only by finding something that is either mortal and blessed or immortal and miserable.

XIV

Can men, though mortal, achieve a happy state of genuine bliss?

WHETHER man can be both blessed and mortal is a question much discussed among men. Some of them have taken a humbler view of their own lot in life and have declared that man cannot possibly enjoy bliss as long as he lives a mortal life. Others on the contrary have with soaring pride dared to say that such mortals as have attained wisdom can be blessed.[1] But if this is so, why is it not rather these same wise men who are given a position midway between miserable mortals and the blessed immortals, since they have happiness in common with the blessed immortals and mortality in common with miserable mortals? For surely, if they are blessed they begrudge nothing to anyone, for what is more

nemini—nam quid miserius invidentia?—et ideo mortalibus miseris, quantum possunt, ad consequendam beatitudinem consulunt, ut etiam inmortales valeant esse post mortem et angelis inmortalibus beatisque coniungi.

XV

De mediatore Dei et hominum, homine Christo Iesu.

Si autem, quod multo credibilius et probabilius disputatur, omnes homines, quamdiu mortales sunt, etiam miseri sint necesse est, quaerendus est medius, qui non solum homo, verum etiam deus sit, ut homines ex mortali miseria ad beatam inmortalitatem huius medii beata mortalitas interveniendo perducat; quem neque non fieri mortalem oportebat, neque permanere mortalem. Mortalis quippe factus est non infirmata Verbi divinitate, sed carnis infirmitate suscepta; non autem permansit in ipsa carne mortalis quam resuscitavit a mortuis; quoniam ipse est fructus mediationis eius, ut nec ipsi propter quos liberandos mediator effectus est in perpetua vel carnis morte remanerent. Proinde mediatorem inter nos et Deum et mortalitatem habere oportuit transeuntem et beatitudinem permanentem, ut per id quod transit congrueret morituris, et ad id quod permanet transferret ex mortuis.

miserable than a grudging spirit? Accordingly they try to the best of their ability to enable miserable mortals to attain bliss, whereby they too may achieve immortality after death and union with the blessed and immortal angels.

XV

On the Mediator between God and man, the man Christ Jesus

But if all men, so long as they are mortal, must also of necessity be miserable—and this is a much more credible and likely thesis—we must seek an intermediary to be not only man but god as well, so that the blessed mortality of this intermediary may lead men by its intervention from mortal misery to blessed immortality. For him there were two requirements. He must not fail to become mortal, yet must not stay permanently mortal. Note that he became mortal, not by any weakening of the divinity of the Word, but by taking upon himself the weakness of the flesh. Yet even in the very flesh he did not remain mortal, since he brought it back to life from the dead, for this is the particular benefit of his mediation, that those for whose liberation he was made Mediator should themselves, like him, no longer remain subject to perpetual death even of the flesh. Accordingly, the Mediator between us and God necessarily had both a temporary mortality and a permanent bliss. His temporary condition made him resemble those destined to die; his permanent condition was the goal to which he transferred them from the company of the dead.

Boni igitur angeli inter miseros mortales et beatos inmortales medii esse non possunt, quia ipsi quoque et beati et inmortales sunt; possunt autem medii esse angeli mali, quia inmortales sunt cum illis, miseri cum istis. His contrarius est mediator bonus, qui adversus eorum inmortalitatem et miseriam et mortalis esse ad tempus voluit, et beatus in aeternitate persistere potuit; ac sic eos et inmortales superbos et miseros noxios, ne inmortalitatis iactantia seducerent ad miseriam, et suae mortis humilitate et suae beatitudinis benignitate destruxit in eis quorum corda per suam fidem mundans ab illorum inmundissima dominatione liberavit.

Homo itaque mortalis et miser longe seiunctus ab inmortalibus et beatis quid eligat medium per quod inmortalitati et beatitudini copuletur? Quod possit delectare in daemonum inmortalitate, miserum est; quod posset offendere in Christi mortalitate, iam non est. Ibi ergo cavenda est miseria sempiterna; hic mors timenda non est, quae non esse potuit sempiterna, et beatitudo amanda est sempiterna. Ad hoc se quippe interponit medius inmortalis et miser, ut ad inmortalitatem beatam transire non sinat, quoniam persistit quod inpedit, id est ipsa miseria;

Thus we see that good angels cannot be mediators between miserable mortals and blessed immortals, because they too are both blessed and immortal; but bad angels can be midway, because they are immortal like those above and miserable like those below. The good Mediator is just the opposite of them. To defeat their immortality and misery, he both chose to be mortal for a time and had the power to keep his blessed state for all eternity. In this way he caused the downfall of the demons, who were arrogant in their immortality and pernicious in their misery. And so they could no longer flaunt their immortality as a lure to lead men astray into misery. By the humiliation of his death and the kind graciousness of his blessed state he destroyed their rule over those hearts that he has cleansed by faith in him and has thus delivered from the most unclean tyranny of the demons.

As for man then, mortal and miserable, far removed from the immortals and the blessed, what intermediary is he to choose to bring about his union with immortality and blessedness? The pleasure that he might take in being immortal like the demons is lost in their misery; the offence that he might find in the mortality of Christ is now a thing of the past. So with the demons man has everlasting misery to fear; with Christ he has, not death to fear, for it has proved powerless to endure, but blessedness to cherish, for it endures forever. The immortal and miserable mediator, in fact, intervenes for the express purpose of preventing man from passing to a blessed immortality, for the obstacle barring man's path is always there, namely misery itself. The mortal and

ad hoc se autem interposuit mortalis et beatus, ut
mortalitate transacta et ex mortuis faceret inmortales, quod in se resurgendo monstravit, et ex
miseris beatos, unde numquam ipse discessit.

Alius est ergo medius malus qui separat amicos;
alius bonus qui reconciliat inimicos. Et ideo multi
sunt medii separatores, quia multitudo quae beata
est unius Dei participatione fit beata; cuius partici-
pationis privatione misera multitudo malorum angelorum, quae se opponit potius ad inpedimentum quam
interponit ad beatitudinis adiutorium, etiam ipsa
multitudine obstrepit quodam modo, ne possit ad
illud unum beatificum bonum perveniri, ad quod ut
perduceremur non multis, sed uno mediatore opus
erat, et hoc eo ipso cuius participatione simus beati,
hoc est Verbo Dei non facto, per quod facta sunt
omnia.

Nec tamen ob hoc mediator est, quia Verbum;
maxime quippe inmortale et maxime beatum
Verbum longe est a mortalibus miseris; sed mediator
per quod homo, eo ipso utique ostendens ad illud non
solum beatum, verum etiam beatificum bonum non
oportere quaeri alios mediatores per quos arbitremur
nobis perventionis gradus esse moliendos, quia
beatus et beatificus Deus factus particeps humanitatis

---

[1] Augustine's use of the qualifying phrase *quodam modo*
suggests that he is using *obstrepit* in its literal sense of " roar
against " rather than in its derived sense of " opposed."

blessed Mediator, on the other hand, intervened for the express purpose, after he had played his part in mortality, both of giving to the dead the immortality that he had made visible in his own resurrection, and of giving to the miserable that blessedness of which he himself had never taken leave.

So there is an evil mediator who separates friends and a good Mediator who reconciles enemies. And the reason why there are many mediators who separate is that the multitude of the blessed derives its blessed state from participation in one God. Being deprived of this participation and consequently miserable, the multitude of bad angels, who oppose themselves as a hindrance to blessedness rather than interpose themselves as a help towards attaining it, by their very number deafen us with their noise, as it were,[1] and block our access to the unique goodness that is the source of bliss. To attain this end, there was no need of many mediators; one alone was enough—one to partake of whom would make us blessed, the uncreated Word of God, through whom all things were created.

That is not to say that he is the Mediator because he is the Word, for the Word, being, as he is, super-latively immortal and superlatively blessed, is far above miserable mortals. Rather he is Mediator by virtue of being man. This is, no doubt, precisely how he makes it plain that to attain the not merely blessed, but bliss-creating final good, we need not seek other mediators by whose aid we might suppose that we must toil upward and reach the goal step by step. We do not need them because a God who is blessed and bliss-creating has become a participator

nostrae compendium praebuit participandae divinitatis suae. Neque enim nos a mortalitate et miseria liberans ad angelos inmortales beatosque ita perducit ut eorum participatione etiam nos inmortales et beati simus; sed ad illam Trinitatem cuius et angeli participatione beati sunt. Ideo quando in forma servi, ut mediator esset, infra angelos esse voluit, in forma Dei supra angelos mansit; idem in inferioribus via vitae qui in superioribus vita.

XVI

An rationabiliter Platonici definierint deos caelestes declinantes terrena contagia hominibus non misceri, quibus ad amicitiam deorum daemones suffragentur.

NON enim verum est quod idem Platonicus ait Platonem dixisse: " Nullus Deus miscetur homini "; et hoc praecipuum eorum sublimitatis ait esse specimen, quod nulla adtrectatione hominum contaminantur. Ergo daemones contaminari fatetur, et ideo eos a quibus contaminantur mundare non possunt omnesque inmundi pariter fiunt, et daemones contrectatione hominum et homines cultu daemonum. Aut si et contrectari miscerique hominibus, nec tamen contaminari daemones possunt,

---

[1] Cf. Hebrews 2.7 and 9.
[2] Philippians 2.7.
[3] *De Deo Socratis* 4.   Cf. Plato, *Symposium* 203 A.

in our humanity and so provided a short and easy path towards our participation in his divinity. For in freeing us from mortality and misery he does not lead us to the immortal and blessed angels, so that by partaking of them we may become ourselves immortal and blessed. Rather he brings us to that Trinity of whom the angels too partake to become blessed. This is why, when he chose to be lower than the angels [1] in the form of a servant,[2] that he might be a Mediator, he remained above the angels in the form of God, being at once the way of life in the world below and life itself in heaven above.

XVI

Were the Platonists right when they described the celestial gods as shunning earthly contacts and refusing to mix with men, who must depend on the help of the demons to secure the gods' friendship?

WE see then that the statement of Plato, quoted by this same Platonist,[3] is not true, namely: " No god mingles with man." And he adds that this is the principal sign of their lofty situation, that they are not contaminated by any contact with men. He admits, then, that the demons are so contaminated, and therefore they cannot purify those by whom they are contaminated; so that all alike become impure, the demons by contact with men and men by their worship of the demons. If, alternatively, the demons can come in contact and mingle with men without becoming contaminated, they must certainly

diis profecto meliores sunt, quia illi si miscerentur, contaminarentur. Nam hoc deorum dicitur esse praecipuum, ut eos sublimiter separatos humana contrectatio contaminare non possit.

Deum quidem summum omnium creatorem, quem nos verum Deum dicimus, sic a Platone praedicari asseverat, quod ipse sit solus qui non possit penuria sermonis humani quavis oratione vel modice conprehendi; vix autem sapientibus viris, cum se vigore animi quantum licuit a corpore removerunt, intellectum huius Dei, id quoque interdum velut in altissimis tenebris rapidissimo coruscamine lumen candidum intermicare. Si ergo supra omnia vere summus Deus intellegibili et ineffabili quadam praesentia, etsi interdum, etsi tamquam rapidissimo coruscamine lumen candidum intermicans, adest tamen sapientium mentibus, cum se quantum licuit a corpore removerunt, nec ab eis contaminari potest, quid est quod isti dii propterea constituuntur longe in sublimi loco, ne contrectatione contaminentur humana? Quasi vero aliud corpora illa aetheria quam videre sufficiat quorum luce terra, quantum sufficit, inlustratur. Porro si non contaminantur sidera cum videntur, quos deos omnes visibiles dicit, nec daemones hominum contaminantur aspectu, quamvis de proximo videantur.

---

[1] *De Deo Socratis* **3**.
[2] *De Deo Socratis* **2**.

be better than the gods, who, if they mingled with men, would be contaminated. For the special virtue of the gods is said to be that they are set apart on a lofty height where contact with men cannot contaminate them.

As for God, the supreme creator of all things, whom we call the true God, Apuleius assures us that, according to Plato's teaching, he is the only one who, because of the poverty of human speech, cannot be even passably described by any form of words. Moreover, he continues, even when wise men have removed themselves by a powerful act of mind as far as possible from the body, the knowledge of this God hardly reaches them, and, when it does on occasion, it darts at lightning speed like a flash of white light through the deepest darkness.[1] If then we are to suppose that the truly supreme God, who is above all things, does visit, occasionally though it be and like a flash of white light though it be, that darts at lightning speed, yet he does draw near to the minds of wise men with a kind of intelligible and ineffable presence when they have withdrawn from the body as far as was permitted, and if we are to suppose that he cannot be contaminated by them, what is the point of placing those gods far away in a lofty abode in order to avoid contamination by contact with men? As if, indeed, those ethereal bodies whose light fulfils the earth's need for illumination fulfilled their function otherwise than by being seen! Moreover, if the heavenly bodies, all of which he describes as visible gods,[2] are not contaminated by being seen, neither are the demons contaminated by the gaze of men, however near they may be when men behold them.

213

An forte vocibus humanis contaminarentur qui
acie non contaminantur oculorum, et ideo daemones
medios habent, per quos eis voces hominum nunti-
entur, a quibus longe absunt, ut incontaminatissimi
perseverent? Quid iam de ceteris sensibus dicam?
Non enim olfaciendo contaminari vel dii possent, si
adessent, vel cum adsunt daemones possunt vivorum
corporum vaporibus humanorum, si tantis sacrificiorum cadaverinis non contaminantur nidoribus.
In gustandi autem sensu nulla necessitate reficiendae
mortalitatis urgentur, ut fame adacti cibos ab hominibus quaerant. Tactus vero in potestate est. Nam
licet ab eo potissimum sensu contrectatio dicta
videatur, hactenus tamen, si vellent, miscerentur
hominibus, ut viderent et viderentur, audirent
et audirentur. Tangendi autem quae necessitas?
Nam neque homines id concupiscere auderent, cum
deorum vel daemonum bonorum conspectu vel
conloquio fruerentur; et si in tantum curiositas
progrederetur ut vellent, quonam pacto quispiam
posset invitum tangere deum vel daemonem, qui
nisi captum non potest passerem?

Videndo igitur visibusque se praebendo et loquendo
et audiendo dii corporaliter misceri hominibus pos-

Or would the gods be contaminated by the sound of the human voice, although they are not contaminated by the sharp dart of the human eye? And is that the reason why the demons are kept in their intermediate position, to report to the gods the speech of men, from whom the gods themselves are far removed, that they may thus continue to be wholly free from contamination? What am I to say now of the remaining senses? For neither could the gods be contaminated by smell, were they present, nor can the demons, when they are present, be contaminated by the exhalations from living human bodies, if they are not contaminated by the reek of so many corpses at sacrifices. As for the sense of taste, they are not hard pressed by any need to repair a mortal body and so driven by hunger to ask men for food. Touch, moreover, is within their own jurisdiction. For although we use the term contact chiefly where the sense of touch is involved, they might, if they wished, limit their mingling with men to seeing and being seen, to hearing and being heard. What need is there, then, for touch? In the first place, men would never be bold enough to lust after such a thing when they were enjoying the sight or the conversation of gods or of good demons. In the second place, even if they went so far in their impertinent meddling as to desire contact, how could any man lay hands on a god or a demon without his consent, when he cannot even touch a sparrow unless it is caught?

So let us suppose that gods might mingle with men corporeally by seeing and letting themselves be seen, and by speaking and hearing. Yet if the

sent. Hoc autem modo daemones si miscentur, ut dixi, et non contaminantur, dii autem contaminarentur, si miscerentur, incontaminabiles dicunt daemones et contaminabiles deos. Si autem contaminantur et daemones, quid conferunt hominibus ad vitam post mortem beatam, quos contaminati mundare non possunt ut eos mundos diis incontaminatis possint adiungere, inter quos et illos medii constituti sunt? Aut si hoc eis beneficii non conferunt, quid prodest hominibus daemonum amica mediatio? An ut post mortem non ad deos homines per daemones transeant, sed simul vivant utrique contaminati ac per hoc neutri beati? Nisi forte quis dicat more spongiarum vel huiusce modi rerum mundare daemones amicos suos, ut tanto ipsi sordidiores fiant, quanto fiunt homines eis velut tergentibus mundiores. Quod si ita est, contaminatioribus dii miscentur daemonibus, qui ne contaminarentur hominum propinquitatem contrectationemque vitarunt. An forte dii possunt ab hominibus contaminatos mundare daemones, nec ab eis contaminari, et eo modo non possent et homines? Quis talia sentiat, nisi quem fallacissimi daemones deceperunt?

Quid quod, si videri et videre contaminat, videntur

demons mingle with men in this way, as I said, without being contaminated, while the gods would be contaminated if they were to mingle with them, they must mean to say that the demons are exempt while the gods are not exempt from contamination. On the other hand, if we suppose that demons too are contaminated, how can they be of service to win for men a life of bliss after death? If they are contaminated themselves, they cannot purify men in order to bring them, once purified, into the company of the uncontaminated gods, between whom and men they have been placed as mediators. But if they cannot confer this boon upon men, what good do men derive from the friendly intervention of the demons? Can the effect of it be that men do not pass after death to the company of the gods by way of the demons, but instead both men and demons live together contaminated and therefore neither of them enjoying happiness? To be sure, someone may say that the demons cleanse their friends in the same way as sponges and suchlike things. They themselves get dirtier to the same extent as men get cleaner while they remove the dirt. But if this is so, then the gods mingle with those who are the more soiled, that is the demons, though they have shunned propinquity and contact with men for fear of contamination. Or can the gods perhaps cleanse the demons, when they are contaminated by men, without being themselves contaminated, even though they could not perform the same service for men? Who would take this view except one led astray by the supremely guileful demons?

If being seen and seeing contaminate, what of the

ab hominibus dii quos visibiles dicit, "clarissima mundi lumina" et cetera sidera, tutioresque sunt daemones ab ista hominum contaminatione, qui non possunt videri, nisi velint? Aut si non videri, sed videre contaminat, negent ab istis clarissimis mundi luminibus, quos deos opinantur, videri homines, cum radios suos terras usque pertendant. Qui tamen eorum radii per quaeque inmunda diffusi non contaminantur, et dii contaminarentur, si hominibus miscerentur, etiamsi esset necessarius in subveniendo contactus? Nam radiis solis et lunae terra contingitur, nec istam contaminat lucem.

XVII

Ad consequendam vitam beatam, quae in participatione est summi boni, non tali mediatore indigere hominem qualis est daemon, sed tali qualis est unus Christus.

MIROR autem plurimum tam doctos homines, qui cuncta corporalia et sensibilia prae incorporalibus et intellegibilibus postponenda iudicaverunt, cum agitur de beata vita, corporalium contrectationum facere mentionem. Ubi est illud Plotini ubi ait: "Fugiendum est igitur ad carissimam patriam, et ibi

---

[1] Apuleius, *De Deo Socratis* 1, quoting Virgil, *Georgics* 1.5–6.

gods whom Apuleius speaks of as visible and as
"most illustrious luminaries of the firmament"[1]
and the other heavenly bodies that are seen by men?
The demons are more secure than they from contamination by men because they cannot be seen
unless they so desire. Or if it is not being seen but
seeing that contaminates, the philosophers must
deny that men are seen by those "most illustrious
luminaries of the firmament" whom they believe to
be gods, when they extend their rays as far as the
earth. Their rays, however, although shed over all
kinds of impure objects, are not themselves contaminated. Would the gods, then, be contaminated
if they were to mingle with men, even if it were
necessary, in helping them, to touch them? For the
rays of the sun and of the moon touch the earth, and
yet the earth does not contaminate their light.

XVII

*That in order to attain a life of bliss, which is
participation in the supreme good, man has need,
not of a mediator like a demon, but of one
such as is Christ alone.*

It causes me the greatest surprise that such learned
men, who decreed that all corporeal and tangible
substances should be held inferior to the incorporeal
and intelligible, should bring up bodily contacts
when it is a question of the blessed life. What has
happened to the saying of Plotinus: "We must
escape then to our beloved fatherland. There is our

pater, et ibi omnia.[1] Quae igitur," inquit, " classis
aut fuga? Similem Deo fieri." Si ergo deo
quanto similior, tanto fit quisque propinquior, nulla
est ab illo alia longinquitas quam eius dissimilitudo.
Incorporali vero illi aeterno et incommutabili tanto
est anima hominis dissimilior, quanto rerum tempora-
lium mutabiliumque cupidior.

Hoc ut sanetur, quoniam inmortali puritati quae
in summo est ea quae in imo sunt mortalia et inmunda convenire non possunt, opus est quidem
mediatore; non tamen tali qui corpus quidem habeat
inmortale propinquum summis, animum autem
morbidum similem infimis—quo morbo nobis invi-
deat potius ne sanemur quam adiuvet ut sanemur—;
sed tali qui nobis infimis ex corporis mortalitate
coaptatus inmortali spiritus iustitia, per quam non
locorum distantia, sed similitudinis excellentia mansit
in summis, mundandis liberandisque nobis vere
divinum praebeat adiutorium. Qui profecto incon-
taminabilis Deus absit ut contaminationem timeret

---

[1] F. Chatillon has shown that the majority of MSS. and
early editions as well as mediaeval citations support the reading, *Fugiendum est igitur ad clarissimam patriam, et ibi patere
tibi omnia.* See *Revue du moyen âge latin*, VIII, 1952, " Ploti-
niana," pp. 273–299. This reading might, as Chatillon says,
have arisen from a wrong division of words, since the oldest
MSS., in particular the seventh-century *Corbeiensis* on which
modern editions are based, has no division between words.
Furthermore, the passage of Plotinus that appears to be the
Greek original of the Latin here supports the reading as given
in the text. See *Enneads* 1.6.8. The change of *carissimam*
to *clarissimam* would have been made to accord with *ibi patere
tibi omnia.*

Father and there is everything. Well, where is the ship, you ask, and how do we escape? By becoming like unto God"?[1] If it is true that the more a man resembles God, the closer he comes to him, then the only way to be far from God is to be unlike him. But the soul of man is the more unlike that eternal and immutable being the more its affections are set on things temporal and changeable.

To remedy this condition, since things below, which are mortal and impure, cannot combine with the immortal purity that is on high, there is certainly need of a mediator, not the sort of mediator, however, who, though he has an immortal body that comes close to the highest, has at the same time an ailing soul that resembles those who are lowest. (His ailment would make him rather begrudge our being cured than give his assistance to effect a cure.) We need the sort of Mediator who is linked to us in our lowest estate by bodily mortality yet is righteous in his immortality of spirit, through which he continued to dwell in the highest region of all, not in any spatial sense, but in the sense that his likeness to God was outstanding. Such a one can provide aid that is truly divine to make us clean and set us free. Far be it from us to imagine that this God, who is un-

---

[1] Augustine appears to have linked together two passages of Plotinus, *Enneads* 1.6.8 (περὶ τοῦ καλοῦ) and 1.2.3 (Περὶ ἀρετῶν). The freedom with which Augustine translates probably indicates that he is quoting from memory. Some scholars, however, take the words *similem deo fieri* to be based not on the passage from Περὶ ἀρετῶν, but on the thought found in *Ennead* 1.6.9: "Let everyone first become godlike and fair, if he is to contemplate God and the fair." See P. Henry, *Plotin et l'Occident* (Louvain, 1934), 108 f.

ex homine quo indutus est, aut ex hominibus inter quos in homine conversatus est. Non enim parva sunt haec interim duo quae salubriter sua incarnatione monstravit, nec carne posse contaminari veram divinitatem, nec ideo putandos daemones nobis esse meliores, quia non habent carnem. Hic est, sicut eum sancta scriptura praedicat, *mediator Dei et hominum, homo Christus Iesus,* de cuius et divinitate, qua patri est semper aequalis, et humanitate, qua nobis factus est similis, non hic locus est ut competenter pro nostra facultate dicamus.

XVIII

Quod fallacia daemonum, dum sua intercessione viam spondet ad Deum, hoc adnitatur, ut homines a via veritatis avertat.

FALSI autem illi fallacesque mediatores daemones, qui, cum per spiritus inmunditiam miseri ac maligni multis effectibus clareant, per corporalium tamen locorum intervalla et per aeriorum corporum levitatem a provectu animorum nos avocare atque avertere moliuntur, non viam praebent ad Deum, sed ne via

---

[1] 1 Timothy 2.5.

questionably above contamination, should fear contamination from the man in whom he clothed himself
or from the men with whom he associated clothed in
a man. For there are two lessons of particular importance demonstrated by his incarnation for our
well-being, to omit for the moment any others,
namely that true divinity cannot be contaminated
by the flesh, and that we must not suppose the
demons to be better than we are merely because
they have no fleshly body. He is, as the holy Scriptures proclaim him, "the Mediator between God and
men, the man Christ Jesus." [1] His divinity sets him
eternally equal with his father, and by his humanity
he was made like unto us. But this is not the place
for us to discuss these points with the competence
permitted by our capacity.

XVIII

*That the wily lure of the demons, while it offers us
assurance of a way to God through their intercession, is really bent on turning men from
the way of truth.*

Moreover, even though those false and fallacious
mediators, the demons, are clearly shown to be
malignant and wretched by many effects of their
activity due to their unclean spirit, nevertheless they
take advantage of the distances that separate objects
in space and of the lightness of their airy bodies, as
they strive to distract and divert us from the spiritual
progress of our souls. Their aim is not to provide
access to God; it is to hinder our keeping to the path

teneatur inpediunt. Quando quidem et in ipsa via corporali—quae falsissima est et plenissima erroris, qua non iter agit iustitia; quoniam non per corporalem altitudinem, sed per spiritalem, hoc est incorporalem, similitudinem ad Deum debemus ascendere —in ipsa tamen via corporali, quam daemonum amici per elementorum gradus ordinant inter aetherios deos et terrenos homines aeriis daemonibus mediis constitutis, hoc deos opinantur habere praecipuum, ut propter hoc intervallum locorum contrectatione non contaminentur humana.

Ita daemones contaminari potius ab hominibus quam homines mundari a daemonibus credunt, et deos ipsos contaminari potuisse, nisi loci altitudine munirentur. Quis tam infelix est ut ista via mundari se existimet ubi homines contaminantes, daemones contaminati, dii contaminabiles praedicantur; et non potius eligat viam ubi contaminantes magis daemones evitentur et ab incontaminabili Deo ad ineundam societatem incontaminatorum angelorum homines a contaminatione mundentur?

of access. For even in the theory of a material path
upward—which is full of delusion and false turns,
and righteousness does not travel by this path, no,
for we must ascend towards God not by bodily eleva-
tion but by spiritual, that is nonmaterial assimilation
to God—even on that route which the friends of
the demons arrange like a ladder with the elements
for steps, putting in the middle of their scheme the
aerial demons between the ethereal gods and earthy
men, even in that scheme the gods are supposed to
enjoy a special advantage in that by being so far off
spatially they escape contamination by contact with
men.

It is thus their belief that demons are contaminated
by men rather than that men are cleansed by
demons, and that the gods themselves would be
liable to contamination if they were not protected by
their lofty location. Who is so unfortunate as to
believe that there is cleansing for him in a path
where, such is their message, men contaminate,
demons are contaminated and gods are liable to contamination? Who would not choose a path that
rather avoids the contaminating demons, a path by
which men may be cleansed from contamination by
a God who cannot be contaminated, that they may
enter the fellowship of angels who are free from
contamination?

XIX

*Quod appellatio daemonum iam nec apud cultores
eorum assumatur in significationem alicuius
boni.*

SED ne de verbis etiam nos certare videamur, quoniam nonnulli istorum, ut ita dixerim, daemonic-
colarum, in quibus et Labeo est, eosdem perhibent
ab aliis angelos dici quos ipsi daemones nuncupant,
iam mihi de bonis angelis aliquid video disserendum,
quos isti esse non negant, sed eos bonos daemones
vocare quam angelos malunt.

Nos autem, sicut scriptura loquitur secundum quam
Christiani sumus, angelos quidem partim bonos,
partim malos, numquam vero bonos daemones legimus; sed ubicumque illarum litterarum hoc nomen
positum reperitur, sive daemones, sive daemonia
dicantur, non nisi maligni significantur spiritus. Et
hanc loquendi consuetudinem in tantum populi
usquequaque secuti sunt ut eorum etiam qui pagani
appellantur et deos multos ac daemones colendos
esse contendunt, nullus fere sit tam litteratus et
doctus qui audeat in laude vel servo suo dicere:
" Daemonem habes "; sed cuilibet [1] hoc dicere

----

[1] quilibet *some MSS. and Hoffmann.*

----

[1] *Daemonicolae,* a word perhaps coined by Augustine himself. Cf. *Confessions* 8.2.4.

XIX

*That the name demons is no longer employed, even
by their worshippers, to indicate any good being.*

But in order not to give the impression that I too
am arguing merely about words, since several of
those demon-worshippers,[1] if I may so designate
them, among whom even Labeo is found,[2] allege that
those whom they term demons are called angels by
others, I see that at this point I must say something
about good angels, whose existence the Platonists
do not deny, although they prefer to call them good
demons rather than angels.

Now as for us, we read, and this is the language of
Scripture by whose guidance we are Christians, sometimes of good and sometimes of bad angels, but never
of good demons;[3] but wherever in Scripture we
find this noun in the text, whether it be expressed in
the masculine (*daemones*) or the neuter form (*daemonia*), it refers only to malign spirits. Moreover,
people everywhere have followed this fashion of
speech to such an extent that even among those who
are called pagans and maintain that we ought to
worship a variety of gods and demons, there is hardly
anyone so well read and educated as to dare to say as
a compliment even to his slave: " You are possessed
of a demon," for no matter to whom he chose to

---

[2] Probably Cornelius Labeo, who wrote a treatise, now lost,
on Romano-Etruscan religion in the third century of our era.
However, he is identified by some with Antistius Labeo, jurist
and antiquarian of the Augustan age. See Book 2.11.

[3] Cf. above, Book 8.14.

voluerit, non se aliter accipi quam maledicere
voluisse dubitare non possit. Quae igitur nos causa
compellit ut post offensionem aurium tam multarum
ut iam paene sint omnium, quae hoc verbum non
nisi in malam partem audire consuerunt, quod
diximus cogamur exponere, cum possimus angelorum
nomine adhibito eandem offensionem quae nomine
daemonum fieri poterat evitare?

XX

De qualitate scientiae quae daemones superbos facit.

QUAMQUAM etiam ipsa origo huius nominis, si divinos intueamur libros, aliquid adfert cognitione dig-
nissimum. Daemones enim dicuntur—quoniam
vocabulum Graecum est—ab scientia nominati. Apostolus autem spiritu sancto locutus ait: *Scientia
inflat, caritas vero aedificat;* quod recte aliter non
intellegitur nisi scientiam tunc prodesse, cum caritas
inest; sine hac autem inflare, id est in superbiam
inanissimae quasi ventositatis extollere. Est ergo
in daemonibus scientia sine caritate, et ideo tam
inflati, hoc est tam superbi sunt, ut honores divinos
et religionis servitutem quam vero Deo deberi sciunt
sibi satis egerint exhiberi, et quantum possunt et

---

[1] i.e. δαίμονες from δαήμονες, "knowing." Cf. Plato,
Cratylus 398 B, referring to Hesiod, *Works and Days* 120–125.
Also Lactantius, *Divinae Institutiones* 2.14.6, and Martianus
Capella 2.154.
[2] 1 Corinthians 8.1.

address this remark, he could be in no doubt that it would be taken as a deliberate curse. What compelling reason is there then to make us offend all the ears, now so numerous as to be almost universal, which have become accustomed to hearing this word used only in an evil sense, and then to feel obliged to explain what we said, instead of using the word angel and so avoiding the offence that might have been given by use of the term demon?

XX

The kind of knowledge on which the demons pride themselves.

THE etymology of this term, however, also contributes a lesson well worth learning, if we scrutinize the sacred books. The demons—for the work is Greek —received their name because of their knowledge.[1] Now the Apostle, speaking by inspiration of the Holy Spirit, says: " Knowledge puffs up, love builds up ";[2] which makes correct sense only when taken to mean that knowledge is of no advantage when there is no love in it. Without love it puffs up, that is to say it raises a man to an arrogance that is nothing but hollow flatulence. Well, the demons have such knowledge without love, and as a result they are so puffed up, that is so arrogant, that they have bent their best efforts to obtain for themselves the divine honours and religious homage that they know should be paid to the true God alone, and, as far as they can and among whomsoever they can, they are still at

apud quos possunt adhuc agant. Contra superbiam
porro daemonum, qua pro meritis possidebatur genus
humanum, Dei humilitas quae in Christo [1] apparuit,
quantam virtutem habeat, animae hominum nesciunt
inmunditia elationis inflatae, daemonibus similes
superbia, non scientia.

XXI

*Ad quem modum Dominus voluerit daemonibus
innotescere.*

IPSI autem daemones etiam hoc ita sciunt ut eidem
Domino infirmitate carnis induto dixerint: *Quid
nobis et tibi, Iesu Nazarene? Venisti perdere nos?*
Clarum est in his verbis quod in eis et tanta scientia
erat, et caritas non erat. Poenam suam quippe
formidabant ab illo, non in illo iustitiam diligebant.
Tantum vero eis innotuit quantum voluit; tantum
autem voluit quantum oportuit. Sed innotuit non
sicut angelis sanctis, qui eius, secundum id quod Dei
Verbum est, participata aeternitate perfruuntur,
sed sicut eis terrendis innotescendum fuit ex quorum
tyrannica quodam modo potestate fuerat liberaturus
praedestinatos in suum regnum et gloriam semper
veracem et veraciter sempiternam.

Innotuit ergo daemonibus non per id quod est vita
aeterna et lumen incommutabile quod inluminat

---

[1] in forma servi *some MSS. and Migne.*

---

[1] Mark 1.24; Matthew 8.29.

work. Furthermore, the souls of men, when they are puffed up by the uncleanness of their own conceit, copying the pride of the demons, not their knowledge, do not know what great virtue there is in the humility of God made manifest in Christ as a bulwark against the arrogance of the demons to which the human race was once enslaved by its own fault.

XXI

How far our Lord chose to become known to the demons.

THE demons themselves, however, know even this virtue so well that they said to the Lord when he was clothed in the weakness of the flesh: " What have we to do with you, Jesus of Nazareth? Have you come to destroy us? " [1] It is clear from these words both that they had a great deal of knowledge and that they had no love.   No doubt they feared punishment from him and had no love for his righteousness. But he let himself be known to them only so far as he chose, and he chose to be known only so far as was proper. He became known to them, however, not as he is known to the holy angels, who constantly enjoy him as the Word of God and have their part with him in eternal life, but with such knowledge as was required to terrify those from whose tyrannical power, so to speak, he was about to deliver those predestined for his kingdom and for a glory that is always genuine and genuinely eternal.

He became known then to the demons, not through his being life eternal and the light unchangeable

pios, cui videndo per fidem quae in illo est corda mundantur, sed per quaedam temporalia suae virtutis effecta et occultissimae signa praesentiae, quae angelicis sensibus etiam malignorum spirituum potius quam infirmitati hominum possent esse conspicua. Denique quando ea paululum supprimenda iudicavit et aliquanto altius latuit, dubitavit de illo daemonum princeps eumque temptavit, an Christus esset explorans, quantum se temptari ipse permisit, ut hominem quem gerebat ad nostrae imitationis temperaret exemplum. Post illam vero temptationem, cum angeli, sicut scriptum est, ministrarent ei, boni utique et sancti ac per hoc spiritibus inmundis metuendi et tremendi, magis magisque innotescebat daemonibus quantus esset, ut ei iubenti, quamvis in illo contemptibilis videretur carnis infirmitas, resistere nullus auderet.

XXII

Quid intersit inter scientiam sanctorum angelorum et scientiam daemonum.

His igitur angelis bonis omnis corporalium temporaliumque rerum scientia qua inflantur daemones vilis est; non quod earum ignari sint, sed quod illis Dei qua sanctificantur caritas cara est, prae cuius

---

[1] Matthew 4.11.

that shines on the truly religious, whose hearts, when they see it, are cleansed through faith in it, but by certain temporal effects of his power and certain signs that reveal his presence however deeply concealed. This was evidence that would be more clearly visible to the angelic senses even of malign spirits than to the weak powers of men. Consequently, when he judged that such signs should be to some extent suppressed, and when he hid himself a good deal deeper, the prince of the demons became uncertain of him and tempted him, trying to discover whether he was Christ, but only so far as he himself allowed himself to be tempted. His purpose was to shape the human person in which he played his part into a model that we might copy. After that temptation, however, when the angels, as it is written, ministered to him,[1] that is, the good and holy angels, who were therefore bound to cause fear and trembling in unclean spirits, his greatness became gradually better known to the demons, so that when he gave commands, however contemptible the infirmity of the flesh might seem to be in him, none dared to resist him.

XXII

The difference between the knowledge that the holy angels have and that of the demons.

CONSEQUENTLY the good angels hold cheap all the knowledge of things material and temporal that gives the demons such a swollen notion of themselves; not that they are ignorant in such matters, but that the love of God whereby they are sanctified is dear to

non tantum incorporali, verum etiam incommutabili
et ineffabili pulchritudine, cuius sancto amore
inardescunt, omnia quae infra sunt et quod illud est
non sunt seque ipsos inter illa contemnunt, ut ex toto
quod boni sunt eo bono, ex quo boni sunt, per-
fruantur.   Et ideo certius etiam temporalia et mutabilia ista noverunt, quia eorum principales causas in
Verbo Dei conspiciunt, per quod factus est mundus;
quibus causis quaedam probantur, quaedam repro-
bantur, cuncta ordinantur.

Daemones autem non aeternas temporum causas
et quodam modo cardinales in Dei sapientia contem-
plantur, sed quorundam signorum nobis occultorum
maiore experientia multo plura quam homines
futura prospiciunt; dispositiones quoque suas aliquando praenuntiant. Denique saepe isti, numquam illi omnino falluntur.   Aliud est enim temporalibus temporalia et mutabilibus mutabilia coniectare
eisque temporalem et mutabilem modum suae
voluntatis et facultatis inserere, quod daemonibus
certa ratione permissum est; aliud autem in aeternis
atque incommutabilibus Dei legibus, quae in eius
sapientia vivunt, mutationes temporum praevidere
Deique voluntatem, quae tam certissima quam
potentissima est omnium, spiritus eius participatione

234

them. In comparison with its beauty, which is not
only immaterial but also immutable and ineffable as
well, and which makes them glow with a holy passion,
they despise all things below it and all things, including themselves, that are not what it is, in order
to enjoy thoroughly, with all the power of their goodness, the good which is the source of their goodness.
It follows that they also know with greater certainty
those temporal and changeable things, because they
can discern the prime causes of them in the Word of
God, by whom the world was made. In the light of
these causes, some things win approval, some dis-
approval; all things are put in their place.

The demons on the contrary do not fix their gaze
on the eternal causes, the hinges as it were, of
temporal events, which are found in God's wisdom,
though they do foresee many more future events
than we do by their greater acquaintance with certain
signs that are hidden from men. Sometimes too they
announce in advance events that they themselves
intend to bring about. Consequently the demons
are often mistaken, the angels absolutely never. For
it is one thing to guess at temporal matters from
temporal, and changeable matters from changeable,
and to introduce into them the temporal and changeable workings of one's own will and capacity, and this
is a thing that the demons may do within fixed
limits; but it is quite another to foresee in the light
of the eternal and immutable laws of God, which
derive their existence from his wisdom, the changes
that time will bring, and to discern, by partaking of
his spirit, the will of God, which is as absolutely certain as it is universally powerful. This gift has

cognoscere; quod sanctis angelis recta discretione
donatum est. Itaque non solum aeterni, verum
etiam beati sunt. Bonum autem quo beati sunt
Deus illis est, a quo creati sunt. Illius quippe
indeclinabiliter participatione et contemplatione
perfruuntur.

XXIII

*Nomen deorum falso ascribi diis gentium, quod tamen
et angelis sanctis et hominibus iustis ex divinarum
scripturarum auctoritate commune est.*

Hos si Platonici malunt deos quam daemones
dicere eisque adnumerare quos a summo Deo
conditos deos scribit eorum auctor et magister Plato,
dicant quod volunt; non enim cum eis de verborum
controversia laborandum est. Si enim sic inmortales
ut tamen a summo Deo factos, et si non per se ipsos,
sed ei a quo facti sunt adhaerendo beatos esse dicunt,
hoc dicunt quod dicimus, quolibet eos nomine
appellent.

Hanc autem Platonicorum esse sententiam, sive
omnium sive meliorum, in eorum litteris inveniri
potest. Nam et de ipso nomine, quod huius modi
inmortalem beatamque creaturam deos appellant,
ideo inter nos et ipsos paene nulla dissensio est,

---

[1] Plato, *Timaeus* 40 A; Cicero, *Timaeus* 10.

justly been reserved and bestowed upon the holy angels. It is this gift which makes them not only eternal but also blessed. Moreover, the good whereby they are blessed is the God by whom they were created, for they never cease to enjoy unfailingly their partaking of him and their absorption in the sight of him.

XXIII

The name gods is mistakenly used of the gods of the gentiles; on the other hand the authority of the holy Scriptures grants it both to holy angels and to righteous men.

IF the Platonists prefer to call the angels gods rather than demons and to include them among those whom their founder and master Plato describes as gods created by the supreme God,[1] let them say what they please, for we must not engage in laboured argument with them over words. For if they mean that these beings are immortal, but with the understanding that they were created by the most high God, and happy, not indeed of themselves, but by clinging to him by whom they were created, they say the same as we, whatever name they choose to give to them.

That this is the view of the Platonists, whether of all of them or of the better among them, can be discovered in their writings. For even in the matter of the name itself, that is their using the term gods for created beings of this kind that are immortal and blessed, there is practically no quarrel between them and us on that score, for we too read in our

237

quia et in nostris sacris litteris legitur: *Deus deorum dominus locutus est,* et alibi: *Confitemini deo deorum,* et alibi: *Rex magnus super omnes deos.* Illud autem ubi scriptum est: *Terribilis est super omnes deos,* cur dictum sit deinceps ostenditur. Sequitur enim: *Quoniam omnes dii gentium daemonia, Dominus autem caelos fecit.* *Super omnes* ergo *deos* dixit, sed *gentium,* id est quos gentes pro diis habent, quae sunt *daemonia*; ideo *terribilis,* sub quo terrore Domino dicebant: *Venisti perdere nos?* Illud vero ubi dicitur: *Deus deorum,* non potest intellegi deus daemoniorum; et *rex magnus super omnes deos* absit ut dicatur rex magnus super omnia daemonia. Sed homines quoque in populo Dei eadem scriptura deos appellat. *Ego,* inquit, *dixi, dii estis et filii Excelsi omnes.* Potest itaque intellegi horum deorum deus, qui dictus est *deus deorum,* et super hos deos rex magnus, qui dictus est *rex magnus super omnes deos.*

Verum tamen cum a nobis quaeritur: Si homines dicti sunt dii quod in populo Dei sunt, quem per angelos vel per homines alloquitur Deus, quanto magis inmortales eo nomine digni sunt qui ea fruuntur beatitudine ad quam Deum colendo cupiunt homines pervenire, quid respondebimus nisi non frustra in scripturis sanctis expressius homines nuncupatos deos quam illos inmortales et beatos,

---

1 Psalm 50.1.   4 Psalm 96.4–5.
2 Psalm 136.2.   5 Mark 1.24.
3 Psalm 95.3.   6 Psalm 82.6.

sacred writings: " The God of gods, the Lord has
spoken," [1] and in another passage: " Give thanks
to the God of gods," [2] and again: " A great king
above all gods." [3] And when it is written: " He is
to be feared above all gods," the meaning is immediately made clear, for the following words are: " For
all the gods of the gentiles are demons, but the Lord
made the heavens." [4] Thus the psalmist said "above
all gods," but added " of the gentiles," that is those
whom the gentiles look upon as gods, but who are
demons. As for the phrase " to be feared," that
refers to their fear when they said to the Lord:
" Have you come to destroy us?" [5] But the expression " God of gods " cannot be understood as meaning god of demons; and as for " a great king above
all gods," far be it from meaning a great king above
all demons. Rather the same Scripture speaks also
of men who belong to God's people as " gods." In
the words of the psalmist, "·I have said ' You are
gods, sons of the Most High, all of you.' " [6] Thus
we may understand that he who is called " God of
gods " is God of gods in this sense, and that when he
is called " a great king above all gods," it is above
gods in this sense that he is a great king.

Nevertheless, when we are asked: " If men are
called gods because they belong to the people of God,
to whom God speaks through angels or through men,
how much more worthy of that name are the immortal
beings who enjoy the very happiness that men would
fain arrive at by worshipping God," what are we to
reply? Well, we can only say that it is not without
reason that in the holy Scriptures men are called
gods more explicitly than those who are immortal

quibus nos aequales futuros in resurrectione promittitur, ne scilicet propter illorum excellentiam aliquem eorum nobis constituere deum infidelis auderet infirmitas? Quod in homine facile est evitare. Et evidentius dici debuerunt homines dii in populo Dei ut certi ac fidentes fierent eum esse Deum suum qui dictus est *deus deorum*; quia etsi appellentur dii inmortales illi et beati qui in caelis sunt, non tamen dicti sunt dii deorum, id est dii hominum in populo Dei constitutorum, quibus dictum est: *Ego dixi, dii estis et filii Excelsi omnes*. Hinc est quod ait apostolus: *Etsi sunt qui dicuntur dii, sive in caelo sive in terra, sicuti sunt dii multi et domini multi, nobis tamen unus Deus Pater, ex quo omnia et nos in ipso, et unus Dominus Iesus Christus, per quem omnia et nos per ipsum.*

Non multum ergo de nomine disceptandum est, cum res ipsa ita clareat ut ab scrupulo dubitationis aliena sit. Illud vero, quod nos ex eorum inmortalium beatorum numero missos esse angelos dicimus qui Dei voluntatem hominibus adnuntiarent, illis autem non placet, quia hoc ministerium non per illos quos deos appellant, id est inmortales et beatos, sed per daemones fieri credunt, quos inmortales tantum, non etiam beatos audent dicere, aut certe ita in-

---

[1] 1 Corinthians 8.5–6.

and blessed, and whose equals, so runs the promise, we shall be in the resurrection. The reason is, of course, to ensure our not, in the weakness of our faith, rashly giving one of them the status of a god because of their lofty position. It is easy to refrain from so honouring a man. Also, it was proper for mortals among the people of God to be called gods more clearly, in order to make them confident and certain that he was their God who was called " God of gods." For, even if those immortal and blessed personages who are in heaven should be called gods, yet they never have been called gods of gods, that is gods of men who are members of the people of God, to whom it was said: " I have said ' You are gods, sons of the Most High, all of you.' " Hence the saying of the Apostle: " Although there be so-called gods, whether in heaven or on earth—as there are many gods and many lords—yet for us there is one God, the father, from whom came all things and for whom we exist, and one lord, Jesus Christ, through whom came all things and through whom we exist." [1]

So there is no need to argue at length about the name, since the fact itself is so plain as to be exempt from all scruple of doubt. When we assert, however, that angels chosen from among the immortals and the blessed have been sent to make known to men the will of God, the Platonists do not agree with us, because they believe that such service is performed, not by those whom they call gods, namely the immortal and blessed ones, but by the demons whom they call immortal only and do not venture to call blessed. Or if they call them both immortal and blessed, they at least do so with the understanding

mortales et beatos ut tamen daemones bonos, non
deos sublimiter conlocatos et ab humana contrectatione semotos, quamvis nominis controversia videatur,
tamen ita detestabile est nomen daemonum ut hoc
modis omnibus a sanctis angelis nos removere
debeamus.

Nunc ergo ita liber iste claudatur ut sciamus inmortales et beatos, quodlibet vocentur, qui tamen
facti et creati sunt, medios non esse ad inmortalem
beatitudinem perducendis mortalibus miseris, a
quibus utraque differentia separantur. Qui autem
medii sunt communem habendo inmortalitatem cum
superioribus, miseriam cum inferioribus, quoniam
merito malitiae miseri sunt, beatitudinem quam non
habent invidere nobis possunt potius quam praebere.
Unde nihil habent amici daemonum quod nobis
dignum adferant cur eos tamquam adiutores colere
debeamus, quos potius ut deceptores vitare debemus.
Quos autem bonos et ideo non solum inmortales,
verum etiam beatos deorum nomine sacris et sacrificiis propter vitam beatam post mortem adipiscendam colendos putant, qualescumque illi sint et
quolibet vocabulo digni sint, non eos velle per tale
religionis obsequium nisi unum Deum coli, a quo
creati et cuius participatione beati sunt, adiuvante
ipso in sequenti libro diligentius disseremus.

that these are good demons, not gods established in
lofty regions and remote from contact with men.
Although the discussion appears to be purely
semantic, the name demons is so detestable that we
must take all precautions to avoid using it is connection with the holy angels.

The time has come, therefore, to end this book with
a statement of our conclusion: we know that the
immortal and blessed ones, who, whatever they are
to be called, were in any case made and created, are
not intermediaries whose purpose is to guide unhappy
mortals to eternal bliss. They are separated from
mortals by a twofold distinction. On the other hand,
those who are in the intermediate position, having immortality in common with those above and misery in
common with those below them—and deserving their
misery because of the evil in their hearts—have the
power rather to grudge than to grant us the bliss that
they do not possess. It follows that the friends of
the demons can offer us no reason worth our consideration why we should worship them as benefactors; rather we ought to shun them as frauds.
Those, moreover, who are good and on that account
not only immortal, but also blessed, whom they think
it prudent to worship with rites and sacrifices under
the name of gods, in order to secure a happy life
after death, whatever their character and whatever
title they deserve—those beings do not want such
religious worship to be offered to any but the one
God by whom they were created and by communion
with whom they are blessed. With the help of that
same God, we shall discuss this point more thoroughly
in the next book.

BOOK X

LIBER X

I

*Veram beatitudinem sive angelis sive hominibus per
unum Deum tribui etiam Platonicos definisse;
sed utrum hi quos ob hoc ipsum colendos
putant uni tantum Deo, an etiam sibi
sacrificari velint, esse
quaerendum.*

OMNIUM certa sententia est qui ratione quoquo
modo uti possunt beatos esse omnes homines velle.
Qui autem sint vel unde fiant dum mortalium
quaerit infirmitas, multae magnaeque controversiae
concitatae sunt in quibus philosophi sua studia et otia
contriverunt, quas in medium adducere atque discutere et longum est et non necessarium. Si enim
recolit qui haec legit quid in libro egerimus octavo
in eligendis philosophis cum quibus haec de beata
vita quae post mortem futura est quaestio tractaretur, utrum ad eam uni Deo vero qui etiam
effector est deorum, an plurimis diis religione sacrisque serviendo pervenire possimus, non etiam hic
eadem repeti expectat, praesertim cum possit rele

---

[1] Cf. above, Book 8.5.

BOOK X

I

Even the Platonists have restricted the bestowal of true
blessedness, whether upon angels or upon men, to
the one God; but the question is whether the
beings who in the opinion of these philosophers
must be worshipped for the sake of this very
blessedness, require sacrifices to be made
only to the one God or to
themselves as well.

It is the established view of everyone who is in
any way capable of using reason that all men want to
be blessed. Yet whenever men, weak as they are,
raise the question who are blessed or what makes
them so, they kindle a host of fierce debates on which
philosophers have exhausted their efforts and spent
their leisure. To bring them up now and discuss
them would not only be tedious but there is no need
to do so. For if the reader of these words recollects
my treatment in Book VIII,[1] when I was selecting
philosophers who might contribute to my disquisi-
tion on the blessed life that is to come after death,
asking whether it is to be won by giving allegiance
and worship to the one true God who is also the
creator of gods, or to a large number of gods, he is
not expecting a repetition of the same arguments
here, the more so since he can refresh his memory by

gendo, si forte oblitus est, adminiculare memoriam. Elegimus enim Platonicos omnium philosophorum merito nobilissimos, propterea quia sapere potuerunt licet inmortalem ac rationalem vel intellectualem hominis animam nisi participato lumine illius Dei, a quo et ipsa et mundus factus est, beatam esse non posse; ita illud quod omnes homines appetunt, id est vitam beatam, quemquam isti assecuturum negant qui non illi uni optimo, quod est incommutabilis Deus, puritate casti amoris adhaeserit.

Sed quia ipsi quoque sive cedentes vanitati errorique populorum sive, ut ait apostolus, *evanescentes in cogitationibus suis* multos deos colendos ita putaverunt vel putari voluerunt ut quidam eorum etiam daemonibus divinos honores sacrorum et sacrificiorum deferendos esse censerent, quibus iam non parva ex parte respondimus, nunc videndum ac disserendum est, quantum Deus donat, inmortales ac beati in caelestibus sedibus dominationibus, principatibus potestatibus constituti, quos isti deos et ex quibus quosdam vel bonos daemones vel nobiscum angelos nominant, quo modo credendi sint velle a nobis religionem pietatemque servari; hoc est, ut apertius dicam, utrum etiam sibi an tantum Deo suo, qui etiam noster est, placeat eis ut sacra faciamus et sacrificemus, vel aliqua nostra seu nos ipsos religionis ritibus consecremus.

---

[1] Romans 1 21.
[2] Colossians 1.16.

rereading the passage if he happens to have forgotten it. In fact I selected the Platonists, who are justly the most renowned of all philosophers, because they had the good sense to see that the soul of man, though it is immortal and rational or intellectual, yet cannot be blessed unless it partakes of the light shed by God, who created the soul itself and the Universe. Consequently they assert that no man will obtain what all men eagerly desire, namely, a blessed life, who has not clung with the purity of a chaste love to the one supreme good, which is the unchangeable God.

Nevertheless, whether they too surrendered to the foolish and mistaken popular notions or whether, as the Apostle says, "they became futile in their thinking," [1] they also believed, or chose to have it believed, that many gods should be worshipped, so that some of them considered it a duty to pay divine honours of worship and sacrifice even to demons. To these I have already in large part replied. What I have to do now, as God grants me power, is to consider and discuss the immortal and blessed creatures who are established in heavenly thrones and dominions, principalities and powers,[2] whom the Platonists call gods and to some of whom they give the name either of good demons, or, as we do, of angels. What are we to believe that they require of us in order to maintain the laws of religious duty and respect? In plainer terms, is it their will that we should offer worship and sacrifices to them too and consecrate some of our possessions or ourselves by religious rites to them or only to their God, who is also ours?

Hic est enim divinitati vel, si expressius dicendum est, deitati debitus cultus, propter quem uno verbo significandum, quoniam mihi satis idoneum non occurrit Latinum, Graeco ubi necesse est insinuo quid velim dicere. Λατρείαν quippe nostri, ubicumque sanctarum scripturarum positum est, interpretati sunt servitutem. Sed ea servitus quae debetur hominibus, secundum quam praecipit apostolus servos dominis suis subditos esse debere, alio nomine Graece nuncupari solet; λατρεία vero secundum consuetudinem qua locuti sunt qui nobis divina eloquia condiderunt aut semper aut tam frequenter ut paene semper ea dicitur servitus quae pertinet ad colendum Deum. Proinde si tantummodo cultus ipse dicatur, non soli Deo deberi videtur. Dicimur enim colere etiam homines, quos honorifica vel recordatione vel praesentia frequentamus. Nec solum ea quibus nos religiosa humilitate subicimus, sed quaedam etiam quae subiecta sunt nobis perhibentur coli. Nam ex hoc verbo et agricolae et coloni et incolae vocantur, et ipsos deos non ob aliud appellant caelicolas nisi quod caelum colant, non utique venerando, sed inhabitando, tamquam caeli quosdam colonos; non sicut appellantur coloni, qui condicionem debent genitali solo, propter agriculturam sub

---

[1] Cf. *City of God* 7.1.
[2] Ephesians 6.5; Titus 2.9.
[3] *Douleia.* Cf. Augustine, *Quaestiones in Heptateuchum* 2.94, where *douleia* is said to be due to God as Lord, but *latreia* only to God as God.

For this is the worship that we owe to divinity or, if we must speak more explicitly, to deity.[1] Since there is need for a single word to describe this, and since no really satisfactory one in Latin comes to my mind, I shall slip in a Greek word where necessary to convey my meaning. To be sure, wherever *latreia* occurs in the holy Scriptures, our translators have rendered it " service." But the service owed to men, in regard to which the Apostle enjoins upon slaves that they must be submissive to their masters,[2] is usually referred to by another word in Greek,[3] whereas *latreia*, according to the usage of those who have set down the word of God in writing, is employed always, or so constantly as to be all but always, of service connected with the worship of God. Consequently, if we were simply to use the Latin word *cultus*, this seems to mean service not reserved for God alone. For we are said to " cultivate " (*colere*) men too, when we give them constant honourable mention or honours by our actual presence. We speak also of ourselves as " cultivating " not only things to which we yield homage with religious humility but also certain things subordinate to ourselves. For this word gives us the derivatives *agricolae* (cultivators of the land), *coloni* (settlers) and *incolae* (inhabitants), and the gods themselves are called *caelicolae* for no other reason than that they " cultivate " the sky, not of course by worshipping it, but by dwelling in it, as if they were a kind of celestial settlers. Here settler has not the meaning it has when used of serfs (*coloni*) who owe their status to the soil on which they were born and are so called because they cultivate land under bondage to its

dominio possessorum, sed, sicut ait quidam Latini eloquii magnus auctor:

Urbs antiqua fuit, Tyrii tenuere coloni.

Ab incolendo enim colonos vocavit, non ab agri-cultura. Hinc et civitates a maioribus civitatibus velut populorum examinibus conditae coloniae nuncu-pantur. Ac per hoc cultum quidem non deberi nisi Deo propria quadam notione verbi huius omnino verissimum est; sed quia et aliarum rerum dicitur cultus, ideo Latine uno verbo significari cultus Deo debitus non potest.

Nam et ipsa religio quamvis distinctius non quem-libet, sed Dei cultum significare videatur—unde isto nomine interpretati sunt nostri eam quae Graece θρησκεία dicitur—tamen quia Latina loquendi con-suetudine, non inperitorum, verum etiam doctissi-morum, et cognationibus humanis atque adfinitatibus et quibusque necessitudinibus dicitur exhibenda religio, non eo vocabulo vitatur ambiguum cum de cultu deitatis vertitur quaestio, ut fidenter dicere valeamus religionem non esse nisi cultum Dei, quoniam videtur hoc verbum a significanda ob-servantia propinquitatis humanae insolenter auferri.

Pietas quoque proprie Dei cultus intellegi solet,

owners, but rather the meaning expressed by a certain master of Latin speech:

> There was an ancient city which was held
> By Tyrian settlers.[1]

Here Virgil called them *coloni* because they were inhabitants in that place, not because they cultivated the land. Thus it comes that cities founded by swarms of people, as it were, hiving off from larger cities, are called colonies. So it is perfectly true that *cultus* (worship) in a certain fundamental sense of the word is due to none save God, but, as *cultus* is used also in connection with other objects, it is for that reason impossible in Latin to convey in one word the meaning " worship due to God."

Moreover, the very term *religio* too, although it would seem to indicate more precisely not any worship, but the worship of God—and this is the reason why our translators have used it to render the Greek word *threskeia*—yet in Latin usage, and that not of the ignorant but of the most cultured also, we say that religion is to be observed in dealing with human relationships, affinities and ties of every sort. Hence this term does not secure us against ambiguity when used in discussing the worship paid to God. We cannot say confidently that *religio* means only the worship of God, since we should thus clearly be violating usage by abolishing one meaning of the word, namely, the observance of duties in human relationships.

Pietas, too, which the Greeks call *eusebeia*, is usually

[1] Virgil, *Aeneid* 1.12.

quam Graeci εὐσέβειαν vocant. Haec tamen et
erga parentes officiose haberi dicitur. More autem
vulgi hoc nomen etiam in operibus misericordiae
frequentatur; quod ideo arbitror evenisse quia
haec fieri praecipue mandat Deus eaque sibi vel pro
sacrificiis vel prae sacrificiis placere testatur. Ex
qua loquendi consuetudine factum est ut et Deus
ipse dicatur pius; quem sane Graeci nullo suo sermonis usu εὐσεβῆν vocant, quamvis εὐσέβειαν pro
misericordia illorum etiam vulgus usurpet. Unde
in quibusdam scripturarum locis, ut distinctio certior
appareret, non εὐσέβειαν, quod ex bono cultu, sed
θεοσέβειαν, quod ex Dei cultu compositum resonat,
dicere maluerunt. Utrumlibet autem horum nos
uno verbo enuntiare non possumus.

Quae itaque λατρεία Graece nuncupatur et Latine
interpretatur servitus, sed ea qua colimus Deum;
vel quae θρησκεία Graece, Latine autem religio
dicitur, sed ea quae nobis est erga Deum; vel quam
illi θεοσέβειαν, nos vero non uno verbo exprimere, sed
Dei cultum possumus appellare, hanc ei tantum
Deo deberi dicimus qui verus est Deus facitque suos
cultores deos. Quicumque igitur sunt in caelestibus
habitationibus inmortales et beati, si nos non amant
nec beatos esse nos volunt, colendi utique non sunt.
Si autem amant et beatos volunt, profecto inde

---

[1] For *pius* in the sense " merciful," see Vulgate, 2 Chronicles
30.9, Ecclesiasticus 2.13 (A.V. 2.11) and Judith 7.20. The
derivative " pity " gets its English meaning from this usage.

[2] Cf. 1 Timothy 2.10 and Augustine, *Enchiridion* 1.2.

[3] Cf. Psalm 82.6.

understood in its strict sense to refer to the worship of God. Yet this word is also used of obligations dutifully performed towards parents. Moreover, by popular usage the word is frequently used of works of mercy. This has happened, I believe, because God especially enjoins the performance of works of this kind and assures us that they are pleasing to him in place of or in preference to sacrifice. From this fashion of speaking it has come about that God himself is called *pius*.[1] But the Greeks of course never call him *eusebēs* (pious) in their own language, although with them too popular speech appropriates the word *eusebeia* (piety) for mercy. Therefore in certain passages of Scripture, to make the distinction clearer, they preferred to employ not *eusebeia*, which means " good worship," but *theosebeia*, a compound made up of the Greek words for " worship of God." [2] But we are still unable to render either one of these words by a single Latin word.

So what the Greeks call *latreia* is translated into Latin as *servitus*, but it is the service by which we worship God. What the Greeks call *threskeia* is called in Latin *religio*, but it is the religious duty owed by us to God. What the Greeks call *theosebeia* we cannot express in a single word, but we can call it the worship of God. This we say is owed to that God alone who is the true God and makes gods of his worshippers.[3] Whoever then the immortal and blessed beings may be who dwell in heavenly habitations, if they do not love us or wish us to be blessed, they are certainly not to be worshipped. But if they do love us and wish us to be blessed, assuredly they wish us to receive our blessedness from the same source as they;

volunt unde et ipsi sunt; an aliunde ipsi beati, aliunde nos?

II

De superna inluminatione quid Plotinus Platonicus senserit.

SED non est nobis ullus cum his excellentioribus philosophis in hac quaestione conflictus. Viderunt enim suisque litteris multis modis copiosissime mandaverunt hinc illos unde et nos fieri beatos, obiecto quodam lumine intellegibili, quod Deus est illis et aliud est quam illi, a quo inlustrantur ut clareant atque eius participatione perfecti beatique subsistant.

Saepe multumque Plotinus asserit sensum Platonis explanans ne illam quidem quam credunt esse universitatis animam aliunde beatam esse quam nostram, idque esse lumen quod ipsa non est, sed a quo creata est et quo intellegibiliter inluminante intellegibiliter lucet. Dat etiam similitudinem ad illa incorporea de his caelestibus conspicuis amplisque corporibus, tamquam ille sit sol et ipsa sit luna. Lunam quippe solis obiectu inluminari putant. Dicit ergo ille magnus Platonicus animam rationalem,

---

[1] Cf. Plotinus, *Enneads* 5.6.4.19–22.
[2] Cf. Plotinus, *Enneads* 5.1.10.10–13.
[3] Cf. Plotinus, *Enneads* 5.6.4.16–19.

256

or is our blessedness derived from one source, theirs
from another?

II

The opinion of the Platonist Plotinus on illumination from on high.

But on this point there is no conflict between us
and these more outstanding of the philosophers.
For they saw and have set down in their writings in a
variety of ways and with abundant eloquence their
opinion that these beings derive their blessedness
from the same source as we ourselves do, from a
certain intelligible light cast upon them, which is
God to them and is different from themselves, and
which illumines them so that they are enlightened,
and by their participation in it exist in a state of perfect blessedness.[1]

Plotinus asserts often and emphatically, in ex-
pounding the doctrine of Plato, that not even that
soul which they believe to be the soul of the universe derives its blessedness from any other source
than does our own, and that the light is something
distinct from the soul. Rather it is that by which
the soul was created and by whose intelligible illumination the soul is made bright with an intelligible
light.[2] He goes on to draw a comparison between
these bodiless beings and the vast and prominent
bodies in the sky, likening God to the sun and the
soul to the moon. They believe of course that the
moon derives its light from the rays of the sun.[3] So
this great Platonist declares that a rational soul, or

257

sive potius intellectualis dicenda sit, ex quo genere
etiam inmortalium beatorumque animas esse intellegit, quos in caelestibus sedibus habitare non
dubitat, non habere supra se naturam nisi Dei, qui
fabricatus est mundum, a quo et ipsa facta est; nec
aliunde illis supernis praeberi vitam beatam et
lumen intellegentiae veritatis quam unde praebetur
et nobis, consonans evangelio, ubi legitur: *Fuit
homo missus a Deo, cui nomen erat Iohannes; hic venit
in testimonium, ut testimonium perhiberet de lumine, ut
omnes crederent per eum. Non erat ille lumen, sed ut
testimonium perhiberet de lumine. Erat lumen verum
quod inluminat omnem hominem venientem in hunc
mundum.* In qua differentia satis ostenditur animam
rationalem vel intellectualem, qualis erat in Iohanne,
sibi lumen esse non posse, sed alterius veri luminis
participatione lucere. Hoc et ipse Iohannes fatetur,
ubi ei perhibens testimonium dicit: *Nos omnes de
plenitudine eius accepimus.*

III

*De vero Dei cultu, a quo Platonici, quamvis creatorem
universitatis intellexerint, deviarunt colendo angelos
seu bonos seu malos honore divino.*

Quae cum ita sint, si Platonici vel quicumque alii
ista senserunt cognoscentes Deum sicut Deum glori-

---

[1] Cf. Plotinus, *Enneads* 5.1.10.12–18.

[2] John 1.6–9.

[3] John 1.16. Augustine evidently quotes these words as
part of the prophecy of John the Baptist, although they are
more usually taken to be the Evangelist's own words.

perhaps we ought rather to say intellectual,—and in this class he includes all the souls of the immortal and blessed, of whose dwelling in heavenly seats he has no doubt—a rational soul, he says, has no natural being above it except God, who created the world and by whom the soul itself was also made.[1] Nor can these beings on high obtain a blessed life and the light for understanding the truth from any other source than that whence we too obtain it. In saying this he agrees with the Gospel, where we read: "There was a man sent from God, whose name was John. He came to be a witness, to bear witness to the light, that all might believe through him. He was not the light, but came to bear witness to the light. It was the true light that enlightens every man coming into this world."[2] This distinction shows clearly that the rational or intellectual soul, such as John had, cannot be its own light, but shines by sharing in some of the other, the true light. John himself confesses this when, bearing witness to Him, he says: "We have all received some of his abundant fulness."[3]

III

The true worship of God, from which the Platonists,
although recognizing that he created the universe,
went astray when they worshipped angels,
whether good or bad, with honour
due to God.

THIS being so, if the Platonists or any others who held the same view, when they recognized God, had glorified him as God and given thanks to him, and

ficarent et gratias agerent nec evanescerent in cogitationibus suis nec populorum erroribus partim auctores fierent, partim resistere non auderent, profecto confiterentur et illis inmortalibus ac beatis nobis mortalibus ac miseris, ut immortales ac beati esse possimus, unum Deum deorum colendum qui et noster est et illorum.

Huic nos servitutem quae λατρεία Graece dicitur sive in quibusque sacramentis sive in nobis ipsis debemus. Huius enim templum simul omnes et singuli templa sumus, quia et omnium concordiam et singulos inhabitare dignatur; non in omnibus quam in singulis maior, quoniam nec mole distenditur nec partitione minuitur. Cum ad illum sursum est, eius est altare cor nostrum; eius Unigenito eum sacerdote placamus; ei cruentas victimas caedimus, quando usque ad sanguinem pro eius veritate certamus; eum suavissimo adolemus incenso, cum in eius conspectu pio sanctoque amore flagramus; ei dona eius in nobis nosque ipsos vovemus et reddimus; ei beneficiorum eius sollemnitatibus festis et diebus statutis dicamus sacramusque memoriam, ne volumine temporum ingrata subrepat oblivio; ei sacrificamus hostiam humilitatis et laudis in ara cordis igne fervidam caritatis.

Ad hunc videndum, sicut videri poterit, eique cohaerendum ab omni peccatorum et cupiditatum

---

[1] Romans 1.21.
[2] 1 Corinthians 3.16–17.
[3] Hebrews 12.4.
[4] Psalm 116.17.

had not become futile in their thinking,[1] in some cases themselves originating popular error, while in others they merely lacked the courage to take a stand against existing error, they would undoubtedly admit that both those immortal and blessed beings, and we too who are mortal and wretched, are bound, in order that we may attain immortality and blessedness, to worship the one God of gods who is both our God and theirs.

To him we owe the service which is called in Greek *latreia*, whether this service is embodied in certain sacraments or is within our very selves. For all of us together are his temple and all of us individually his temples,[2] since he deigns to dwell both in the united heart of all and in each one separately. He is no greater in the heart of all men than in each individual, since he is neither enlarged by addition nor made less by division. When we lift our hearts to him, our hearts are his altar; with his only begotten Son as our priest we seek his favour. We sacrifice bleeding victims to him when we fight in defence of his truth even unto blood;[3] we offer him the sweetest incense when in his sight we burn with pious and holy love, when we vow, and pay the vow, to devote to him his gifts bestowed on us and to devote ourselves with them; when we dedicate and consecrate to him a memorial of his benefits in solemn feasts on appointed days, lest, as time unrolls its scroll, a thankless forgetfulness should creep in; when we offer him on the altar of our hearts a sacrifice of humility and praise[4] kindled by the fire of our love.

In order to see him, so far as he can be seen, and to cling to him, we are cleansed from every stain caused

malarum labe mundamur et eius nomine consecra-
mur. Ipse enim fons nostrae beatitudinis, ipse
omnis appetitionis est finis. Hunc eligentes vel
potius religentes—amiseramus enim neglegentes—
hunc ergo religentes, unde et religio dicta perhibetur,
ad eum dilectione tendimus, ut perveniendo quiesca-
mus, ideo beati quia illo fine perfecti. Bonum
enim nostrum, de cuius fine inter philosophos magna
contentio est, nullum est aliud quam illi cohaerere,
cuius unius anima intellectualis incorporeo, si dici
potest, amplexu veris impletur fecundaturque virtutibus.

Hoc bonum diligere in toto corde, in tota anima et
in tota virtute praecipimur; ad hoc bonum debemus
et a quibus diligimur duci, et quos diligimus ducere.
Sic complentur duo illa praecepta, in quibus tota
lex pendet et prophetae: *Diliges Dominum Deum
tuum in toto corde tuo et in tota anima tua et in tota mente
tua*, et: *Diliges proximum tuum tamquam te ipsum.* Ut
enim homo se diligere nosset, constitutus est ei finis
quo referret omnia quae ageret ut beatus esset; non
enim qui se diligit aliud vult esse quam beatus. Hic
autem finis est adhaerere Deo. Iam igitur scienti
diligere se ipsum, cum mandatur de proximo dili-
gendo sicut se ipsum, quid aliud mandatur nisi ut ei,
quantum potest, commendet diligendum Deum?

---

[1] Cicero, *De Natura Deorum* 2.28.72, likewise derived *religio*
from *relegere* rather than from *religare* (to bind).
[2] Matthew 22.37, 39   [3] Psalm 73.28.
[4] Cf. Augustine, *Letter* 155.11.

by sins and evil desires, and are consecrated in his name. For he is the fount of our blessedness, he is the goal of all our striving. In electing him, or rather re-electing him, for we had lost him by our neglecting him, in re-electing him then—and this is also said to be the derivation of the word "religion"[1]—we make our way towards him through our love, that when we reach him, we may have rest, being blessed because made perfect by him who is our goal. For our good, the supreme good that is the great subject of dispute among philosophers, is nothing but to cling to him, the sole being by whose incorporeal embrace the intellectual soul is, if we may put it so, impregnated and made to give birth to true virtues.

To love this good with all our hearts, with all our souls, and with all our strength, is what we are enjoined to do. Towards this good it is our due to be led by those who love us and our duty to lead those whom we love. In this way those two commandments are fulfilled on which depend all the law and the prophets: "You shall love the Lord your God with all your heart, and with all your soul, and with all your mind" and "You shall love your neighbour as yourself."[2] For in order that man should know what it means to love himself, a goal has been appointed for him, to which he is to direct all his efforts to achieve blessedness; for he who loves himself wants nothing else but to be blessed. Now this goal is to cleave to God.[3] So when the man who now knows how to love himself is commanded to love his neighbour as himself, what does this mean but that, as far as he can, he is to exhort his neighbour to love God.[4] This is the worship of God, this is true

Hic est Dei cultus, haec vera religio, haec recta pietas, haec tantum Deo debita servitus.

Quaecumque igitur inmortalis potestas quantalibet virtute praedita si nos diligit sicut se ipsam, ei vult esse subditos ut beati simus cui et ipsa subdita beata est. Si ergo non colit Deum, misera est quia privatur Deo; si autem colit Deum, non vult se coli pro Deo. Illi enim potius divinae sententiae suffragatur et dilectionis viribus favet qua scriptum est: *Sacrificans diis eradicabitur, nisi Domino soli.*[2]

IV

Quod uni vero Deo sacrificium debeatur.

NAM, ut alia nunc taceam, quae pertinent ad religionis obsequium quo colitur Deus, sacrificium certe nullus hominum est qui audeat dicere deberi nisi deo. Multa denique de cultu divino usurpata sunt quae honoribus deferrentur humanis, sive humilitate nimia sive adulatione pestifera; ita tamen ut, quibus ea deferrentur, homines haberentur, qui dicuntur colendi et venerandi, si autem multum eis additur, et adorandi. Quis vero sacrificandum censuit nisi ei

---

[1] Cf. *De Doctrina Christiana* 1.29.30.
[2] Exodus 22.20.

religion, this is genuine piety, this is the service
due only to God.

Whatever immortal power there be then, endowed
with virtue however great, if it loves us as itself, it
wishes us, in order to be blessed, to be the subjects
of Him in submission to whom it is itself blessed.[1]
Consequently if it fails to worship God, it is miserable,
because it is deprived of God; but if on the other
hand it does worship God, it has no will to be worshipped itself in place of God. For it rather endorses
and supports with the strength of loyal love that
decree of God in which it is written: " Whoever
sacrifices to any God, save to the Lord only, shall be
utterly destroyed."[2]

IV

Sacrifice is due only to the true God.

SACRIFICE certainly, we see, and no man living
dare deny it, is a rite that belongs to God alone. Let
me say nothing at the moment about other kinds of
service by which God is worshipped. There are indeed many kinds of worship that have been appro-
priated from the service of God to be conferred upon
men for their honour, an abuse that may come either
from carrying humility too far or from the pestilential
practice of flattery. Yet those who received such
tribute were still considered only men. They are
spoken of as men worthy of worship, or of reverence,
or even, if we choose to bestow still more honour, men
worthy of being addressed in prayer. But who ever
thought it right to offer sacrifice except to one who

265

quem deum aut scivit aut putavit aut finxit? Quam
porro antiquus sit in sacrificando Dei cultus duo illi
fratres Cain et Abel satis indicant, quorum maioris
Deus reprobavit sacrificium, minoris aspexit.

V

*De sacrificiis quae Deus non requirit, sed ad signi-
ficationem eorum offerri voluit quae requirit.*

Quis autem ita desipiat ut existimet aliquibus usibus Dei esse necessaria quae in sacrificiis offeruntur?
Quod cum multis locis divina scriptura testetur, ne
longum faciamus, breve illud de psalmo commemorare suffecerit: *Dixi Domino, Deus meus es tu, quoniam
bonorum meorum non eges.* Non solum igitur pecore
vel qualibet alia re corruptibili atque terrena, sed ne
ipsa quidem iustitia hominis Deus egere credendus
est, totumque quod recte colitur Deus homini prodesse, non Deo. Neque enim fonti se quisquam
dixerit consuluisse, si biberit; aut luci, si viderit.

Nec quod ab antiquis patribus alia sacrificia facta
sunt in victimis pecorum, quae nunc Dei populus
legit, non facit, aliud intellegendum est nisi rebus
illis eas res fuisse significatas quae aguntur in nobis,

---

[1] Genesis 4.4–5.
[2] Psalm 16.2. The Hebrew of this passage is of uncertain
meaning. Augustine's Latin follows the Septuagint, which
gives ὅτι τῶν ἀγαθῶν μου οὐ χρείαν ἔχεις.

he either knew or considered or pretended was God? Moreover, the antiquity of sacrifice as a form of divine worship is sufficiently proved by the two brothers, Cain and Abel: God rejected the sacrifice of the elder of these, but had regard for that of the younger.[1]

V

The sacrifices that God does not require but that he chose should be offered as symbols of those that he does require.

But who would be so foolish as to think that the objects offered in sacrifices are needed by God for any particular purposes? The folly of this is attested by holy Scripture in many passages, but, not to be tedious, let it suffice to cite that brief text from the Psalm: " I have said to the Lord, ' Thou art my God, for thou needest not my goods.' "[2] We are to believe, then, that God has no need either of man's flocks and herds or of any other thing that is corruptible or earthbound. Not only that, but he has no need even of man's righteousness, so we must believe; and everything done in the due worship of God benefits man, not God. For no man would say that he intended to help a spring when he drank from it, or a light when he saw by it.

As for those other sacrifices offered by the patriarchs of old, using sacrifical victims taken from their flocks or herds—which at the present day God's people encounter in their reading without doing the same—we are to take them only as meaning that

ad hoc ut inhaereamus Deo et ad eundem finem proximo consulamus. Sacrificium ergo visibile invisibilis sacrificii sacramentum, id est sacrum signum est. Unde ille paenitens apud prophetam vel ipse propheta quaerens Deum peccatis suis habere propitium: *Si voluisses*, inquit, *sacrificium, dedissem utique; holocaustis non delectaberis. Sacrificium Deo spiritus contritus; cor contritum et humiliatum Deus non spernet.*

Intueamur quem ad modum, ubi Deum dixit nolle sacrificium, ibi Deum ostendit velle sacrificium. Non vult ergo sacrificium trucidati pecoris, et vult sacrificium contriti cordis. Illo igitur quod eum nolle dixit, hoc significatur quod eum velle subiecit. Sic itaque illa Deum nolle dixit quo modo ab stultis ea velle creditur, velut suae gratia voluptatis. Nam si ea sacrificia quae vult—quorum hoc unum est, cor contritum et humiliatum dolore paenitendi—nollet eis sacrificiis significari quae velut sibi delectabilia desiderare putatus est, non utique de his offerendis in lege vetere praecepisset. Et ideo mutanda erant oportuno certoque iam tempore, ne ipsi Deo desiderabilia vel certe in nobis acceptabilia, ac non potius

---

[1] Psalm 51.16–17.

the old practices foreshadowed our present worship, whose purpose is to enable us to cleave to God and to help our neighbour to the same end. Sacrifice then is the visible ritual of an invisible sacrifice, that is, it is a sacred symbol. That is why the penitent man according to the prophet, or perhaps the prophet himself, seeking forgiveness from God for his sins, says: "If thou hadst wished for a sacrifice, I would indeed have given it, but thou wilt take no delight in burnt offerings. The sacrifice acceptable to God is a contrite spirit; a contrite and humbled heart God will not despise." [1]

Let us consider how in the same passage, where he said that God does not desire sacrifice, he also made it clear that God does desire sacrifice. That is, what God does not want is the sacrifice of a slaughtered beast; what he does want is the sacrifice of a contrite heart. Therefore, the sacrifice that he says God does not want is symbolic of the one that, as he then adds, God does want. So too in saying that God does not want that kind of sacrifices, he means that God does not require them as if they were for his own pleasure, as stupid people suppose. For if he did not want those sacrifices that he does require—and there is but one, a heart contrite and humbled with the sorrow of repentance—to be seen symbolically in the sacrifices that he was thought to want for his own pleasure, he surely would not have enjoined in his ancient law that these must be offered. The reason, moreover, why they had to be altered at the opportune and already chosen moment was to prevent anyone from believing that such sacrifices were desirable in God's own eyes, or at least acceptable as

quae his significata sunt crederentur. Hinc et alio loco psalmi alterius: *Si esuriero,* inquit, *non dicam tibi; meus est enim orbis terrae et plenitudo eius. Numquid manducabo carnes taurorum aut sanguinem hircorum potabo?* tamquam diceret: Utique si mihi essent necessaria, non a te peterem quae habeo in potestate. Deinde subiungens quid illa significent: *Immola,* inquit, *Deo sacrificium laudis et redde Altissimo vota tua et invoca me in die tribulationis, et eximam te et glorificabis me.*

Item apud alium prophetam: *In quo,* inquit, *adprehendam Dominum, assumam Deum meum excelsum? Si adprehendam illum in holocaustis, in vitulis anniculis? Si acceptaverit Dominus in milibus arietum aut in denis milibus hircorum pinguium? Si dedero primogenita mea inpietatis, fructum ventris mei pro peccato animae meae? Si adnuntiatum est tibi, homo, bonum? Aut quid Dominus exquirat a te nisi facere iudicium et diligere misericordiam et paratum esse ire cum Domino Deo tuo?* Et in huius prophetae verbis utrumque distinctum est satisque declaratum illa sacrificia per se ipsa non requirere Deum, quibus significantur haec sacrificia quae requirit Deus. In epistula quae inscribitur ad Hebraeos: *Bene facere,* inquit, *et communicatores esse nolite oblivisci; talibus enim sacrificiis placetur Deo.* Ac per hoc ubi scriptum est: *Misericordiam volo quam sacrificium* nihil aliud quam sacrificium sacrificio praelatum oportet intellegi; quoniam illud quod ab omnibus appellatur

---

[1] Psalm 50.12–13. [3] Micah 6.6–8.
[2] Psalm 50.14–15. [4] Hebrews 13.16.
[5] Hosea 6.6.

our offering rather than those things of which they
are symbols. Hence he says in another passage of a
different Psalm: " If I grow hungry, I shall not tell
you; for the world is mine and its fulness. Shall I
eat the flesh of bulls, or drink the blood of goats? " [1]
As if he were to say: In any case, if I had to have
them, I should not ask you for them, for I have them
at my command. Then he appends an explanation
of his words: " Offer to God a sacrifice of thanksgiving, and pay your vows to the Most High: and
call upon me in the day of trouble; and I will deliver
you and you shall glorify me." [2]

Likewise in the words of another prophet: " With
what shall I reach up to the Lord, and attain to my
God on high? Shall I come before him with burnt
offerings, with calves a year old? Will the Lord
accept me with thousands of rams or with tens of
thousands of fat he-goats? Shall I give my first
born for my transgression, the fruit of my belly for
the sin of my soul? Have you been told, O man,
what is good? Or what does the Lord require of
you, but to do justice, and to love mercy, and to be
ready to walk with the Lord your God." [3] In the
words of this prophet too the two things are set apart,
and it is made quite clear that God does not require
for their own sake the old sacrifices, which symbolize
the sacrifices that God does require. In the epistle entitled to the Hebrews it is said: " Do not forget to do
good and to share what you have, for such sacrifices
are pleasing to God" [4] And so, where it is written:
" I want mercy, and not sacrifice," [5] this must be
understood to mean merely that one kind of sacrifice is preferred to another. For that which all men

sacrificium signum est veri sacrificii. Porro autem
misericordia verum sacrificium est; unde dictum est
quod paulo ante commemoravi: *Talibus enim sacri-*
ficiis placetur Deo. Quaecumque igitur in ministerio
tabernaculi sive templi multis modis de sacrificiis
leguntur divinitus esse praecepta, ad dilectionem
Dei et proximi significando referuntur. *In his* enim
duobus praeceptis, ut scriptum est, *tota lex pendet et*
prophetae.

VI

De vero perfectoque sacrificio.

PROINDE verum sacrificium est omne opus quo [1] agitur ut sancta societate inhaereamus Deo, relatum
scilicet ad illum finem boni quo veraciter beati esse
possimus. Unde et ipsa misericordia qua homini
subvenitur, si non propter Deum fit, non est sacrificium. Etsi enim ab homine fit vel offertur, tamen
sacrificium res divina est, ita ut hoc quoque vocabulo
id Latini veteres appellaverint. Unde ipse homo
Dei nomine consecratus et Deo votus, in quantum
mundo moritur ut Deo vivat, sacrificium est. Nam
et hoc ad misericordiam pertinet quam quisque in
se ipsum facit. Propterea scriptum est: *Miserere*
animae tuae placens Deo.

Corpus etiam nostrum cum temperantia castigamus,
si hoc, quem ad modum debemus, propter Deum

----

[1] quod *some MSS. and Migne.*

----

[1] Matthew 22.40.
[2] Ecclesiasticus 30.24 (Vulgate).

call sacrifice is a symbol of the true sacrifice. Furthermore, mercy is the true sacrifice; it is referred to in the words that I have quoted just above: " For such sacrifices are pleasing to God." All the divine commandments, then, that we read concerning sacrifices to be performed in many ways in the service of tabernacle or temple point symbolically to the love of God and of our neighbour. For " on these two commandments," so it is written, " depend all the law and the prophets." [1]

VI

The true and perfect sacrifice.

THUS the true sacrifice is every act whose purpose is that we may cling to God in a holy fellowship, that is, every act governed by that final good whereby we may be truly blessed. Hence it also follows that the very act of mercy that succours some man is no sacrifice if it is not performed for the sake of God. For even though sacrifice is carried out or offered by man, it still belongs to God, so much so that the ancient Latins actually called it *res divina* or God's business. Therefore a man who is consecrated in the name of God and dedicated to God, in so far as he dies to the world that he may live to God, is himself a sacrifice. For this too is grounded in mercy, the mercy that the individual bestows on himself. This explains the text: " Show mercy on your soul by pleasing God." [2]

Our body too is a sacrifice when we discipline it by self-control, if we do so, as we ought, for the sake of

facimus, ut non exhibeamus membra nostra arma iniquitatis peccato, sed arma iustitiae Deo, sacrificium est. Ad quod exhortans apostolus ait: *Obsecro itaque vos, fratres, per miserationem Dei, ut exhibeatis corpora vestra hostiam vivam, sanctam, Deo placentem, rationabile obsequium vestrum.* Si ergo corpus, quo inferiore tamquam famulo vel tamquam instrumento utitur anima, cum eius bonus et rectus usus ad Deum refertur, sacrificium est, quanto magis anima ipsa cum se refert ad Deum, ut igne amoris eius accensa formam concupiscentiae saecularis amittat eique tamquam incommutabili formae subdita reformetur, hinc ei placens quod ex eius pulchritudine acceperit, fit sacrificium! Quod idem apostolus consequenter adiungens: *Et nolite*, inquit, *conformari huic saeculo; sed reformamini in novitate mentis vestrae ad probandum vos quae sit voluntas Dei, quod bonum et bene placitum et perfectum.*

Cum igitur vera sacrificia opera sint misericordiae sive in nos ipsos sive in proximos, quae referuntur ad Deum; opera vero misericordiae non ob aliud fiant nisi ut a miseria liberemur ac per hoc ut beati simus —quod non fit nisi bono illo de quo dictum est: *Mihi autem adhaerere Deo bonum est*—, profecto efficitur ut tota ipsa redempta civitas, hoc est congregatio societasque sanctorum, universale sacrificium offeratur Deo per sacerdotem magnum qui etiam se ipsum

---

[1] Romans 6.13.
[2] Romans 12.1.
[3] The Latin would also allow " kindled by the fire of God's love (for it)."
[4] Romans 12.2.
[5] Psalm 73.28.

God, and do not yield our members to sin as instruments of wickedness, but to God as instruments of righteousness.[1] To this the Apostle exhorts us when he says: "I appeal to you, therefore, brethren, by the mercy of God, to present your bodies as a living sacrifice, holy and acceptable to God, which is your reasonable service."[2] Therefore, if the body, which being inferior is used by the soul as a servant or instrument, is a sacrifice when its good and right use is directed to God, how much more does the soul become a sacrifice when it directs itself to God, so that kindled by the fire of love for him[3] it discards its former mould derived from wordly concupiscence and is moulded anew by subjection to God as to a model that is not subject to change, becoming beautiful in his sight by the reflections of his beauty that it has received. It is the same thing that the Apostle says in his next words when he adds: "And do not shape yourselves in conformity with this world, but be transformed by a renovation of heart, that you may yourselves have judgement to know what is the will of God, that which is good and acceptable and perfect."[4]

Therefore, since true sacrifices are works of mercy, whether mercy shown to ourselves or to our neighbours, and are directed to God, and since, on the other hand, works of mercy are done with no other object than to release us from misery and so to make us blessed—a state which cannot arise save through that good of which it was said: "But for me it is good to cling to God"[5]—it assuredly follows that all this redeemed city, which is to say the assembly and fellowship of the saints, is offered to God as a

obtulit in passione pro nobis, ut tanti capitis corpus essemus, secundum formam servi. Hanc enim obtulit, in hac oblatus est, quia secundum hanc mediator est, in hac sacerdos, in hac sacrificium est. Cum itaque nos hortatus esset apostolus ut exhibeamus corpora nostra hostiam vivam, sanctam, Deo placentem, rationabile obsequium nostrum, et non conformemur huic saeculo, sed reformemur in novitate mentis nostrae ad probandum quae sit voluntas Dei, quod bonum et bene placitum et perfectum, quod totum sacrificium nos ipsi sumus: *Dico enim*, inquit, *per gratiam Dei quae data est mihi, omnibus qui sunt in vobis, non plus sapere quam oportet sapere, sed sapere ad temperantiam; sicut unicuique Deus partitus est mensuram fidei. Sicut enim in uno corpore multa membra habemus, omnia autem membra non eosdem actus habent, ita multi unum corpus sumus in Christo; singuli autem alter alterius membra, habentes dona diversa secundum gratiam quae data est nobis.* Hoc est sacrificium Christianorum: *multi unum corpus in Christo.* Quod etiam sacramento altaris fidelibus noto frequentat ecclesia, ubi ei demonstratur quod in ea re quam offert, ipsa offeratur.

---

[1] Cf. Philippians 2.7.

[2] Romans 12.3–6.

[3] The reference is to the Mass, which is the renewal of Christ's passion and sacrifice. When the Church, which embodies Christ, renews his sacrifice in the Eucharist, one may say that the Church itself is offered as a sacrifice to God.

universal sacrifice through the High Priest who in his passion offered even himself for us in the shape of a slave [1] that we might be the body of so great a head. For it was this shape that he offered, in this that he was offered, because in consequence of this he is mediator, in this he is priest, in this he is a sacrifice. So after having exhorted us to present our bodies as a living sacrifice, holy and acceptable to God, which is our reasonable service, and not to shape ourselves in conformity with this world, but to be transformed by the renovation of our heart, that we may have judgement to know what is the will of God, that which is good and acceptable and perfect, the whole sacrifice being ourselves, the Apostle continues, " For by the grace of God given to me I bid every one among you not to think of himself more highly than he ought to think, but to think with sober judgement, each according to the measure of faith which God has assigned to him. For as in one body we have many members, and all the members do not have the same function, so we, though many, are one body in Christ, but individually members one of another, having gifts that differ according to the grace given to us." [2] This is the Christian sacrifice: "though many, one body in Christ." And this sacrifice the Church continually celebrates in the rite of the altar well known to the faithful, in which it is made clear to her that in her offering she herself is offered to God.[3]

VII

*Quod sanctorum angelorum ea sit in nos dilectio ut
nos non suos, sed unius veri Dei velint esse
cultores.*

MERITO illi in caelestibus sedibus constituti inmortales et beati, qui creatoris sui participatione congaudent, cuius aeternitate firmi, cuius veritate certi, cuius munere sancti sunt, quoniam nos mortales et miseros ut inmortales beatique simus misericorditer diligunt, nolunt nos sibi sacrificari, sed ei cuius et ipsi nobiscum sacrificium se esse noverunt. Cum ipsis enim sumus una civitas Dei, cui dicitur in psalmo: *Gloriosissima dicta sunt de te, civitas Dei;* cuius pars in nobis peregrinatur, pars in illis opitulatur. De illa quippe superna civitate, ubi Dei voluntas intellegibilis atque incommutabilis lex est, de illa superna quodam modo curia—geritur namque ibi cura de nobis—ad nos ministrata per angelos sancta illa scriptura descendit ubi legitur: *Sacrificans diis eradicabitur, nisi Domino soli.* Huic scripturae, huic legi, praeceptis talibus tanta sunt adtestata miracula ut satis appareat cui nos sacrificari velint inmortales ac beati, qui hoc nobis volunt esse quod sibi.

---

[1] Psalm 87.3.
[2] The play on the words *curia* and *cura* depends on a false etymology.
[3] Exodus 22.20.

VII

*The holy angels have such love for us that they
want us to be worshippers, not of themselves,
but of the one true God.*

WELL may those immortal and blessed beings
established in heavenly abodes, rejoicing together in
their union with their creator, enjoying security
because he is eternal, certainty because of his truth,
and sanctity by his gift, be unwilling that we should
sacrifice to themselves, choosing rather that we
should sacrifice to him whose sacrifice they know
themselves to be along with us, for they mercifully
love us mortal and wretched creatures to the end that
we may be immortal and blessed. For with them we
form one city of God, the city to whom it is said in the
Psalm: " Glorious things are spoken of thee, O city
of God." [1] This city has two divisions, one consisting
of us, sojourning in an alien land, the other of them,
lending us their aid. It is, be it noted, from that city
on high where God's will, intelligible and immutable,
is the law, from that lofty senate, so to speak, of care-
takers (*curia*)—for care (*cura*) is there taken for us [2]—
that the holy Scripture came down to us by angelic
ministry which reads: " Whoever sacrifices to any
god, save to the Lord only, shall be utterly destroyed." [3] This Scripture, this law, these and
similar precepts have been attested by so many
miracles that it is abundantly evident to whom the
immortal and blessed beings would have us sacrifice,
inasmuch as they want us to have what they have.

VIII

De miraculis quae Deus ad conroborandam fidem
piorum etiam per angelorum ministerium
promissis suis adhibere dignatus est.

Nam nimis vetera si commemorem, longius quam
sat est revolvere videbor quae miracula facta sint
adtestantia promissis Dei, quibus ante annorum
milia praedixit Abrahae quod in semine eius omnes
gentes benedictionem fuerant habiturae. Quis enim
non miretur eidem Abrahae filium peperisse coniu-
gem sterilem eo tempore senectutis quo parere nec
fecunda iam posset, atque in eiusdem Abrahae
sacrificio flammam caelitus factam inter divisas
victimas cucurrisse, eidemque Abrahae praedictum
ab angelis caeleste incendium Sodomorum, quos
angelos hominibus similes hospitio susceperat et per
eos de prole ventura Dei promissa tenuerat, ipsoque
inminente iam incendio miram de Sodomis per
eosdem angelos liberationem Loth filii fratris eius,
cuius uxor in via retro respiciens atque in salem
repente conversa magno admonuit sacramento
neminem in via liberationis suae praeterita desiderare
debere ?

Illa vero quae et quanta sunt quae iam per Moysen
pro populo Dei de iugo servitutis eruendo in Aegypto

---

[1] Genesis 18.18. [3] Genesis 15.17.
[2] Genesis 21.2. [4] Genesis 18.2–21.
[5] Genesis 19.17–26.

VIII

*The miracles by which God has seen fit to confirm
his promises, even through the ministry of
the angels, in order to fortify the faith
of believers.*

Now if I rehearse events too long past, I shall be
thought unduly tedious in reviewing the miracles
that took place in support of God's promises, by which
thousands of years ago he foretold to Abraham that
in his seed all nations should obtain a blessing.[1]
For who could think it no miracle that a barren wife
bore a son to this same Abraham at a time of life
when even a fruitful woman could no longer bear a
child,[2] or that when the same Abraham was sacrificing, a flame descended from heaven and passed
rapidly between the pieces of the victim,[3] or that the
fire from heaven that would destroy Sodom was foretold
to the same Abraham by angels whom he had received
as guests in the likeness of men and through whom he
had obtained God's promises concerning the son
that was to be his,[4] or that when the fire itself was
already threatening, the same angels miraculously
saved from Sodom Abraham's brother's son, Lot,
whose wife, by looking backwards on the way and
being straightway turned into salt, provided a solemn
and sacred warning that no man who has set his foot
on the path of salvation ought to yearn again for
what he has left behind.[5]

And again, what miracles, what great miracles were
accomplished in Egypt through the agency of Moses
in order that God's people should be rescued from the

mirabiliter gesta sunt, ubi magi Pharaonis, hoc est
regis Aegypti qui populum illum dominatione de-
primebat, ad hoc facere quaedam mira permissi sunt
ut mirabilius vincerentur! Illi enim faciebant vene-
ficiis et incantationibus magicis quibus sunt mali
angeli, hoc est daemones, dediti; Moyses autem
tanto potentius quanto iustius, nomine Dei qui
fecit caelum et terram, servientibus angelis eos facile
superavit. Denique in tertia plaga deficientibus
magis decem plagae per Moysen magna mysteriorum
dispositione completae sunt, quibus ad Dei populum
dimittendum Pharaonis et Aegyptiorum dura corda
cesserunt. Moxque paenituit, et cum abscedentes
Hebraeos consequi conarentur, illis diviso mari per
siccum transeuntibus unda hinc atque hinc in sese
redeunte cooperti et oppressi sunt.

Quid de illis miraculis dicam quae, cum in deserto
idem populus ductaretur, stupenda divinitate cre-
buerunt: aquas quae bibi non poterant misso in eas
sicut Deus praeceperat ligno amaritudine caruisse
sitientesque satiasse; manna esurientibus venisse de
caelo et, cum esset colligentibus constituta mensura,
quidquid amplius quisque collegerat exortis vermibus
putruisse, ante diem vero sabbati duplum collectum,

---

[1] Exodus 7–8.7.
[2] Exodus 14.
[3] Exodus 15.23–25.

yoke of slavery! On this occasion the wizards of Pharaoh, that is, the king of Egypt who was oppressing that people with his tyranny, were allowed to perform some miracles, simply that they might be outdone by even greater marvels. For they worked their deeds by the sorceries and magic incantations to which the bad angels, that is demons, have devoted themselves. But Moses, as much more powerful as more righteous, in the name of God who made heaven and earth, with angels as his ministers overcame them with ease.[1] Then the magicians failed with the third plague, and the full number of ten plagues was completed by Moses in a great array of miraculous works, whereupon the bad hearts of Pharaoh and the Egyptians gave way and they let God's people go. Presently they regretted it and tried to overtake the Hebrews in their flight. Then the sea parted and allowed the Hebrews to cross on dry ground, but its waters returned from the one side and the other to bury and overwhelm the Egyptians.[2]

What am I to say of the miracles that came thick and fast by the amazing exercise of divine power, when the same people was being guided through the desert? There was water unfit for drinking that lost its bitterness when a piece of wood was dropped into it, as God had enjoined, and satisfied their thirst?[3] There was manna that fell from the sky when they were hungry so that, when they had gathered the appointed quantity, any that had been gathered beyond this became foul with worms that appeared in it; and yet when a double quantity was gathered on the day before the sabbath, because it was not lawful to gather it on the sabbath day, it did not become foul

quia sabbato colligere non licebat, nulla putredine violatum; desiderantibus carne vesci, quae tanto populo nulla sufficere posse videbatur, volatilibus castra completa et cupiditatis ardorem fastidio satietatis extinctum; obvios hostes transitumque prohibentes atque proeliantes orante Moyse manibusque eius in figuram crucis extentis nullo Hebraeorum cadente prostratos; seditiosos in populo Dei ac sese ab ordinata divinitus societate dividentes ad exemplum visibile invisibilis poenae vivos terra dehiscente submersos; virga percussam petram tantae multitudini abundantia fluenta fudisse; serpentum morsus mortiferos, poenam iustissimam peccatorum, in ligno exaltato atque prospecto aeneo serpente sanatos, ut et populo subveniretur adflicto, et mors morte destructa velut crucifixae mortis similitudine signaretur? Quem sane serpentem propter facti memoriam reservatum cum postea populus errans tamquam idolum colere coepisset, Ezechias rex religiosa potestate Deo serviens cum magna pietatis laude contrivit.

---

[1] Exodus 16; Numbers 11.31–34.
[2] Exodus 17.8–16.
[3] Numbers 16.23–34
[4] Exodus 17.6–7; Numbers 20.8–11.
[5] 2 Kings 18.4.

and polluted. When they longed for meat to eat, thinking that no amount could possibly satisfy so great a multitude, the camp was filled with birds and their eager hunger was drowned in the distaste that comes from satiety.[1] When enemies planted themselves in their path and tried to bar their way by offering battle, Moses prayed with his arms extended in the shape of a cross, and they were laid low without the loss of a single Hebrew.[2] When rebellious members appeared among God's people and would have separated themselves from the divinely ordained society, as a visible demonstration of invisible punishment they were swallowed up alive when the earth opened wide for them.[3] A rock struck by a rod poured forth running water ample for that great multitude.[4] The deadly bites of serpents, a very just punishment for sinners, were healed when a brazen serpent was raised aloft on a wooden pole for all to see, not only in order to bring relief to a tormented nation, but also to show symbolically by a representation of death crucified, as it were, the destruction of death by death. This serpent, it is true, which had been preserved in memory of this miracle, had later come to receive idolatrous worship when the nation went astray, but King Hezekiah, using his power in the service of God and religion, broke it in pieces, and won high praise for his pious devotion.[5]

IX

De inlicitis artibus erga daemonum cultum, in quibus
Porphyrius Platonicus quaedam probando,
quaedam quasi inprobando versatur.

HAEC et alia multa huiusce modi, quae omnia commemorare nimis longum est, fiebant ad commendandum unius Dei veri cultum et multorum falsorumque
prohibendum. Fiebant autem simplici fide atque
fiducia pietatis, non incantationibus et carminibus
nefariae curiositatis arte compositis, quam vel
magian vel detestabiliore nomine goetian vel honorabiliore theurgian vocant qui quasi conantur ista
discernere et inlicitis artibus deditos alios damnabiles,
quos et maleficos vulgus appellat—hos enim ad
goetian pertinere dicunt—alios autem laudabiles
videri volunt, quibus theurgian deputant; cum
sint utrique ritibus fallacibus daemonum obstricti
sub nominibus angelorum.

Nam et Porphyrius quandam quasi purgationem
animae per theurgian, cunctanter tamen et pudibunda quodam modo disputatione promittit; reversionem vero ad Deum hanc artem praestare cuiquam
negat; ut videas eum inter vitium sacrilegae curiosi-

IX

*The illicit arts employed in the worship of demons,
in which the Platonist Porphyry is versed,
giving approval to some and denying
approval, it would seem, to others.*

THESE miracles and many others of a similar kind,
to enumerate all of which would be tedious, were
performed in order to promote the worship of the one
true God and to forbid that of the many false gods.
Moreover, they were performed through simple faith
and pious trust in God, not by means of incantations
and charms, products of an art that wickedly meddles
with the occult, an art that they call either magic or,
using a more hateful name, witchcraft or, using a
more honourable one, theurgy. This terminology is
employed by those who make as if an attempt to distinguish two kinds of magic. They would have it
thought that among those who devote themselves to
these illicit arts, some deserve condemnation—whom
the common people also call warlocks or witches, and
these they say are concerned with witchcraft—while
others, to whom they give credit for theurgy, are
praiseworthy. And yet both groups alike are
devotees of the fraudulent rites of demons masquerading under the names of angels.

In fact Porphyry too puts forward a sort of purification, as it were, of the soul through the practice
of theurgy, though with hesitation and a shamefaced
sort of argument. He asserts, however, that this art
cannot provide for any man a path back to God. So
you may see his judgement wavering between alter-

tatis et philosophiae professionem sententiis alter-
nantibus fluctuare. Nunc enim hanc artem tamquam
fallacem et in ipsa actione periculosam et legibus
prohibitam cavendam monet; nunc autem velut eius
laudatoribus cedens utilem dicit esse mundandae
parti animae, non quidem intellectuali, qua rerum
intellegibilium percipitur veritas nullas habentium
similitudines corporum; sed spiritali, qua corporalium rerum capiuntur imagines. Hanc enim dicit
per quasdam consecrationes theurgicas, quas teletas
vocant, idoneam fieri atque aptam susceptioni
spirituum et angelorum et ad videndos deos. Ex
quibus tamen theurgicis teletis fatetur intellectuali
animae nihil purgationis accedere quod eam faciat
idoneam ad videndum Deum suum et perspicienda
ea quae vere sunt. Ex quo intellegi potest qualium
deorum vel qualem visionem fieri dicat theurgicis
consecrationibus, in qua non ea videntur quae vere
sunt. Denique animam rationalem sive, quod magis
amat dicere, intellectualem, in sua posse dicit
evadere, etiamsi quod eius spiritale est nulla theurgica fuerit arte purgatum; porro autem a theurgo
spiritalem purgari hactenus ut non ex hoc ad inmortalitatem aeternitatemque perveniat.

---

[1] It is generally thought that Augustine is drawing in this
chapter upon Porphyry's lost treatise Περὶ ἀνόδου ψυχῆς,
On the Ascent of the Soul. This is the work mentioned below,
Chapter XXIX, as *De Regressu Animae.* Augustine must
have been long familiar with Marius Victorinus' Latin version.
The distinction between the intellectual and spiritual parts of
the soul was taken by Porphyry from Plotinus. See *Enneads,*
1.1 and 5.3.9. In the Neoplatonic system the intellectual is
the soul's third and highest phase. This portion of the soul

natives, the crime of sacrilegious occult practices and
the open career of a philosopher. For at one time he
warns us to beware of this art as being delusive and
dangerous in actual practice, as well as prohibited
by law, while at another, as if giving in to those who
praise it, he says that it does service in purifying one
part of the soul, not, to be sure, the intellectual part,
which apprehends the truth of intelligible things that
have no bodily likenesses, but the spiritual part,
whereby we receive the images of corporeal things.[1]
For this part, he says, after certain theurgic initiations
which are called *teletae*, mystic rites, becomes fit and
suitable for the entertainment of spirits and angels
and capable of seeing gods. Still, he admits that the
intellectual soul receives no purification from these
theurgic *teletai* such as might make it fit to behold its
own God and to perceive the things that truly exist.
From this it can be deduced what kind of gods they
are or what kind of seeing it is that he says is produced
by these theurgic initiations, a seeing that affords no
sight of what really exists. Next he declares that it
is possible for the rational or, as he prefers to call it,
the intellectual soul to escape into its own realm,
even though the spiritual part of it has never been
purified by any art of theurgy. Furthermore, he
says, the purification of the spiritual part by the
theurgist does not go so far as by itself to lead all the
way to immortality and eternity.

achieves understanding through instantaneous intuition. In
contrast, the spiritual or middle phase judges sensations and
learns through the process of discursive reasoning. Augustine
adopts and develops this distinction in the twelfth book of
De Genesi ad Litteram.

Quamquam itaque discernat a daemonibus angelos, aeria loca esse daemonum, aetheria vel empyria disserens angelorum, et admoneat utendum alicuius daemonis amicitia, quo subvectante vel paululum a terra possit elevari quisque post mortem, aliam vero viam esse perhibeat ad angelorum superna consortia. Cavendam tamen daemonum societatem expressa quodam modo confessione testatur, ubi dicit animam post mortem luendo poenas cultum daemonum a quibus cicumveniebatur horrescere; ipsamque theurgian quam velut conciliatricem angelorum deorumque commendat apud tales agere potestates negare non potuit quae vel ipsae invideant purgationi animae, vel artibus serviant invidorum, querelam de hac re Chaldaei nescio cuius expromens: " Conqueritur," inquit, " vir in Chaldaea bonus purgandae animae magno in molimine frustratos sibi esse successus, cum vir ad eadem potens tactus invidia adiuratas sacris precibus potentias alligasset ne postulata concederent. Ergo et ligavit ille," inquit, " et iste non solvit." Quo indicio dixit apparere theurgian esse tam boni conficiendi quam mali et apud deos et apud homines disciplinam; pati etiam deos et ad illas perturbationes passionesque deduci quas communiter daemonibus et hominibus Apuleius adtribuit, deos tamen ab eis aetheriae sedis altitudine

Accordingly, although he distinguishes angels from demons, explaining that the demons have their habitation in the air while the angels dwell in the aether or empyrean, and although he advises making use of the friendship of some demon, by whose support an individual can rise, though ever so little, above the earth after death, yet he acknowledges that it is another way that leads to fellowship on high with the angels. Moreover, he explicitly asserts in a kind of confession that we must beware of any fellowship with the demons. I mean where he says that the soul, in expiating after death the guilt it has incurred, is aghast at the worship of the demons by which it was ensnared. He was also unable to deny that the very theurgy which he commends as winning the favour of angels and gods has to do with powers that either themselves begrudge the purification of the soul or are enslaved by the magic art of those who do so. He recounts the complaint of some Chaldaean on this subject: "A good man in Chaldaea," he says, "complains that though he made tremendous efforts to purify a soul, he was frustrated short of success because a man with great power of the same sort, who was infected by envy, had bound the powers adjured by his holy prayers not to grant his request. "So," Porphyry adds, "one man fastened the bonds, and the other could not loosen them." He concluded from this evidence that theurgy is clearly a science capable of performing good as well as evil among both gods and men, and that the gods too endure and are subject to the agitations and emotions which Apuleius attributed to demons and men in common, though he set the gods apart by the greater height of

separans et Platonis asserens in illa discretione
sententiam.

X

*De theurgia, quae falsam purgationem animis
daemonum invocatione promittit.*

Ecce nunc alius Platonicus, quem doctiorem ferunt,
Porphyrius, per nescio quam theurgicam disciplinam
etiam ipsos deos obstrictos passionibus et perturbationibus dicit, quoniam sacris precibus adiurari
tenerique potuerunt ne praestarent animae purgationem, et ita terreri ab eo qui imperabat malum
ut ab alio qui poscebat bonum per eandem artem
theurgicam solvi illo timore non possent et ad
dandum beneficium liberari.

Quis non videat haec omnia fallacium daemonum
esse commenta, nisi eorum miserrimus servus et a
gratia veri liberatoris alienus? Nam si haec apud
deos agerentur bonos, plus ibi utique valeret bene-
ficus purgator animae quam malevolus inpeditor.
Aut si diis iustis homo pro quo agebatur purgatione
videbatur indignus, non utique ab invido territi nec,
sicut ipse dicit, per metum valentioris numinis
inpediti, sed iudicio libero id negare debuerunt.

---

[1] The reference is perhaps to the *Epinomis*, or *Supplement
to the Laws*, a dialogue widely, but not universally, believed
both in ancient and in modern times to be the work of Plato.
On the separation between gods and demons, see *Epinomis*
984 D–985 B.

their ethereal abode. In this distinction he upheld the opinion of Plato.[1]

X

Theurgy, which promises a fraudulent purification of souls by the invocation of demons.

Now here is another Platonist, Porphyry, who is said to be more learned, declaring that through some theurgic practice or other even the gods themselves are held bound by passions and disturbing emotions, for it was possible, when they were adjured by holy prayers, for them to be restrained from providing purification for a soul. They were, he says, so intimidated by one who demanded evil of them that another man, who required good of them, using the same theurgic art, could not secure their release and obtain their freedom to grant the good thing asked for.

Who could fail to see that all these things are the invention of deceitful demons, unless, he were their abject slave, and untouched by the grace of the true Liberator? For if those concerned in the business had been good gods, surely the man of good will who wished to purify the soul would prevail with them over the man of ill will who stood in the way. Or if just gods decided that the man whose cause was being advocated was unfit for purification, surely they must have refused it not because they were frightened by a malicious agent or, as Porphyry himself says, because they were shackled by fear of a more powerful divinity, but of their own free will. Besides, it is

Mirum est autem quod benignus ille Chaldaeus qui theurgicis sacris animam purgare cupiebat, non invenit aliquem superiorem deum qui vel plus terreret atque ad bene faciendum cogeret territos deos, vel ab eis terrentem compesceret ut libere bene facerent; si tamen theurgo bono sacra defuerunt quibus ipsos deos quos invocabat animae purgatores prius ab illa timoris peste purgaret. Quid enim causae est cur deus potentior adhiberi possit a quo terreantur, nec possit a quo purgentur? An invenitur deus qui exaudiat invidum et timorem diis incutiat ne bene faciant; nec invenitur deus qui exaudiat benevolum et timorem diis auferat ut bene faciant?

O theurgia praeclara, o animae praedicanda purgatio, ubi plus imperat inmunda invidentia quam inpetrat pura beneficentia! Immo vero malignorum spirituum cavenda et detestanda fallacia, et salutaris audienda doctrina. Quod enim qui has sordidas purgationes sacrilegis ritibus operantur quasdam mirabiliter pulchras, sicut iste commemorat, vel angelorum imagines vel deorum tamquam purgato spiritu vident—si tamen vel tale aliquid vident— illud est quod apostolus dicit: *Quoniam satanas transfigurat se velut angelum lucis.* Eius enim sunt illa phantasmata qui miseras animas multorum falsorumque deorum fallacibus sacris cupiens inretire et

---

[1] 2 Corinthians 11.14.

strange that the good Chaldaean who desired to
purify a soul by theurgic rites did not discover some
higher-ranking god who might either inspire greater
terror and so compel the terrified gods to do good, or
repress the terrifier so as to leave them free to do good.
Presumably the good theurgist had no rites by which
to purge in advance from the disease of fear the very
gods whom he called upon to purge or purify a soul.
But why? For why could not a more powerful god,
if one could be summoned to terrify them, not be
summoned to purify them? If a god is found to hear
the prayer of the malicious and strike fear into the
gods to prevent them from doing good, can no god be
found to hear the prayer of the well-disposed and to
deliver the gods from fear so that they may become
benefactors?

O glorious theurgy, O gospel to be cried abroad,
this purification of the soul where the power of
filthy malice is greater than the appeal of unstained
beneficence. No, no! not so, but hateful spirits
playing tricks that we must distrust and denounce,
while we open our ears to the teaching that saves.
What of it that those who work these sordid purifica-
tions by irreligious rites behold with supposedly
purified spirits certain visions of angels or of gods—
wondrously beautiful visions according to his account,
if indeed they really see anything of the kind? It is
as the apostle says: " For Satan transforms himself
to look like an angel of light." [1] For those phantoms
come from him who, hoping to ensnare unhappy souls
by delusive rites of many false gods and to turn them
away from the true worship of the true God, the
worship by which alone they are cleansed and healed,

a vero veri Dei cultu, quo solo mundantur et sanatur,
avertere, sicut de Proteo dictum est,

> formas se vertit in omnes,[1]

hostiliter insequens, fallaciter subveniens, utrobique
nocens.

XI

De epistula Porphyrii ad Anebontem Aegyptium, in qua petit de diversitate daemonum se doceri.[2]

MELIUS sapuit iste Porphyrius cum ad Anebontem
scripsit Aegyptium, ubi consulenti similis et quaerenti
et prodit artes sacrilegas et evertit. Et ibi quidem
omnes daemones reprobat, quos dicit ob inpru-
dentiam trahere humidum vaporem et ideo non in
aethere, sed in aere esse sub luna atque in ipso
lunae globo; verum tamen non audet omnes fallacias
et malitias et ineptias quibus merito movetur omnibus daemonibus dare. Quosdam namque benignos
daemones more appellat aliorum, cum omnes
generaliter inprudentes esse fateatur.

Miratur autem quod non solum dii alliciantur
victimis, sed etiam compellantur atque cogantur
facere quod homines volunt; et si corpore et incor-
poralitate dii a daemonibus distinguuntur, quo

---

[1] Virgil, *Georgics* 4.411.
[2] Porphyry's lost *Letter to Anebon*, a searching critique of
popular religion, is known to us from the citations here and in
Eusebius' *Praeparatio Evangelica* 3. 4 and 5. 8–10 and from
the reply of Iamblichus, the work entitled *De Mysteriis*. For

" transforms himself," as was said of Proteus, " into every shape."[1] Whether pursuing us as a foe, or offering help in the guise of a friend, he is in both cases harmful to us.

XI

*The letter of Porphyry to Anebon, the Egyptian,
in which he asks for instruction about the
differences among demons.*

PORPHYRY showed more wisdom in writing to Anebon, the Egyptian, when, assuming the rôle of an inquirer asking for advice, he both exposes these sacrilegious arts and lays them waste.[2] Indeed in this letter he rejects all the demons, who, he says, are so foolish as to be attracted by moist fumes [3] and must therefore dwell, not in the aether, but in the air below the moon and on the lunar globe itself. Nevertheless, he does not venture to ascribe to all demons every kind of cheat, malice and absurdity at which he is justifiably indignant. For, following the practice of others, he calls some of the demons benign, although he admits that as a general rule they are all witless.

Moreover, he expresses surprise that gods are not only enticed by victims, but are even actually compelled and forced to do the will of men; and if gods are distinguished from demons by being

the surviving fragments of the *Letter*, see G. Parthey, *Iamblichi de mysteriis liber* (1857).

[3] The smoke of sacrifices is meant.

modo deos esse existimandum sit solem et lunam et
visibilia cetera in caelo, quae corpora esse non
dubitat; et si dii sunt, quo modo alii benefici, alii
malefici esse dicantur; et quo modo incorporalibus,
cum sint corporei, coniungantur.

Quaerit etiam veluti dubitans utrum in divinan-
tibus et quaedam mira facientibus animae sint
passiones an aliqui spiritus extrinsecus veniant per
quos haec valeant; et potius venire extrinsecus
conicit, eo quod lapidibus et herbis adhibitis et
alligent quosdam, et aperiant clausa ostia, vel aliquid
eius modi mirabiliter operentur. Unde dicit alios
opinari esse quoddam genus cui exaudire sit proprium, natura fallax, omniforme, multimodum, simu-
lans deos et daemones et animas defunctorum, et hoc
esse quod efficiat haec omnia quae videntur bona
esse vel prava; ceterum circa ea quae vere bona sunt
nihil opitulari, immo vero ista nec nosse, sed et male
conciliare et insimulare atque inpedire nonnumquam
virtutis sedulos sectatores, et plenum esse temeritatis
et fastus, gaudere nidoribus, adulationibus capi, et
cetera quae de hoc genere fallacium malignorumque
spirituum qui extrinsecus in animam veniunt human-

bodiless while the demons have bodies, he wonders how we can believe that the sun and moon and the other objects visible in the sky are gods, for he has no doubt that they are bodies; and, if they are gods, how some are classed as beneficent and others as maleficent, and, since they are material bodies, how they are bound to immaterial beings.

He asks, too, as if he were in doubt, whether diviners and those who perform certain marvels draw their power to do so from emotions affecting the soul or from spirits of some kind coming from without. He ventures a guess that spirits come from without, because it is by the use of stones and herbs that they both cast a spell on certain people and open closed doors or perform some other marvel of this kind. This, he says, is why some think there is a class of beings whose special function is to hear prayers, creatures by nature deceitful, capable of adopting any form, versatile, assuming the semblance of gods, demons and the ghosts of dead men; and it is this class of being that performs all these acts that appear to us to be good or perverted. But where really good things are in question, they render no assistance. On the contrary, they are not even aware of such goodness. No, they win men over to evil ways, accuse them falsely, and sometimes put obstacles in the path of persistent seekers after virtue. Full of presumption and arrogance, they take pleasure in the odour of sacrifice and are an easy prey to flattery. Porphyry does not support as a convinced believer these and all other such statements about this kind of fraudulent and malign spirits who enter into the soul from

osque sensus sopitos vigilantesve deludunt non
tamquam sibi persuasa confirmat, sed tam tenuiter
suspicatur aut dubitat ut haec alios asserat opinari.
Difficile quippe fuit tanto philosopho cunctam dia-
bolicam societatem vel nosse vel fidenter arguere
quam quaelibet anicula Christiana nec cunctatur
esse, et liberrime detestatur. Nisi forte iste et
ipsum ad quem scribit Anebontem tamquam talium
sacrorum praeclarissimum antistitem et alios talium
operum tamquam divinorum et ad deos colendos
pertinentium admiratores verecundatur offendere.

Sequitur tamen et ea velut inquirendo commemorat quae sobrie considerata tribui non possunt
nisi malignis et fallacibus potestatibus. Quaerit
enim cur tamquam melioribus invocatis quasi
peioribus imperetur ut iniusta praecepta hominis
exsequantur; cur adtrectatum re Veneria non
exaudiant inprecantem, cum ipsi ad incestos quos-
que concubitus quoslibet ducere non morentur; cur
animantibus suos antistites oportere abstinere de-
nuntient, ne vaporibus profecto corporeis polluantur,
ipsi vero et aliis vaporibus inliciantur et nidoribus
hostiarum, cumque a cadaveris contactu prohibeatur
inspector, plerumque illa cadaveribus celebrentur;
quid sit quod non daemoni vel alicui animae defuncti,

without and play tricks on the senses of men whether asleep or awake, but he ever so faintly indicates his sceptical or mistrustful feeling by his declaration that these are the opinions of others. No doubt it was not easy for so great a philosopher either to recognize or to oppose boldly the whole diabolical organization that any little old woman of Christian faith has no doubt exists and feels free to denounce. It may be of course that Porphyry reveres Anebon himself, to whom he is writing, too much to affront him, since he is the most eminent high priest of such rites, as well as some others who were impressed by such effects as the work of gods and belonging to the worship of the gods.

He continues, however, and, still speaking as an inquirer, enumerates things of a sort that, coolly weighed, can only be ascribed to malign and fraudulent powers. For instance he asks why it is that, when powers have been invoked because they are presumably superior, they are then commanded as if they were inferior to carry out some man's unrighteous commands; why they refuse to hear the prayers of a man who is tainted by sexual intercourse, although they themselves do not scruple to lead all and sundry into unchaste unions; why they insist upon their priests' abstaining from animal food, obviously to avoid pollution from the reek of bodies, while they themselves are attracted by other aromas and by the savoury odours of victims and, although the initiated are forbidden to touch a corpse, their rites usually employ corpses; why it is that a man who is in the grip of some wickedness or other hurls threats, not at a demon or at the ghost of some dead man, but

sed ipsi soli et lunae aut cuicumque caelestium homo
vitio cuilibet obnoxius intendit minas eosque territat
falso ut eis extorqueat veritatem. Nam et caelum
se conlidere comminatur et cetera similia homini
inpossibilia, ut illi dii tamquam insipientissimi pueri
falsis et ridiculis comminationibus territi quod im-
peratur efficiant. Dicit etiam scripsisse Chaere-
monem quendam, talium sacrorum vel potius sacri-
legiorum peritum, ea quae apud Aegyptios sunt
celebrata rumoribus vel de Iside vel de Osiri marito
eius maximam vim habere cogendi deos ut faciant
imperata quando ille qui carminibus cogit ea se
prodere vel evertere comminatur, ubi se etiam
Osiridis membra dissipaturum terribiliter dicit, si
facere iussa neglexerint.

Haec atque huius modi vana et insana hominem
diis minari, nec quibuslibet, sed ipsis caelestibus et
siderea luce fulgentibus, nec sine effectu, sed
violenta potestate cogentem atque his terroribus ad
facienda quae voluerit perducentem, merito Porphyrius admiratur; immo vero sub specie mirantis
et causas rerum talium requirentis dat intellegi illos
haec agere spiritus quorum genus superius sub
aliorum opinatione descripsit, non, ut ipse posuit,
natura, sed vitio fallaces, qui simulant deos et animas

---

[1] An Egyptian priest, Stoic philosopher and teacher of the
Emperor Nero. Among his works were treatises on comets
(cited by Origen, *Contra Celsum* 1. 59) and on the Egyptian
priesthood. The latter is cited by St. Jerome (*Adversus
Iovinianum* 2. 13), who calls Chaeremon *Stoicus, vir elo-
quentissimus*. But Strabo the geographer describes him as a
fraud, if indeed the Chaeremon he knew is the same as the
above. See *Geography* 17.806.

at the sun itself and the moon or at any heavenly body whatever, terrorizing them with imaginary disaster in order to extort a real favour from them. For he threatens that he will shatter the heavens and do the other similar things that are humanly impossible, expecting those gods, as if they were the most witless children, to carry out his commands in terror of his unreal and laughable threats.   Porphyry also says that a certain Chaeremon,[1] an expert in such religious or rather sacrilegious rites, wrote that the performances among the Egyptians that report adventures either of Isis or of her husband Osiris are most efficacious in compelling the gods to carry out orders when the man who compels them by his incantations threatens to publish or to abolish their mysteries, including even the terrible threat that he will scatter abroad the dismembered limbs of Osiris, if the gods fail to perform his commands.

That a man should utter these idle and crazy threats and others like them to the gods, and not just to any gods, but to the gods of heaven themselves who shine with stellar light, and that not without result, but actually compelling them by violent mastery and moving them by terrifying threats to do his will, is justly a source of wonder to Porphyry.   Or rather, while appearing to wonder and to seek explanations for such things, he lets it be understood that this is the work of spirits whose characteristics he earlier recorded as if quoting the opinion of others.   The spirits are fraudulent, not, as he himself put it, by nature, but by a fault, pretending to be gods and the ghosts of dead men; but they do not pretend to be demons, as he says they do, for clearly they are

defunctorum, daemones autem non, ut ait ipse,
simulant, sed plane sunt. Et quod ei videtur herbis
et lapidibus et animantibus et sonis certis quibusdam ac vocibus et figurationibus atque figmentis,
quibusdam etiam observatis in caeli conversione
motibus siderum fabricari in terra ab hominibus
potestates idoneas variis effectibus exsequendis,
totum hoc ad eosdem ipsos daemones pertinet ludi-
ficatores animarum sibimet subditarum et voluptaria
sibi ludibria de hominum erroribus exhibentes.

Aut ergo re vera dubitans et inquirens ista Porphyrius ea tamen commemorat quibus convincantur
et redarguantur, nec ad eas potestates quae nobis ad
beatam vitam capessendam favent, sed ad deceptores
daemones pertinere monstrentur; aut, ut meliora
de philosopho suspicemur, eo modo voluit hominem
Aegyptium talibus erroribus deditum et aliqua
magna se scire opinantem non superba quasi auctoritate doctoris offendere, nec aperte adversantis alter-
catione turbare, sed quasi quaerentis et discere
cupientis humilitate ad ea cogitanda convertere et
quam sint contemnenda vel etiam devitanda
monstrare.

Denique prope ad epistulae finem petit se ab eo
doceri quae sit ad beatitudinem via ex Aegyptia
sapientia. Ceterum illos quibus conversatio cum
diis ad hoc esset ut ob inveniendum fugitivum vel
praedium comparandum, aut propter nuptias vel
mercaturam vel quid huius modi mentem divinam

demons. As for his view that it is by the use of
herbs, stones, animals, certain particular sounds and
words, drawings and plastic representations, even by
observing certain planetary movements in the
revolving vault of heaven, that men create on earth
powers capable of accomplishing all sorts of results,
all this has to do with those same demons who play
tricks on souls that are in subjection to them and
stage as a delicious treat for themselves comedies of
human error.

Either then Porphyry is actually in doubt and is
therefore inquiring into these practices, but still
records the evidence that will invalidate them and
rebut their claims, and demonstrate that they have
nothing to do with those powers which support us
in the search for a happy life, but have to do rather
with guileful demons; or else, to give a philosopher
the benefit of the doubt, he chose by this means to
avoid affronting an Egyptian who was devoted to
such mistaken practices and who believed that he
possessed some great truths. Thus Porphyry did not
arrogantly assume the authority of a teacher, nor
upset him with the arguments of a declared opponent;
he assumed the humble status of an inquirer who is
eager to learn, in order to make him stop and think
about these practices and to prove to him how worthy
of contempt or even of avoidance they are.

Finally, near the end of his letter, he asks Anebon
to teach him the way to happiness according to
Egyptian philosophy. As for those who deal with
the gods only to disturb the divine mind for such
purposes as finding a runaway slave, or getting possession of a field, or arranging a marriage, or making a

305

inquietarent, frustra eos videri dicit coluisse sapientiam; illa etiam ipsa numina cum quibus conversarentur, etsi de ceteris rebus vera praedicerent, tamen quoniam de beatitudine nihil cautum nec satis idoneum monerent, nec deos illos esse nec benignos daemones, sed aut illum qui dicitur fallax, aut humanum omne commentum.

XII

De miraculis quae per sanctorum angelorum
ministerium Deus verus operatur.

VERUM quia tanta et talia geruntur his artibus ut universum modum humanae facultatis excedant, quid restat nisi ut ea quae mirifice tamquam divinitus praedici vel fieri videntur nec tamen ad unius Dei cultum referuntur, cui simpliciter inhaerere fatentibus quoque Platonicis et per multa testantibus solum beatificum bonum est, malignorum daemonum ludibria et seductoria inpedimenta, quae vera pietate cavenda sunt, prudenter intellegantur?

Porro autem quaecumque miracula sive per angelos sive quocumque modo ita divinitus fiunt ut Dei unius, in quo solo beata vita est, cultum religionemque

sale, or something of the kind, these people, he says,
seem to have cultivated wisdom to no purpose.
Moreover, although these same deities with whom
they had such dealings may have been accurate in
their pronouncements on every other subject, yet
they had no advice to give that was other than rash
and inadequate on the subject of happiness. Therefore, he says, they can be neither gods nor friendly
demons; either they are that demon who is called
the Deceiver or else no more than a tissue of human
fancy.

XII

*The miracles that are wrought by the true God
through the ministry of the holy angels.*

But the fact is that, with the help of these arts,
marvels are wrought of a character and magnitude
that go beyond all the limits of man's power. What
conclusion remains save to understand wisely that
such miracles as appear to be prophesied or actually
accomplished by an act of God, but yet have no connection with worship of the one God—whole-hearted
clinging to whom is the one good that brings happiness, as the Platonists too bear witness with many
proofs in support of their belief— are but tricks played
by malign demons and alluring traps which true piety
must strive to avoid.

On the other hand, whatever miracles are so
wrought by God either through angels or by whatever
means that they give support to the worship and
religion of the one God, in whom alone is a blessed

commendent, ea vere ab eis vel per eos qui nos
secundum veritatem pietatemque diligunt fieri ipso
Deo in illis operante credendum est. Neque enim
audiendi sunt qui Deum invisibilem visibilia miracula
operari negant, cum ipse etiam secundum ipsos
fecerit mundum, quem certe visibilem negare non
possunt. Quidquid igitur mirabile fit in hoc mundo
profecto minus est quam totus hic mundus, id est
caelum et terra et omnia quae in eis sunt, quae certe
Deus fecit. Sicut autem ipse qui fecit, ita modus
quo fecit occultus est et inconprehensibilis homini.
Quamvis itaque miracula visibilium naturarum
videndi assiduitate viluerint, tamen, cum ea sapienter
intuemur, inusitatissimis rarissimisque maiora sunt.
Nam et omni miraculo quod fit per hominem, maius
miraculum est homo.

Quapropter Deus, qui fecit visibilia caelum et
terram, non dedignatur facere visibilia miracula in
caelo vel terra, quibus ad se invisibilem colendum
excitet animam adhuc visibilibus deditam; ubi vero
et quando faciat, incommutabile consilium penes
ipsum est in cuius dispositione iam tempora facta
sunt quaecumque futura sunt. Nam temporalia
movens temporaliter non movetur, nec aliter novit
facienda quam facta, nec aliter invocantes exaudit
quam invocaturos videt. Nam et cum exaudiunt

life to be found—these we must truly believe to be
the work of those who love us in accord with religious
truth, acting either on their own or as instruments,
while God himself is active in them. For again we
must not give ear to those who say that no invisible
God works visible miracles, since even in their view
he himself created the universe, which they surely
must admit is visible. Now any marvellous thing
that is wrought in this universe is assuredly less than
this whole universe, that is, heaven and earth and all
things that in them are, which God assuredly created.
But the means by which he created it are as hidden
and incomprehensible to man as he is himself who
created it. No matter then how cheap the natural
marvels, that we can see, have come to be held because they are always before us, yet whenever we
contemplate them with the eye of wisdom, we see
that they are greater marvels than the least familiar
and rarest of miracles; for man is greater even than
any miracle performed by any man's agency.

Wherefore God, who made the visible heaven and
earth, does not disdain to perform visible miracles in
heaven or on earth, whereby he may quicken the
soul, hitherto given up to visible things, to worship
him, the invisible; but where and when he performs
them depends on an unchangeable plan that rests in
the keeping of him alone in whose ordered design all
the days to come have already been created. For
though he creates the movement in time of things
temporal, he himself does not move in time; and his
view of things that are to be done is no different from
his view of things already done. Nor does he hearken
in one way to those who are calling upon him and in

angeli eius, ipse in eis exaudit, tamquam in vero nec manu facto templo suo, sicut in hominibus sanctis suis, eiusque temporaliter fiunt iussa aeterna eius lege conspecta.

XIII

De invisibili Deo, qui se visibilem saepe praestiterit,
non secundum quod est, sed secundum quod
poterant ferre cernentes.

NEC movere debet quod, cum sit invisibilis, saepe visibiliter patribus apparuisse memoratur. Sicut enim sonus quo auditur sententia in silentio intellegentiae constituta non est hoc quod ipsa, ita et species qua visus est Deus in natura invisibili constitutus non erat quod ipse. Verum tamen ipse in eadem specie corporali videbatur, sicut illa sententia ipsa in sono vocis auditur; nec illi ignorabant invisibilem Deum in specie corporali, quod ipse non erat, se videre. Nam et loquebatur cum loquente Moyses et ei tamen dicebat: *Si inveni gratiam ante te, ostende mihi temet ipsum, scienter ut videam te.*

Cum igitur oporteret Dei legem in edictis angelo-

---

[1] Exodus 33.13.

another way perceive those who will call upon him
later. For even when his angels answer prayers, it
is he who answers within them, for there he is in his
true temple not made with hands, just as he is in the
temple formed by his saints among men; and his
commands are executed in time, though they are
seen in one view by his eternal law.

XIII

The invisible God, who has often presented himself
in visible form, not as he really is, but to suit
the capacity of those who beheld him.

Nor should it disturb us that, although God is invisible, he is said to have often appeared to our fathers
in visible form. For just as the sound by which we
hear a thought that was first formulated in the silence
of mental activity, is not the same thing as the thought
itself, just so the visible form in which God was seen,
even though he is by nature an invisible being, was
not the same as God himself. Nevertheless it was God
himself who was seen in the same bodily form, just
as it is the thought itself that is heard in the sound
of the voice. Nor were our fathers unaware that it
was the invisible God in bodily form that they beheld, although God himself was not the bodily form.
For Moses spoke to God, who spoke to him in return,
and yet he could say to him: " If I have found favour
in thy sight, show me thyself, that I may see and
know thee." [1]

So when it was fitting that the law of God should be
delivered in an awe-inspiring manner by means of

rum terribiliter dari, non uni homini paucisve sapientibus, sed universae genti et populo ingenti, coram eodem populo magna facta sunt in monte, ubi lex per unum dabatur, conspiciente multitudine metuenda et tremenda quae fiebant. Non enim populus Israel sic Moysi credidit quem ad modum suo Lycurgo Lacedaemonii, quod a Iove seu Apolline leges quas condidit accepisset. Cum enim lex dabatur populo qua coli unus iubebatur Deus, in conspectu ipsius populi, quantum sufficere divina providentia iudicabat, mirabilibus rerum signis et motibus apparebat ad eandem legem dandam creatori servire creaturam.

XIV

*De uno Deo colendo non solum propter aeterna,
sed etiam propter temporalia beneficia, quia
universa in ipsius providentiae
potestate consistunt.*

Sicut autem unius hominis, ita humani generis, quod ad Dei populum pertinet, recta eruditio per quosdam articulos temporum tamquam aetatum profecit accessibus, ut a temporalibus ad aeterna

---

[1] Cf. Acts 7.53.
[2] Cf. Plutarch, *Lycurgus* 6.

angelic proclamations,[1] not to one man or to a few wise men, but to a whole nation and a great people, mighty works were brought to pass in the sight of that same people on the mountain where the law was handed down through one man, while the multitude looked on and saw such works as must cause fear and trembling. For the people of Israel did not come to believe in Moses in any such way as the Spartans put faith in their Lycurgus—because he was reported to have received from Jupiter or Apollo the laws that he established.[2] No, when the law was delivered to the people by which they were commanded to worship the one God, there were miraculous signs in nature and earthquakes enacted in sight of that same people, in such number as divine providence deemed sufficient; and this showed them that the created world was co-operating with the creator as his instrument, to the end that the delivery of the law might take place.

XIV

The one God must be worshipped to secure temporal as well as eternal benefits, because all things are as they are under the mighty hand of his providence.

THE true education of the human race, at least as far as God's people were concerned, was like that of an individual. It advanced by steps in time, as the individual's does when a new stage of life is reached. Thus it mounted from the level of temporal things to a level where it could grasp the eternal, and from

capienda et a visibilibus ad invisibilia surgeretur; ita sane ut etiam illo tempore quo visibilia promittebantur divinitus praemia, unus tamen colendus commendaretur Deus, ne mens humana vel pro ipsis terrenis vitae transitoriae beneficiis cuiquam nisi vero animae creatori et domino subderetur.

Omnia quippe quae praestare hominibus vel angeli vel homines possunt in unius esse Omnipotentis potestate quisquis diffitetur, insanit. De providentia certe Plotinus Platonicus disputat eamque a summo Deo, cuius est intellegibilis atque ineffabilis pulchritudo, usque ad haec terrena et ima pertingere flosculorum atque foliorum pulchritudine conprobat; quae omnia quasi abiecta et velocissime pereuntia decentissimos formarum suarum numeros habere non posse confirmat nisi inde formentur ubi forma intellegibilis et incommutabilis simul habens omnia perseverat. Hoc Dominus Iesus ibi ostendit ubi ait: *Considerate lilia agri, non laborant neque neunt. Dico autem vobis quia nec Salomon in tota gloria sua sic amictus est sicut unum ex eis. Quod si faenum agri, quod hodie est et cras in clibanum mittitur, Deus sic vestit, quanto magis vos, modicae fidei?*

Optime igitur anima humana adhuc terrenis desideriis infirma ea ipsa quae temporaliter exoptat

---

[1] Enneads 3.2.13.18–29. This treatise (3.2) is entitled Περὶ προνοίας, *On Providence.*
[2] Matthew 6.28–30.

visible things to a grasp of invisibles. Note, however, that even at the stage where visible rewards from God were promised, the command was given that the one God must be worshipped. The human heart was not permitted to yield homage to any but the soul's true creator and lord, even to secure the worldly advantages of a fleeting life.

Assuredly if anyone denies that all things that either angels or other men can bestow upon men are controlled by the mighty hand of the Almighty and of none other, he is raving mad. Providence is without doubt a subject that the Platonist Plotinus discusses[1]. He demonstrates that providence reaches down from the most high God, to whom belong intellectual and inexpressible beauty, all the way to things here on earth and proves it by the beauty that is seen in tiny flowers and in leaves. All these, he maintains, inasmuch as they are so lowly and fade so fleetingly, could not possibly have such perfectly designed harmony in their proportions, should they not derive from a region where intellectual and immutable beauty continues to exist while at the same time it dwells in all things. This is what the Lord Jesus points out when he says: " Consider the lilies of the field; they neither toil nor spin; yet I tell you, even Solomon in all his glory was not arrayed like one of these. But if God so clothes the grass of the field, which today is alive and tomorrow is thrown into the oven, will he not much more clothe you, O men of little faith? " [2]

Very good it is, therefore, when the human soul, still weak in its earthly lusts, makes a habit of looking only to the one God even for the lowest kind of goods,

bona infima atque terrena vitae huic transitoriae necessaria et prae illius vitae sempiternis beneficiis contemnenda, non tamen nisi ab uno Deo expectare consuescit, ut ab illius cultu etiam in istorum desiderio non recedat ad quem contemptu eorum et ab eis aversione perveniat.

XV

De ministerio sanctorum angelorum, quo providentiae Dei serviunt.

Sic itaque divinae providentiae placuit ordinare temporum cursum ut, quem ad modum dixi et in actibus apostolorum legitur, lex in edictis angelorum daretur de unius veri Dei cultu, in quibus et persona ipsius Dei, non quidem per suam substantiam, quae semper corruptibilibus oculis invisibilis permanet, sed certis indiciis per subiectam creatori creaturam, visibiliter appareret et syllabatim per transitorias temporum morulas humanae linguae vocibus loqueretur, qui in sua natura non corporaliter sed spiritaliter, non sensibiliter sed intellegibiliter, non temporaliter sed, ut ita dicam, aeternaliter nec incipit loqui nec desinit; quod apud illum sincerius

---

[1] Acts 7.53.

that it seeks in its temporal existence, that are need-
ful for this fleeting life, though contemptible in comparison with the everlasting boons of life hereafter.
Yet by turning to God even in its desire for them, the
soul is kept true to the worship of him to whom it may
attain only by despising and turning from them.

XV

The ministry of the holy angels, whereby they serve God's providence.

HERE, then, is the way in which divine providence
saw fit to arrange the succession of temporal periods.
It was arranged, as I have said and as we read in
the Acts of the Apostles,[1] that the law should be
laid down in the form of angelic pronouncements
concerning the worship of the one true God. In the
midst of his messengers the person of God himself
actually made a visible appearance, not, it is true, in
his real substance, which remains ever invisible
to corruptible eyes, but by unmistakable signs
shown by creation obedient to its creator. He
also spoke in words of human speech syllable by
syllable, giving to each its brief moment of fleeting
time, although in his own being he uses
language that is not physical but spiritual, not addressed to the sense but to the mind, not the language
of time but, if I may put it that way, the language
of eternity, which he never starts to speak, nor ever
ceases to speak. His ministers and messengers near
him, who in blessed immortality have his immutable
truth ever present for their profit, hear his words in

audiunt, non corporis aure, sed mentis, ministri eius et nuntii, qui eius veritate incommutabili perfruuntur inmortaliter beati; et quod faciendum modis ineffabilibus audiunt et usque in ista visibilia atque sensibilia perducendum, incunctanter atque indifficulter efficiunt.

Haec autem lex distributione temporum data est, quae prius haberet, ut dictum est, promissa terrena, quibus tamen significarentur aeterna, quae visibilibus sacramentis celebrarent multi, intellegerent pauci. Unius tamen Dei cultus apertissima illic et vocum et rerum omnium contestatione praecipitur, non unius de turba, sed qui fecit caelum et terram et omnem animam et omnem spiritum, qui non est quod ipse. Ille enim fecit, haec facta sunt, atque ut sint et bene se habeant eius indigent a quo facta sunt.

XVI

An de promerenda beata vita his angelis sit credendum qui se coli exigunt honore divino; an vero illis qui non sibi, sed uni Deo sancta praecipiunt religione serviri.

Quibus igitur angelis de beata et sempiterna vita credendum esse censemus? Utrum eis qui se religionis ritibus coli volunt sibi sacra et sacrificia

greater purity with the ear not of the body, but of the mind. Hearing by means inexpressible what they must do and what must be conveyed all the way to our visible and sensible world, they get it done without delay or difficulty.

Moreover, the delivery of the law took place at intervals of time, so that there came earlier as has been said, promises of earthly gifts. These were, however, symbols of eternal counterparts that in the shape of visible rites found many to participate as celebrants, though but few to penetrate their meaning. Nevertheless, the combined testimony of all the words and ceremonies presented in that law enjoins in the plainest terms the worship of one God, and not one of a throng of gods, but the God who made heaven and earth and every animate or spiritual being that is not identical with himself. For he made them, they were created, and they need him by whom they were created in order to exist and be in good condition.

XVI

To secure the happy life promised, should we put confidence in the angels who demand divine honours for their own worship, or in those, on the other hand, who enjoin sacred rites and services, not for themselves, but for God alone?

GIVING our considered opinion, then, in which kind of angels are we to place our confidence, where life, blessed and everlasting, is at stake? In those who want to be worshipped themselves with religious

flagitantes a mortalibus exhiberi, an eis qui hunc
omnem cultum uni Deo creatori omnium deberi
dicunt eique reddendum vera pietate praecipiunt
cuius et ipsi contemplatione beati sunt et nos futuros
esse promittunt? Illa namque visio Dei tantae
pulchritudinis visio est et tanto amore dignissima
ut sine hac quibuslibet aliis bonis praeditum atque
abundantem non dubitet Plotinus infelicissimum
dicere. Cum ergo ad hunc unum quidam angeli,
quidam vero ad se ipsos latria colendos signis mirabilibus excitent, et hoc ita ut illi istos coli prohibeant,
isti autem illum prohibere non audeant, quibus potius
sit credendum, respondeant Platonici, respondeant
quicumque philosophi, respondeant theurgi vel
potius periurgi; hoc enim sunt omnes illae artes
vocabulo digniores; postremo respondeant homines,
si ullus naturae suae sensus, quod rationales creati
sunt, ex aliqua parte vivit in eis; respondeant,
inquam, eisne sacrificandum sit diis vel angelis qui
sibi sacrificari iubent, an illi uni cui iubent hi qui et
sibi et istis prohibent?

Si nec isti nec illi ulla miracula facerent, sed tantum

---

[1] *Enneads* 1.6.7.30–39.
[2] Cf. Acts 19.19, where the term τὰ περίεργα is used of the
illicit practice of magic.

ceremonies, browbeating mortals into offering rites
and sacrifices to them, or in those who say that all
this worship is the exclusive right of the one God,
creator of all things, and who instruct us with true
religious devotion that we are bound to honour in
our rites him whom it is bliss to contemplate, both
for them now and, as they promise, for us in time to
come? For to see God in that way is a vision of such
beauty and is altogether deserving of love so great
that Plotinus does not scruple to declare that without
it, no matter how well endowed even to superfluity
a man may be with any goods, no matter what, he is
entirely miserable.[1] Since, then, some angels stir
us by signs and wonders to worship the one God,
while others egg us on to pay religious honours to
themselves—but with the difference that the first
party prohibits the worship of the second, yet the
second is not so bold as to prohibit the worship of
God—in which party are we to put our faith? For
a reply let us turn to the Platonists, to philosophers
of every persuasion, to dealers in theurgy, or rather
in *periergy*, rash meddling with the occult,[2] for that
is a more appropriate term for such arts. Lastly,
let us turn to men, if any awareness of their own
status as beings created rational is alive, however
diluted, in their consciousness. Let them reply,
I say, and tell us whether we are to sacrifice to those,
whether gods or angels, who bid men sacrifice to
themselves, or to that one God whose worship is enjoined by those angels who forbid the offering of
worship either to themselves or to those others.

If neither the one party nor the other performed
miracles, but merely laid down orders, the one en-

321

praeciperent, alii quidem ut sibi sacrificaretur, alii
vero id vetarent, sed uni tantum iuberent Deo, satis
deberet pietas ipsa discernere quid horum de fastu
superbiae, quid de vera religione descenderet. Plus
etiam dicam: si tantum hi mirabilibus factis humanas
animas permoverent qui sacrificia sibi expetunt, illi
autem qui hoc prohibent et uni tantum Deo sacrificari iubent nequaquam ista visibilia miracula facere
dignarentur, profecto non sensu corporis, sed ratione
mentis praeponenda eorum esset auctoritas. Cum
vero Deus id egerit ad commendanda eloquia veritatis suae, ut per istos inmortales nuntios non sui
fastum, sed maiestatem illius praedicantes faceret
maiora, certiora, clariora miracula, ne infirmis piis
illi qui sacrificia sibi expetunt falsam religionem
facilius persuaderent eo quod sensibus eorum
quaedam stupenda monstrarent, quem tandem ita
desipere libeat ut non vera eligat quae sectetur, ubi
et ampliora invenit quae miretur?

Illa quippe miracula deorum gentilium quae commendat historia—non ea dico quae intervallis temporum occultis ipsius mundi causis, verum tamen sub
divina providentia constitutis et ordinatis monstrosa
contingunt; quales sunt inusitati partus animalium

joining sacrifice to themselves, the others forbidding this, but ordaining sacrifice solely to one God, religious feeling unaided should be able to discern which instruction is delivered from a pinnacle of arrogance and which from the abode of true religion. I will go even further. If those who solicit worship for themselves were alone in using miracles to stir men's souls with wonders, while those who forbid sacrifice to themselves and ordain sacrifice to God alone never deigned to perform such visible miracles, surely the authority of the latter should be preferred as resting not on the body and its sensations but on the mind and its reasoning. But God has in fact, in order to reinforce the proclamation of his truth, taken care to perform by the hand of those immortal messengers who cry abroad not their own arrogance but his majesty, miracles more striking, more certain and more celebrated. He would not permit the party who claim sacrifice for themselves to make an easier pray of the weaker believer, converting him to a false religion by displaying wonders to his senses to dumbfound them. Is there anyone then so enamoured of folly that his choice is not plain: to follow the path of truth, the path on which he also finds a wider range of miracles to wonder at?

Let us take up the miracles presented by history as performed by the gods that are worshipped by the pagans. I do not mean those portentous events which occur from time to time for obscure reasons belonging to the natural world itself, reasons which nevertheless are shaped and regulated by the overruling power of divine providence. Such are the freakish births of animals and unusual manifestations

et caelo terraque rerum insolita facies, sive tantum
terrens sive etiam nocens, quae procurari atque
mitigari daemonicis ritibus fallacissima eorum astutia
perhibentur; sed ea dico quae vi ac potestate eorum
fieri satis evidenter apparet, ut est quod effigies
deorum Penatium quas de Troia Aeneas fugiens
advexit de loco in locum migrasse referuntur; quod
cotem Tarquinius novacula secuit; quod Epidaurius
serpens Aesculapio naviganti Romam comes adhaesit;
quod navem qua simulacrum matris Phrygiae vehe-
batur tantis hominum boumque conatibus inmobilem
redditam una muliercula zona alligatam ad suae
pudicitiae testimonium movit et traxit; quod virgo
Vestalis de cuius corruptione quaestio vertebatur
aqua inpleto cribro de Tiberi neque perfluente
abstulit controversiam—haec ergo atque huius modi
nequaquam illis quae in populo Dei facta legimus
virtute ac magnitudine conferenda sunt; quanto
minus ea quae illorum quoque populorum qui tales
deos coluerunt legibus iudicata sunt prohibenda
atque plectenda, magica scilicet vel theurgica!
Quorum pleraque specie tenus mortalium sensus
imaginaria ludificatione decipiunt, quale est lunam
deponere, " donec suppositas," ut ait Lucanus,

---

[1] Cf. Servius Danielis on Virgil, *Aeneid* 1.270; Valerius
Maximus 1.8.7; Ps. Aurelius Victor, *Origo Gentis Romanae*
17.2–3.

[2] Cicero, *De Divinatione* 1.17.32; Livy 1.36.4–5.

[3] Livy, Epitome 11; Ovid, *Metamorphoses* 15.622–744;
Valerius Maximus 1.8.2.

[4] Cicero, *De Haruspicum Responsis* 13.27; Ovid, *Fasti*
4.295–326.

in the heavens and on earth, some merely alarming, others harmful as well. Their menace is said to be dispelled and mitigated by demonic rites, such is the craft and utter deceit of the demons. No, I mean those marvels that we have evidence enough to show were brought about by the might and power of the demons. For instance, it is reported that the images of the Penates which Aeneas carried with him when he fled from Troy moved by themselves from one place to another;[1] that Tarquin cut a whetstone with a razor;[2] that the serpent of Epidaurus attached itself to Aesculapius and accompanied him on his voyage to Rome;[3] that the ship on which travelled the statue of the Phrygian mother, after resisting all the mighty efforts of men and oxen to move it, was set in motion and drawn along by a frail woman who had attached her girdle to it in proof of her chastity;[4] that a Vestal Virgin whose purity was in question settled all controversy by filling a sieve with water from the Tiber which did not escape through the holes.[5] These marvels, then, and others like them can by no means be compared in power and scale with those that we read were performed among the people of God. How much less can we compare those practices which, even by the legal ordinances of the nations that worshipped such gods, were judged worthy of being forbidden and punished, that is works of magic or, if you like, theurgy! Most of them are mere specious illusions that cheat men's senses by playing upon their imagination, like the trick of drawing down the moon " until " as Lucan says, " from

[5] Valerius Maximus 8.1.5; Dionysius of Halicarnassus, *Antiquitates Romanae* 2.69.

" propior despumet in herbas "; quaedam vero etsi
nonnullis piorum factis videantur opere coaequari,
finis ipse quo discernuntur incomparabiliter haec
nostra ostendit excellere. Illis enim multi tanto
minus sacrificiis colendi sunt quanto magis haec
expetunt; his vero unus commendatur Deus, qui se
nullis talibus indigere et scripturarum suarum testi-
ficatione et eorundem postea sacrificiorum remotione
demonstrat.

Si ergo angeli sibi expetunt sacrificium, praepon-
endi eis sunt qui non sibi, sed Deo creatori omnium,
cui serviunt. Hinc enim ostendunt quam sincero
amore nos diligant, quando per sacrificium non sibi,
sed ei nos subdere volunt cuius et ipsi contemplatione
beati sunt, et ad eum nos pervenire a quo ipsi non
recesserunt. Si autem angeli qui non uni sed
plurimis sacrificia fieri volunt, non sibi, sed eis diis
volunt quorum deorum angeli sunt, etiam sic eis prae-
ponendi sunt illi qui unius Dei deorum angeli sunt,
cui sacrificari sic iubent ut alicui alteri vetent, cum
eorum nullus huic vetet cui uni isti sacrificari iubent.

Porro si, quod magis indicat eorum superba fal-

---

[1] *De Bello Civili* 6.506. The ancient witches of Thessaly
were thought to have the power of drawing the moon down to
earth by their incantations. See Aristophanes, *Clouds* 749–
756; Virgil, *Eclogue* 8.70; Horace, *Epode* 5.45–46. That the
moon produces dew was also a common belief of antiquity.
See the references given by Housman on Manilius 4.501.

[2] Augustine refers probably to the prodigies by which the
gods sought to exact from their devotees the performance of
such expiatory ceremonies (called *procurationes*) as athletic
games, sacrifices, lustral processions and *lectisternia*. For
examples, see Livy 21.62 and 22.9–10.

close at hand she foams her dew upon the plants below." [1] Even though certain of these miracles, it is true, appear to match in effect some of those performed by the saints, the ends that they serve are different, and consideration of these ends makes it plain that our wonders are incomparably superior. Their miracles show that the multitude of gods is so much the less deserving of sacrificial worship the more they demand it. [2] Our miracles, however, support the worship of the one God, who makes it clear that he has no need of such things, both by the witness of his own Scriptures and by the eventual suppression of these same sacrifices.

If, then, there are angels who demand sacrifices for themselves, we must prefer to them those who demand worship not for themselves, but for God the creator of all things, whom they serve. For in this they show how genuine is their love for us, since they desire to bring us by our sacrifice into subjection not to themselves but to him in contemplation of whom they too find happiness, and they want us to reach him from whom they have never departed. If, on the other hand, angels who desire sacrifice to be performed not to one, but to several gods, want it not for themselves but for those gods whose angels they are, even so we must prefer to them those who are the angels of the one God of gods. They command us to worship him and forbid the worship of any second god, although none of those others forbids the worship of him whose angels issue the decree that sacrifice is to be offered to him alone.

Moreover if, as is rather suggested by their arrogant trickery, they are neither good angels nor the

lacia, nec boni nec bonorum deorum angeli sunt, sed
daemones mali qui non unum solum ac summum
Deum, sed se ipsos sacrificiis coli volunt, quod maius
quam unius Dei contra eos eligendum est praesi-
dium, cui serviunt angeli boni qui non sibi, sed illi
iubent ut sacrificio serviamus cuius nos ipsi sacrificium esse debemus?

XVII

De arca testamenti miraculisque signorum quae ad
commendandam legis ac promissionis auctoritatem
divinitus facta sunt.

PROINDE lex Dei, quae in edictis data est angelorum, in qua unus Deus deorum religione sacrorum
iussus est coli, alii vero quilibet prohibiti, in arca erat
posita, quae arca testimonii nuncupata est. Quo
nomine satis significatur non Deum, qui per illa
omnia colebatur, circumcludi solere vel contineri
loco, cum responsa eius et quaedam humanis sensibus
darentur signa ex illius arcae loco, sed voluntatis eius
hinc testimonia perhiberi; quod etiam ipsa lex erat
in tabulis conscripta lapideis et in arca, ut dixi,
posita, quam tempore peregrinationis in heremo cum
tabernaculo, quod similiter appellatum est tabernaculum testimonii, cum debita sacerdotes venera-
tione portabant; signumque erat quod per diem
nubes apparebat, quae sicut ignis nocte fulgebat;

---

[1] Cf. Acts 7.53.
[2] Cf. Exodus 25.22 and Numbers 7.89.

angels of good gods but evil demons who wish sacrifice to be offered not to one god, unique and supreme, but to themselves, what stronger protection can we choose against them than that of the one God who is served by good angels? They command us to serve by sacrifice, not themselves, but him to whom we ought ourselves to be the sacrifice that we bring.

XVII

The ark of the testimony and the miraculous signs wrought by God to support the authority of his laws and his promise.

HENCE the law of God, as delivered in pronouncements of angels,[1] the law in which it is laid down that the one God of gods is to be worshipped by religious rites, but no other gods whatever, was deposited in a chest that has received the name of ark of the testimony. This name clearly indicates, not that our God, who was worshipped in all these rites, made a practice of being boxed up and shut into one place, though his answers and certain signs intelligible to human senses were vouchsafed from the enclosed space of the ark,[2] but rather that testimonies to his will were noised abroad from it. For the law itself was also engraved on tablets of stone and deposited, as I have said, in the ark. During the wandering in the wilderness it was carried with due reverence by the priests along with a tabernacle likewise called the tabernacle of the testimony. And there was a sign, a cloud that was visible through the day and

quae nubes cum moveretur, castra movebantur, et ubi staret, castra ponebantur.

Reddita sunt autem illi legi magni miraculi testimonia praeter ista quae dixi, et praeter voces quae ex illius arcae loco edebantur. Nam cum terram promissionis intrantibus eadem arca transiret, Iordanes fluvius ex parte superiore subsistens et ex inferiore decurrens et ipsi et populo siccum praebuit transeundi locum. Deinde civitatis, quae prima hostilis occurrit more gentium deos plurimos colens, septiens eadem arca circumacta muri repente ceciderunt, nulla manu oppugnati, nullo ariete percussi. Post haec etiam cum iam in terra promissionis essent et eadem arca propter eorum peccata fuisset ab hostibus capta, hi qui ceperant in templo eam dei sui, quem prae ceteris colebant, honorifice conlocarunt abeuntesque clauserunt, apertoque postridie simulacrum cui supplicabant invenerunt conlapsum deformiterque confractum. Deinde ipsi prodigiis acti deformiusque puniti arcam divini testimonii populo unde ceperant reddiderunt. Ipsa autem redditio qualis fuit! Inposuerunt eam plaustro eique iuvencas a quibus vitulos sugentes abstraxerant subiunxerunt et eas quo vellent ire siverunt, etiam

---

[1] Cf. Exodus 13.21–22.
[2] Cf. Exodus 40.36–37.
[3] Cf. Joshua 3.16–17.
[4] Cf. Joshua 6.15–20.

blazed like a fire in the night.[1] When this cloud moved, they broke camp, and where it stood still, they pitched camp.[2]

Moreover, apart from these wonders already mentioned, and apart from the spoken words that issued from the space enclosed in that ark, other great marvels bore witness to the law. For instance, as they were entering the promised land and this same ark started to cross over the Jordan, the river halted its flow from upstream while it continued to flow downstream, thereby providing a dry crossing for both ark and people.[3] In the second place, the walls of the first city that resisted them, a city that worshipped many gods, as the pagans do, suddenly fell down flat when that same ark had been carried around them seven times,[4] although no human hand had struck a blow nor battering ram shattered them. Later, too, when they were already settled in the promised land, and in punishment for their sins the ark had been captured by their enemies, those who had taken it deposited it ceremoniously in the temple of the god whom they especially worshipped, closed the doors and went away. On the next day when they opened the doors, they found the statue to which they offered their prayers fallen to the ground and smashed to ugly lumps. Soon after, impelled by signs and more grievously punished by an unsightly affliction, of their own accord they restored the ark of the divine testimony to the people from whom they had taken it. And what an occasion the restoration was! They placed the ark on a waggon and yoked to it heifers whose suckling calves they had taken away, and they allowed the heifers to go where they

hic vim divinam explorare cupientes. At illae sine duce homine atque rectore ad Hebraeos viam pertinaciter gradientes nec revocatae mugitibus esurientium filiorum magnum sacramentum suis cultoribus reportarunt.

Haec atque huius modi Deo parva sunt, sed magna terrendis salubriter erudiendisque mortalibus. Si enim philosophi praecipueque Platonici rectius ceteris sapuisse laudantur, sicut paulo ante commemoravi, quod divinam providentiam haec quoque rerum infima atque terrena administrare docuerunt numerosarum testimonio pulchritudinum quae non solum in corporibus animalium, verum in herbis etiam faenoque gignuntur, quanto evidentius haec adtestantur divinitati quae ad horam praedicationis eius fiunt, ubi ea religio commendatur quae omnibus caelestibus, terrestribus, infernis sacrificari vetat, uni Deo tantum iubens, qui solus diligens et dilectus beatos facit eorumque sacrificiorum tempora imperata praefiniens eaque per meliorem sacerdotem in melius mutanda praedicens non ista se appetere, sed per haec alia potiora significare testatur, non ut ipse his honoribus sublimetur, sed ut nos ad eum colendum

---

[1] Cf. I Samuel 4–6.
[2] Above, Book 10.14.

pleased, desiring to search out the divine power in this way also. Then the heifers without men's guidance or control directed their steps unswervingly towards the Hebrews and, unmoved by the lowing of their hungry offspring, carried the most sacred object back to those who held it in reverence.[1]

These miracles and others of their kind are trivial in the sight of God but of great importance in their power to induce wholesome awe and provide sound instruction for mortals. Now philosophers, and especially the Platonists, enjoy a reputation for coming nearer to true wisdom than the rest of mankind because, as I remarked a little while ago,[2] they have taught that divine providence controls even the lowest of earthly things, adducing as evidence the harmony and beauty displayed by nature, not merely in the forms of animals, but even in plants and grasses. How much more convincing, however, is the added evidence of God's existence provided by the miracles that are performed at the moment when God makes his proclamation in which he commands us to embrace that religion which forbids sacrifice to any other power in heaven or on earth or under the earth, and bids us sacrifice to the one God only, who alone by loving us and inspiring our love for him makes us blessed. When he set a limit to the period during which these sacrifices were ordained, and declared in advance that they must be changed for the better by a better priest, he bore witness that he himself has no relish for these humbler rites, but used them to symbolize others that are superior. He was not concerned for himself, to be exalted by such marks of honour, but for us, that we might be kindled by

333

eique cohaerendum igne amoris eius accensi, quod
nobis, non illi, bonum est, excitemur.

XVIII

*Contra eos qui de miraculis quibus Dei populus
eruditus est, negant ecclesiasticis libris esse
credendum.*

AN dicet aliquis ista falsa esse miracula nec fuisse
facta, sed mendaciter scripta? Quisquis hoc dicit,
si de his rebus negat omnino ullis litteris esse
credendum, potest etiam dicere nec deos ullos
curare mortalia. Non enim se aliter colendos esse
persuaserunt nisi mirabilium operum effectibus,
quorum et historia gentium testis est, quarum dii
se ostentare mirabiles potius quam utiles ostendere
potuerunt. Unde hoc opere nostro, cuius hunc iam
decimum librum habemus in manibus, non eos suscepimus refellendos qui vel ullam esse vim divinam
negant vel humana non curare contendunt, sed eos
qui nostro Deo conditori sanctae et gloriosissimae
civitatis deos suos praeferunt, nescientes eum ipsum
esse etiam mundi huius visibilis et mutabilis invisibilem et incommutabilem conditorem et vitae beatae

---

[1] The Latin could also mean " the flame of His love for us."

the flame of our love for him [1] and stirred to worship
him and cleave to him, which is good, not for him,
but for us.

XVIII

*A reply to those who assert that the books of the
Church are not to be believed in their account
of the miracles performed for the instruction
of God's people.*

WILL someone tell us that the miracles referred to
are a sham, that they never took place, but were the
lying invention of those who wrote of them? Anyone who says that, denying the authority on such
topics of any written work whatever, may well also
deny that there are gods who concern themselves
with mortal needs. For the gods won men to worship
them in no other way but by the performance of
wondrous works. Pagan history too bears witness to
such works, though the pagan gods were better able
to display their miraculous powers than to show any
real good that they did. This has led me in this work
of mine, upon the tenth book of which I am now engaged, to omit any effort to refute either those who
deny that any divine power exists at all or those who
maintain that any such power is unconcerned about
human events. I speak rather to those who follow
their own gods in preference to our God, the founder
of a holy and most glorious city, because they do not
know that he is himself the invisible and unchangeable
founder of this visible and changeable world too, and
the only real dispenser of the blessed life, which comes

non de his quae condidit, sed de se ipso verissimum largitorem.

Eius enim propheta veracissimus ait: *Mihi autem adhaerere Deo bonum est.* De fine boni namque inter philosophos quaeritur, ad quod adipiscendum omnia officia referenda sunt. Nec dixit iste: Mihi autem divitiis abundare bonum est, aut insigniri purpura et sceptro vel diademate excellere, aut, quod nonnulli etiam philosophorum dicere non erubuerunt: Mihi voluptas corporis bonum est; aut quod melius velut meliores dicere visi sunt: Mihi virtus animi mei bonum est; sed: *Mihi*, inquit, *adhaerere Deo bonum est.* Hoc eum docuerat cui uni tantummodo sacrificandum sancti quoque angeli eius miraculorum etiam contestatione monuerunt. Unde et ipse sacrificium eius factus erat, cuius igne intellegibili correptus ardebat, et in eius ineffabilem incorporeumque complexum sancto desiderio ferebatur.

Porro autem si multorum deorum cultores—qualescumque deos suos esse arbitrentur—ab eis facta esse miracula vel civilium rerum historiae vel libris magicis sive, quod honestius putant, theurgicis credunt, quid causae est cur illis litteris nolint credere ista facta esse quibus tanto maior debetur fides quanto super omnes est magnus cui uni soli sacrificandum esse praecipiunt?

---

[1] Psalm 73.28.
[2] The Epicureans, cf. Cicero, *De Finibus* 2.1.2.
[3] The Stoics.
[4] Cf. Exodus 22.20.

not from the material things that he created, but from God himself.

Indeed, his wholly veracious prophet says: "But for me it is good to cling to God." [1] Now among philosophers there is argument about the supreme good, to the attainment of which all our responsible acts should be directed. And the psalmist did not say: "For me it is good to have riches in abundance," nor "to be decked out in imperial purple and have sceptre and diadem to mark my superiority," nor, as some even of the philosophers have not blushed to say: "For me the pleasure of the body is good," [2] nor, as the nobler philosophers, it is thought, have said more nobly: "For me the moral strength of my mind is good." [3] No, the psalmist said, "For me it is good to cling to God." This teaching he had received from Him who is alone entitled to sacrifice, as his holy angels have also pointed out, and confirmed their message by the evidence of miracles. [4] He had thus been led to become himself a sacrifice to God, by whose intelligible flame he was caught up and set afire, and into whose ineffable and incorporeal embrace his holy longing carried him.

Furthermore, if the worshippers of many gods, whatever be the qualities that they assign to them, believe that their gods have performed miracles, putting faith in recorded history or in books of magic, that is, to use the term that they consider more respectable, theurgy, what excuse have they for refusing to credit our miracles? They are found in records that deserve as much more confidence as He is great above all others to whom alone these records direct us to sacrifice.

XIX

*Quae ratio sit visibilis sacrificii, quod uni
vero et invisibili Deo offerri docet
vera religio.*

QUI autem putant haec visibilia sacrificia diis aliis
congruere, illi vero tamquam invisibili invisibilia et
maiora maiori meliorique meliora, qualia sunt purae
mentis et bonae voluntatis officia, profecto nesciunt
haec ita signa esse illorum, sicut verba sonantia signa
sunt rerum. Quocirca sicut orantes atque laudantes
ad eum dirigimus significantes voces cui res ipsas in
corde quas significamus offerimus, ita sacrificantes
non alteri visibile sacrificium offerendum esse noverimus quam illi cuius in cordibus nostris invisibile
sacrificium nos ipsi esse debemus. Tunc nobis
favent nobisque congaudent atque ad hoc ipsum nos
pro suis viribus adiuvant angeli quique virtutesque
superiores et ipsa bonitate ac pietate potentiores.
Si autem illis haec exhibere voluerimus, non libenter
accipiunt, et cum ad homines ita mittuntur ut eorum
praesentia sentiatur, apertissime vetant. Sunt
exempla in litteris sanctis. Putaverunt quidam deferendum angelis honorem vel adorando vel sacrificando qui debetur Deo, et eorum sunt admonitione

XIX

*The principle of visible sacrifice which, by the
tenets of true religion, is offered to the
one true and invisible God.*

As for those who think that these visible sacrifices
are appropriately offered to other gods, but that
God, inasmuch as he is invisible, greater and better,
should receive invisible, greater and better sacrifices,
for instance the due oblation of a pure heart and a good
will, they are surely unaware that these visible
sacrifices are symbols of the invisible, just as spoken
words are symbols of the realities to which they refer.
Therefore, just as in prayer and praise we address
to him words that have a meaning and offer him in our
hearts the actual things which this meaning represents, so in sacrifice let us be aware that visible
sacrifice should be offered to none other than to him
whose invisible sacrifice we ourselves ought to be in
our hearts. It is then that we have the approval of
all the angels, who rejoice with us and, as far as in
them lies, help us to do this very thing, as do the
higher spiritual beings whose greater power comes
from their very goodness and devotion to God. But
if we show any desire to offer them such worship, they
are unwilling to accept it. So too when they are sent
to men in such guise that their presence is observed,
they refuse most explicitly any worship offered.
There are instances of this in sacred literature.
Certain men have supposed it proper by worship or
sacrifice to do honour to the angels such as is due to
God, but the angels themselves forbade them to do

prohibiti iussique hoc ei deferre cui uni fas esse noverunt.

Imitati sunt angelos sanctos etiam sancti homines Dei. Nam Paulus et Barnabas in Lycaonia facto quodam miraculo sanitatis putati sunt dii, eisque Lycaonii victimas immolare voluerunt; quod a se humili pietate removentes eis in quem crederent adnuntiaverunt Deum.

Nec ob aliud fallaces illi superbe sibi hoc exigunt nisi quia vero Deo deberi sciunt. Non enim re vera, ut ait Porphyrius et nonnulli putant, cadaverinis nidoribus, sed divinis honoribus gaudent. Copiam vero nidorum magnam habent undique, et si amplius vellent, ipsi sibi poterant exhibere. Qui ergo divinitatem sibi arrogant spiritus, non cuiuslibet corporis fumo, sed supplicantis animo delectantur, cui decepto subiectoque dominentur, intercludentes iter ad Deum verum, ne sit homo illius sacrificium, dum sacrificatur cuipiam praeter illum.

XX

De summo veroque sacrificio quod ipse Dei et hominum mediator effectus est.

UNDE verus ille mediator, in quantum formam servi accipiens mediator effectus est Dei et hominum,

---

[1] Cf. Judges 13.16; Tobit 12.16–18; Revelation 19.10, 22.8–9.   [2] Acts 14.7–17.
[3] Cf. above, Book 10.11.   [4] Cf. Philippians 2.7.

so and told them to pay this tribute to him to whom alone, as they knew, it could be paid without sin.[1]

The example of these holy angels was also followed by holy men of God. Paul and Barnabas in Lycaonia were taken for gods when they worked a miraculous cure, and the Lycaonians wanted to sacrifice victims to them; but they in humble piety rejected this tribute and preached to them the God in whom they must believe.[2]

The sole reason why those deceitful spirits arrogantly demand this homage for themselves is that they know that it belongs to the true God. For they actually take pleasure not in the reek of corpses, as Porphyry says and a good many think, but in divine honours.[3] Surely they have a great abundance of such odours on all sides, and should they desire still more, they could easily produce more for themselves. The spirits, we conclude, who usurp divine status for themselves take delight, not in the fumes rising from any sort of body, but in the soul of a suppliant over whom, once he is cheated and enslaved, they may lord it thereafter, barring his way to the true God, because they would not see a man become a sacrifice to Him, and a man's way is barred as long as he offers sacrifice to anyone save Him.

XX

The true and supreme sacrifice which the Mediator between God and man became.

THEREFORE, he who is the true Mediator—inasmuch as by taking the form of a servant [4] he became

homo Christus Iesus, cum in forma Dei sacrificium cum Patre sumat, cum quo et unus Deus est, tamen in forma servi sacrificium maluit esse quam sumere, ne vel hac occasione quisquam existimaret cuilibet sacrificandum esse creaturae. Per hoc et sacerdos est, ipse offerens, ipse et oblatio.[1] Cuius rei sacramentum cotidianum esse voluit ecclesiae sacrificium, quae cum ipsius capitis corpus sit, se ipsam per ipsum discit offerre. Huius veri sacrificii multiplicia variaque signa erant sacrificia prisca sanctorum, cum hoc unum per multa figuraretur, tamquam verbis multis res una diceretur, ut sine fastidio multum commendaretur. Huic summo veroque sacrificio cuncta sacrificia falsa cesserunt.[2]

XXI

De modo potestatis daemonibus datae ad glorificandos sanctos per tolerantiam passionum, qui aerios spiritus non placando ipsos, sed in Deo permanendo vicerunt.

MODERATIS autem praefinitisque temporibus etiam potestas permissa daemonibus ut hominibus quos

---

[1] I Timothy 2.5.

[2] The Emperor Constantine had prohibited by law the public sacrifice of victims in the temples, although such rites were permitted to continue in private houses. See Eusebius, *Vita Constantini* 2.45 and *Codex Theodosianus* 16.10.2. But in A.D. 391 and 392 Theodosius, who was under the influence of St. Ambrose, issued laws declaring all pagan sacrifices, whether public or private, punishable as acts of treason. *Codex Theodosianus* 16.10.10–12.

the Mediator between God and men, the man Christ Jesus [1]—in the form of God accepts sacrifice along with the Father, together with whom he is one God. Yet in the form of a servant he chose to be himself the sacrifice rather than to receive it, so that even this might not be taken by anyone as a precedent for sacrificing to a creature, no matter of what sort. In this way he is at the same time the priest, since it is he who offers the sacrifice, and he is the offering as well. This is the act that he chose should be symbolized in the sacrament of the Church's daily sacrifice, for the Church of Christ, being the body of which he is the head, is taught to offer itself through him. This is the real sacrifice of which the early sacrifices of the saints were the manifold and varied symbols, for this one thing was symbolized in many forms, just as if one were to refer to a single object by many different words in order to emphasize it strongly without being repetitiously dull. It is to this supreme and true sacrifice that all false sacrifices have yielded and vanished.[2]

XXI

The measure of power granted the demons for the glorification of the saints through their strength to endure suffering; for the saints triumphed over the spirits of the air, not by doing their pleasure, but by abiding in God.

MOREOVER at periods of time measured and defined in advance, power is actually granted to the demons to stir up men who are possessed by them and so to

possident excitatis inimicitias adversus Dei civitatem
tyrannice exerceant sibique sacrificia non solum ab
offerentibus sumant et a volentibus expetant, verum
etiam ab invitis persequendo violenter extorqueant,
non solum perniciosa non est, sed etiam utilis invenitur ecclesiae, ut martyrum numerus impleatur;[1]
quos civitas Dei tanto clariores et honoratiores cives
habet, quanto fortius adversus impietatis peccatum
et usque ad sanguinem certant.[2]

Hos multo elegantius, si ecclesiastica loquendi
consuetudo pateretur, nostros heroas vocaremus.
Hoc enim nomen a Iunone dicitur tractum, quod
Graece Iuno Ἥρα appellatur, et ideo nescio quis
filius eius secundum Graecorum fabulas Heros
fuerit nuncupatus,[3] hoc videlicet veluti mysticum
significante fabula, quod aer Iunoni deputetur, ubi
volunt cum daemonibus heroas habitare, quo nomine
appellant alicuius meriti animas defunctorum. Sed
a contrario martyres nostri heroes nuncuparentur
si, ut dixi, usus ecclesiastici sermonis admitteret,
non quo eis esset cum daemonibus in aere societas,
sed quod eosdem daemones, id est aerias vincerent
potestates et in eis ipsam, quidquid putatur significare, Iunonem, quae non usquequaque inconveni-

---

[1] Cf. Revelation 6.11.
[2] Cf. Hebrews 12.4.
[3] No son of Hera by this name appears to be known elsewhere.
[4] See *City of God*, Book 4.10 and A. S. Pease on Cicero, *De
Natura Deorum* 2.66. Some scholars believe that the name
Hera is indeed etymologically related to "hero" (ἥρως), but
Augustine's further implication that these words are connected with *aer* perpetuates an etymological fancy widespread
in antiquity, especially among the Stoics.

wreak their hatred against the city of God. These
demons are so tyrannical that they are not content
with accepting sacrifice from those who offer it and
demanding it from willing worshippers, but they
even persecute the unwilling and try to exact it by
violence and torture. This power is so far from
being destructive to the Church that it is actually
found to do her a service, since it adds new martyrs
and helps make up their full number; [1] and the city of
God holds her martyred citizens in greater honour
and higher repute in such measure as they fight with
fortitude against the sin of denying their religion,
even to the shedding of their blood.[2]

If the Church's traditional canon of style permitted
such a term, we might more neatly dub them " our
heroes." This name is said to have been derived
from Juno, because in Greek Juno is called Hera,
and therefore one or another of her sons, according
to Greek mythology, was called Heros.[3] Now the
cryptic meaning of the myth is this. The air (*aer*) is
counted as Juno's realm,[4] and there, they would have
it, the heroes dwell together with the demons. By
heroes they mean such souls of the departed as
earned distinction to some degree in this life. Our
martyrs, in contrast, would receive the appellation
heroes—if, as I said, ecclesiastical style admitted this
term—not because they and the demons could be
members of one community in the air, but because
they overcame these same demons, that is to say,
powers of the air, and in company with them Juno
herself, whatever her particular significance is
thought to be. It is not altogether unfitting that
the poets depict her as hostile to manly qualities

enter a poetis inducitur inimica virtutibus et caelum petentibus viris fortibus invida.

Sed rursus ei succumbit infeliciter ceditque Vergilius, ut, cum apud eum illa dicat:

Vincor ab Aenea,

ipsum Aenean admoneat Helenus quasi consilio religioso et dicat:

Iunoni cane vota libens, dominamque potentem
Supplicibus supera donis.

Ex qua opinione Porphyrius, quamvis non ex sua sententia, sed ex aliorum, dicit bonum deum vel genium non venire in hominem nisi malus fuerit ante placatus; tamquam fortiora sint apud eos numina mala quam bona, quando quidem mala inpediunt adiutoria bonorum nisi eis placata dent locum, malisque nolentibus bona prodesse non possunt; nocere autem mala possunt, non sibi valentibus resistere bonis. Non est ista verae veraciterque sanctae religionis via; non sic Iunonem, hoc est aerias potestates piorum virtutibus invidentes, nostri martyres vincunt. Non omnino, si dici usitate posset, heroes nostri supplicibus donis, sed virtutibus divinis Heran superant. Commodius quippe Scipio Africanus est cognominatus quod virtute Africam vicerit, quam si hostes donis placasset ut parcerent.

---

[1] *Aeneid* 7.310.
[2] *Aeneid* 3.438-9.

and jealous of courageous men whose goal is heaven.

But once again Virgil unfortunately falls down and surrenders to her. For although he represents her as saying in one passage,

> I am defeated by Aeneas,[1]

yet Aeneas himself is exhorted by Helenus with what purports to be religious advice in the words:

> To Juno gladly chant your prayers and overbear
> That mighty queen with suppliant gifts.[2]

This sentiment leads Porphyry to the conclusion— which he expresses not as his own opinion but as that of others—that no god or genius enters a man unless an evil god or genius has first been appeased. This implies that in their system evil spirits are more powerful than good, inasmuch as the evil spirits, so they say, prevent good spirits from giving aid unless they are first appeased and so make room for them. Unless the evil spirits consent, the good are powerless to help; but evil spirits can always do hurt because the good spirits are not strong enough to resist them. This is not the way of true and truly holy religion; not thus do our martyrs overcome Juno, which is to say the powers of the air that envy the valour of the god-fearing. Our heroes, if usage permitted us so to call them, do not in the least resort to gifts to over-bear Hera, but to valour that comes from God. Surely it was better that Scipio should win his sur-name Africanus by conquering Africa valorously, than by appeasing the enemy with gifts and persuad-ing them to have mercy.

SAINT AUGUSTINE

XXII

Unde sit sanctis adversum daemones potestas et unde cordis vera purgatio.

VERA pietate homines Dei aeriam potestatem inimicam contrariamque pietati exorcizando eiciunt, non placando, omnesque temptationes adversitatis eius vincunt orando non ipsam, sed Deum suum adversus ipsam. Non enim aliquem vincit aut subiugat nisi societate peccati. In eius ergo nomine vincitur qui hominem adsumpsit egitque sine peccato ut in ipso sacerdote ac sacrificio fieret remissio peccatorum, id est per mediatorem Dei et hominum, hominem Christum Iesum, per quem facta peccatorum purgatione reconciliamur Deo. Non enim nisi peccatis homines separantur a Deo, quorum in hac vita non fit nostra virtute sed divina miseratione purgatio, per indulgentiam illius, non per nostram potentiam; quia et ipsa quantulacumque virtus quae dicitur nostra illius est nobis bonitate concessa. Multum autem nobis in hac carne tribueremus nisi usque ad eius depositionem sub venia viveremus. Propterea ergo nobis per Mediatorem praestita est gratia ut polluti carne peccati carnis peccati similitudine mundaremur. Hac Dei gratia, qua in nos ostendit magnam misericordiam suam, et

---

[1] Cf. Ephesians 2.2. [2] I Timothy 2.5.
[3] Romans 8.3.

XXII

*The source of the saints' power in fighting against
demons and the source of the heart's true
cleansing.*

It is by true piety that men of God cast out the
power of the air,[1] the enemy and adversary of piety,
that is, by exorcizing, not by appeasing it; they
overcome all temptations that the struggle with it
brings forth by appealing, not to the enemy, but to
their own God against the enemy. For that power
neither conquers nor enthralls any man unless he
join it by some act of sin. It follows that any victory over it is won in the name of Him who took
human form and lived without sin in order to accom-
plish the remission of sins by being himself both
priest and sacrifice, that is, the mediator between
God and men, the man Christ Jesus,[2] through whom
we are cleansed of sin and reconciled to God. For
nothing but sin separates men from God, and our
sins are cleansed, not by any virtue of ours, but by
God's mercy, thanks to his indulgence and not to our
own power, for even the very virtue that is called
ours, however little it be, is a free grant of his bounty.
We might indeed give much of the credit to ourselves
while we are in this flesh of ours, were it not that until
we lay this flesh aside, we live subject to his pardon.
For this reason, therefore, grace was granted to us
through the Mediator to the end that we who were
polluted by sinful flesh might be cleansed by " the
likeness of sinful flesh." [3] Thanks to this grace of
God, by which he manifests his great compassion to-

in hac vita per fidem regimur, et post hanc vitam per ipsam speciem incommutabilis veritatis ad perfectionem plenissimam perducemur.

XXIII

De principiis in quibus Platonici purgationem animae esse profitentur.

DICIT etiam Porphyrius divinis oraculis fuisse responsum nos non purgari lunae teletis atque solis, ut hinc ostenderetur nullorum deorum teletis hominem posse purgari. Cuius enim teletae purgant, si lunae solisque non purgant, quos inter caelestes deos praecipuos habent? Denique eodem dicit oraculo expressum principia posse purgare, ne forte, cum dictum esset non purgare teletas solis et lunae, alicuius alterius dei de turba valere ad purgandum teletae crederentur.

Quae autem dicat esse principia tamquam Platonicus, novimus. Dicit enim Deum Patrem et Deum Filium, quem Graece appellat paternum intellectum vel paternam mentem; de Spiritu autem sancto aut nihil aut non aperte aliquid dicit; quamvis quem alium dicat horum medium, non intellego. Si enim tertiam, sicut Plotinus ubi de tribus principalibus

---

[1] For *teletae* (" mysteries ") see above, Book 10.9.

[2] See Cyril of Alexandria, *Contra Iulianum*, I, *Patrologia Graeca* 76.553 B, where the passage of Porphyry to which Augustine refers is quoted. Cyril points out that Porphyry sets forth Plato's opinion concerning these three " principles "

wards us, we are guided in this life by our faith, and
we shall be conducted after this life to our goal, the
utmost plenitude of perfection, by the actual sight of
truth immutable in ideal form.

XXIII

*The principles on which the Platonists teach that
purification of the soul depends.*

EVEN Porphyry says that divine oracles once
declared that we are not cleansed by mysteries of the
moon or of the sun, in order to let it be shown on this
basis that man cannot be purified by mystic rites of
any gods.[1] For whose mystic rites can cleanse, if
not those of the sun and moon, which they esteem
as chief among the celestial gods? Consequently,
he says, the aforesaid oracle was a declaration that
principles have the power to purify, lest his readers,
when informed that the mystic rites of sun and
moon do not cleanse, should perhaps suppose that
rites of some other god, one of the common herd, had
cleansing power.

Now we know what he as a Platonist means by
principles. He means God the Father and God the
Son, whom he calls in Greek the intellect or mind of
the Father; concerning the Holy Spirit, however,
he says either nothing or nothing directly, although
I do not understand whom else he means when he
speaks of one midway between these two.[2] For
if, like Plotinus when he is discussing the three

(ἀρχαί), the third of which was the Soul, ἡ τοῦ κόσμου ψυχή,
translated below by Augustine as *natura animae*.

substantiis disputat, animae naturam etiam iste
vellet intellegi, non utique diceret horum medium,
id est Patris et Filii medium. Postponit quippe
Plotinus animae naturam paterno intellectui; iste
autem cum dicit medium, non postponit, sed interponit. Et nimirum hoc dixit, ut potuit sive ut voluit,
quod nos sanctum Spiritum, nec Patris tantum nec
Filii tantum, sed utriusque Spiritum dicimus.
Liberis enim verbis loquuntur philosophi, nec in
rebus ad intellegendum difficillimis offensionem
religiosarum aurium pertimescunt. Nobis autem ad
certam regulam loqui fas est, ne verborum licentia
etiam de rebus quae his significantur impiam gignat
opinionem.

XXIV

*De uno veroque principio quod solum naturam
humanam purgat atque renovat.*

Nos itaque ita non dicimus duo vel tria principia
cum de Deo loquimur, sicut nec duos deos vel tres
nobis licitum est dicere, quamvis de unoquoque
loquentes, vel de Patre vel de Filio vel de Spiritu
sancto, etiam singulum quemque Deum esse fatea-

---

[1] *Enneads* 5.1, entitled Περὶ τῶν τριῶν ἀρχικῶν ὑποστάσεων,
De Tribus Principalibus Substantiis.
[2] *Enneads* 5.1.3.
[3] Cf. below, Book 11.10.

principle substances,[1] Porphyry too meant us to
understand by the third term the elemental soul,
he certainly would not use the words " midway
between these two," that is between the Father and
the Son. For Plotinus considers the elemental soul
inferior to the intellect of the Father,[2] but Porphyry,
when he says " midway between," places it, not
below, but in between the Father and the Son. So
then he must have meant, employing such language
as he had at his command or chose to use, the same one
as we when we speak of the Holy Spirit, which means
not the Spirit of the Father alone or of the Son alone,
but the Spirit of both of them. For philosophers
use words loosely, and in matters that are most
difficult to understand they are not over careful to
avoid giving offence to pious ears. But religion
requires me to follow a fixed rule in my use of language, for fear that some verbal licence may give rise
to a mistaken view, contrary to religious truth, of the
matters to which the words refer.

XXIV

*The one true principle which alone cleanses
and renews human nature.*

CONSEQUENTLY in discussing God I do not speak of
two principles, or three, any more than I may law-
fully say that we have two gods or three, although
when we speak of any one of the persons, whether
Father, Son or Holy Spirit, we freely declare that
each singly is God; and yet we do not say, like the
Sabellian heretics,[3] that the Father is the same as the

353

mur, nec dicamus tamen quod haeretici Sabelliani,
eundem esse Patrem qui est et Filius, et eundem
Spiritum sanctum qui est et Pater et Filius, sed
Patrem esse Filii Patrem, et Filium Patris Filium, et
Patris et Filii Spiritum sanctum nec Patrem esse
nec Filium. Verum itaque dictum est non purgari
hominem nisi principio, quamvis pluraliter apud eos
sint dicta principia.

Sed subditus Porphyrius invidis potestatibus de
quibus et erubescebat, et eas libere redarguere
formidabat, noluit intellegere Dominum Christum
esse principium cuius incarnatione purgamur. Eum
quippe in ipsa carne contempsit quam propter sacrificium nostrae purgationis adsumpsit, magnum
scilicet sacramentum ea superbia non intellegens
quam sua ille humilitate deiecit verus benignusque
Mediator, in ea se ostendens mortalitate mortalibus
quam maligni fallacesque mediatores non habendo se
superbius extulerunt miserisque hominibus adiutorium deceptorium velut inmortales mortalibus promiserunt. Bonus itaque verusque Mediator ostendit
peccatum esse malum, non carnis substantiam vel
naturam, quae cum anima hominis et suscipi sine
peccato potuit et haberi, et morte deponi et in melius
resurrectione mutari; nec ipsam mortem, quamvis
esset poena peccati, quam tamen pro nobis sine
peccato ipse persolvit, peccando esse vitandam, sed

---

[1] These words are directed against the Manichaeans, who
regarded the flesh as essentially evil. Augustine had himself
been an adherent of this sect early in life.

Son and that the Holy Spirit is the same as the Father
and the Son. We say that the Father is Father of the
Son and that the Son is Son of the Father, while the
Holy Spirit is the spirit of both Father and Son but
is neither Father nor Son. It was, then, a just
observation that only by a principle can man be
purified, although philosophers use the plural
" principles " in their books.

But Porphyry was the thrall of malicious powers
and he was both ashamed of them and at the same
time held them in too much awe to dispute against
them freely. He chose not to see that the Lord
Christ is the principle by whose incarnation we are
purified. Indeed, he despised him in the very
flesh that he took upon him in order to be sacrificed
for our cleansing. It is obvious that pride blinded
Porphyry to the great sacred truth, the same pride
that our great and gracious Mediator cast down by his
humility, when he showed himself to mortals clothed
in that mortality for the lack of which malevolent
and deceitful mediators too proudly lauded themselves
and spoke as immortals to wretched mortals with
promises of help that were only a snare. Thus the
good and true Mediator has demonstrated that
flesh in its substance and nature is no evil, but sin
alone is.[1] For a body of flesh with a human soul
could be put on and kept on without sin; the body
could be laid aside at death and changed for a better
one by rising again. He also demonstrated that
death itself, although it is the penalty of sin—a
penalty, however, that he himself paid in full for us
without any sin of his own—is nothing that we should
seek to escape by sinful means. Rather, if a way

355

potius, si facultas datur, pro iustitia perferendam.
Ideo enim solvere potuit moriendo peccata, quia et
mortuus est, et non pro peccato.

Hunc ille Platonicus non cognovit esse principium;
nam cognosceret purgatorium. Neque enim caro
principium est aut anima humana, sed Verbum per
quod facta sunt omnia. Non ergo caro per se ipsa
mundat, sed per Verbum a quo suscepta est cum
Verbum caro factum est et habitavit in nobis. Nam de
carne sua manducanda mystice loquens, cum hi
qui non intellexerunt offensi recederent dicentes:
Durus est hic sermo, quis eum potest audire? respondit
manentibus ceteris: *Spiritus est qui vivificat, caro
autem non prodest quicquam.*

Principium ergo suscepta anima et carne et animam credentium mundat et carnem. Ideo quaerentibus Iudaeis quis esset respondit se esse principium. Quod utique carnales, infirmi, peccatis
obnoxii et ignorantiae tenebris obvoluti nequaquam
percipere possemus nisi ab eo mundaremur atque
sanaremur per hoc quod eramus et non eramus.
Eramus enim homines, sed iusti non eramus; in
illius autem incarnatione natura humana erat, sed

---

[1] John 1.14.
[2] John 6.60, 63.
[3] John 8.25. Jesus' answer as given here by Augustine is
based on a mistranslation of the Greek. The Vulgate version,
Principium, qui et loquor vobis, arises from the same mis-
understanding. The Revised Standard Version gives, "Jesus
said to them, 'Even what I have told you from the begin-

opens, we should endure to die in the cause of righteousness. For his death gained him the power to redeem from sin because he both died and died for no sin of his own.

But our Platonist did not recognize him as the principle, for if he did, he would recognize him as the cleanser. For neither is the flesh the principle, nor the human soul, but rather the Word by which all things were made is the principle. Hence flesh does not purify by its own power. What purifies is the Word that clothed itself in flesh when " the Word became flesh and dwelt among us."[1] For when he was speaking in parables of the eating of his flesh, and those who did not understand took offence and withdrew with the remark: " This is a hard saying, who can listen to it?" he replied to those who remained: " It is the Spirit that gives life, the flesh is of no avail."[2]

The principle, then, having put on soul and flesh, purifies both the soul of believers and also their flesh. This is why, when the Jews asked who he was, he replied that he was the principle.[3] Carnal as we are, weak, liable to sin, and shrouded in the darkness of ignorance, assuredly we should be totally unable to gain sight of this principle if it did not cleanse and heal us by means of the thing that we were and the thing that we were not. For we were men, but we were not upright;[4] yet in his incarnation the nature that he assumed was human nature, but upright and

ning.' " This is grammatically possible, as Augustine's version is not; but there is much disagreement over the precise meaning of the Greek.

[4] Cf. Augustine, *Letter* 140.10.

iusta, non peccatrix erat. Haec est mediatio qua manus lapsis iacentibusque porrecta est; hoc est semen dispositum per angelos, in quorum edictis et lex dabatur qua et unus Deus coli iubebatur et hic Mediator venturus promittebatur.

XXV

Omnes sanctos et sub legis tempore et sub prioribus saeculis in sacramento et fide Christi iustificatos fuisse.

Huius sacramenti fide etiam iusti antiqui mundari pie vivendo potuerunt, non solum antequam lex populo Hebraeo daretur—neque enim eis praedicator Deus vel angeli defuerunt—, sed ipsius quoque legis temporibus, quamvis in figuris rerum spiritalium habere videretur promissa carnalia, propter quod vetus dicitur testamentum. Nam et prophetae tunc erant, per quos, sicut per angelos, eadem promissio praedicata est, et ex illorum numero erat cuius tam magnam divinamque sententiam de boni humani fine paulo ante commemoravi: *Mihi autem adhaerere Deo bonum est.*

In quo plane psalmo duorum testamentorum, quae dicuntur vetus et novum, satis est declarata distinctio.

---

[1] Augustine cites here and below, Chapter XXXII, an erroneous Latin version of Galatians 3.19. In our Greek text, as in the Vulgate, the law, not the descendant, is designated or ordained by the angels. Augustine later recog-

not sinful. This is the mediation by which a hand is reached out to those who have fallen and are lying on the ground. This is the descendant designated by the angels,[1] by whose words of command the law too was delivered [2] that bids us worship one God and promises the coming of this Mediator.

XXV

All the saints who lived at the time of the law and in earlier ages have been justified by faith in the holy truth of Christ's incarnation.

By their faith in this religious truth just men of old were also enabled to purify themselves by a life of piety, not only before the law was given to the Jewish people—for they never lacked a preacher; they had both God and his angels—but also during the era of the law itself, although when it used symbolic language to refer to spiritual matters, it gave the appearance of containing promises of carnal things, and for this reason it is called the Old Testament. For by this time there were prophets also, whose mouth proclaimed the same promise as had the angels, and one of their number was he whose great and divine saying about the supreme good of man I mentioned a short time ago: " But for me it is good to cling to God." [3]

Surely in this psalm the distinction between the two Testaments, the Old and the New as they are

nized the mistranslation that led him into error, and he corrected himself in *Retractations* 2.24(51)2.

[2] Acts 7.53.

[3] Psalm 73.28: cf. above, Book 10.18.

Propter carnales enim terrenasque promissiones,
cum eas impiis abundare perspiceret, dicit pedes
suos paene fuisse commotos et effusos in lapsum
propemodum gressus suos, tamquam frustra Deo
ipse servisset, cum ea felicitate quam de illo expectabat contemptores eius florere perspiceret; seque
in rei huius inquisitione laborasse, volentem cur ita
esset adprehendere, donec intraret in sanctuarium
Dei et intellegeret in novissima eorum qui felices
videbantur erranti. Tunc eos intellexit in eo quod
se extulerunt, sicut dicit, fuisse deiectos et defecisse
ac perisse propter iniquitates suas; totumque illud
culmen temporalis felicitatis ita eis factum tamquam
somnium evigilantis qui se repente invenit suis quae
somniabat fallacibus gaudiis destitutum. Et quoniam in hac terra vel in civitate terrena magni sibi
videbantur: *Domine*, inquit, *in civitate tua imaginem
eorum ad nihilum rediges.*

Quid huic tamen utile fuerit etiam ipsa terrena
non nisi ab uno vero Deo quaerere, in cuius potestate
sunt omnia, satis ostendit ubi ait: *Velut pecus factus
sum apud te, et ego semper tecum. Velut pecus* dixit
utique " non intellegens." " Ea quippe a te desiderare debui quae mihi cum impiis non possunt esse
communia, non ea[1] quibus eos cum abundare cer-
nerem, putavi me incassum tibi servisse, quando et

---

[1] non ea *Migne: omitted in MSS.*

---

[1] Psalm 73.2.
[2] Psalm 73.3, 16–17.
[3] Cf. Vulgate Psalm 72.20.
[4] Psalm 73.22–23.

called, is quite clearly drawn. For because of carnal and earthly promises of which he saw that the wicked had an abundance, the psalmist says that his feet had almost stumbled and his steps had well nigh slipped,[1] as if his serving God must have been in vain, since he could plainly see that men who set God at naught enjoyed the very prosperity that he looked for at God's hand. Moreover, he says that he had tried hard to solve the problem, for he longed to discover some explanation of the facts, until, on entering the sanctuary of God, he came to understand the ultimate fate of those whom he had made the mistake of regarding as fortunate.[2] Then he saw that in their very pride they had been, as he says, cast down and had passed away and been destroyed because of their iniquities, and that the summit of temporal prosperity had been changed for them to a sort of dream from which the dreamer wakes and suddenly finds himself stripped of the illusory joys that were his while he dreamed. And since here on earth, that is, in the earthly city they thought themselves important, " Lord," he says, " in thy city thou wilt reduce their image to nothing." [3]

He shows clearly, however, why it was expedient for him to seek even earthly goods from none save the one true God, in whose power are all things, when he says: " I am become like a beast before thee, and I am continually with thee." [4] " As a beast," he said, meaning " without understanding." In other words, " I ought to have desired from thee things that I cannot have in common with the impious, not the kind of thing that made me think, when I saw the wicked luxuriating in such blessings, that I must

361

illi haec haberent qui tibi servire noluissent. Tamen
ego semper tecum, quia etiam in talium rerum desiderio
deos alios non quaesivi." Ac per hoc sequitur:
*Tenuisti manum dexterae meae, in voluntate tua deduxisti
me, et cum gloria adsumpsisti me;* tamquam ad sini-
stram cuncta illa pertineant quae abundare apud
impios cum vidisset paene conlapsus est. *Quid enim
mihi est*, inquit, *in caelo, et a te quid volui super terram?*
Reprehendit se ipsum iusteque sibi displicuit quia,
cum tam magnum bonum haberet in caelo—quod
post intellexit—rem transitoriam, fragilem et quodam modo luteam felicitatem a suo Deo quaesivit in
terra. *Defecit*, inquit, *cor meum et caro mea, Deus
cordis mei*, defectu utique bono ab inferioribus ad
superna; unde in alio psalmo dicitur: *Desiderat et
deficit anima mea in atria Domini;* item in alio:
Defecit in salutare tuum anima mea. Tamen cum de
utroque dixisset, id est de corde et carne deficiente,
non subiecit: Deus cordis et carnis meae, sed *Deus
cordis mei.* Per cor quippe caro mundatur. Unde
dicit Dominus: *Mundate quae intus sunt, et quae foris
sunt munda erunt.*

Partem deinde suam dicit ipsum Deum, non aliquid ab eo, sed ipsum. *Deus* inquit, *cordis mei, et pars*

---

[1] Psalm 73. 23–24.
[2] i.e. to the ill-omened or sinister side.
[3] Psalm 73.25.
[4] Psalm 73.26.
[5] Psalm 84.2.
[6] Psalm 119.81.
[7] Matthew 23.26.

have served thee in vain, since they too who had
refused to serve thee had them. Still," he says,
" ' I am continually with thee,' because even while I
longed for such things I did not seek other gods."
So he goes on: " My right hand hast thou held, thou
hast guided me with thy counsel, and with thy glory
hast thou taken me up," [1] thus implying that all the
things that existed in abundance among the impious
and caused him almost to faint at the sight belonged
to the left hand.[2] " For what have I in heaven," he
says, " and what have I desired from thee upon
earth? " [3] He berated himself and was justifiably
at odds with himself because, although he possessed
so great a blessing in heaven—as he later realized—
he sought from his God a fleeting thing, a brittle
prosperity, made of clay, so to speak, on earth.
" My heart and my flesh have failed me, God of my
heart," he says,[4] meaning a failure in the right
direction, an ascent from lower things to higher
things. Hence in another psalm we read: " My
soul fails with longing for the courts of the Lord." [5]
So in another place: " My soul has failed awaiting
thy salvation." [6] Yet, though he had spoken of the
failure of both heart and flesh, he did not add:
" God of my heart and flesh," but only " God of
my heart." It is by the heart, we must note, that
the flesh is purified. This is why the Lord says:
" Cleanse what is in the cup and the outside will be
clean." [7]

Then he says that his portion is God himself, not
something from God, but God himself. " God of my
heart," he says, and " God is my portion for ever,"
because among the many blessings that people select

mea Deus in saecula; quod inter multa quae ab hominibus eliguntur, ipse illi placuerit eligendus. *Quia
ecce,* inquit, *qui longe se faciunt a te, peribunt; perdidisti
omnem qui fornicatur abs te,* hoc est, qui multorum
deorum vult esse prostibulum. Unde sequitur illud
propter quod et cetera de eodem psalmo dicenda visa
sunt: *Mihi autem adhaerere Deo bonum est,* non longe
ire, non per plurima fornicari. Adhaerere autem
Deo tunc perfectum erit cum totum quod liberandum
est fuerit liberatum.

Nunc vero fit illud quod sequitur: *Ponere in Deo
spem meam. Spes* enim *quae videtur, non est spes;
quod enim videt quis, quid et sperat?* ait apostolus. *Si
autem quod non videmus speramus, per patientiam ex-
pectamus.* In hac autem spe nunc constituti agamus
quod sequitur, et simus nos quoque pro modulo nostro
angeli Dei, id est nuntii eius, adnuntiantes eius
voluntatem et gloriam gratiamque laudantes. Unde
cum dixisset: *Ponere in Deo spem meam, ut adnuntiem,*
inquit, *omnes laudes tuas in portis filiae Sion.*

Haec est gloriosissima civitas Dei; haec unum
Deum novit et colit; hanc angeli sancti adnuntiaverunt, qui nos ad eius societatem invitaverunt
civesque suos in illa esse voluerunt; quibus non placet

---

[1] Psalm 73.26–27.
[2] Psalm 73.28.
[3] Psalm 73.28. Cf. Vulgate, Psalm 72.28.
[4] Romans 8.24 f.
[5] See Vulgate Psalm 72.28, Septuagint 73.28. The words
in portis filiae Sion are not found in the Hebrew text and hence

for themselves he has determined on God himself as the right choice. "For behold," he says, "those who put themselves far from thee shall perish; thou hast destroyed every man that goes a whoring from thee," [1] that is, who chooses to play the harlot with many gods. From this follows the sentence that explains why I thought fit to quote the other passages from this same psalm. "But for me it is good to cling to God," [2] not to go far away from him and not to go whoring after many. But clinging to God will be complete only when all that was destined for freedom has been freed.

But the next words set forth what is already going on: "To put my hope in God." [3] For as the Apostle says, "Hope that is seen is not hope. For why should anyone hope for what he sees? But if we hope for what we do not see, we wait for it with patience." [4] Established now in this hope, let us do what naturally follows, and let us too in our small measure be angels of God, that is, his messengers, proclaiming his will and praising his glory and his grace. Thus when he had said: "to put my hope in God," he added: "that I may recount all thy praises in the gates of the daughter of Zion." [5]

This is the most glorious City of God, the city that knows and worships one God, the city proclaimed by the holy angels who have invited us into their fellowship and have willed us to be their fellow citizens therein. They do not desire us to worship them as if

are omitted in the Authorized and Revised Standard Versions. They do appear in the Septuagint and passed thence into the early Latin translations and into the Vulgate. Cf. also Psalm 9.14.

ut eos colamus tamquam nostros deos, sed cum eis et illorum et nostrum Deum; nec eis sacrificemus, sed cum ipsis sacrificium simus Deo.

Nullo itaque dubitante qui haec deposita maligna obstinatione considerat, omnes inmortales beati, qui nobis non invident—neque enim si inviderent, essent beati—, sed potius nos diligunt ut et nos cum ipsis beati simus, plus nobis favent, plus adiuvant quando unum Deum cum illis colimus, Patrem et Filium et Spiritum sanctum, quam si eos ipsos per sacrificia coleremus.

XXVI

De inconstantia Porphyrii inter confessionem veri Dei et cultum daemonum fluctuantis.

NESCIO quo modo, quantum mihi videtur, amicis suis theurgis erubescebat Porphyrius. Nam ista utcumque sapiebat, sed contra multorum deorum cultum non libere defendebat. Et angelos quippe alios esse dixit, qui deorsum descendentes hominibus theurgicis divina pronuntient; alios autem, qui in terris ea quae Patris sunt et altitudinem eius profunditatemque declarent. Num igitur hos angelos, quorum ministerium est declarare voluntatem Patris, credendum est velle nos subdi nisi ei cuius nobis adnuntiant voluntatem? Unde optime admonet etiam ipse Platonicus imitandos eos potius quam invo-

they were our gods, but to worship with them the God who is theirs and ours; nor do they want us to sacrifice to them, but to be with them a sacrifice to God.

So without any doubt on the part of anyone who has laid aside his malignant obstinacy and considers these things, those blessed immortals, all of them, regard us not with ill-will—indeed if they did bear ill-will they would not be blessed—but rather with love, that we too like them may be happy. They show us more favour and help us more when we worship with them the one God, Father, Son, and Holy Spirit, than they would if we were to worship them themselves with sacrifices.

XXVI

Porphyry wavers unsteadily between confessing the true God and worshipping demons.

SOMEHOW or other, as far as I can see, Porphyry used to blush for his friends the theurgists. For he knew quite well the arguments that I have been using, but he never came out frankly to fight against polytheism. He even said, in fact, that there are angels of two kinds, those who come down to earth to make divine pronouncements to theurgists, and those who live on earth and declare the truth of the Father, his height and his depth. Surely then we cannot be expected to believe that these angels, whose task is to declare the will of the Father, wish us to be subject to any other than to him whose will they report to us? Hence even our Platonist himself quite rightly advises us to imitate them rather than invoke them.

candos. Non itaque debemus metuere ne inmortales et beatos uni Deo subditos non eis sacrificando offendamus. Quod enim non nisi uni vero Deo deberi sciunt, cui et ipsi adhaerendo beati sunt, procul dubio neque per ullam significantem figuram, neque per ipsam rem quae sacramentis significatur, sibi exhiberi volunt. Daemonum est haec arrogantia superborum atque miserorum, a quibus longe diversa est pietas subditorum Deo nec aliunde quam illi cohaerendo beatorum. Ad quod bonum percipiendum etiam nobis sincera benignitate oportet ut faveant, neque sibi arrogent quo eis subiciamur, sed eum adnuntient sub quo eis in pace sociemur.

Quid adhuc trepidas, o philosophe, adversus potestates et veris virtutibus et veri Dei muneribus invidas habere liberam vocem? Iam distinxisti angelos qui Patris adnuntiant voluntatem ab eis angelis qui ad theurgos homines nescio qua deducti arte descendunt. Quid adhuc eos honoras ut dicas pronuntiare divina? Quae tandem divina pronuntiant qui non voluntatem Patris adnuntiant? Nempe illi sunt quos sacris precibus invidus alligavit ne praestarent animae purgationem, nec a bono, ut dicis, purgare cupiente ab illis vinculis solvi et suae potestati reddi potuerunt. Adhuc dubitas haec maligna esse daemonia, vel te fingis fortasse nescire, dum

---

[1] Cf. above, Book 10.9.

We ought not, consequently, to be afraid of offending those immortal and happy beings who are subject to one God, by not offering sacrifice to them. For they know that sacrifice is due only to the one true God, in clinging to whom their own happiness consists. Without question, therefore, they do not want to receive such worship, neither the symbolic sacrifice that points to truth, nor the true sacrifice that is symbolized in the rites. Such arrogance befits proud and unhappy demons, and from them it is a long way to the piety of those who are subject to God and derive their happiness only from clinging to him. That we too may win this boon, it behoves them to show us favour by genuine kindness and not to claim for themselves a service that would make us their subjects; rather must they proclaim him under whose rule we will be their fellow citizens in peace.

Why are you so afraid, you philosopher, to raise your voice freely against powers that are hostile to the true virtues and bounties of the true God? You have already set apart the angels who proclaim the will of the Father from those who are attracted by some sort of cunning art and come down to visit theurgists. Why do you honour them so far as to say that they make divine revelations? What divine revelations can it be that they make when they do not proclaim the will of the Father? Clearly they are the same spirits that a malicious man inhibited by incantations from granting purification to a soul: and not even a good man, so you say, who wished to purify it, could release them from the inhibition and restore them to their proper power.[1] Do you still doubt that these are spiteful demons, or are you perhaps

non vis theurgos offendere, a quibus curiositate deceptus ista perniciosa et insana pro magno beneficio didicisti? Audes istam invidam non potentiam, sed pestilentiam, et non dicam dominam, sed, quod tu fateris, ancillam potius invidorum isto aere transcenso levare in caelum et inter deos vestros etiam sidereos conlocare, vel ipsa quoque sidera his opprobriis infamare?

XXVII

De impietate Porphyrii, qua etiam Apulei transcendit errorem.

QUANTO humanius et tolerabilius consectaneus tuus Platonicus Apuleius erravit, qui tantummodo daemones a luna et infra ordinatos agitari morbis passionum mentisque turbelis honorans eos quidem, sed volens nolensque confessus est; deos tamen caeli superiores ad aetheria spatia pertinentes, sive visibiles quos conspicuos lucere cernebat, solem ac lunam et cetera ibidem lumina, sive invisibiles quos putabat, ab omni labe istarum perturbationum quanta potuit disputatione secrevit!

Tu autem hoc didicisti non a Platone, sed a Chaldaeis magistris, ut in aetherias vel empyrias mundi sublimitates et firmamenta caelestia extolleres vitia

---

[1] Cf. Eusebius, *Praeparatio Evangelica* 4.9–10.

[2] The astral gods are the planets, which are below the "fixed" stars.

[3] Cf. above, Book 9.8; Apuleius, *De Deo Socratis* 12.

pretending not to know, for fear of offending the
theurgists from whom, lured by the urge to meddle,
you learned those baneful and senseless tricks as if
they were some great and good thing?[1]   How dare
you exalt that malicious influence, not power but
pestilence, not queen but slave girl of the malicious
as you yourself confess, till it rises through your air to
heaven and you give it a place even among your astral
gods,[2] if you do not actually make the stars themselves
infamous by your attributing such shame to them.

XXVII

The impiety of Porphyry, which surpasses even the error of Apuleius.

How much more humane and tolerable was the
error of Apuleius, your fellow Platonist, who, for all
that he held the lunar and sublunar demons in high
regard, admitted in spite of himself that they alone
are disturbed by the virus of passion and by mental
storms![3]   When it came, however, to the higher gods
in the sky with their position in the realm of aether,
whether they were visible and his eyes beheld them
shining bright—that is, the sun, the moon and the
other luminaries in those regions—or whether they
were invisible and merely objects of his thought, he
used all his power of argument to set them apart
from any stain of such storms of passion.

But you were not so schooled by Plato; it was
from Chaldaean schoolmasters that you learned to
elevate human failings to ethereal or empyrean
heights in the universe and to celestial firmaments, in

371

humana, ut possent dii vestri theurgis pronuntiare
divina; quibus divinis te tamen per intellectualem
vitam facis altiorem, ut tibi videlicet tamquam
philosopho theurgicae artis purgationes nequaquam
necessariae videantur; sed aliis eas tamen inportas,
ut hanc veluti mercedem reddas magistris tuis, quod
eos qui philosophari non possunt ad ista seducis quae
tibi tamquam superiorum capaci esse inutilia confiteris; ut videlicet quicumque a philosophiae virtute
remoti sunt, quae ardua nimis atque paucorum est, te
auctore theurgos homines, a quibus non quidem in
anima intellectuali, verum saltem in anima spiritali
purgentur, inquirant, et quoniam istorum quos
philosophari piget incomparabiliter maior est multitudo, plures ad secretos et inlicitos magistros tuos
quam ad scholas Platonicas venire cogantur. Hoc
enim tibi inmundissimi daemones, deos aetherios
se esse fingentes, quorum praedicator et angelus
factus es, promiserunt, quod in anima spiritali
theurgica arte purgati ad Patrem quidem non
redeunt, sed super aerias plagas inter deos aetherios
habitabunt.

Non audit ista hominum multitudo propter quos a
daemonum dominatu liberandos Christus advenit.
In illo enim habent misericordissimam purgationem

---

[1] Cf. above, Book 10.10.
[2] Cf. above, Book 10.9.
[3] For the distinction between the spiritual and intellectual
soul, see above, Book 10.9.
[4] Cf. Eusebius, *Praeparatio Evangelica* 4.4.

order that your kind of gods might deliver divine messages to theurgists.[1] It is true that by virtue of your intellectual life you raise yourself above these divine messages. You, being a philosopher, we must assume, can see that for you no such rite of cleansing by theurgic art is necessary in the least![2] Yet for all that you bring in such rites for the benefit of others, for you want to pay your debt to your teachers, and you do it by decoying those who are incapable of becoming philosophers into practices that you admit are of no value to you, you who are capable of higher things. Evidently you want all who are turned away from the pursuit of philosophic excellence, which is too lofty for all but a few, to seek out theurgists on your recommendation, in order to obtain catharsis at least of their spiritual, though not, to be sure, of their intellectual soul.[3] And since the number of those who have no stomach for philosophy is incomparably the greater, more are forced to resort to your clandestine and illegal teachers than to the Platonic schools. For this is the promise you received from those foul, foul demons who pretend that they are gods of the aether, whose prophet and messenger you have become, namely, that those who have been cleansed in their spiritual soul by the theurgic art, though they do not, to be sure, return to the father, yet they will dwell above the realm of air among the aetherial deities.

A deaf ear is turned to all this nonsense by the host of men whom Christ came to set free from the tyranny of the demons.[4] For in him they find the most compassionate cleansing of mind, of spirit, and of body. It was for this purpose that he put on the

et mentis et spiritus et corporis sui. Propterea quippe totum hominem sine peccato ille suscepit, ut totum quo constat homo a peccatorum peste sanaret. Quem tu quoque utinam cognovisses eique te potius quam vel tuae virtuti, quae humana, fragilis et infirma est, vel perniciosissimae curiositati sanandum tutius commisisses. Non enim te decepisset, quem vestra, ut tu ipse scribis, oracula sanctum inmortalemque confessa sunt; de quo etiam poeta nobilissimus poetice quidem, quia in alterius adumbrata persona, veraciter tamen si ad ipsum referas, dixit:

> Te duce, si qua manent sceleris vestigia nostri,
> Inrita perpetua solvent formidine terras.

Ea quippe dixit quae etiam multum proficientium in virtute iustitiae possunt propter huius vitae infirmitatem, etsi non scelera, scelerum tamen manere vestigia, quae non nisi ab illo salvatore sanantur de quo iste versus expressus est. Nam utique non hoc a se ipso se dixisse Vergilius in eclogae ipsius quarto ferme versu indicat, ubi ait:

> Ultima Cumaei venit iam carminis aetas;

unde hoc a Cumaea Sibylla dictum esse incunctanter apparet.

---

[1] Cf. *City of God*, Book 19.23.

[2] Virgil, *Eclogue* 4.13 f. This is the so-called Messianic Eclogue frequently cited by the Fathers as prophetic of Christ's coming. But St. Jerome, most scholarly of the Fathers, states flatly that the Christian interpretation of this poem is childish nonsense. See Jerome, *Letter* 53.7.

whole man, except for his sin, in order to cleanse
man, and all that goes to make a man, from the in-
fection of his sins. Would that you too had learned
to know him and had entrusted yourself to him for a
surer healing rather than either to your own virtue
which, being human, is brittle and precarious, or to
that utterly fatal practice of meddling with the occult.
For he would not have played you false, whose holiness and immortality, as you yourself say in writing,
have been acknowledged by your oracles.[1] And the
most renowned of poets also said of him by poetic
symbolism, be it noted, for it was another's portrait
that he sketched, and yet it was a true description
if applied to Christ himself:

> With you as guide, such traces of our crimes
> As linger shall be done away; no more
> Shall terror through the years hold fast the earth.[2]

Clearly he speaks of such traces as may well linger,
in those who are making great progress in the virtue
of righteousness, because of the insecurity of our
life here. There may be no more crimes, but there
are traces; and such things have no healing except
by the saviour of whom these verses speak. For
clearly Virgil indicates that he did not deliver these
verses as his own when he says in the fourth line, I
think, of the same Eclogue:

> The final age has come as Cumae's song foretold.[3]

On this evidence we may without hesitation declare
that these are the words of the Sibyl of Cumae.

---

[3] Virgil, *Eclogue* 4.4.

Theurgi vero illi vel potius daemones deorum
speciem figurasque fingentes inquinant potius quam
purgant humanum spiritum falsitate phantasmatum
et deceptoria vanarum ludificatione formarum.
Quo modo enim purgent hominis spiritum qui
inmundum habent proprium? Alioquin nullo modo
carminibus invidi hominis ligarentur ipsumque inane
beneficium quod praestaturi videbantur aut metu
premerent aut simili invidentia denegarent. Sufficit
quod purgatione theurgica neque intellectualem
animam, hoc est mentem nostram, dicis posse
purgari, et ipsam spiritalem, id est nostrae animae
partem mente inferiorem, quam tali arte purgari
posse asseris, inmortalem tamen aeternamque non
posse hac arte fieri confiteris. Christus autem vitam
promittit aeternam; unde ad eum mundus vobis
quidem stomachantibus, mirantibus tamen stupenti-
busque concurrit. Quid prodest quia negare non
potuisti errare homines theurgica disciplina et quam
plurimos fallere per caecam insipientemque sententiam atque esse certissimum errorem agendo et
supplicando ad principes angelosque decurrere, et
rursum, quasi ne operam perdidisse videaris ista
discendo, mittis homines ad theurgos, ut per eos
anima spiritalis purgetur illorum qui non secundum
intellectualem animam vivunt?

But those theurgists, or rather the demons, when they create false shapes and likenesses of gods, defile rather than cleanse the spirit of man with their sham apparitions and the fraudulent delusion of their bodiless phantoms. For how are they to cleanse the spirit of man when their own spirit is filthy? Otherwise they could by no means be bound by the incantations of a malicious man, nor would they suppress in fear, or refuse with malice equal to his, that same boon, illusory as it was, that they were expected to confer. We are content with your admission that it is impossible for the intellectual soul, that is, our mind, to be cleansed by theurgic purgation and that the spiritual soul itself, which is the part of our soul that ranks below the mind and, so you assert, may be cleansed by such practices, cannot for all that be rendered immortal and eternal by it. But Christ promises eternal life; and this is why, though you are vexed, but withal amazed and struck dumb too, the world is flocking to him. What do you gain by contradicting yourself? You could not deny that men go wrong when they school themselves in theurgic practices, and that they delude as many as they can with their blind and silly dogma, and that it is most certainly a mistake to resort with sacrifices and prayers to principalities and angels; but on the other hand, as if to cover up your waste of effort spent to learn this nonsense, you direct men to the theurgists for the cleansing of the spiritual souls of those whose lives are not guided by the intellectual soul.

XXVIII

*Quibus persuasionibus Porphyrius obcaecatus non
potuerit veram sapientiam, quod est Christus,
agnoscere.*

MITTIS ergo homines in errorem certissimum,
neque hoc tantum malum te pudet, cum virtutis et
sapientiae profitearis amatorem; quam si vere ac
fideliter amasses, *Christum Dei virtutem et Dei sapientiam* cognovisses nec ab eius saluberrima humilitate
tumore inflatus vanae scientiae resiluisses.

Confiteris tamen etiam spiritalem animam sine
theurgicis artibus et sine teletis, quibus frustra di-
scendis elaborasti, posse continentiae virtute purgari.
Aliquando etiam dicis quod teletae non post mortem
elevant animam, ut iam nec eidem ipsi quam spiritalem vocas aliquid post huius vitae finem prodesse
videantur; et tamen versas haec multis modis et
repetis, ad nihil aliud, quantum existimo, nisi ut
talium quoque rerum quasi peritus appareas et
placeas inlicitarum artium curiosis, vel ad eas facias

---

[1] *Sapientiae amatorem* translates literally the Greek
φιλόσοφος, philosopher.

[2] I Corinthians 1.24. *Virtus* here, as so often in Augustine,
translates Greek δύναμις, literally " power." The Authorized
and Revised Standard Versions, based directly on the Greek,
translate " Christ, the power of God and the wisdom of God."
But the philosopher is the lover of virtue, not of power, and
Augustine apparently understands *virtus* as virtue here.

[3] The word *resiluisses* indicates, according to some, that
Porphyry had once been a Christian, but had apostatized.

XXVIII

*The arguments that blinded Porphyry and prevented
him from recognizing the true wisdom, which
is Christ.*

So you direct men into the most undoubted error
and you are not ashamed of committing so great a
wrong, although you profess to be a lover of virtue
and wisdom; [1] whereas if you had loved them truly
and faithfully, you would have come to know " Christ
the virtue of God and the wisdom of God," [2] instead
of being so puffed up with pride in your own empty
knowledge that you recoiled in shock [3] from his
supremely health-giving humility.

Still, you do admit that even the spiritual soul can,
without the aid of the theurgic arts and rites, which
you have wasted so much effort to learn, be purified
by the virtue of continence. You also say on occasion
that rites do not raise the soul after death, so that it is
evident now that they procure no benefit after the
termination of this life even for that very same part
of the soul that you call spiritual. And yet you
treat these matters in a great variety of ways and
keep recurring to them—to no other purpose, so
far as I can judge, than to give yourself the air of one
expert in such things too and to win the approval
of those who pry into forbidden arts, or else yourself
to win new fanciers of such things. But you did well
to point out that this art is dangerous for either of two

Socrates, the Church historian, supports this view. See his
Ecclesiastical History 3.23. But the authority of Socrates is
suspect, and *resiluisses* does not necessarily imply a previous
attachment to Christianity and later rejection.

ipse curiosos. Sed bene quod metuendam dicis hanc artem vel legum periculis vel ipsius actionis. Atque utinam hoc saltem abs te miseri audiant et inde, ne illic absorbeantur, abscedant aut eo penitus non accedant.

Ignorantiam certe et propter eam multa vitia per nullas teletas purgari dicis, sed per solum πατρικὸν νοῦν, id est paternam mentem sive intellectum, qui paternae est conscius voluntatis. Hunc autem Christum esse non credis; contemnis enim eum propter corpus ex femina acceptum et propter crucis opprobrium, excelsam videlicet sapientiam spretis atque abiectis infimis idoneus de superioribus carpere. At ille implet quod prophetae sancti de illo veraciter praedixerunt: *Perdam sapientiam sapientium et prudentiam prudentium reprobabo.* Non enim suam in eis perdit et reprobat quam ipse donavit, sed quam sibi arrogant qui non habent ipsius.

Unde commemorato isto prophetico testimonio sequitur et dicit apostolus: *Ubi sapiens? ubi scriba? ubi conquisitor huius saeculi? Nonne stultam fecit Deus sapientiam huius mundi? Nam quoniam in Dei sapientia non cognovit mundus per sapientiam Deum, placuit Deo per stultitiam praedicationis salvos facere credentes. Quoniam quidem Iudaei signa petunt et Graeci sapientiam quaerunt; nos autem,* inquit, *praedicamus Christum crucifixum, Iudaeis quidem scandalum,*

---

[1] Cf. above, Book 10.23.
[2] I Corinthians 1.19; cf. Isaiah 29.14.

reasons, either the peril of its illegality or the peril involved in the very exercise of the art. And would that your unhappy audience might lend an ear at least to these words of yours and depart from the sink that would swallow them, or never come near it at all.

You say, it is true, that ignorance and the many vices to which it gives rise can never be cleansed by any rites, but only by *patrikos nous*, that is the mind or intellect of the Father, which knows the Father's will.[1] But you do not believe that this is identical with Christ, for you despise him because of the body that came to him from a woman and because of the reproach of the cross. We are to understand evidently that you are one who may properly spurn and reject lowly things and gather a lofty wisdom from higher sources. But He fulfills the true prophecy spoken of him by the holy prophets: " I will destroy the wisdom of the wise and reject the prudence of the prudent." [2] This wisdom, note, that in them he destroys and rejects is not his own wisdom that he himself gave them, but the wisdom that those who lack his wisdom arrogantly lay claim to as their own.

This is why the Apostle, after citing the evidence of this prophecy, goes on to say: " Where is the wise man? Where is the scribe? Where is the debater of this age? Has not God made foolish the wisdom of the world? For since, in the wisdom of God, the world did not find God out by wisdom, God saw fit to use the folly of our preaching to save those who believe. For Jews ask for signs and Greeks seek wisdom, but we," he says, " preach Christ crucified, a stumbling-block to Jews and folly to Gentiles, but

*gentibus autem stultitiam, ipsis vero vocatis Iudaeis et
Graecis Christum Dei virtutem et Dei sapientiam; quoniam stultum Dei sapientius est hominibus, et infirmum
Dei fortius est hominibus.* Hoc quasi stultum et
infirmum tamquam sua virtute sapientes fortesque
contemnunt. Sed haec est gratia quae sanat in-
firmos non superbe iactantes falsam beatitudinem
suam, sed humiliter potius veram miseriam confitentes.

XXIX

*De incarnatione Domini nostri Iesu Christi, quam
confiteri Platonicorum erubescit impietas.*

Praedicas Patrem et eius Filium, quem vocas paternum intellectum seu mentem, et horum medium,
quem putamus te dicere Spiritum sanctum, et more
vestro appellas tres deos. Ubi, etsi verbis indisci-
plinatis utimini, videtis tamen qualitercumque et
quasi per quaedam tenuis imaginationis umbracula
quo nitendum sit; sed incarnationem incommutabilis
Filii Dei, qua salvamur ut ad illa quae credimus vel
ex quantulacumque parte intellegimus venire possimus, non vultis agnoscere. Itaque videtis utcumque, etsi de longinquo, etsi acie caligante, patriam in
qua manendum est, sed viam qua eundum est non
tenetis.

---

[1] I Corinthians, 1.20–25.
[2] See above, Book 10.23.

to those who are called, both Jews and Greeks, Christ the power of God and the wisdom of God. For the foolishness of God is wiser than men, and the weakness of God is stronger than men." [1] This is what they despise as foolish and weak, as if they were wise and strong by virtue of their own excellence. But this is the grace that heals the weak who do not proudly boast of a false happiness of their own, but rather confess humbly their genuine misery.

XXIX

The incarnation of our Lord Jesus Christ, which the irreligion of the Platonists blushes to acknowledge.

You proclaim the Father and his Son, whom you call the intellect or the mind of the Father, and one intermediate between these two, by whom we suppose you mean the Holy Spirit; [2] and, as is the custom of your school, you call them three gods. Here, although the terms you employ are ill-considered, yet you and your school do perceive however poorly, as in a shadowy presentation of faint images, the goal towards which we ought to strive. But when it comes to the incarnation of the unchangeable Son of God, by which we are saved and so are enabled to attain the ends that we see by faith and in part, ever so little though it be, by knowledge, all of you refuse to accept it. Thus you see, in some sort of way, although it be from a long way off and with clouded vision, the homeland in which we are to abide, but your feet are not on the road that leads to it.

Confiteris tamen gratiam, quando quidem ad Deum per virtutem intellegentiae pervenire paucis dicis esse concessum. Non enim dicis: Paucis placuit, vel: Pauci voluerunt; sed cum dicis esse concessum, procul dubio Dei gratiam, non hominis sufficientiam confiteris. Uteris etiam hoc verbo apertius ubi Platonis sententiam sequens nec ipse dubitas in hac vita hominem nullo modo ad perfectionem sapientiae pervenire, secundum intellectum tamen viventibus omne quod deest providentia Dei et gratia post hanc vitam posse compleri.

O si cognovisses Dei gratiam per Iesum Christum dominum nostrum ipsamque eius incarnationem, qua hominis animam corpusque suscepit, summum esse exemplum gratiae videre potuisses. Sed quid faciam? Scio me frustra loqui mortuo, sed quantum ad te adtinet; quantum autem ad eos qui te magnipendunt et te vel qualicumque amore sapientiae vel curiositate artium quas non debuisti discere diligunt, quos potius in tua compellatione alloquor, fortasse non frustra. Gratia Dei non potuit gratius commendari quam ut ipse unicus Dei Filius in se incommutabiliter manens indueretur hominem et spiritum [1] dilectionis suae daret hominibus homine medio, qua [2] ad illum ab hominibus veniretur qui tam longe erat inmortalis a mortalibus incommutabilis a com-

[1] spiritum *coni. Weyman:* spem *MSS. Migne Welldon:* speciem *coni. Dombart* (= *exemplum*).
[2] quo *MS. a* (*saec. X*) *Migne Welldon.*

---

[1] Cf. *Phaedo* 66B–67B.

Still, you acknowledge the existence of grace, since you say that it has been granted to only a few to attain to God by the strength of their intelligence. For you do not say: " A few decided to attain " or " A few chose "; no, when you say: " It has been granted," you are undoubtedly bearing witness to the grace of God, and not to any self-sufficiency of man. Indeed, you resort to this formula more openly still when, following Plato's view,[1] you yourself state without hesitation that in this life man by no means arrives at perfect wisdom, yet those who live on an intellectual level may find their want fully supplied after this life by God's providence and grace.

Oh, if only you could have recognized the grace of God through Jesus Christ our Lord and especially his incarnation, whereby he put on the soul and the body of a man, you might have seen that this is the supreme example of grace. But what am I to do? I know that it is useless for me to speak to one who is dead; but that applies only to you. There are those who hold you in high esteem and affection through love of wisdom, whatever the quality of that love may be, or else through the urge to meddle with those arts that you should never have studied, and I address my urgent appeal rather to them than to you, but in your name and perhaps not without success. The grace of God could not have commended itself in more gracious form than it did. The only Son of God, while remaining unchangeably in his own character, himself put on humanity and bestowed upon men through the mediation of a man the spirit of God's love. That love provided a way for men to come to him who was so far from the mortal, immortal

mutabilibus, iustus ab impiis beatus a miseris. Et quia naturaliter indidit nobis ut beati inmortalesque esse cupiamus, manens beatus suscipiensque mortalem ut nobis tribueret quod amamus, perpetiendo docuit contemnere quod timemus.

Sed huic veritati ut possetis adquiescere, humilitate opus erat, quae cervici vestrae difficillime persuaderi potest. Quid enim incredibile dicitur, praesertim vobis qui talia sapitis quibus ad hoc credendum vos ipsos admonere debeatis; quid, inquam, vobis incredibile dicitur cum dicitur Deus adsumpsisse humanam animam et corpus? Vos certe tantum tribuitis animae intellectuali, quae anima utique humana est, ut eam consubstantialem paternae illi menti quem Dei Filium confitemini fieri posse dicatis. Quid ergo incredibile est, si aliqua una intellectualis anima modo quodam ineffabili et singulari pro multorum salute suscepta est? Corpus vero animae cohaerere ut homo totus et plenus sit, natura ipsa nostra teste cognoscimus. Quod nisi usitatissimum esset, hoc profecto esset incredibilius; facilius quippe in fidem recipiendum est, etsi humanum divino, etsi mutabile incommutabili, tamen spiritum spiritui, aut ut verbis utar quae in usu habetis, incorporeum incorporeo, quam corpus incorporeo cohaerere.

An forte vos offendit inusitatus corporis partus ex

as he was; from the changeable, unchangeable as he was; from the impious, righteous as he was; from the unhappy, blest as he was. And because he imbued our nature with the desire to be happy and immortal, he, by remaining happy while he put on mortality in order to grant us the thing we love, taught us by his suffering to despise the thing we fear.

But for you to acquiesce in this truth, you had need of humility, a thing very hard for your stiff neck to accept. For what is incredible in the statement—especially for men like you whose philosophy is such as should prompt you of yourselves to believe it—what, I say, is incredible in the statement that God assumed a human soul and body? Obviously, you have enough respect for the intellectual soul, which is in any case a human soul, to enable you to say that it can be made consubstantial with the mind of the Father, which you acknowledge to be the Son of God. What then is so incredible if one intellectual soul was assumed by some unique and ineffable means for the salvation of many? Surely we learn from the evidence of our own nature that the body is united to the soul to produce a man whole and complete. If this were not such a common experience, it would certainly be a harder thing to believe. For it is easier to accept and believe in a union of spirit with spirit, or, to employ the vocabulary of your school, of incorporeal with incorporeal, even though the human be joined to the divine, the mutable to the immutable, than it is to accept a union of incorporeal with corporeal.

Or can it be that you find a stumbling-block in the

387

virgine? Neque hoc debet offendere, immo potius ad pietatem suscipiendam debet adducere, quod mirabilis mirabiliter natus est.

An vero quod ipsum corpus morte depositum et in melius resurrectione mutatum iam incorruptibile neque mortale in superna subvexit, hoc fortasse credere recusatis intuentes Porphyrium in his ipsis libris, ex quibus multa posui, quos de regressu animae scripsit, tam crebro praecipere omne corpus esse fugiendum ut anima possit beata permanere cum Deo? Sed ipse potius ista sentiens corrigendus fuit, praesertim cum de anima mundi huius visibilis et tam ingentis corporeae molis cum illo tam incredibilia sapiatis. Platone quippe auctore animal esse dicitis mundum et animal beatissimum, quod vultis esse etiam sempiternum. Quo modo ergo nec umquam solvetur a corpore, nec umquam carebit beatitudine, si, ut beata sit anima, corpus est omne fugiendum? Solem quoque istum et cetera sidera non solum in libris vestris corpora esse fatemini, quod vobiscum omnes homines et conspicere non cunctantur et dicere; verum etiam altiore, ut putatis, peritia haec esse animalia beatissima perhibetis et cum his corporibus sempiterna. Quid ergo est quod, cum vobis fides Christiana suadetur, tunc

---

[1] *Timaeus* 30 f.

unexampled birth of his body from a virgin? This should be no obstacle either. On the contrary, it ought rather to be an inducement to you to embrace our faith, that a marvellous person was born in a marvellous way.

Or do you really refuse to believe, perhaps, that he bore aloft his body itself, laid aside in death, changed for the better in the resurrection, and now incorruptible and mortal no longer? Do you refuse to believe this because you see Porphyry so often insisting, in those very books *On the Return of the Soul* from which I have often quoted, that the soul must avoid all union with a body in order to abide forever happy with God? But it was rather Porphyry himself who was in need of correction when he held such a view, particularly inasmuch as you have such incredible notions in common with him concerning the soul of this visible world, that is, of so huge a corporeal mass. I mean that you follow Plato,[1] and maintain that the universe is a living being, and not only alive but supremely happy, and you would even have it eternal. How then can it be that its soul will never be detached from its body and yet will never be deprived of happiness, if a soul to be happy must avoid every kind of body? There is the sun, too, and the other heavenly luminaries, which you acknowledge in your books are bodies, and all men join you in seeing this plainly and saying so without scruple. And in addition, you, with that higher wisdom that you claim, maintain that these are supremely happy beings that live forever united with their bodies. Why is it, then, that when the Christian faith is recommended to you, you immediately forget or pretend to be un-

389

obliviscimini, aut ignorare vos fingitis quid disputare aut docere soleatis? Quid causae est cur propter opiniones vestras quas vos ipsi oppugnatis Christiani esse nolitis, nisi quia Christus humiliter venit et vos superbi estis? Qualia sanctorum corpora in resurrectione futura sint, potest aliquanto scrupulosius inter Christianarum scripturarum doctissimos disputari; futura tamen sempiterna minime dubitamus, et talia futura quale sua resurrectione Christus demonstravit exemplum. Sed qualiacumque sint, cum incorruptibilia prorsus et inmortalia nihiloque animae contemplationem qua in Deo figitur inpedientia praedicentur vosque etiam dicatis esse in caelestibus inmortalia corpora inmortaliter beatorum, quid est quod, ut beati simus, omne corpus fugiendum esse opinamini, ut fidem Christianam quasi rationabiliter fugere videamini, nisi quia illud est quod iterum dico: Christus est humilis, vos superbi?

An forte corrigi pudet? Et hoc vitium non nisi superborum est. Pudet videlicet doctos homines ex discipulis Platonis fieri discipulos Christi, qui piscatorem suo spiritu docuit sapere ac dicere: *In principio erat Verbum, et Verbum erat apud Deum, et Deus erat*

acquainted with a doctrine that you make a practice of upholding in debate and including in your instruction? Why is it that because of opinions of yours with which you yourselves are in conflict you refuse to become Christians, except that Christ came in humble guise and you are proud? It is possible that those who are most learned in the Christian writings may debate among themselves just what kind of bodies the saints will assume in the resurrection with a little too much anxious concern over small points. Yet we have no doubt at all that their bodies will be eternal and will be like the prototype that Christ made manifest in his resurrection. But whatever they may be like in detail, the declaration is made in our preaching that they are absolutely incorruptible and immortal and offer no obstacle to the contemplation of God in which the soul is constantly engaged. You too yourselves declare that there are in the celestial regions immortal bodies of beings whose happiness is immortal. Then why do you cling to the opinion that, for the sake of our happiness, we must avoid every kind of body, in order to give the impression that you have some semblance of reason for avoiding the Christian faith, unless it is true, as I say once again: " Christ is humble, you are proud " ?

Are you perhaps embarrassed to admit correction? This weakness too is found only in the proud. It is an embarrassment, we must assume, for scholars to become followers of Christ, instead of followers of Plato, of Christ who by his spirit imbued a fisherman with wisdom to think, and taught him to say: " In the beginning was the Word, and the Word was with

Verbum. Hoc erat in principio apud Deum. Omnia per ipsum facta sunt, et sine ipso factum est nihil quod factum est. In ipso vita erat, et vita erat lux hominum, et lux in tenebris lucet, et tenebrae eam non conprehenderunt. Quod initium sancti evangelii, cui nomen est secundum Iohannem, quidam Platonicus, sicut a sancto sene Simpliciano, qui postea Mediolanensi ecclesiae praesedit episcopus, solebamus audire, aureis litteris conscribendum et per omnes ecclesias in locis eminentissimis proponendum esse dicebat. Sed ideo viluit superbis Deus ille magister, quia *Verbum caro factum est et habitavit in nobis*; ut parum sit miseris quod aegrotant nisi se etiam in ipsa aegritudine extollant et de medicina qua sanari poterant erubescant. Non enim hoc faciunt ut erigantur, sed ut cadendo gravius affligantur.

XXX

Quanta Platonici dogmatis Porphyrius refutaverit et dissentiendo correxerit.

Si post Platonem aliquid emendare existimatur indignum, cur ipse Porphyrius nonnulla et non parva emendavit? Nam Platonem animas hominum post

---

[1] John 1.1–5.

[2] A.D. 397–400.

[3] The Platonist in question has been identified by some as Marius Victorinus, fourth-century Neoplatonic philosopher, rhetorician, and grammarian, who was converted to Christianity. It would appear, to be sure, that Augustine is speaking of a Neoplatonist who became a Christian, but there must have been many such in Milan. Moreover, admiration for Neoplatonic doctrine was widespread among the educated Christians;

God, and the Word was God. This Word was in the beginning with God. All things were made through him, and without him was nothing made that was made. In him was life, and the life was the light of men; and the light shines in the darkness, and the darkness did not lay hold of it." [1] This is the beginning of the holy Gospel, called the Gospel according to John. These are the words which, as that saintly old man Simplicianus, who later took his seat as bishop in charge of the church at Milan,[2] always told us, a certain Platonist used to say should be inscribed in letters of gold and displayed in the most prominent place in every church.[3] Yet this is the reason why God the great teacher was held cheap in the eyes of the proud, because: "The Word became flesh and dwelt among us." [4] So it is not enough for these unfortunates to be sick. They must even take pride in their sickness and blush to take the medicine that had power to cure them. What they achieve by such tactics is not to rise healed, but to suffer a fall that aggravates their malady.

XXX

How many points of Platonic doctrine Porphyry refuted and corrected by his dissent.

If it is is thought to be disgraceful to improve upon anything that Plato said, why did Porphyry himself improve upon several of his doctrines, and important ones at that? For nothing is more certain than that

hence it is impossible to identify this particular Platonist with any certainty.
  [4] John 1.14.

mortem revolvi usque ad corpora bestiarum scripsisse certissimum est. Hanc sententiam Porphyrii doctor tenuit et Plotinus; Porphyrio tamen iure displicuit. In hominum sane non sua quae dimiserant, sed alia nova corpora redire humanas animas arbitratus est. Puduit scilicet illud credere, ne mater fortasse filium in mulam revoluta vectaret; et non puduit hoc credere ubi revoluta mater in puellam filio forsitan nuberet. Quanto creditur honestius quod sancti et veraces angeli docuerunt, quod prophetae Dei spiritu acti locuti sunt, quod ipse quem venturum Salvatorem praemissi nuntii praedixerunt, quod missi apostoli qui orbem terrarum evangelio repleverunt,— quanto, inquam, honestius creditur reverti animas semel ad corpora propria quam reverti totiens ad diversa! Verum tamen, ut dixi, ex magna parte correctus est in hac opinione Porphyrius, ut saltem in solos homines humanas animas praecipitari posse sentiret, beluinos autem carceres evertere minime dubitaret.

Dicit etiam ad hoc Deum animam mundo dedisse, ut materiae cognoscens mala ad Patrem recurreret

---

[1] *Phaedrus* 249 B; *Phaedo* 81 E; *Timaeus* 42 C; *Republic* 10.618 A–620 D.

[2] *Enneads* 3.4.2; 4.3.12.

Plato said in writing that after death the souls of
men return to earth in a cycle and pass even into the
bodies of animals.[1]   This theory was held by Plotinus
also,[2] the teacher of Porphyry, but Porphyry was
right to reject it.   He held that human souls return
to earth and enter human bodies, not indeed those
they had discarded, but new and different ones.   He
was ashamed, apparently, to adopt the Platonic
theory, for fear that a mother, returning to earth in
the form of a mule, might perhaps carry her son on
her back.   Yet he was not ashamed to believe in a
doctrine by which a mother, returning in the form of
a girl, might perhaps marry her son. How much
more respectable is the belief, in accord with what
holy and truthful angels have taught men, with what
the prophets, moved by the spirit of God, announced,
with the words of the Saviour himself, whose coming
was foretold by messengers sent in advance, and with
the preaching of the apostles whom he sent forth
and who covered the whole earth with the gospel—
how much more respectable it is, I say, to believe
that souls return once to their own bodies than to
believe that they return so many times to all sorts of
bodies!   However, as I said, Porphyry has to a great
extent corrected the error of this doctrine, in so far
at least as he held that human souls can only be cast
down into human bodies, and did not have the slightest hesitation in abolishing incarceration of souls in
the bodies of monstrous beasts.

He also says that God's purpose in giving a soul
to the world was that it might recognize the evils
inherent in material things and so return to the
Father, and never again find itself held fast and

nec aliquando iam talium polluta contagione teneretur. Ubi etsi aliquid inconvenienter sapit—magis enim data est corpori ut bona faceret; non enim mala disceret si non faceret—, in eo tamen aliorum Platonicorum opinionem et non in re parva emendavit, quod mundatam ab omnibus malis animam et cum Patre constitutam numquam iam mala mundi huius passuram esse confessus est. Qua sententia profecto abstulit quod esse Platonicum maxime perhibetur, ut mortuos ex vivis, ita vivos ex mortuis semper fieri; falsumque esse ostendit quod Platonice videtur dixisse Vergilius, in campos Elysios purgatas animas missas—quo nomine tamquam per fabulam videntur significari gaudia beatorum—ad fluvium Letheum evocari, hoc est ad oblivionem praeteritorum:

> Scilicet inmemores supera ut convexa revisant
> Rursus et incipiant in corpora velle reverti.

Merito displicuit hoc Porphyrio quoniam re vera credere stultum est ex illa vita quae beatissima esse non poterit nisi de sua fuerit aeternitate certissima, desiderare animas corruptibilium corporum labem et inde ad ista remeare, tamquam hoc agat summa purgatio, ut inquinatio requiratur. Si enim quod perfecte mundantur hoc efficit, ut omnium obliviscantur malorum, malorum autem oblivio facit corporum desiderium, ubi rursus implicentur malis, profecto erit infelicitatis causa summa felicitas et stultitiae causa perfectio sapientiae et inmunditiae

---

[1] Cf. Plato, *Phaedo* 70 C.
[2] Aeneid 6.750 f.

polluted by their contagion. Here, to be sure, there is some impropriety in his view, since the soul is rather given to the body to do good, for it would not learn evil if it did no evil. Still, he corrected the opinion of other Platonists, and in no small matter, when he admitted that the soul, once cleansed from all evil and firmly joined to the Father, will never again suffer the evils of this world. By this verdict he definitely discarded a particularly notorious dogma ascribed to Plato, the view that, as the dead derive from the living, so the living derive from the dead.[1] He also revealed as fiction the words of Virgil, spoken presumably under Platonic influence, and telling of purified souls dispatched to the Elysian fields—an allegorical name, it seems, for the joys of the blessed —and summoned to the river Lethe, that is to forgetfulness of the past:

> So that with memory erased they may
> Again behold the vault on high and start
> To grow desirous of return to bodies.[2]

Porphyry was right to reject this doctrine, for it is really stupid to believe that, from a life that cannot be absolutely happy if it is not entirely convinced that its bliss is everlasting, souls should hanker after the foulness of corruptible bodies, as if it were the purpose of perfect purgation to create a demand for defilement. For if perfect purification causes them to forget all past ills, and if this forgetting of ills creates a longing for bodies, in which to be again entangled in ills, it inevitably follows that supreme happiness must be a source of unhappiness, perfect wisdom of folly and perfect purification of impurity.

397

causa summa mundatio. Nec veritate ibi beata erit
anima, quamdiucumque erit, ubi oportet fallatur ut
beata sit. Non enim beata erit nisi secura; ut
autem secura sit, falso putabit semper se beatam
fore, quoniam aliquando erit et misera. Cui ergo
gaudendi causa falsitas erit, quo modo de veritate
gaudebit? Vidit hoc Porphyrius purgatamque animam ob hoc reverti dixit ad Patrem, ne aliquando iam
malorum polluta contagione teneatur. Falso igitur
a quibusdam est Platonicis creditus quasi necessarius
orbis ille ab eisdem abeundi et ad eadem revertendi.
Quod etiamsi verum esset, quid hoc scire prodesset,
nisi forte inde se nobis auderent praeferre Platonici,
quia id nos in hac vita iam nesciremus quod ipsi in
alia meliore vita purgatissimi et sapientissimi fuerant
nescituri et falsum credendo beati futuri? Quod si
absurdissimum et stultissimum est dicere, Porphyrii
profecto est praeferenda sententia his qui animarum
circulos alternante semper beatitate et miseria
suspicati sunt. Quod si ita est, ecce Platonicus in
melius a Platone dissentit; ecce vidit quod ille non
vidit, nec post talem ac tantum magistrum refugit
correctionem, sed homini praeposuit veritatem.

---

[1] Cf. the proverb: " Plato is a friend, but a greater friend
is the truth " (*amicus Plato, magis amica veritas*). See also
Cicero, *Tusculan Disputations* 1.17.39.

Nor will the soul in truth be happy in a state where, no matter how long it remains in it, it must be fooled if it is to be happy. For it will not be happy unless it be free from anxiety; but to be free from anxiety, it will falsely suppose its happiness to be eternal—falsely, for the time will also come when it will be wretched. How then can a man rejoice in truth, when the cause of his rejoicing is untruth? Porphyry saw the force of this and to meet it, declared that the purged soul returns to the Father, to escape from being stained ever again by contact with ills and so held down. Certain Platonists, then, were wrong when they accepted as necessary the cycle of continual going and coming from the same to the same. But even if this were true, what would be the advantage of knowing it? Would the Platonists have the effrontery to rate themselves as better than we because we were already in this life ignorant of a fact of which they themselves in another and better life and at the height of purification and wisdom were going to be ignorant, when they were to be kept happy by believing what was not in fact true? And if it is the height of absurdity and folly to say that, Porphyry's view is surely more acceptable than that of those who conceived of souls as swinging in a circle between alternate joy and misery. If this is so, here we have a Platonist adopting a different view from Plato's, and a better one. Mark him well. He saw what Plato failed to see. Nor did he, coming after so great, so wise a master, boggle at correcting his error. He loved truth more than the man.[1]

XXXI

Contra argumentum Platonicorum quo animam
humanam Deo asserunt esse coaeternam.

CUR ergo non potius divinitati credimus de his rebus
quas humano ingenio pervestigare non possumus,
quae animam quoque ipsam non Deo coaeternam,
sed creatam dicit esse, quae non erat? Ut enim
hoc Platonici nollent credere, hanc utique causam
idoneam sibi videbantur adferre, quia nisi quod
semper ante fuisset sempiternum deinceps esse non
posset; quamquam et de mundo et de his quos in
mundo deos a Deo factos scribit Plato, apertissime
dicat eos esse coepisse et habere initium, finem
tamen non habituros, sed per conditoris potentissi-
mam voluntatem in aeternum mansuros esse perhibeat. Verum id quo modo intellegant invenerunt,
non esse hoc videlicet temporis, sed substitutionis
initium. "Sicut enim," inquiunt, "si pes ex
aeternitate semper fuisset in pulvere, semper ei
subesset vestigium, quod tamen vestigium a calcante
factum nemo dubitaret, nec alterum altero prius
esset, quamvis alterum ab altero factum esset,
sic," inquiunt, "et mundus atque in illo dii creati
et semper fuerunt semper existente qui fecit, et
tamen facti sunt."

Numquid ergo, si anima semper fuit, etiam miseria

---

[1] *Timaeus* 41 B.

XXXI

A contradiction of the Platonic theory that the human soul is co-eternal with God.

WHY, then, do we not prefer to believe the divine word in regard to matters that no human insight can search out? Divine authority tells us that the soul itself, like other things, is not co-eternal with God but was created, having no existence before. The Platonists certainly thought they had a good reason for refusing to accept this. They argued that if a thing had not been eternal in time past, it could not be eternal in the future. And yet both when Plato speaks of the universe and when he speaks of the gods whom he says that God created in the universe, he declares in no uncertain terms that they came into being and had a beginning, yet they will have no end;[1] rather, he assures us, they will endure for ever by virtue of the all-powerful will of their creator. But his followers have found a way to understand this. They say that he meant the beginning, not of a period of time, but of a dependence. "For," they say, "if from all eternity a foot had always been implanted in the dust, its print would always be there underneath it. Yet nobody would have any doubt that the print had been made by the planter of the foot; and the one would not be earlier than the other, although one would have been made by the other. So," they add, "the world itself and the gods created in it have been there eternally during the eternal existence of him who created them, and yet they were created."

Well, then, if the soul has always existed, are we to

eius semper fuisse dicenda est? Porro si aliquid in illa quod ex aeterno non fuit esse coepit ex tempore, cur non fieri potuerit ut ipsa esset ex tempore quae antea non fuisset? Deinde beatitudo quoque eius post experimentum malorum firmior et sine fine mansura, sicut iste confitetur, procul dubio coepit ex tempore, et tamen semper erit cum ante non fuerit.

Illa igitur omnis argumentatio dissoluta est qua putatur nihil esse posse sine fine temporis nisi quod initium non habet temporis. Inventa est enim animae beatitudo, quae cum initium temporis habuerit, finem temporis non habebit. Quapropter divinae auctoritati humana cedat infirmitas, eisque beatis et inmortalibus de vera religione credamus qui sibi honorem non expetunt quem Deo suo, qui etiam noster est, deberi sciunt, nec iubent ut sacrificium faciamus nisi ei tantum cuius et nos cum illis, ut saepe dixi et saepe dicendum est, sacrificium esse debemus, per eum sacerdotem offerendi qui in homine quem suscepit, secundum quem et sacerdos esse voluit, etiam usque ad mortem sacrificium pro nobis dignatus est fieri.

say that its misery too has always existed. If not, we go on to ask why, if some condition of the soul that has not existed from eternity began to exist from some moment in time, why should it have been impossible for the soul itself to come into being at a certain moment, although it had no existence before? In the second place the soul's happiness, which after its trial of evil is more secure and is destined to endure forever, as Porphyry admits, undoubtedly also began at a given moment, and yet it will exist forever, though it had no previous existence.

So then the whole argument in support of the view that nothing can be without an end in time unless it also had no beginning in time falls apart. For we have discovered a contrary instance: although the happiness of the soul had a beginning in time, it will still have no ending in time. Therefore let human weakness yield to divine authority, and on the subject of true religion let us trust those happy and immortal beings who do not seek for themselves the honour that they know is due to their God, who is also ours. They bid us sacrifice to him alone whose sacrifice we too along with them are duty-bound to be, as I have often said and must often say in future. We must be offered as a sacrifice, and the minister of the sacrifice must be He who in the human form that he took upon himself and in which he chose also to serve as priest, deigned to become a sacrifice for us even unto death.

SAINT AUGUSTINE

XXXII

De universali via animae liberandae, quam Porphyrius
male quaerendo non repperit, et quam sola gratia
Christiana reseravit.

HAEC est religio quae universalem continet viam
animae liberandae, quoniam nulla nisi hac liberari
potest. Haec est enim quodam modo regalis via,
quae una ducit ad regnum, non temporali fastigio
nutabundum, sed aeternitatis firmitate securum.

Cum autem dicit Porphyrius in primo iuxta finem
de regressu animae libro nondum receptum in unam [1]
quandam sectam quod [2] universalem contineat viam
animae liberandae, vel a philosophia verissima
aliqua vel ab Indorum moribus ac disciplina, aut
inductione Chaldaeorum aut alia qualibet via, nondumque in suam notitiam eandem viam historiali
cognitione perlatam, procul dubio confitetur esse
aliquam, sed nondum in suam venisse notitiam. Ita
ei non sufficiebat quidquid de anima liberanda
studiosissime didicerat sibique vel potius aliis nosse
ac tenere videbatur. Sentiebat enim adhuc sibi de-
esse aliquam praestantissimam auctoritatem quam
de re tanta sequi oporteret. Cum autem dicit vel a
philosophia verissima aliqua nondum in suam
notitiam pervenisse sectam quae universalem con-

---

[1] receptam unam *Migne.*
[2] quae *a few MSS., Migne, and Hoffmann.*

XXXII

The universal path to the deliverance of the soul.
Porphyry failed to find it because his search
was wrongly conducted. The grace of
Christ alone has disclosed it.

THIS is the religion that embodies a universal path
to the liberation of the soul, since no soul can be
liberated by any way but this. For this is a sort of
royal road that alone leads to the kingdom, a kingdom not doomed to sway uneasily upon a pinnacle of
time but solidly founded on eternity.

Now when Porphyry says towards the end of his
first book *On the Return of the Soul* that no one system
of thought has yet embraced a doctrine that embodies a universal path to the liberation of the soul,
no, neither the truest of philosophies, nor the moral
ideas and practices of the Indians, nor the initiation
of the Chaldaeans, nor any other way of life, and adds
that this same path has not yet been brought to his
attention in the course of his research into history, he
is undoubtedly acknowledging that some such path
exists though it had not yet come to his attention.
So dissatisfied was he with the results of his devoted
study of the liberation of the soul and with what his
reputation, higher in the eyes of others than in his
own, credited him with discovering and maintaining.
For he judged that there was some pre-eminent
authority missing, in whose steps he ought to follow
on a matter of such great moment. Moreover, when
he says that even the truest of philosophies has never
yet brought to his attention a system that embodies

tineat viam animae liberandae, satis, quantum arbitror, ostendit vel eam philosophiam in qua ipse philosophatus est non esse verissimam, vel ea non contineri talem viam. Et quo modo iam potest esse verissima qua non continetur haec via? Nam quae alia via est universalis animae liberandae nisi qua universae animae liberantur ac per hoc sine illa nulla anima liberatur? Cum autem addit et dicit: "Vel ab Indorum moribus ac disciplina, vel ab inductione Chaldaeorum vel alia qualibet via," manifestissima voce testatur neque illis quae ab Indis neque illis quae a Chaldaeis didicerat hanc universalem viam liberandae animae contineri; et utique se a Chaldaeis oracula divina sumpsisse, quorum adsiduam commemorationem facit, tacere non potuit.

Quam vult ergo intellegi animae liberandae universalem viam nondum receptam vel ex aliqua verissima philosophia vel ex earum gentium doctrinis quae magnae velut in divinis rebus habebantur quia plus apud eas curiositas valuit quorumque angelorum cognoscendorum et colendorum, nondumque in suam notitiam historiali cognitione perlatam? Quaenam ista est universalis via nisi quae non suae cuique genti propria, sed universis gentibus quae communis esset divinitus inpertita est?

Quam certe iste homo non mediocri ingenio prae-

a universal path to the liberation of the soul, he makes it sufficiently clear, in my opinion, that the philosophy that he professed is either not the truest, or no such way is found in it. And how can a philosophy be in that case the truest, when no such path is embodied within it? For what else is a universal way of liberating the soul than a way by which all souls universally are liberated, and consequently no soul is liberated without it. When he adds to his statement: " nor the moral ideas and practices of the Indians, nor the initiation of the Chaldaeans, nor any other way of life," he bears witness in the clearest possible terms that this universal path to the liberation of the soul is embodied neither in what he had learned from the Indians nor in what he had learned from the Chaldaeans. In any case he could not conceal the fact that he took over from the Chaldaeans the divine oracles to which he constantly refers.

What then does he mean us to understand by the universal path to the liberation of the soul? It has not yet been acquired either from any philosophy, even the truest, or from the systems of those nations whose high reputation in a field supposedly divine was due to the greater strength of their superstitious zeal to discover and worship the particular classes of angels. Nor has it yet been brought to his attention in the course of his research into history. What can this universal path be, unless it is a way that is not the exclusive property of any one nation but has been divinely communicated for all the nations universally to share?

Porphyry, a man endowed with no ordinary intellect, certainly has no doubt that there is such a

ditus esse non dubitat. Providentiam quippe divinam sine ista universali via liberandae animae genus
humanum relinquere potuisse non credit. Neque
enim ait non esse, sed hoc tantum bonum tantumque
adiutorium nondum receptum, nondum in suam
notitiam esse perlatum; nec mirum. Tunc enim
Porphyrius erat in rebus humanis quando ista
liberandae animae universalis via, quae non est alia
quam religio Christiana, oppugnari permittebatur ab
idolorum daemonumque cultoribus regibusque terrenis, propter asserendum et consecrandum
martyrum numerum, hoc est testium veritatis, per
quos ostenderetur omnia corporalia mala pro fide
pietatis et commendatione veritatis esse toleranda.
Videbat ergo ista Porphyrius et per huius modi
persecutiones cito istam viam perituram et propterea
non esse ipsam liberandae animae universalem putabat, non intellegens hoc quod eum movebat et quod
in eius electione perpeti metuebat ad eius confirma-
tionem robustioremque commendationem potius
pertinere.

Haec est igitur animae liberandae universalis via,
id est universis gentibus divina miseratione concessa,
cuius profecto notitia ad quoscumque iam venit et
ad quoscumque ventura est, nec debuit nec debebit
ei dici: Quare modo? et: Quare sero? quoniam
mittentis consilium non est humano ingenio pene-
trabile. Quod sensit etiam iste, cum dixit nondum

---

[1] The persecutions of the Christians by the Emperors
Decius (249–251), Diocletian (284–305) and his colleague
Maximian fell within Porphyry's lifetime (232/3–c. 305).

path. He does not believe that Providence, not Divine Providence certainly, could have left the human race without such a universal path to the liberation of the soul. For he does not deny that it exists but tells us merely that this so great boon and succour has not yet been acquired nor as yet been brought to his attention. This is not surprising, for when Porphyry was on earth, this universal path to the liberation of the soul, which is none other than the Christian religion, was with God's permission attacked by those who worshipped idols and demons and by the kings of the earth.[1] God permitted this in order to establish and consecrate the full number of martyrs, that is, of witnesses to the truth, who were instruments to demonstrate that all bodily ills must be endured in loyalty to the cause of religion and to spread the truth. Porphyry must have seen all this and thought that this path would shortly be destroyed by such persecutions and therefore was not itself the universal way to the liberation of the soul. He did not realize that the very persecutions that troubled him and the very sufferings that he feared if he chose that way, contributed rather to found it more solidly and to spread it more vigorously.

This then is the universal path to the liberation of the soul, that is, a path granted to all nations universally by divine compassion. No matter who they may be to whom report of it has already come, or shall come in the future, no man, assuredly, has been or will be justified in asking the one who sent it: " Why at this moment? " or " Why so late? " since the sender is one whose purpose is inscrutable to human wit. Even Porphyry adopted this view when

receptum hoc donum Dei et nondum in suam notitiam fuisse perlatum. Neque enim propterea verum non esse iudicavit quia nondum in fidem suam receptum fuerat vel in notitiam nondum pervenerat.

Haec est, inquam, liberandorum credentium universalis via, de qua fidelis Abraham divinum accepit oraculum: *In semine tuo benedicentur omnes gentes.* Qui fuit quidem gente Chaldaeus, sed ut talia promissa perciperet et ex illo propagaretur semen dispositum per angelos in manu Mediatoris, in quo esset ista liberandae animae universalis via, hoc est omnibus gentibus data, iussus est discedere de terra sua et de cognatione sua et de domo patris sui.

Tunc ipse primitus a Chaldaeorum superstitionibus liberatus unum verum Deum sequendo coluit, cui haec promittenti fideliter credidit. Haec est universalis via, de qua in sancta prophetia dictum est: *Deus misereatur nostri et benedicat nos; inluminet vultum suum super nos, ut cognoscamus in terra viam tuam, in omnibus gentibus salutare tuum.* Unde tanto post ex Abrahae semine carne suscepta de se ipso ait ipse Salvator: *Ego sum via, veritas et vita.*

Haec est universalis via de qua tanto ante prophetatum est: *Erit in novissimis diebus manifestus*

---

[1] Genesis 22.18.
[2] See Genesis 12.1.
[3] Galatians 3.19. cf. above, Book 10.24.
[4] Cf. City of God Book 16.12.
[5] Psalm 67.1–2.
[6] John 14.6.

he said that this gift of God had not yet been acquired and had not yet come to his attention. He did not, in fact, deny the reality of the gift either on the ground that he had not yet received it as an article of his faith or because it had not yet come to his attention.

This is, I repeat, the universal way of liberation for those who believe. Concerning it the faithful Abraham received the divine prophecy: " In your seed shall all the nations be blest." [1] Abraham was indeed by birth a Chaldaean, but he was commanded to depart from his own country, from his kindred and from his father's house, [2] that he might receive such promises and that from him might spring the descendant that was designated by the angels through the hand of a Mediator, [3] in whom should lie this universal path to the liberation of the soul, that is, a way given to all nations.

At that time he was in the first place liberated from Chaldaean superstitions [4] and began to follow and worship the one true God, in whom he put implicit trust when he made these promises. This is the universal way of which it was said in the holy prophecy: " May God be merciful to us and bless us. May he make his face to shine upon us, that we may recognize thy way upon earth, thy saving power among all nations." [5] It was with reference to this that the Saviour himself so long afterwards, having put on flesh of the line of Abraham, said of himself: " I am the way, the truth, and the life." [6]

This is the universal way of which it was prophesied so long before: " In the last days the mountain of the Lord shall be plainly revealed, set ready on the

mons Domini, paratus in cacumine montium et extolletur super colles, et venient ad eum universae gentes et ingredientur nationes multae et dicent: Venite, ascendamus in montem Domini et in domum Dei Iacob; et adnuntiabit nobis viam suam, et ingrediemur in ea. Ex Sion enim prodiet lex et verbum Domini ab Hierusalem. Via ergo ista non est unius gentis, sed universarum gentium; et lex verbumque Domini non in Sion et Hierusalem remansit, sed inde processit ut se per universa diffunderet. Unde ipse Mediator post resurrectionem suam discipulis trepidantibus ait: *Oportebat impleri quae scripta sunt in lege et prophetis et psalmis de me. Tunc aperuit illis sensum, ut intellegerent scripturas, et dixit eis quia oportebat Christum pati et resurgere a mortuis tertio die et praedicari in nomine eius paenitentiam et remissionem peccatorum per omnes gentes incipientibus ab Hierusalem.*

Haec est igitur universalis animae liberandae via, quam sancti angeli sanctique prophetae prius in paucis hominibus ubi potuerunt Dei gratiam reperientibus et maxime in Hebraea gente, cuius erat ipsa quodam modo sacrata res publica in prophetationem et praenuntiationem civitatis Dei ex omnibus gentibus congregandae, et tabernaculo et templo et sacerdotio et sacrificiis significaverunt et eloquiis quibusdam manifestis, plerisque mysticis praedixerunt; praesens autem in carne ipse Mediator et

---

¹ Isaiah 2.2–3.　　　² Luke 24.44–47.

summit of the mountains, and it shall be raised high above the hills; and all the nations shall come to it. And many peoples shall advance towards it and say: 'Come, let us go up to the mountain of the Lord and into the house of the God of Jacob; and he will proclaim to us his way and we shall enter upon it.' For out of Zion shall go forth the law, and the word of the Lord from Jerusalem." [1] So this path does not belong to one nation, but to all nations: and the law and word of the Lord did not stop short in Zion and Jerusalem but went forth from them to spread abroad everywhere. With reference to this the Mediator himself said after his resurrection to his quaking disciples: "'What is written of me in the law and the prophets and the psalms had to be fulfilled.' Then he opened their minds to understand the Scriptures and said to them that it was necessary for Christ to suffer and on the third day rise from the dead, and that repentance and forgiveness of sins should be preached in his name throughout all nations, beginning from Jerusalem." [2]

This, then, is the universal path to the liberation of the soul, the path to which holy angels and holy prophets pointed symbolically by signs such as the tabernacle, the temple, the priesthood and sacrifices, and foretold by pronouncements which were sometimes clear but for the most part wrapped in mystery. They did so first where they could, to a few men who found favour with God, and especially the Hebrew nation whose very state had been to a certain extent consecrated to prophesy and to announce in advance the City of God which is to be assembled from all nations. But then, when the Mediator was himself present in the flesh, he and his blessed apostles

beati eius apostoli iam testamenti novi gratiam
revelantes apertius indicarunt quae aliquanto occul-
tius superioribus sunt significata temporibus, pro
aetatum generis humani distributione, sicut eam Deo
sapienti placuit ordinare, mirabilium operum divinorum, quorum superius pauca iam posui, con-
testantibus signis. Non enim apparuerunt tantummodo visiones angelicae et caelestium ministrorum
sola verba sonuerunt, verum etiam hominibus Dei
verbo simplicis pietatis agentibus spiritus inmundi de
hominum corporibus ac sensibus pulsi sunt, vitia
corporis languoresque sanati, fera animalia terrarum
et aquarum, volatilia caeli, ligna, elementa, sidera
divina iussa fecerunt, inferna cesserunt, mortui
revixerunt; exceptis ipsius Salvatoris propriis sin-
gularibusque miraculis, maxime nativitatis et resur-
rectionis, quorum in uno maternae virginitatis
tantummodo sacramentum, in altero autem etiam
eorum qui in fine resurrecturi sunt demonstravit
exemplum.

Haec via totum hominem mundat et inmortalitati
mortalem ex omnibus quibus constat partibus prae-
parat. Ut enim non alia purgatio ei parti quaereretur
quam vocat intellectualem Porphyrius, alia ei quam
vocat spiritalem, aliaque ipsi corpori, propterea
totum suscepit veracissimus potentissimusque mun-
dator atque salvator. Praeter hanc viam, quae
partim cum haec futura praenuntiantur, partim cum

from that time on, as they revealed the grace of the New Testament, made known more openly things that in earlier times had been rather more obscurely conveyed in symbolic terms, to suit the parts assigned to different ages of mankind for them to play, as it pleased the wisdom of God to ordain. This revelation was supported by signs, that is the evidence of wondrous works divinely wrought, of which I have given a few examples above. For not only did visions of angels appear, not only were the words of heavenly messengers heard ringing forth, but even men of God, using language of simple piety, drove out unclean spirits from the bodies and minds of men and cured bodily defects and sicknesses. Wild beasts of land and water, the birds of the sky, trees, the elements and the heavenly bodies obeyed the divine commands. Hell retreated and the dead lived again. I have omitted here the miracles that are unique and belong to the Saviour himself, especially those of his nativity and resurrection. In the one he demonstrated solely the holy mystery of his mother's virginity; in the latter he exhibited a pattern to be followed also by those who will rise again on the last day.

This way cleanses the whole man and, mortal as he is, prepares him for immortality in each of his constituent parts. For we need not seek out one kind of purification for the part that Porphyry calls intellectual, and another for that part that he calls spiritual, and still another for the body itself for the reason that our most true and powerful Cleanser and Saviour took upon himself the whole man. Apart from this way, which has never been wanting to the

facta nuntiantur, numquam generi humano defuit,
nemo liberatus est, nemo liberatur, nemo liberabitur.

Quod autem Porphyrius universalem viam animae
liberandae nondum in suam notitiam historiali cognitione dicit esse perlatam, quid hac historia vel in-
lustrius inveniri potest quae universum orbem tanto
apice auctoritatis obtinuit, vel fidelius, in qua ita
narrantur praeterita ut futura etiam praedicantur,
quorum multa videmus impleta, ex quibus ea quae
restant sine dubio speremus implenda?

Non enim potest Porphyrius vel quicumque Platonici etiam in hac via quasi terrenarum rerum et ad
vitam istam mortalem pertinentium divinationem
praedictionemque contemnere, quod merito in aliis
vaticinantibus et quorumlibet modorum vel artium
divinationibus faciunt. Negant enim haec vel
magnorum hominum vel magni esse pendenda, et
recte. Nam vel inferiorum fiunt praesensione
causarum, sicut arte medicinae quibusdem ante-
cedentibus signis plurima eventura valetudini prae-
videntur; vel inmundi daemones sua disposita facta
praenuntiant, quorum ius et in mentibus atque
cupiditatibus iniquorum ad quaeque congruentia

human race—for at one time it is predicted that these things will happen, at other times it is reported that they have happened—no man has been, is being or will be set free.

As for Porphyry's statement that the universal path to the liberation of the soul has never yet been brought to his attention in the course of his historical research, what can be found more striking than the history that has come to dominate the whole world because its authority is the very highest? What can be found more reliable, since in relating the past it predicts the future at the same time, and we see that many of its predictions have been manifestly fulfilled and by the example of these we expect without a doubt that the remainder are also to be fulfilled?

The fact is that neither Porphyry nor any other Platonists can, in dealing with this way, despise divination and the prediction of what may be described as earthly affairs or affairs that belong to this mortal life, as they justly do when it comes to other soothsayers and other divinations, whatever the method or technique that they employ. They say in fact that such predictions are not the concern of great men and are not to be valued highly; and in this they are right. For sometimes these predictions are made by previous observation of secondary factors, as when the physician's art by observing certain antecedent symptoms foresees to a great extent the course that an illness will take. Or again, unclean demons predict the deeds that they have arranged to do, and they assume for themselves the right, as it were, of bringing these about by guiding the thoughts and desires of the unrighteous and inducing them to

417

facta ducendis quodam modo sibi vindicant, et in
materia infima fragilitatis humanae. Non talia
sancti homines in ista universali animarum liber-
andarum via gradientes tamquam magna prophetare
curarunt, quamvis et ista eos non fugerint et ab eis
saepe praedicta sint ad eorum fidem faciendam quae
mortalium sensibus non poterant intimari nec ad
experimentum celeri facilitate perduci.

Sed alia erant vere magna atque divina quae
quantum dabatur cognita Dei voluntate futura
nuntiabant. Christus quippe in carne venturus et
quae in illo tam clara perfecta sunt atque in eius
nomine impleta, paenitentia hominum et ad Deum
conversio voluntatum, remissio peccatorum, gratia
iustitiae, fides piorum et per universum orbem in
veram divinitatem multitudo credentium, culturae
simulacrorum daemonumque subversio et a tempta-
tionibus exercitatio, proficientium purgatio et libera-
tio ab omni malo, iudicii dies, resurrectio mortuorum,
societatis impiorum aeterna damnatio regnumque
aeternum gloriosissimae civitatis Dei conspectu eius
inmortaliter perfruentis in huius viae scripturis
praedicta atque promissa sunt; quorum tam multa
impleta conspicimus ut recta pietate futura esse
cetera confidamus. Huius viae rectitudinem usque

---

[1] Cf. above, Book 9.22.

act in ways that in each case suit these predictions; they operate upon the very dregs of human frailty.[1] It was not such things as these that holy men, as they walked in this universal path for the liberation of souls, took pains to prophesy as if such matters were deemed important, although even the unimportant did not elude them. For they did also frequently predict such things in order to strengthen belief in realities that could not be presented to mortal senses or be brought to the test of experience in any quick and easy way.

But there were other events truly great and divine which they announced as destined to occur, in so far as it was given them to know the will of God, such as the coming of Christ in the flesh with all the glorious things that were accomplished in his person or fulfilled in his name, the repentance of men and the conversion of their wills to God, the remission of sins, the grace of righteousness, the faith of the pious, and the great multitude of men throughout the whole world who believe in true divinity. Such too were the overthrow of idol and demon worship, the trial of the faithful by temptations, the purification of those who persevere and their deliverance from all evil, the day of judgement, the resurrection of the dead, the eternal damnation of the community of unbelievers, and the everlasting reign of the most glorious City of God with perpetual enjoyment of his visible presence. All these were predicted and promised in the sacred writings concerning this way, and we see so many of them fulfilled that with true religion we have confidence that all the others will come to pass. As for those who do not believe and

ad Deum videndum eique in aeternum cohaerendum in sanctarum scripturarum qua praedicatur atque adseritur veritate quicumque non credunt et ob hoc nec intellegunt, oppugnare possunt, sed expugnare non possunt.

Quapropter in decem istis libris, etsi minus quam nonnullorum de nobis expectabat intentio, tamen quorundam studio, quantum verus Deus et Dominus adiuvare dignatus est, satisfecimus refutando contradictiones impiorum, qui conditori sanctae civitatis, de qua disputare instituimus, deos suos praeferunt.

Quorum decem librorum quinque superiores adversus eos conscripti sunt qui propter bona vitae huius deos colendos putant; quinque autem posteriores adversus eos qui cultum deorum propter vitam quae post mortem futura est servandum existimant. Deinceps itaque, ut in primo libro polliciti sumus, de duarum civitatum quas in hoc saeculo perplexas diximus invicemque permixtas exortu et procursu et debitis finibus quod dicendum arbitror, quantum divinitus adiuvabor expediam.

hence cannot know that this path leads straight all the way to a vision of God and everlasting union with him, as is truly asserted and affirmed in the holy Scriptures, they may storm at, but they cannot storm down our stronghold.

So, in these ten books of mine, I have satisfied, although less perfectly than the eager hope of a good many expected of me, yet I have, as far as the true God and Lord has seen fit to give me aid, satisfied the zeal of certain men for the cause by refuting the objections of the irreligious, who prefer their own gods to the Founder of the holy City, the City which is the theme that I have undertaken to discuss.

Of these ten books, the first five were written in answer to those who think that we should worship the gods in order to secure the good things of this life, the second five in answer to those who hold that the worship of gods should be preserved for the sake of life after death. Accordingly, as I promised in the first book, I shall next set forth what I think needs to be said, as far as I receive divine assistance, concerning the origin, the progress and the final merited ends of the two cities that, as I have said, are thoroughly interwoven and blended together in our present age.

BOOK XI

LIBER XI

I

De ea parte operis qua duarum civitatum,
id est caelestis atque terrenae,
initia et fines incipient
demonstrari.

CIVITATEM Dei dicimus cuius ea scriptura testis est
quae non fortuitis motibus animorum, sed plane
summae dispositione providentiae super omnes
omnium gentium litteras omnia sibi genera ingenio-
rum humanorum divina excellens auctoritate subiecit.
Ibi quippe scriptum est: *Gloriosa dicta sunt de te,
civitas Dei;* et in alio psalmo legitur: *Magnus
Dominus et laudabilis nimis in civitate Dei nostri, in
monte sancto eius, dilatans exultationes universae terrae;*
et paulo post in eodem psalmo: *Sicut audivimus, ita
et vidimus, in civitate domini virtutum, in civitate Dei
nostri; Deus fundavit eam in aeternum;* item in alio:
*Fluminis impetus laetificat civitatem Dei, sanctificavit
tabernaculum suum Altissimus; Deus in medio eius non
commovebitur.* His atque huius modi testimoniis,

---

[1] For the supremacy of the Scriptures, see *De Doctrina
Christiana* 2.63.
[2] Psalm 87.3.
[3] Psalm 48.1–2, 8 (Septuagint).
[4] Psalm 46.4–5.

BOOK XI

I

*An introduction to the part of this work in which
the beginnings and the ends of the two cities,
the heavenly and the earthly, will be
discussed.*

By the City of God we mean the city to which the
Scriptures bear witness, the Scriptures that have
gained dominion over every branch of human genius,
not by virtue of any random activity of men's minds
but by the decree of Providence Most High, surpassing every literary work of every nation because of
their divine authority.[1]   They tell us, to wit: " Glorious things are spoken of thee, O city of God ";[2]
and in another psalm we read: " Great is the Lord
and greatly to be praised in the city of our God, in
his holy mountain, spreading far and wide the rejoic-
ings of the whole earth ";   and a little later in the
same psalm: " As we have heard, so have we also
seen in the city of the Lord of hosts, in the city of our
God: God has established it for ever ";[3] and again
in another: " A rushing river makes glad the city of
God, the Most High has sanctified his tabernacle;
God is in the midst of her, he will not be moved."[4]
By these and similar testimonies, which are too many
to cite all of them, we are instructed that there is a

quae omnia commemorare nimis longum est, didicimus esse quandam civitatem Dei, cuius cives esse concupivimus illo amore quem nobis illius conditor inspiravit. Huic conditori sanctae civitatis cives terrenae civitatis deos suos praeferunt ignorantes eum esse Deum deorum, non deorum falsorum, hoc est impiorum et superborum, qui eius incommutabili omnibusque communi luce privati et ob hoc ad quandam egenam potestatem redacti suas quodam modo privatas potentias consectantur honoresque divinos a deceptis subditis quaerunt; sed deorum piorum atque sanctorum, qui potius se ipsos uni subdere quam multos sibi, potiusque Deum colere quam pro Deo coli delectantur.

Sed huius sanctae civitatis inimicis decem superioribus libris, quantum potuimus, domino et rege nostro adiuvante respondimus. Nunc vero quid a me iam expectetur agnoscens meique non inmemor debiti de duarum civitatum, terrenae scilicet et caelestis, quas in hoc interim saeculo perplexas quodam modo diximus invicemque permixtas, exortu et excursu et debitis finibus, quantum valuero, disputare eius ipsius domini et regis nostri ubique opitulatione fretus adgrediar, primumque dicam quem ad modum exordia duarum istarum civitatum in angelorum diversitate praecesserint.

---

[1] See *City of God*, Book 1, preface.

City of God, of which it has become our heart's desire
to be citizens because of the love that its Founder
has inspired in us. The citizens of the earthly city
give preference to their own gods over the Founder
of the holy city, because they do not know that he is
the God of gods, and not of false gods who are impious and proud and who, being deprived of his unchangeable light in which all may share, are thereby
reduced to a kind of poverty-stricken power. They
strive after their own personal privileges, so to speak,
and seek divine honours from their deluded subjects.
He is, rather, the God of pious and holy gods whose
delight it is to do homage to the one God rather than
to receive homage from many others, and to worship
God rather than to be worshipped in place of God.

Well, we have answered the enemies of the holy
city in the ten preceding books, as far as we could,
with the help of our Lord and King. Now, however,
recognizing what is expected of me at this point and
not forgetting my duty, but relying on the ever-
present help of that same Lord and King, I shall
endeavour, as far as I am able, to discuss the origin,
course, and final merited ends of the two cities, by
which I mean the earthly and the heavenly. As I
have said, they are interwoven, as it were, and blended
together in this transitory age.[1] I shall first tell
how these two cities had their first origin in a parting
of the ways among the angels.

II

De cognoscendo Deo, ad cuius notitiam nemo hominum
pervenit nisi per mediatorem Dei et hominum,
hominem Christum Iesum.

MAGNUM est et admodum rarum universam creaturam corpoream et incorpoream consideratam com-
pertamque mutabilem intentione mentis excedere
atque ad incommutabilem Dei substantiam pervenire
et illic discere ex ipso quod cunctam naturam quae
non est quod ipse, non fecit nisi ipse. Sic enim
Deus cum homine non per aliquam creaturam loquitur corporalem, corporalibus instrepens auribus, ut
inter sonantem et audientem aeria spatia verberen-
tur, neque per eius modi spiritalem quae corporum
similitudinibus figuratur, sicut in somnis vel quo alio
tali modo—nam et sic velut corporis auribus loquitur,
quia velut per corpus loquitur et velut interposito
corporalium locorum intervallo; multum enim similia
sunt talia visa corporibus—, sed loquitur ipsa veritate
si quis sit idoneus ad audiendum mente, non corpore.
Ad illud enim hominis ita loquitur quod in homine
ceteris quibus homo constat est melius, et quo ipse
Deus solus est melior.

Cum enim homo rectissime intellegatur vel, si hoc
non potest, saltem credatur factus ad imaginem Dei,
profecto ea sui parte est propinquior superiori Deo

---

[1] Cf. *De Genesi ad Litteram* 12.4-8.
[2] See Genesis 1.26.

II

*On the knowledge of God, to which no man attains
save through the Mediator between God and
men, the man Christ Jesus.*

IT is a great and very unusual thing for a man, after
he has contemplated all creation, corporeal and incorporeal, and found it to be subject to change, to
pass beyond it by concentrated thought and so to
arrive at the unchangeable substance of God, and
there to learn from God himself that all nature that
is not identical with himself has been made by none
other than he. For so it comes that God speaks
to man, not by means of some material creation,
making a noise for material ears by concussion of the
air-filled spaces between the source of sound and the
hearer of it, nor through a spiritual agency [1]
that takes on the form and likeness of bodies, as in dreams
or anything else of that kind; for even in this case
he speaks as if for the ears of a body, because it is
by means of a body that he appears to speak and
with an appearance of material space intervening;
for such imaginary visions are very like bodies. No,
he speaks with the voice of truth itself, if anyone is
attuned to hear him with his mind, not using the body.
He speaks to that in man which is superior to all the
rest of his substance, and which has no superior save
God alone.

Now since intelligence, or if this is impossible, at
any rate faith, quite accurately teaches us that man
was made in the image of God,[2] assuredly he is nearer
to God, who is his superior, by virtue of the part of

429

qua superat inferiores suas, quas etiam cum pecoribus communes habet. Sed quia ipsa mens, cui ratio et intellegentia naturaliter inest, vitiis quibusdam tenebrosis et veteribus invalida est non solum ad inhaerendum fruendo, verum etiam ad perferendum incommutabile lumen, donec de die in diem renovata atque sanata fiat tantae felicitatis capax, fide primum fuerat inbuenda atque purganda. In qua ut fidentius ambularet ad veritatem, ipsa veritas, Deus Dei filius, homine adsumpto, non Deo consumpto, eandem constituit et fundavit fidem, ut ad hominis Deum iter esset homini per hominem Deum. Hic est enim mediator Dei et hominum, homo Christus Iesus. Per hoc enim mediator per quod homo, per hoc et via. Quoniam si inter eum qui tendit et illud quo tendit via media est, spes est perveniendi; si autem desit aut ignoretur qua eundum sit, quid prodest nosse quo eundum sit? Sola est autem adversus omnes errores via munitissima, ut idem ipse sit Deus et homo; quo itur Deus, qua itur homo.

III

De auctoritate canonicae scripturae divino spiritu conditae.

Hic prius per prophetas, deinde per se ipsum, postea per apostolos, quantum satis esse iudicavit,

---

[1] I Timothy 2.5.
[2] See John 14.6; Hebrews 10.20.

himself whereby he rises above his baser parts that he has in common with the beasts as well. But because our very mind, that natural seat of reason and understanding, is enfeebled by certain old faults that obscure its clarity and is prevented not only from embracing and enjoying, but even from enduring the unchangeable light until this mind has been renewed from day to day and so healed, thereby becoming equal to such felicity, it had first to be dipped and soaked in faith and so cleansed. In order that in this faith it might make progress with greater confidence towards the goal of truth, Truth itself, God the son of God, put on manhood without putting off godhead and established and founded this same faith, so that man might find a path to the God of man through the godman. Here then is the Mediator between God and men, the man Christ Jesus.[1] For inasmuch as he is man, he is the Mediator, and as man he is the way.[2] If there is a connecting way between the striver and the goal towards which he is striving, he has hope of reaching it; but if there is none, or if he has no knowledge what way to take, of what avail is it to know the goal that he is to reach? Now the only way that is completely proof against mistakes is the way created when the same person is both God and man, God being the goal and man the way.

III

On the authority of the canonical Scriptures composed by the Divine Spirit.

THIS Mediator first through the prophets, then through himself and later through the apostles, said

locutus etiam scripturam condidit quae canonica nominatur, eminentissimae auctoritatis, cui fidem habemus de his rebus quas ignorare non expedit nec per nos ipsos nosse idonei sumus. Nam si ea sciri possunt testibus nobis quae remota non sunt a sensibus nostris sive interioribus sive etiam exterioribus—unde et praesentia nuncupantur, quod ita ea dicimus esse prae sensibus, sicut prae oculis quae praesto sunt oculis—, profecto ea quae remota sunt a sensibus nostris, quoniam nostro testimonio scire non possumus, de his alios testes requirimus eisque credimus a quorum sensibus remota esse vel fuisse non credimus. Sicut ergo de visibilibus quae non vidimus, eis credimus, qui viderunt, atque ita de ceteris quae ad suum quemque sensum corporis pertinent, ita de his quae animo ac mente sentiuntur —quia et ipse rectissime dicitur sensus, unde et sententia vocabulum accepit—, hoc est de invisibilibus quae a nostro sensu interiore remota sunt, his nos oportet credere qui haec in illo incorporeo lumine disposita didicerunt vel manentia contuentur.

as much as he thought sufficient and in addition
established the Scriptures which are called canonical;
they have pre-eminent authority, and we put faith
in them concerning matters of which it is not good
to be ignorant, but which we are not capable of
knowing by ourselves.   For if we can know and vouch
for those things that are not removed from our senses,
whether these senses are internal or even external—
and that is why such things are spoken of as " present," because we say that they are presented to our
senses, just as what is before our eyes is presented to
them—yet we cannot know and vouch for what is
removed from our senses.   Certainly we must have
other witnesses in these cases and put our trust in
those from whose senses we do not believe these
things to be or to have been removed.   Therefore,
just as in the case of visible objects unseen by us we
believe those who have seen them, and likewise
where the other individual bodily senses are concerned, so with respect to the things that the mind
and heart sense—for the word *sensus* or ' sense ' is
quite correct here and has given us the word *sententia*
or judgement—that is to say, with respect to invisible
things not present to our inner sense, we are bound to
believe those who have learned of them as they are
exhibited under that incorporeal light, or who hold
them in lasting contemplation.

IV

*De conditione mundi, quae nec intemporalis sit, nec
novo Dei ordinata consilio, quasi postea voluerit
quod ante noluerat.*

VISIBILIUM omnium maximus mundus est, invisi-
bilium omnium maximus Deus est. Sed mundum
esse conspicimus, Deum esse credimus. Quod
autem Deus fecerit mundum, nulli tutius credimus
quam ipsi Deo. Ubi eum audivimus? Nusquam
interim nos melius quam in scripturis sanctis, ubi
dixit propheta eius: *In principio fecit Deus caelum
et terram.* Numquidnam ibi fuit iste propheta, quando fecit Deus caelum et terram? Non; sed ibi fuit
sapientia Dei, per quam facta sunt omnia, quae in
animas sanctas etiam se transfert, amicos Dei et prophetas constituit eisque opera sua sine strepitu
intus enarrat. Loquuntur eis quoque angeli Dei,
qui semper vident faciem Patris voluntatemque
eius quibus oportet adnuntiant. Ex his unus erat
iste propheta qui dixit et scripsit: *In principio fecit
Deus caelum et terram.* Qui tam idoneus testis est
per quem Deo credendum sit, ut eodem spiritu Dei
quo haec sibi revelata cognovit, etiam ipsam fidem
nostram futuram tanto ante praedixerit.

---

[1] Genesis 1.1.
[2] Cf. Proverbs 8.27.
[3] Cf. Wisdom 7.27.
[4] Matthew 18.10.

IV

On the creation of the universe, which is neither independent of time nor ordained by a new decision of God, as if he later chose to do what he formerly had not chosen to do.

OF all visible things the universe is the greatest, just as God is the greatest of all that are invisible. But we behold the existence of the universe, while we only believe that God exists. Yet we have no more trustworthy witness than God himself to testify that he made the universe. Where did we hear him speak? Nowhere more clearly as yet than in the holy Scriptures, where his prophet said: "In the beginning God created the heaven and the earth."[1] Was this prophet there when God created the heaven and earth?[2] No, but the wisdom of God, by which all things were created, was there; and this wisdom also passes into holy souls, making them friends of God and mouthpieces for him[3] and giving them noiselessly and inwardly an account of his works. The angels of God as well, who always behold the face of their Father[4] and announce his will to anyone whom it befits to know it, speak to them too. One among these was the prophet who said and wrote: "In the beginning God created the heaven and the earth." And so proper a witness is he to convince us that we should believe in God that, aided by the same spirit of God who revealed this truth for him to know, he also predicted so long beforehand the coming faith that was to be ours.

Sed quid placuit aeterno Deo tunc facere caelum et terram quae antea non fecisset? Qui hoc dicunt, si mundum aeternum sine ullo initio et ideo nec a Deo factum videri volunt, nimis aversi sunt a veritate et letali morbo impietatis insaniunt. Exceptis enim propheticis vocibus mundus ipse ordinatissima sua mutabilitate et mobilitate et visibilium omnium pulcherrima specie quodam modo tacitus et factum se esse et non nisi a Deo ineffabiliter atque invisibiliter magno et ineffabiliter atque invisibiliter pulchro fieri se potuisse proclamat.

Qui autem a Deo quidem factum fatentur, non tamen eum temporis volunt habere, sed suae creationis initium, ut modo quodam vix intellegibili semper sit factus, dicunt quidem aliquid unde sibi Deum videntur velut a fortuita temeritate defendere, ne subito illi venisse credatur in mentem quod numquam ante venisset, facere mundum, et accidisse illi voluntatem novam, cum in nullo sit omnino mutabilis; sed non video quo modo eis possit in ceteris rebus ratio ista subsistere maximeque in anima, quam si Deo coaeternam esse contenderint, unde illi acciderit nova miseria quae numquam antea per aeternum, nullo modo poterunt explicare. Si enim alternasse semper eius miseriam et beatitudinem dixerint, necesse est dicant etiam semper alter-

---

[1] Cf. *Confessions* 11.12.14.
[2] The Neoplatonists in particular. See above, Book 10.31.

But why did the eternal God decide at that time to create the heaven and the earth which hitherto he had not created?[1] If those who speak thus would have it that the universe is eternal, without a beginning, and therefore not created by God, they turn their backs too much on truth and are mortally infected with the deadly plague of irreligion. For, even if no prophet had uttered a word, the universe itself, such is the perfect order of its ever-shifting and constant motions and so fair the spectacle it affords of all things visible—the universe cries aloud, as it were, without saying a word, declaring both that it was created and that it could only have been created by a God who is ineffably and invisibly great and ineffably and invisibly beautiful.

But there are those too[2] who agree that the universe was indeed created by God but refuse to allow it a beginning of time, but only of its creation, so that in some scarcely intelligible way it was always created. They have, to be sure, a point in saying this, for it enables them to suppose that they are defending God against the charge of acting on random impulse. They would not have us believe that the idea suddenly occurred to him, which never had entered his mind before, of creating the universe, and that a new act of will took place in him, although he is utterly unchangeable in any respect. But I do not see how this theory of theirs can stand, when we consider the rest of creation and especially the soul. If they maintain that the soul is co-eternal with God, they will be quite unable to explain the source of any new misery which happens to it for the first time and never happened before in all eternity. For suppose them to

437

naturam; unde illa eos sequetur absurditas, ut etiam cum beata dicitur in hoc utique non sit beata, si futuram suam miseriam et turpitudinem praevidet; si autem non praevidet nec se turpem ac miseram fore, sed beatam semper existimat, falsa opinione sit beata; quo dici stultius nihil potest. Si autem semper quidem per saecula retro infinita cum beatitudine alternasse animae miseriam putant, sed nunc iam de cetero, cum fuerit liberata, ad miseriam non esse redituram, nihilo minus convincuntur numquam eam fuisse vere beatam, sed deinceps esse incipere nova quadam nec fallaci beatitudine; ac per hoc fatebuntur accidere illi aliquid novi, et hoc magnum atque praeclarum, quod numquam retro per aeternitatem accidisset.

Cuius novitatis causam si Deum negabunt in aeterno habuisse consilio, simul eum negabunt beatitudinis eius auctorem, quod nefandae impietatis est; si autem dicent etiam ipsum novo consilio excogitasse ut de cetero sit anima in aeternum beata, quo modo eum alienum ab ea quae illis quoque displicet mutabilitate monstrabunt? Porro si ex tempore creatam, sed nullo ulterius tempore perituram, tamquam numerum, habere initium, sed non habere finem

---

[1] Cf. *City of God*, 12.19.

declare that its misery and blessedness have always
succeeded each other, they must also say that this
shifting from one to the other will go on for ever.
This will involve them in the absurdity that even
when the soul is said to be blessed, it is certainly not
so, in so far at least as it foresees its own misery and
coming shame. If on the other hand it does not
foresee its coming misery and shame, but counts on
being for ever blessed, it must be that it is happy because it is mistaken, which is as stupid a statement
as could well be made.[1] Suppose them to assume,
however, that though for infinite ages past the soul
has known such alternate states of misery and bliss,
yet for the rest of time to come, after its next release from misery, it will not return to it, they are no
less convicted of holding that it never was truly blessed
before but only now begins to be endowed with bliss
of a new sort that is not an illusion. This amounts to
an admission that something new happens to it, a
great and resounding change such as had never
happened before in the eternity of time past.

Now if they refuse to admit that God included in
his eternal purpose some cause of this new experience, they will at the same time be saying that he
was not the author of this blessedness of the soul,
and that is an unspeakably blasphemous statement.
If again they say that he conceived a new purpose,
and decided to make the soul from now on eternally
blessed, how will they show that he is exempt from
the changeability which they also refuse to accept?
Furthermore, if they admit that the soul was created
in time but will never perish in any future time and
that it is like the series of numbers in having a be-

fatentur, et ideo semel expertam miserias, si ab eis
fuerit liberata, numquam miseram postea futuram,
non utique dubitabunt hoc fieri manente incom-
mutabilitate consilii Dei. Sic ergo credant et mundum ex tempore fieri potuisse, nec tamen ideo Deum
in eo faciendo aeternum consilium voluntatemque
mutasse.

V

Tam non esse cogitandum de infinitis temporum
spatiis ante mundum quam nec de infinitis
locorum spatiis extra mundum, quia,
sicut nulla ante ipsum sunt tem-
pora, ita nulla extra ipsum
sunt loca.

DEINDE videndum est, isti qui Deum conditorem
mundi esse consentiunt et tamen quaerunt de mundi
tempore quid respondeamus, quid ipsi respondeant
de mundi loco. Ita enim quaeritur cur potius tunc
et non antea factus sit, quem ad modum quaeri potest
cur hic potius ubi est et non alibi. Nam si infinita
spatia temporis ante mundum cogitant in quibus eis
non videtur Deus ab opere cessare potuisse, similiter
cogitent extra mundum infinita spatia locorum, in
440

ginning but not an end, and that therefore, after experiencing miseries and being released from them, it will never be miserable thereafter, they will certainly have no doubt that this takes place without any impairment of the unchangeability of God's purpose. Similarly, then, let them believe that it was possible for the universe to be created in time, but that God did not on that account change his eternal will and purpose in creating it.

V

We should not try to comprehend the infinite expanses of time preceding the existence of the universe any more than we should the infinite expanses of space outside the universe, because, just as there are no periods of time before it, so there are no positions in space outside it.

Next we must see what reply we should make to those who agree that God is the creator of the universe and yet ask questions about its location in time, and what answer they themselves will make about its location in space. For just as men inquire why it was created at that particular moment and not earlier, so the question may arise why it was created here where it is and not elsewhere. For if they contemplate infinite expanses of time preceding the existence of the universe during which, they are convinced, God could not have remained unoccupied, let them contemplate in the same way infinite posi-

quibus si quisquam dicat non potuisse vacare Omnipotentem, nonne consequens erit ut innumerabiles mundos cum Epicuro somniare cogantur—ea tantum differentia, quod eos ille fortuitis motibus atomorum gigni asserit et resolvi, isti autem opere Dei factos dicturi sunt—, si eum per interminabilem inmensitatem locorum extra mundum circumquaque patentium vacare noluerint, nec eosdem mundos, quod etiam de isto sentiunt, ulla causa posse dissolvi?

Cum his enim agimus qui et Deum incorporeum et omnium naturarum quae non sunt quod ipse creatorem nobiscum sentiunt; alios autem nimis indignum est ad istam disputationem religionis admittere, maxime quod apud eos qui multis diis sacrorum obsequium deferendum putant, isti philosophos ceteros nobilitate atque auctoritate vicerunt, non ob aliud nisi quia longo quidem intervallo, verum tamen reliquis propinquiores sunt veritati.

An forte substantiam Dei, quam nec includunt nec determinant nec distendunt loco, sed eam, sicut de Deo sentire dignum est, fatentur incorporea praesentia ubique totam, a tantis locorum extra mundum spatiis absentem esse dicturi sunt, et uno tantum

---

[1] See above, Book 8.6; *De Vera Religione* 4.7.

tions in space outside the universe. Now if anyone were to say that the Omnipotent could not have been inactive in those places, will it not follow that they are compelled to dream with Epicurus of the existence of countless universes? The only difference will be that he asserts that they come into being and break up again by the random movement of atoms, while they will say that the universes were created by the action of God. It must be so if they will not leave him unproductive throughout the boundless immensity of positions in space that open out in all directions, and if they also extend to those universes their view of this one and conclude that they cannot pass away for any reason.

Note that we are dealing now with those who agree with us that God is both incorporeal and the creator of all creatures that are not identical with himself. For it would be lowering ourselves too far to admit others to this debate on a religious subject. Our strongest reason is that among those who believe that many gods may duly claim the honour of religious service, those of whom I speak have outstripped other philosophers in prestige and authority precisely because, though they are indeed far from the truth, yet for all that they are nearer to it than the rest.[1]

Can these philosophers possibly regard the divine nature as unenclosed, unbounded, and unextended in space, and admit, as right feeling about God requires them to, that it is everywhere incorporeally present in its entirety, while at the same time asserting that it is absent from the vast spaces outside the universe, and is busy with only the one place in which the

443

atque in comparatione illius infinitatis tam exiguo loco in quo mundus est occupatam? Non opinor eos in haec vaniloquia progressuros.

Cum igitur unum mundum ingenti quidem mole corporea, finitum tamen et loco suo determinatum et operante Deo factum esse dicant, quod respondent de infinitis extra mundum locis, cur in eis ab opere Deus cesset, hoc sibi respondeant de infinitis ante mundum temporibus, cur in eis ab opere Deus cessaverit. Et sicut non est consequens ut fortuito potius quam ratione divina Deus non alio, sed isto in quo est loco mundum constituerit, cum pariter infinitis ubique patentibus nullo excellentiore merito posset hic eligi, quamvis eandem divinam rationem qua id factum est nulla possit humana conprehendere, ita non est consequens ut Deo aliquid existimemus accidisse fortuitum quod illo potius quam anteriore tempore condidit mundum, cum aequaliter anteriora tempora per infinitum retro spatium praeterissent nec fuisset aliqua differentia unde tempus tempori eligendo praeponeretur. Quod si dicunt inanes esse hominum cogitationes quibus infinita imaginantur loca, cum locus nullus sit praeter mundum, respondetur eis isto modo inaniter homines cogitare prae-

universe is located, tiny though it is in comparison with the infinite space of which we have spoken? My opinion is that they will stop short of such empty bombast.

We may assume, then, that they declare that there is a single universe of huge material bulk, yet finite, limited to its own place in space, and created by the action of God. Well, when the question arises about the infinite ages of time before the creation of the universe and why God has remained inactive and inoperative during them, they may give themselves the same answer that they give when asked about the infinite spaces outside the universe and why God remains inactive and inoperative in them. Now it is no necessary conclusion that God acted at random rather than by divine reason when he established the universe in no other place than where it is, though the place he chose had no special claim to be preferred over an infinite number of others which extended in every direction and though we must admit that no human reason can grasp the divine reason that dictated such action. But it is equally illogical to suppose that God was moved by a random whim to establish the universe at that particular time rather than earlier, although it is true that earlier periods of time had been elapsing, all in the same manner, throughout the infinite extent of the past and no difference can be found that might cause one time to be chosen rather than another. But they may say that it is idle for man to contemplate infinite regions of space, since there is no place outside the universe. Our reply to them is that by the same token it is idle for man to contemplate bygone eras

445

terita tempora vacationis Dei, cum tempus nullum
sit ante mundum.

VI

*Creationis mundi et temporum unum esse principium
nec aliud alio praeveniri.*

Si enim recte discernuntur aeternitas et tempus
quod tempus sine aliqua mobili mutabilitate non est,
in aeternitate autem nulla mutatio est, quis non
videat quod tempora non fuissent nisi creatura fieret
quae aliquid aliqua motione mutaret, cuius motionis
et mutationis cum aliud atque aliud, quae simul esse
non possunt, cedit atque succedit, in brevioribus
vel productioribus morarum intervallis tempus
sequeretur? Cum igitur Deus, in cuius aeternitate
nulla est omnino mutatio, creator sit temporum et
ordinator, quo modo dicatur post temporum spatia
mundum creasse non video, nisi dicatur ante mundum iam aliquam fuisse creaturam cuius motibus
tempora currerent.

Porro si litterae sacrae maximeque veraces ita dicunt in principio fecisse Deum caelum et terram ut
nihil antea fecisse intellegatur, quia hoc potius in
principio fecisse diceretur si quid fecisset ante cetera
cuncta quae fecit, procul dubio non est mundus factus

---

[1] St. Augustine frequently takes up the problem of time, its
essential nature, and its relationship to eternity, e.g. *City of
God*, 10. 31 and 12. 15; *Confessions* 11.14.17; *Sermon*
117.10.VII. Boethius in his *Consolation of Philosophy*, Book

in which God did nothing, since there is no time
before a universe exists.

VI

*The creation of the universe and of units of time
had one and the same beginning, and neither
came before the other.*

For if eternity and time are rightly distinguished
in that time does not exist without some movement
and change, while there is no change in eternity, who
could not see that time would not have existed unless
something had been created to cause change by
some movement?[1] Since the different stages of this
movement and change cannot exist simultaneously,
one stage gives way and another takes its place; time
is based on the shorter or longer intervals between the
stages. Therefore, since God, in whose eternity
there is no change at all, is the creator and regulator
of periods of time, I do not see how it can be said
that he created the universe after lapses of time, unless we say that before the universe was created there
was already in existence some created body whose
movements could mark the passage of time.

Furthermore, if the sacred and wholly true Scriptures say that in the beginning God created the
heaven and the earth and mean us to understand by
this that he had created nothing before that because
if he had created anything before all the other things
that he created, he would rather be said to have

5.6 sets forth at length the different characteristics of time and
eternity.

in tempore, sed cum tempore. Quod enim fit in tempore, et post aliquod fit et ante aliquod tempus; post id quod praeteritum est, ante id quod futurum est; nullum autem posset esse praeteritum, quia nulla erat creatura cuius mutabilibus motibus ageretur. Cum tempore autem factus est mundus si in eius conditione factus est mutabilis motus, sicut videtur se habere etiam ordo ille primorum sex vel septem dierum, in quibus et mane et vespera nominantur, donec omnia quae his diebus Deus fecit sexto perficiantur die septimoque in magno mysterio Dei vacatio commendetur. Qui dies cuius modi sint, aut perdifficile nobis aut etiam inpossibile est cogitare, quanto magis dicere.

VII

De qualitate primorum dierum, qui etiam antequam
sol fieret vesperam et mane traduntur habuisse.

VIDEMUS quippe istos dies notos non habere vesperam nisi de solis occasu nec mane nisi de solis exortu; illorum autem priores tres dies sine sole peracti sunt, qui die quarto factus refertur. Et primitus quidem lux verbo Dei facta atque inter ipsam et tenebras Deus separasse narratur et eandem lucem vocasse

---

[1] For this symbolic significance, see below, Chapters VIII and XXXI.

created this in the beginning, there can be no doubt that the universe was created not in time but along with time. For what is created in time is created both after and before some extent of time, after the past and before the future; but there could have been no past time because there was no created body by whose changing motions time could be enacted. Now the universe was created along with time if in the course of its framing a changing motion was created; this condition is seen fulfilled even in the recorded sequence of the first six or seven days. In that sequence both morning and evening are mentioned daily until everything that God created on those days was finished on the sixth; and on the seventh God's resting is brought in with profound symbolic significance.[1] What these days were like it is highly difficult or even impossible for us to imagine, let alone say.

VII

On the character of the first days, which are said to have had morning and evening before the sun was created.

WE see, I mean to say, that days as we know them have an evening only as a result of sunset and a morning only as a result of sunrise. But the first three days of creation passed without any sun; the sun is reported to have been created on the fourth day. Scripture tells us that originally at least light was created by the word of God, and God is said to have divided the light from the darkness and to have

449

diem, tenebras autem noctem; sed qualis illa sit lux
et quo alternante motu qualemque vesperam et
mane fecerit, remotum est a sensibus nostris, nec
ita ut est intellegi a nobis potest, quod tamen sine
ulla haesitatione credendum est. Aut enim aliqua
lux corporea est, sive in superioribus mundi partibus
longe a conspectibus nostris sive unde sol postmodum
accensus est; aut lucis nomine significata est sancta
civitas in sanctis angelis et spiritibus beatis, de qua
dicit apostolus: *Quae sursum est Hierusalem, mater
nostra aeterna in caelis;* ait quippe et alio loco:
*Omnes enim vos filii lucis estis et filii diei; non sumus
noctis neque tenebrarum;* si tamen et vesperam diei
huius et mane aliquatenus congruenter intellegere
valeamus.

Quoniam scientia creaturae in comparatione
scientiae Creatoris quodam modo vesperascit, itemque lucescit et mane fit cum et ipsa refertur ad laudem
dilectionemque Creatoris; nec in noctem vergitur
ubi non Creator creaturae dilectione relinquitur.
Denique scriptura cum illos dies dinumeraret ex
ordine, nusquam interposuit vocabulum noctis. Non
enim ait alicubi: Facta est nox; sed: *Facta est vespera et factum est mane dies unus.* Ita dies secundus
et ceteri. Cognitio quippe creaturae in se ipsa

---

1 Genesis 1.3–4.
2 Galatians 4.26.
3 I Thessalonians 5.5.
4 Genesis 1.5.

called the light day and the darkness night.[1]   But the nature of that light, by what shift back and forth it caused morning and evening and what kind of thing evening and morning were are questions that are far beyond the reach of our perception.   Nor can our understanding see the way in which it is true, though that it is true we must believe untroubled by doubt.   For either there exists a physical light, whether in the upper regions of the universe far beyond our power of sight or some light from which derived the later inflammation of the sun, or else the word light was used of that holy city, composed of holy angels and blessed spirits, of which the Apostle says: " The Jerusalem that is above, our eternal mother in heaven." [2]   Note that he says elsewhere too: " For you are all sons of light and sons of the day; we are not of the night or of darkness." [3] The only question is whether we are able to find a meaning for the evening and the morning of such a day that will fit this interpretation to some extent.

Well, since the knowledge of a created being may be likened, in comparison with the Creator's knowledge, to the onset of the darkness of evening, we may find likewise a growing dawn or morning when our knowledge is focused on the praise and love of the Creator; and there is no lapse into night when the Creator is not deserted for love of a created thing.   Accordingly, although the Scripture enumerated those first days in order, it nowhere inserted the the word night.   It never says: " Night was made," but instead: " There was made evening and there was made morning, one day." [4]   So also the second day and all the rest.   We must note that the know-

decoloratior est, ut ita dicam, quam cum in Dei
sapientia cognoscitur, velut in arte qua facta est.
Ideo vespera quam nox congruentius dici potest;
quae tamen, ut dixi, cum ad laudandum et amandum
refertur Creatorem, recurrit in mane. Et hoc cum
facit in cognitione sui ipsius, dies unus est; cum in
cognitione firmamenti, quod inter aquas inferiores et
superiores caelum appellatum est, dies secundus;
cum in cognitione terrae ac maris omniumque gignen-
tium, quae radicibus continuata sunt terrae, dies
tertius; cum in cognitione luminarium maioris et
minoris omniumque siderum, dies quartus; cum in
cognitione omnium ex aquis animalium natatilium
atque volatilium, dies quintus; cum in cognitione
omnium animalium terrenorum atque ipsius hominis,
dies sextus.

VIII

*Quae qualisque intellegenda sit Dei requies qua post
opera sex dierum requievit in septimo.*

Cum vero in die septimo requiescit Deus ab omnibus operibus suis et sanctificat eum, nequaquam est
accipiendum pueriliter, tamquam Deus laboraverit

---

[1] See below, Chapter XXIX.

ledge of created entities when seen by themselves is dim and faded, so to speak, in comparison with their brilliance when seen in the realm of God's wisdom, and, as it were, in the design according to which they were made.[1] Therefore the term evening is more appropriate than night. Still, as I have said, night in its course becomes morning again when the creature returns to praise and love of the Creator. And when the creature does this in recognition of itself, that is one day; but when it does so in recognition of the firmament which, lying between the lower and the upper waters, was called heaven, it is the second day. When it does so with recognition of the earth, the sea, and all things that come to life from the earth and are bound to earth by their roots, it is the third day; when it does so with recognition of the greater and lesser luminaries and all the stars, it is the fourth day; when it does so in the recognition of all living things that swim in the waters and of all that fly, it is the fifth day; and when it does so in recognition of every beast of the earth and of man himself, it is the sixth day.

VIII

*How we are to understand God's rest and what sort
of rest it was with which, after six days
of work, he rested on the seventh.*

WHEN, however, God rests from all his work on the seventh day and sanctifies it, this statement must not be childishly taken to mean that God toiled as he worked; for " he commanded and they were

453

operando, qui *dixit et facta sunt* verbo intellegibili et
sempiterno, non sonabili et temporali. Sed requies
Dei requiem significat eorum qui requiescunt in Deo,
sicut laetitia domus laetitiam significat eorum qui
laetantur in domo, etiamsi non eos domus ipsa, sed
alia res aliqua laetos facit. Quanto magis, si eadem
domus pulchritudine sua faciat laetos habitatores, ut
non solum eo loquendi modo laeta dicatur quo significamus per id quod continet id quod continetur—
sicut "theatra plaudunt, prata mugiunt," cum in illis
homines plaudunt, in his boves mugiunt—; sed etiam
illo quo significatur per efficientem id quod efficitur;
sicut laeta epistula dicitur, significans eorum laetitiam
quos legentes efficit laetos. Convenientissime itaque, cum Deum requievisse prophetica narrat
auctoritas, significatur requies eorum qui in illo
requiescunt et quos facit ipse requiescere; hoc etiam
hominibus, quibus loquitur et propter quos utique
conscripta est, promittente prophetia, quod etiam
ipsi post bona opera quae in eis et per eos operatur
Deus, si ad illum prius in ista vita per fidem quodam
modo accesserint, in illo habebunt requiem sempiternam. Hoc enim et sabbati vacatione ex praecepto legis in vetere Dei populo figuratum est, unde
suo loco diligentius arbitror disserendum.

---

1 Psalm 148.5; 33.9.
2 Cf. Hebrews 4.4–11.
3 See *De Genesi ad Litteram* 4.8.15–4.12.23.
4 i.e. the writer of Genesis.
5 *City of God*, Book 22.30.

created." [1] The word of his command was not a
sound in the ear and transitory, but spiritual and
eternal. No, God's resting signifies the rest of
those who rest in God,[2] just as the gladness of a house
signifies the gladness of those who are glad in the
house. This is true even if it is not the house itself
but some other thing that makes them glad; how
much more is this the case if that same house makes
those who live in it glad by its beauty! [3] It is
accordingly called glad, not only by the figure of
speech whereby we use the container for the contained; we say for example that theatres applaud
or meadows low, whereas these are the places where
men applaud and cattle low, but also by the figure
that puts the cause for the effect. So, for example,
we speak of a letter as joyful when we have in mind
the joy of those who are made joyful by reading it.
Accordingly, it is quite proper that, when the prophetic author [4] reports that God rested, he means by
God's rest the rest of those who rest in God and of
whose rest he is the cause. The prophecy is also a
promise to mankind, since it is addressed to man and
was certainly recorded for his benefit, a promise that
men too after the good works that God works in them
and through them, if they have beforehand in this
life made their way to him, as it were, by the path of
faith, will find eternal rest in him. For this rest is
also referred to symbolically in the commandment of
the law enjoining a rest from labour on the sabbath
day among the ancient people of God. This is a
matter that I must discuss more thoroughly in its
proper place.[5]

IX

*De angelorum conditione quid secundum divina testi-
monia sentiendum sit.*

Nunc, quoniam de sanctae civitatis exortu dicere
institui et prius quod ad sanctos angelos adtinet
dicendum putavi, quae huius civitatis et magna pars
est et eo beatior quod numquam peregrinata, quae
hinc divina testimonia suppetant, quantum satis
videbitur, Deo largiente explicare curabo. Ubi de
mundi constitutione sacrae litterae loquuntur, non
evidenter dicitur utrum vel quo ordine creati sint
angeli; sed si praetermissi non sunt, vel caeli nomine,
ubi dictum est: *In principio fecit Deus caelum et
terram*, vel potius lucis huius de qua loquor significati
sunt. Non autem esse praetermissos hinc existimo, quod scriptum est requievisse Deum in die
septimo ab omnibus operibus suis quae fecit, cum
liber ipse ita sit exorsus: *In principio fecit Deus
caelum et terram*; ut ante caelum et terram nihil
aliud fecisse videatur. Cum ergo a caelo et terra
coeperit, atque ipsa terra, quam primitus fecit, sicut
scriptura consequenter eloquitur, invisibilis et incomposita nondumque luce facta utique tenebrae

---

[1] Genesis 1.1.   [2] Genesis 2.2.

IX

What conclusion we should reach, relying on scriptural evidence, about the creation of angels.

Since I have taken it upon me to speak of the origin of the holy city and have thought fit to speak first of the holy angels who not only form a large part of it but are all the more blessed because they have known no pilgrimage in this world, I shall now, as far as God is gracious to me, attempt to explain the information that is furnished on this topic by the evidence of God's word, and at such length as shall seem appropriate. When holy Scripture speaks of the creation of the universe, it does not say clearly whether, or at what point, the angels were created; but if they have not been omitted, they are either meant by the word heaven, where Scripture says, " In the beginning God created the heaven and the earth," [1] or they are rather included in the meaning of that light of which I have spoken. My reason for thinking that they have not been omitted is the statement that God rested on the seventh day from all his works which he had done,[2] combined with the statement with which the book opens. " In the beginning God created the heaven and the earth," which implies, apparently, that he created nothing before he created the heaven and the earth. Thus the heaven and the earth were the beginning of creation. And the earth itself, which he made in the beginning was, as Scripture goes on to say, invisible and inchoate; and as light had not yet been created, certainly darkness was

457

fuerint super abyssum, id est super quandam terrae
et aquae indistinctam confusionem—ubi enim lux non
est, tenebrae sint necesse est—, deinde omnia creando
disposita sint, quae per sex dies consummata narrantur, quo modo angeli praetermitterentur, tamquam
non essent in operibus Dei a quibus in die septimo
requievit?

Opus autem Dei esse angelos hic quidem etsi non
praetermissum, non tamen evidenter expressum est;
sed alibi hoc sancta scriptura clarissima voce testatur.
Nam et in hymno trium in camino virorum cum
praedictum esset: *Benedicite omnia opera Domini
Dominum*, in executione eorundem operum etiam
angeli nominati sunt; et in psalmo canitur: *Laudate
Dominum de caelis, laudate eum in excelsis; laudate
eum omnes angeli eius, laudate eum omnes virtutes eius;
laudate eum sol et luna, laudate eum omnes stellae et
lumen; laudate eum caeli caelorum, et aquae quae super
caelos sunt, laudent nomen Domini; quoniam ipse dixit,
et facta sunt; ipse mandavit, et creata sunt.* Etiam hic
apertissime a Deo factos esse angelos divinitus dictum est, cum eis inter cetera caelestia commemoratis infertur ad omnia: *Ipse dixit, et facta sunt.* Quis
porro audebit opinari post omnia ista quae sex diebus
enumerata sunt angelos factos? Sed etsi quisquam
ita desipit, redarguit istam vanitatem illa scriptura
paris auctoritatis ubi Deus dicit: *Quando facta sunt*

---

[1] Daniel 3.57 (Septuagint and Vulgate. Not in the
Hebrew).
[2] Psalm 148.1–5.

over the deep—by which is meant an indiscriminate mixture of earth and water—, for where there is no light there must be darkness. But if all things were then given their place in the work of creation, which is said to have been finished in six days, how could the angels be omitted as if they were not included among God's works from which he rested on the seventh day?

Still, even if the fact that the angels are the work of God is not omitted here, it is not explicitly stated; but it is attested elsewhere in no uncertain terms by holy Scripture. For in the hymn of the three men in the furnace, after the words: " Bless the Lord, all ye works of the Lord," [1] the angels are also mentioned in the following list of these same works. In a psalm too occur the words of a hymn: " Praise the Lord from the heavens, praise him on the heights! Praise him, all his angels; praise him all his powers! Praise him, ye sun and moon; praise him, all ye stars and light! Praise him, ye highest heavens, and let the waters above the heavens praise the name of the Lord! For he spoke and they were made; he commanded and they were created." [2] Here too we are told by God's word most plainly that the angels were made by God, for they are mentioned among the other heavenly things, regarding all of which the Psalmist adds the statement: " He spoke and they were made." Furthermore, who will dare to believe that the angels were created only after all the works enumerated that were created in six days? Why, even if any man is so foolish, his folly is confuted by the scriptural passage of equal authority where God says: " When the stars were created, all my angels

sidera, laudaverunt me voce magna omnes angeli mei.
Iam ergo erant angeli quando facta sunt sidera.
Facta sunt autem quarto die. Numquidnam ergo
die tertio factos esse dicemus? Absit. In promptu
est enim quid illo die factum sit. Ab aquis utique
terra discreta est et distinctas sui generis species duo
ista elementa sumpserunt et produxit terra quidquid
ei radicitus inhaeret. Numquidnam secundo? Ne
hoc quidem. Tunc enim firmamentum factum est
inter aquas superiores et inferiores caleumque appellatum est; in quo firmamento quarto die facta sunt
sidera.

Nimirum ergo si ad istorum dierum opera Dei
pertinent angeli, ipsi sunt illa lux quae diei nomen
accepit, cuius unitas ut commendaretur, non est
dictus dies primus, sed dies unus. Nec alius est dies
secundus aut tertius aut ceteri; sed idem ipse unus
ad inplendum senarium vel septenarium numerum
repetitus est propter septenariam cognitionem;
senariam scilicet operum quae fecit Deus, et septi-
mam quietis Dei. Cum enim dixit Deus: *Fiat lux*,
et facta est lux, si recte in hac luce creatio intellegitur
angelorum, profecto facti sunt participes lucis
aeternae, quod est ipsa incommutabilis sapientia Dei,

---

[1] Job 38.7 (Septuagint).
[2] Augustine believes that God, having no need to work
within time, created all parts of the universe simultaneously.
Hence the six days of creation described in Genesis have a
purely symbolic meaning. This meaning is set forth below,
Book 11.30 and 31. Cf. *De Genesi ad Litteram* 4.1 and 7.28

praised me with a great shout."[1] So then there must have been angels when the stars were created. But the stars were created on the fourth day. Shall we say then that the angels were created on the third day? Certainly not, for we have the record of what was created on that day. The earth was separated from the waters and those two elements took on their separate forms each of its own kind; then the earth brought forth whatever is attached to it by roots. What of the second day? Neither will that do, for the firmament was created on that day between the upper and the lower waters and called heaven; and in this firmament on the fourth day the stars were created.

Surely then if the angels are included among the works of God on those six days, they are the light that received the name day; and in order to emphasize its oneness for us, the day was not called " the first day " but " one day." Nor is the second, third or any remaining day a different day, but the same expression " one day " was repeated in order to complete the number six or seven, and so to make us aware of the sevenfold series—the sixfold series, that is, of the days of works wrought by God, plus the seventh when God rested.[2] For when God said: " Let there be light " and light was created, if we are right in interpreting this light as the act of creating the angels, surely, then, they have been made partakers of the eternal light, which is naught but the unchangeable wisdom of God itself, by which

and *De Genesi contra Manichaeos* 1.23.35 ff. See also J. De Blic, *Le processus de la création d'après saint Augustin* in *Mélanges Cavallera*, 1948, pp. 180–184.

SAINT AUGUSTINE

per quam facta sunt omnia, quem dicimus unigenitum Dei filium; ut ea luce inluminati qua creati,
fierent lux et vocarentur dies participatione incommutabilis lucis et diei, quod est verbum Dei, per
quod et ipsi et omnia facta sunt. *Lumen* quippe
*verum, quod inluminant omnem hominem venientem in
hunc mundum*, hoc inluminat et omnem angelum
mundum, ut sit lux non in se ipso, sed in Deo; a quo
si avertitur angelus, fit inmundus; sicut sunt omnes
qui vocantur inmundi spiritus, nec iam lux in
Domino, sed in se ipsis tenebrae, privati participatione lucis aeternae. Mali enim nulla natura est;
sed amissio boni mali nomen accepit.

X

*De simplici et incommutabili trinitate Dei Patris et
Dei Filii et Dei Spiritus sancti, unius Dei, cui
non est aliud qualitas aliudque substantia.*

Est itaque bonum solum simplex et ob hoc solum
incommutabile, quod est Deus. Ab hoc bono creata
sunt omnia bona, sed non simplicia et ob hoc mutabilia. Creata sane, inquam, id est facta, non genita.
Quod enim de simplici bono genitum est, pariter
simplex est et hoc est quod illud de quo genitum est;

---

[1] Cf. John 1.9; 8.12; 12.46.
[2] John 1.9.
[3] The pun on *mundus* " world " and *mundus* " clean " cannot be captured in English. For the same pun, see *City of
God*, Book 7.26.
[4] See Plotinus, *Enneads* 3.2.5.

all things were made, and which we call the only-begotten Son of God.[1] Thus the angels, illumined by the light that created them, became light and were called " day " because they took part in that unchangeable light, the day that is the Word of God, by which both they and all other things were made. For " the true light that enlightens every man coming into the world "[2] enlightens also every pure[3] angel so that he is light, not in himself, but in God. If the angel turns away from God, he becomes unclean, as are all those who are called unclean spirits. They are no longer light in the Lord but darkness in themselves, since they have lost their participation in eternal light. For evil has in itself no substance; rather the loss of what is good has received the name evil.[4]

X

On the simple and unchangeable Trinity of God
the Father, God the Son and God the Holy
Spirit, one God, in whom quality and
substance are not two different
things.

THERE is accordingly a good which alone is simple and therefore alone is unchangeable, namely God. By this good have been created all good things, but they are not simple and therefore are changeable. Note that I say that they were created, that is to say made, not begotten. For what was begotten from simple good is likewise simple, and this is the same as that from which it is begotten. These two

quae duo Patrem et Filium dicimus; et utrumque hoc
cum spiritu suo unus Deus est; qui spiritus Patris et
Filii Spiritus sanctus propria quadam notione huius
nominis in sacris litteris nuncupatur.

Alius est autem quam Pater et Filius, quia nec
Pater est nec Filius; sed " alius " dixi, non " aliud,"
quia et hoc pariter simplex pariterque incommutabile
bonum est et coaeternum.   Et haec trinitas unus est
Deus; nec ideo non simplex, quia trinitas.   Neque
enim propter hoc naturam istam boni simplicem
dicimus, quia Pater in ea solus aut solus Filius
aut solus Spiritus sanctus, aut vero sola est ista
nominis trinitas sine subsistentia personarum, sicut
Sabelliani haeretici putaverunt; sed ideo simplex
dicitur, quoniam quod habet hoc est, excepto quod
relative quaeque persona ad alteram dicitur.   Nam
utique Pater habet Filium, nec tamen ipse est Filius
et Filius habet Patrem, nec tamen ipse est Pater.[1]
In quo ergo ad semet ipsum dicitur, non ad alterum,
hoc est quod habet; sicut ad se ipsum dicitur vivus
habendo utique vitam, et eadem vita ipse est.

Propter hoc itaque natura dicitur simplex, cui non
sit aliquid habere quod vel possit amittere; vel aliud
sit habens, aliud quod habet; sicut vas aliquem
liquorem aut corpus colorem aut aer lucem sive fer-
vorem aut anima sapientiam.   Nihil enim horum est
id quod habet; nam neque vas liquor est nec corpus
color nec aer lux sive fervor neque anima sapientia

---

[1] et Filius—Pater *omitted by some MSS.*

---

[1] The Sabellians held that the persons of the Trinity are
merely different modes or aspects of a unified Godhead.

we call the Father and the Son, and both with their Spirit are one God. This Spirit of the Father and the Son is called in the sacred Writings holy with a certain special meaning attached to the word.

Now the Holy Spirit is another person than the Father and the Son, because he is neither the Father nor the Son. But I have called him another person, not a different thing, because he is, like them, the simple and, like them, the unchangeable good and is co-eternal. And this Trinity is one God, and it is none the less simple because it is a Trinity. For we do not say that this substance of good is simple because the Father alone is in it, or the Son alone, or the Holy Spirit alone. Nor is it, on the other hand, only nominally a Trinity without reality of persons, as the Sabellian heretics have thought,[1] but it is called simple because it is what it has, save in so far as each person is spoken of in relation to another. For without question the Father has a Son, but is not the Son; and the Son has a Father, but is not the Father. Therefore it is in respect to himself and not to the other that he is what he has; for example, he is said in respect to himself to be alive surely by having life, and he is himself this life.

Now the reason why something is called a simple substance is this, because it does not possess anything that it can lose, or, to put it another way, because it is not different from what it has, for example, a jar has some liquid in it, a body has colour, the air light or heat and the soul wisdom. Now none of these is what it has, that is, the jar is not the liquid, nor is the body colour, nor is the air light or heat, nor is the soul wisdom. This is why these things can also suffer loss

est. Hinc est quod etiam privari possunt rebus quas
habent, et in alios habitus vel qualitates verti atque
mutari, ut et vas evacuetur umore quo plenum est,
et corpus decoloretur et aer tenebrescat sive frigescat
et anima desipiat. Sed etsi sit corpus incorruptibile,
quale sanctis in resurrectione promittitur, habet
quidem ipsius incorruptionis inamissibilem qualitatem, sed manente substantia corporali non hoc est
quod ipsa incorruptio. Nam illa etiam per singulas
partes corporis tota est nec alibi maior, alibi minor;
neque enim ulla pars est incorruptior quam altera;
corpus vero ipsum maius est in toto quam in parte;
et cum alia pars est in eo amplior, alia minor, non
ea quae amplior est incorruptior quam quae minor.
Aliud est itaque corpus, quod non ubique sui totum
est, alia incorruptio, quae ubique eius tota est,
quia omnis pars incorruptibilis corporis etiam ceteris
inaequalis aequaliter incorrupta est. Neque enim
verbi gratia, quia digitus minor est quam tota manus,
ideo incorruptibilior manus quam digitus. Ita
cum sint inaequales manus et digitus, aequalis est
tamen incorruptibilitas manus et digiti. Ac per
hoc quamvis a corpore incorruptibili inseparabilis
incorruptibilitas sit, aliud est tamen substantia qua
corpus dicitur, aliud qualitas eius qua incorruptibile
nuncupatur. Et ideo etiam sic non hoc est quod
habet.

of the things that they have and may be converted
and changed to take on other conditions or qualities;
for example a jar may be emptied of the liquid that
fills it, the body may lose its colour, the air may become dark or cold and the soul may lose its wisdom.
True, there is an incorruptible body, such as is
promised to the saints in the resurrection, and this
body cannot, I grant, lose the quality of incorruption
which it has, yet its bodily substance persists, and so
it is not the same thing as the incorruptibility itself.
For that quality exists entire in all the individual
parts of the body, nor is it more in one part or less in
another, for no one part is more incorruptible than
another. The body itself is, however, greater in the
whole than in the part; yet, though one part of it is
larger and another smaller, the part which is larger
is no more incorruptible than that which is smaller.
Therefore the body, which is not present in its entirety in each of its parts, is one thing, while
incorruptibility is another, being present in its entirety in every part of the body, since every part of
the incorruptible body, even if it be unequal to all
other parts, is equally incorruptible. For, to give
an instance, though the finger is smaller than the
whole hand, the hand is not on that account more incorruptible than the finger. So although hand and
finger are unequal, yet the hand and the finger are
equal in their incorruptibility. It follows that,
although incorruptibility is inseparable from an incorruptible body, yet the substance by virtue of which
it is described as body is one thing, the quality by which
it is called incorruptible is another. That is why, in
spite of this inseparability, the body is not what it has.

Anima quoque ipsa, etiamsi semper sit sapiens, sicut erit cum liberabitur in aeternum, participatione tamen incommutabilis sapientiae sapiens erit, quae non est quod ipsa. Neque enim si aer infusa luce numquam deseratur, ideo non aliud est ipse, aliud lux qua inluminatur. Neque hoc ita dixerim quasi aer sit anima, quod putaverunt quidam qui non potuerunt incorpoream cogitare naturam. Sed habent haec ad illa etiam in magna disparilitate quandam similitudinem, ut non inconvenienter dicatur sic inluminari animam incorpoream luce incorporea simplicis sapientiae Dei, sicut inluminatur aeris corpus luce corporea; et sicut aer tenebrescit ista luce desertus—nam nihil sunt aliud quae dicuntur locorum quorumque corporalium tenebrae quam aer carens luce—, ita tenebrescere animam sapientiae luce privatam.

Secundum hoc ergo dicuntur illa simplicia quae principaliter vereque divina sunt, quod non aliud est in eis qualitas, aliud substantia, nec aliorum participatione vel divina vel sapientia vel beata sunt. Ceterum dictus est in scripturis sanctis Spiritus sapientiae multiplex, eo quod multa in sese habeat; sed quae habet, haec et est, et ea omnia unus est. Neque enim multae, sed una sapientia est, in qua sunt infiniti quidam eique finiti[1] thensauri rerum

---

[1] infinita quaedam eique infiniti *MSS. FGBat* (finiti *t*): immensi quidam atque infiniti *Migne*: infiniti eidemque indefiniti *Welldon*.

---

[1] e.g. Anaximenes and Diogenes, the presocratics, as well as some of the Stoics. Even some Christian thinkers came near to this view. See Tertullian, *De Anima* 9.

The soul itself, too, even if it be wise without end, as it will be when it is redeemed for eternity, will, for all that, be wise because it participates in unchangeable wisdom, which is not the same thing as the soul itself. For even if the air is never bereft of the light that suffuses it, this does not mean that the air is not one thing and the light that illumines it something different. Nor do I mean by this that the soul is air, as some have thought who could not conceive of an incorporeal nature.[1] Yet great as is their disparity, the two things, soul and air, have a certain similarity, enough to let us say without impropriety that the incorporeal soul is illumined by the incorporeal light of the simple wisdom of God, just as the corporeal air is illumined by corporeal light. And as the air becomes dark when this light abandons it—for what is called darkness in any corporeal region is nothing but air minus light [2]—so the soul becomes dark when deprived of the light of wisdom.

According to this principle, then, those things are called simple that are fundamentally and truly divine, because in them quality and substance are the same; and they are themselves divine or wise or happy without being so by participation in something not themselves. Nevertheless, in the holy Scriptures the Spirit of wisdom is described as manifold,[3] because wisdom contains many things in itself; but what it contains it also is, and it, being one, is all these things that it contains. For wisdom is not many things, but one, in which are an infinite number of storehouses of intelligible

[2] Cf. *De Genesi contra Manichaeos* 1.4.7.
[3] Wisdom 7.22.

intellegibilium, in quibus sunt omnes invisibiles atque incommutabiles rationes rerum etiam visibilium et mutabilium, quae per ipsam factae sunt. Quoniam Deus non aliquid nesciens fecit, quod nec de quolibet homine artifice recte dici potest; porro si sciens fecit omnia, ea utique fecit quae noverat. Ex quo occurrit animo quiddam mirum, sed tamen verum, quod iste mundus nobis notus esse non posset, nisi esset; Deo autem nisi notus esset, esse non posset.

XI

An eius beatitudinis quam sancti angeli ab initio sui semper habuerunt, etiam illos spiritus qui in veritate non steterunt participes fuisse credendum sit.

QUAE cum ita sint, nullo modo quidem secundum spatium aliquod temporis prius erant spiritus illi tenebrae quos angelos dicimus; sed simul ut facti sunt, lux facti sunt; non tamen tantum ita creati ut quoquo modo essent et quoquo modo viverent; sed etiam inluminati, ut sapienter beateque viverent. Ab hac inluminatione aversi quidam angeli non obtinuerunt excellentiam sapientis beataeque vitae, quae procul dubio non nisi aeterna est aeternitatisque

---

[1] Cf. *City of God*, Book 12.9.

realities—but for wisdom a finite number. Among these are all the invisible and unchangeable ideas even of changeable and visible things, patterns created by wisdom itself. For God did not make anything without knowledge, nor can that rightly be said even of any human craftsman, no matter who. Moreover, if he made everything with knowledge, it surely follows that what he made he knew. From this there arises in the mind a strange and wonderful thought, which is nevertheless true, that this universe of ours could not be known to us if it did not exist; but it could not exist if it were not known to God.

XI

Are we to believe that those spirits too who did not remain fixed in the truth partook of the happiness that the holy angels possessed from the beginning of their existence?

THIS being so, those spirits which we call angels were never previously darkness in any way or for any period of time, but from the moment they were created, they were created as beings of light.[1] Yet they were not created merely so as to exist and live in any way whatever, but they were also created enlightened, so as to live wisely and happily. Certain angels who turned their backs on this enlightenment did not obtain the outstanding boon of a wise and happy life, for that without any doubt, in order to be at all, must be eternal and confidently certain of its eternity. But they still have a life of reason, un-

suae certa atque secura; sed rationalem vitam
licet insipientem sic habent ut eam non possint
amittere, nec si velint.

Quatenus autem, antequam peccassent, illius
sapientiae fuerint participes, definire quis potest?
In eius tamen participatione aequales fuisse istos
illis qui propterea vere pleneque beati sunt quoniam
nequaquam de suae beatitudinis aeternitate falluntur, quo modo dicturi sumus? Quando quidem si
aequales in ea fuissent, etiam isti in eius aeternitate
mansissent pariter beati quia pariter certi. Neque
enim sicut vita, quamdiucumque fuerit, ita aeterna
vita veraciter dici poterit, si finem habitura sit; si
quidem vita tantummodo vivendo, aeterna vero finem
non habendo nominata est. Quapropter quamvis
non quidquid aeternum continuo beatum sit—
dicitur enim etiam poenalis ignis aeternus—, tamen
si vere perfecteque beata vita non nisi aeterna est,
non erat talis istorum, quandoque desitura et propterea non aeterna, sive id scirent, sive nescientes
aliud putarent; quia scientes timor, nescientes error
beatos esse utique non sinebat. Si autem hoc ita
nesciebant ut falsis incertisve non fiderent, sed
utrum sempiternum an quandoque finem habiturum
esset bonum suum, in neutram partem firma ad-
sensione ferrentur, ipsa de tanta felicitate cunctatio
eam beatae vitae plenitudinem quam in sanctis angelis
esse credimus non habebat. Neque enim beatae

472

wisely rational though it may be, and on such a tenure that they cannot lose it, not even if they so wish.

But who can clearly determine to what extent they partook of that wisdom before they had sinned? Again, how shall we say that they had equal possession of it with those who are fully and truly happy precisely because they are in no way mistaken in thinking that their happiness is eternal? For surely if they had been equal sharers in this wisdom, they too would have continued to be eternally happy equally with the others, since they must have been equally certain of the future. For happiness is like life; however long it is, it cannot truly be called eternal life if it is destined to have an end; life is life because someone is alive, but it is qualified as eternal only if it has no end. It follows that, though eternity does not automatically ensure happiness, for it is said that hell fire is eternal, yet, if we assume that life is not truly and completely happy unless it is eternally so, then they did not enjoy that sort of life, for their life of happiness was to come to an end some day and therefore was not eternal, whether they knew this to be true or, not knowing, had some other notion. For if they knew this, then fear, and if they did not know it, ignorance, assuredly prevented their being happy. But if their not knowing came to this, that they put no trust in false or uncertain hopes, but could not take the decisive step of believing with steadfast conviction either that their happiness was eternal or that it was destined to end some day, this indecision on the vital question of their happiness was itself a negation of the fully happy life

vitae vocabulum ita contrahimus ad quasdam signi-
ficationis angustias ut solum Deum dicamus beatum;
qui tamen vere ita beatus est ut maior beatitudo esse
non possit, in cuius comparatione quod angeli beati
sunt summa quadam sua beatitudine, quanta esse in
angelis potest, quid aut quantum est?

XII

*De comparatione beatitudinis iustorum necdum
obtinentium promissionis divinae praemium
et primorum in paradiso hominum
ante peccatum.*

NEC ipsos tantum, quod adtinet ad rationalem vel
intellectualem creaturam beatos nuncupandos putamus. Quis enim primos illos homines in paradiso
negare audeat beatos fuisse ante peccatum, quamvis
sua beatitudo quam diuturna vel utrum aeterna esset
incertos—esset autem aeterna, nisi peccassent—,
cum hodie non inpudenter beatos vocemus quos
videmus iuste ac pie cum spe futurae inmortalitatis
hanc vitam ducere sine crimine vastante conscien-
tiam, facile inpetrantes peccatis huius infirmitatis
divinam misericordiam. Qui licet de suae perseverantiae praemio certi sint, de ipsa tamen perse-

which, we believe, the holy angels enjoy. For we do not so narrowly restrict the meaning of the expression " happy life " as to assert that God alone is happy, although, to be sure, he is so truly happy that no greater happiness can exist. Although the angels are happy with a happiness of their own, as great as angels can enjoy, yet in comparison with God's happiness, what does that amount to, what is its greatness?

XII

A comparison between the happiness of the righteous,
who have not yet received the prize divinely
promised, and that of the first man and
woman in paradise before they sinned.

NOR are the angels the only beings belonging to the rational or intellectual level of creation whom we think worthy to be termed happy. For who would dare to deny that those first human beings in paradise were happy before they sinned, although they were uncertain how long their happiness would last and whether it was eternal—and eternal it would have been had they not sinned—who, I say, would deny that they were happy, inasmuch as in our own day we are not overbold when we call happy those whom we see leading a righteous and religious life in the hope of immortality to come, having no sense of guilt to ravage their conscience, easily obtaining divine mercy for the sins to which our present weakness is liable? And although they are assured of a reward if they persevere, they are found to have no

verantia sua reperiuntur incerti. Quis enim hominum se in actione provectuque iustitiae persevera-
turum usque in finem sciat, nisi aliqua revelatione ab
illo fiat certus qui de hac re iusto latentique iudicio
non omnes instruit, sed neminem fallit?

Quantum itaque pertinet ad delectationem praesentis boni, beatior erat primus homo in paradiso
quam quilibet iustus in hac infirmitate mortali;
quantum autem ad spem futuri, beatior quilibet in
quibuslibet cruciatibus corporis cui non opinione,
sed certa veritate manifestum est sine fine se habiturum omni molestia carentem societatem angelorum
in participatione summi Dei quam erat ille homo
sui casus incertus in magna illa felicitate paradisi.

XIII

*An ita unius felicitatis omnes angeli sint
creati ut neque lapsuros se possent
nosse qui lapsi sunt, et post ruinam
labentium perseverantiae suae
praescientiam acceperint
qui steterunt.*

Quocirca cuivis iam non difficulter occurrit utroque coniuncto effici beatitudinem quam recto pro-

---

[1] This chapter should be compared with the fuller treatment of the same topic in *De Dono Perseverantiae* and *De
Correptione et Gratia.*

guarantee of that same perseverance. For what man can know that he will persevere to the end in the practice and promotion of righteousness, unless he is given that assurance by some revelation from him who with righteous, though inscrutable, judgement, does not instruct all men on this matter, yet deceives no one?

As far, then, as the enjoyment of present good is concerned, the first man in paradise was happier than any righteous man we care to choose who is subject to our mortal weakness. But where hope for the future is concerned, any man who does not merely think but knows with the certainty of truth that he will enjoy endless fellowship, free from all trouble, among the angels, participating in the being of God the most high, is happier, to whatever bodily torture he is submitted, than was the man who amid the great felicity of paradise was yet uncertain of his fate.[1]

XIII

Were all the angels created in a common state of
felicity, so that not only did those who fell
have no way of knowing that they were
destined to fall, but those who stood
firm acquired a certainty of their
future steadfastness only
after the downfall of
those who lapsed?

It is now easily seen by anyone from what has been said, that the happiness that a rational being craves as his proper goal is achieved when these two condi-

posito intellectualis natura desiderat, hoc est, ut et bono incommutabili quod Deus est, sine ulla molestia perfruatur et in eo se in aeternum esse mansurum nec ulla dubitatione cunctetur nec ullo errore fallatur. Hanc habere angelos lucis pia fide credimus; hanc nec antequam caderent habuisse angelos peccatores, qui sua pravitate illa luce privati sunt, consequenti ratione colligimus; habuisse tamen aliquam, etsi non praesciam, beatitudinem, si vitam egerunt ante peccatum, profecto credendi sunt.

Aut si durum videtur, quando facti sunt angeli, alios credere ita factos ut non acciperent praescientiam vel perseverantiae vel casus sui, alios autem ita ut veritate certissima aeternitatem suae beatitudinis nossent, sed aequalis felicitatis omnes ab initio creati sunt, et ita fuerunt donec isti qui nunc mali sunt ab illo bonitatis lumine sua voluntate cecidissent, procul dubio multo est durius nunc putare angelos sanctos aeternae suae beatitudinis incertos, et ipsos de semet ipsis ignorare quod nos de illis per scripturas sanctas nosse potuimus. Quis enim catholicus Christianus ignorat nullum novum diabolum ex bonis angelis ulterius futurum, sicut nec istum in societatem bonorum angelorum ulterius rediturum? Veritas

tions occur together, namely that he should enjoy continuously and without any troublesome interruption the unchangeable good which is God, and that he should not be held back by any doubt or be misled by any error of judgement so as to lack full assurance that he will eternally continue to enjoy it. With religious faith we believe that the angels of light have such happiness. And we gather by a logical conclusion that the sinning angels who were deprived of that light by their misconduct did not enjoy such happiness even before they fell. Yet if they lived any life at all before their sin, we must surely suppose that they enjoyed some degree of happiness, even though it did not include knowledge of the future.

But there is a difficulty in supposing that when the angels were created, some were made incapable of acquiring knowledge either of their constancy or of their fall, while others were created knowing with unshakeable certainty that their happiness would be everlasting. No, all were created, to begin with, equal in felicity and so they continued until those who are now evil angels had of their own free will fallen away from the light of goodness. But there can be no doubt that it would be much more difficult to suppose that the holy angels are even now uncertain of their eternal happiness, and that they themselves do not know about themselves what we have been able to learn about them through the holy Scriptures. For what Catholic Christian does not know that no new devil will ever from now on come forth from among the good angels just as he knows that our present devil will never return to

quippe in evangelio sanctis fidelibusque promittit quod erunt aequales angelis Dei; quibus etiam promittitur quod ibunt in vitam aeternam. Porro autem si nos certi sumus numquam nos ex illa inmortali felicitate casuros, illi vero certi non sunt, iam potiores, non aequales eis erimus. Sed quia nequaquam Veritas fallit et aequales eis erimus, profecto etiam ipsi certi sunt suae felicitatis aeternae. Cuius illi allii quia certi non fuerunt—non enim erat eorum aeterna felicitas cuius certi essent, quae finem habitura—, restat ut aut inpares fuerint, aut si pares fuerunt, post istorum ruinam illis certa scientia suae sempiternae felicitatis accesserit.

Nisi forte quis dicat id quod Dominus ait de diabolo in evangelio: *Ille homicida erat ab initio et in veritate non stetit*, sic esse accipiendum ut non solum homicida fuerit ab initio, id est initio humani generis, ex quo utique homo factus est quem decipiendo posset occidere, verum etiam ab initio suae conditionis in veritate non steterit et ideo numquam beatus cum sanctis angelis fuerit, suo recusans esse subditus creatori et sua per superbiam velut privata potestate laetatus, ac per hoc falsus et fallax, quia nec quisquam potestatem Omnipotentis evadit, et qui per piam subiectionem noluit tenere quod vere

---

[1] Matthew 22.30.
[2] Matthew 25.46.
[3] John 8.44.

fellowship with the good angel? For Truth in the Gospel promises to the saints and the faithful that they will be equal with the angels of God,[1] and they are assured in addition that they will enter into eternal life.[2] But if we are sure that we shall never fall from eternal felicity while the angels on the contrary are not sure, that would make us their superiors, not their equals. But Truth cannot at all lead us astray and we shall be their equals; hence they too are sure of their everlasting felicity. Those sinning angels were not sure of this, for they had no eternal felicity to be sure of, since their felicity was one that would end. So we must conclude either that the angels were unequal in rank or, if they were actually once equal, it was after the fall of the sinning angels that the others acquired certain knowledge of their own everlasting felicity.

But perhaps someone may say that the words that the Lord used of the devil in the Gospel, " He was a murderer from the beginning, and did not abide by the truth," [3] are to be taken to mean, not merely that he was a murderer from the beginning, that is from the beginning of the human race and in any case from the time when a human being was created who might be lured to death by his guile, but further that even from the beginning of his own existence he did not abide by the truth and therefore was never happy together with the holy angels. He refused to be second to his creator, and was so proud that he exulted in his power as if it were something of his own, and in so doing he was deceived and a deceiver. For no one ever escapes the power of the Omnipotent and he who refuses to hold to the true reality in

481

est adfectat per superbam elationem simulare quod non est, ut sic intellegatur etiam quod beatus Iohannes apostolus ait: *Ab initio diabolus peccat,* hoc est, ex quo creatus est, iustitiam recusavit quam nisi pia Deoque subdita voluntas habere non posset.

Huic sententiae quisquis adquiescit, non cum illis haereticis sapit, id est Manichaeis, et si quae aliae pestes ita sentiunt, quod suam quandam propriam tamquam ex adverso quodam principio diabolus habeat naturam mali; qui tanta vanitate desipiunt ut, cum verba ista evangelica in auctoritate nobiscum habeant, non adtendant non dixisse Dominum: A veritate alienus fuit; sed: *In veritate non stetit,* ubi a veritate lapsum intellegi voluit, in qua utique si stetisset, eius particeps factus beatus cum sanctis angelis permaneret.

XIV

Quo genere locutionis dictum sit de diabolo quod in veritate non steterit, quia veritas non est in eo.

SUBIECIT autem indicium, quasi quaesissemus, unde ostendatur quod in veritate non steterit, atque ait:

---

[1] 1 John 3.8.
[2] John 8.44.

reverent submission takes it upon himself in his proud conceit to pretend what does not exist. We may consequently see this meaning in the words of the blessed apostle John as well: "The devil has sinned from the beginning,"[1] that is, from the moment when he was created he rejected the righteousness that only a reverent will and one submissive to God could possess.

Whoever accepts this conclusion is at odds with those heretical Manichaeans or with any other pestilential sect that holds, as they do, that the devil derives as if from a certain contrary principle a natural evil substance that is peculiar to him. So great is the folly of their error that although they, like us, acknowledge the authority of those words in the Gospel, they fail to notice that the Lord did not say: "He was no adherent of the truth," but: "He did not abide by the truth." By this he meant it to be understood that the devil had lapsed from the truth. Certainly if he had stood firm in it, he would have been made a partaker in it and would continue to be in a state of bliss with the holy angels.

XIV

The figure of speech used in saying of the devil that he did not abide by the truth, because the truth is not in him.

MOREOVER, our Lord also gave us, as if we had asked for it, a sign to demonstrate that the devil did not abide by the truth, where the Gospel says: "Because the truth is not in him."[2] Now the truth

Quia non est veritas in eo. Esset autem in eo, si in illa stetisset. Locutione autem dictum est minus usitata. Sic enim videtur sonare: *In veritate non stetit, quia veritas non est in eo*, tamquam ea sit causa ut in veritate non steterit quod in eo veritas non sit; cum potius ea sit causa ut in eo veritas non sit, quod in veritate non stetit. Ista locutio est et in psalmo: *Ego clamavi, quoniam exaudisti me Deus*; cum dicendum fuisse videatur: Exaudisti me Deus, quoniam clamavi. Sed cum dixisset: " *Ego clamavi*," tamquam ab eo quaereretur unde se clamasse monstraret, ab effectu exauditionis Dei clamoris sui ostendit affectum; tamquam diceret: " Hinc ostendo clamasse me, quoniam exaudisti me."

XV

Quid sentiendum sit de eo quod dictum est: Ab initio diabolus peccat.

ILLUD etiam quod ait de diabolo Iohannes: *Ab initio diabolus peccat*, non intellegunt, si natura talis est, nullo modo esse peccatum. Sed quid respondetur propheticis testimoniis, sive quod ait Esaias sub figurata persona principis Babyloniae diabolum notans: *Quo modo cecidit Lucifer, qui mane oriebatur;*

---

[1] Psalm 17.6.
[2] 1 John 3.8.

would be in him had he stood firm in it, but the
language employed is rather unusual. For the words,
" He did not abide by the truth because the truth is
not in him," sound as if his not abiding by the truth
were the effect of truth not being in him, although the
case is rather that his not abiding by the truth is
cause and the truth not being in him is effect. The
same figure is used again in the psalm: " I called
upon thee, for thou hast answered me, O God," [1]
although it seems as if the psalmist should have said:
" Thou hast answered me, O God, because I called
upon thee." But after saying: " I called upon
thee," then as if someone were asking him how he
could prove that he had called, he uses the effect,
namely God's answering his call, to prove his own act
directed to that end, as if he were saying: " Hereby
I make it clear that I called upon thee, that thou hast
answered me."

XV

How are we to interpret the statement: " The devil has sinned from the beginning "?

As for what John says about the devil: " The devil
has sinned from the beginning," [2] some do not understand that, if we have here a statement about his
sinful nature, there is no such thing as sin. But
what can be said to rebut the testimony of the
prophets? Isaiah represents the devil symbolically
as the prince of Babylon and apostrophizes him thus:
" How Lucifer has fallen, who used to rise in the

sive quod Hiezechiel: *In deliciis paradisi Dei fuisti,
omni lapide pretioso ornatus es?* Ubi intellegitur
fuisse aliquando sine peccato. Nam expressius ei
paulo post dicitur: *Ambulasti in diebus tuis sine vitio.*
Quae si aliter convenientius intellegi nequeunt,
oportet etiam illud quod dictum est: *In veritate non
stetit,* sic accipiamus quod in veritate fuerit, sed non
permanserit; et illud quod *ab initio diabolus peccat,*
non ab initio ex quo creatus est peccare putandus est,
sed ab initio peccati, quod ab ipsius superbia coeperit
esse peccatum.

Nec illud quod scriptum est in libro Iob, cum de
diabolo sermo esset: *Hoc est initium figmenti Domini,
quod fecit ad inludendum ab angelis suis*—cui consonare
videtur et psalmus ubi legitur: *Draco hic, quem
finxisti ad inludendum ei*—sic intellegendum est ut
existimemus talem ab initio creatum cui ab angelis
inluderetur, sed in hac poena post peccatum ordi-
natum. Initium ergo eius figmentum est Domini;
non enim est ulla natura etiam in extremis infimisque

---

[1] Isaiah 14.12 (Septuagint). Lucifer ("light-bearer") in
this biblical passage is properly an epithet of the King of
Babylon. The Christians, taking this passage in conjunction
with Luke 10.18, used Lucifer as a synonym for Satan. To the
pagans Lucifer meant the morning-star, the planet Venus.
Because of this pagan usage, the Revised Standard Version
renders Lucifer as "Day Star" in Isaiah 14.12.

[2] Ezekiel 28.13 (Septuagint).

morning!" [1] Ezekiel says: "You were in the delights of God's paradise, you were adorned with every precious stone." [2] Here it is understood that there was a time when he was without sin. In fact a little later he is told more explicitly: "You walked blameless in your days," [3] And if no other more fitting interpretation of these passages can be found, then we must also accept the statement: "He did not abide by the truth," as meaning that he was in the truth but did not remain in it permanently, and the words: "The devil has sinned from the beginning," as meaning that he is not to be supposed to sin from his beginning, when he was created, but from the beginning of his sin, because it was by his pride that sin first came to be.

Then there is the statement in the book of Job where the devil was being discussed: "This is the beginning of the Lord's handiwork, which he made to be a laughing-stock for his angels." [4] With this passage the psalm too appears to agree in which we read: "This serpent which thou didst form to be a laughing-stock." [5] But the words in Job are not to be interpreted by assuming that the devil was created from the beginning as a fit subject for the angels to make fun of, but that he was consigned to this punishment after his sin. He started, then, as the handiwork of the Lord, for there is no natural creature even among the least significant and lowest animal-

---

[3] Ezekiel 28.15 (Septuagint).

[4] Job 40.19 (Septuagint). The reference is to Behemoth, which Augustine interprets as a type of the devil.

[5] Psalm 104.26. (Cf. Septuagint Psalm 103.26). Leviathan too is here regarded as the devil. See Chapter XVII below.

bestiolis quam non ille constituit, a quo est omnis
modus, omnis species, omnis ordo, sine quibus nihil
rerum inveniri vel cogitari potest; quanto magis
angelica creatura, quae omnia cetera quae Deus
condidit naturae dignitate praecedit!

XVI

De gradibus et differentiis creaturarum,
quas aliter pendit usus utilitatis,
aliter ordo rationis.

IN his enim quae quoquo modo sunt et non sunt
quod Deus est a quo facta sunt, praeponuntur viventia non viventibus, sicut ea quae habent vim gignendi
vel etiam appetendi his quae isto motu carent; et in
his quae vivunt, praeponuntur sentientia non
sentientibus, sicut arboribus animalia; et in his
quae sentiunt, praeponuntur intellegentia non in-
tellegentibus, sicut homines pecoribus; et in his
quae intellegunt, praeponuntur inmortalia mortalibus, sicut angeli hominibus. Sed ista praeponuntur
naturae ordine; est autem alius atque alius pro suo
cuiusque usu aestimationis modus, quo fit ut quaedam sensu carentia quibusdam sentientibus prae-

cules that was not wrought by him. From him comes
every measure, every form, every pattern, and apart
from his measure, form, and pattern nothing can be
found existing or imagined to exist. How much
more then is he the author of the created being of
angels, a kind of being that is superior in the natural
scale of values to all the rest of God's creation!

XVI

The grades and distinctions among created beings,
which are weighed in one way by the scales
of utility, in another by the scales of
rational order.

Now among those created things which exist in
whatever measure and whose being is not that of
God who created them, those that are alive are above
those that are not, just as those which have the power
of generation or even of aspiration are superior to
those which lack such an urge. Again among those
that have life the sentient are superior to those that
lack sensation; thus animals are superior to trees.
Again among those that have sensation, those with
understanding are superior to those that lack it; so
men are superior to cattle; and among those with
understanding the immortal are superior to the
mortal; in this way angels are superior to men. But
these are examples of status according to natural
order. There are, however, other standards of value
that vary according to the proper use of each created
thing, and by this system we rank certain things that
lack sensation above certain sentient beings. We go

ponamus, in tantum ut si potestas esset ea prorsus de natura rerum auferre vellemus, sive quem in ea locum habeant ignorantes, sive etiamsi sciamus nostris ea commodis postponentes. Quis enim non domui suae panem habere quam mures, nummos quam pulices malit? Sed quid mirum, cum in ipsorum etiam hominum aestimatione, quorum certe natura tantae est dignitatis, plerumque carius comparetur equus quam servus, gemma quam famula?

Ita libertate iudicandi plurimum distat ratio considerantis a necessitate indigentis seu voluptate cupientis, cum ista quid per se ipsum in rerum gradibus pendat, necessitas autem quid propter quid expetat cogitat, et ista quid verum luci mentis appareat, voluptas vero quid iucundum corporis sensibus blandiatur spectat. Sed tantum valet in naturis rationalibus quoddam veluti pondus voluntatis et amoris ut, cum ordine naturae angeli hominibus, tamen lege iustitiae boni homines malis angelis praeferantur.

so far in such cases as to wish, if we had the power, to banish the latter from nature altogether, either because we do not know where they naturally fit or because in spite of our knowledge we still put our own interests first. For who would not rather have bread in his house than mice, or money rather than fleas? But why should this surprise us? When it comes to evaluating men themselves, who surely rank very high in nature, a horse often brings a higher price than a slave, or a jewel more than a servant girl.

So in point of freedom of judgement, the rationality of a thoughtful man is poles apart from the necessity felt by a man in want or the calculus of pleasure applied by one who is ruled by desire. Reason weighs a thing according to its intrinsic place in the great scale of being; necessity, however, calculates what it must obtain and for what reason. Reason considers what will appear to the inner light of the mind as being true; but pleasure keeps in view the question what pleasant thing will gratify the physical senses. In the case of rational creatures, however, a good will and a right love add so much weight to the scales, you might say, that, although in the natural order angels rank above men, yet by the law of righteousness good men are rated above bad angels.

SAINT AUGUSTINE

XVII

*Vitium malitiae non naturam esse, sed contra na-
turam, cui ad peccandum non Conditor
causa est, sed voluntas.*

PROPTER naturam igitur, non propter malitiam dia-
boli, dictum recte intellegimus: *Hoc est initium
figmenti Domini*. Quia sine dubio, ubi est vitium
malitiae, natura non vitiata praecessit. Vitium
autem ita contra naturam est ut non possit nisi
nocere naturae Non itaque esset vitium recedere
a Deo nisi naturae cuius id vitium est potius com-
peteret esse cum Deo. Quapropter etiam voluntas
mala grande testimonium est naturae bonae. Sed
Deus sicut naturarum bonarum optimus creator est,
ita malarum voluntatum iustissimus ordinator; ut
cum illae male utuntur naturis bonis, ipse bene utatur etiam voluntatibus malis. Itaque fecit ut diabolus institutione illius bonus, voluntate sua malus, in
inferioribus ordinatus inluderetur ab angelis eius, id
est, ut prosint temptationes eius sanctis quibus eas
obesse desiderat. Et quoniam Deus, cum eum conderet, futurae malignitatis eius non erat utique
ignarus et praevidebat quae bona de malo eius esset

---

[1] Job 40.19.

XVII

*The vice consisting of malice is not a substantial
reality of nature, but is against nature; it is
led to sinful action not by the Creator,
but by the will.*

IT is the essential nature, then, not the wicked will
of the devil that we rightly assume to be meant in
the words: " This is the beginning of the Lord's
handiwork." [1] For no doubt where the vice of
malice occurs, it must have been preceded by a
created nature that was free from vice. Now vice is
so contrary to nature that it is inevitably detrimental
to it. Accordingly, it would not be vicious to with-
draw from God if it were not more fitting for the
created nature whose withdrawal is vice to remain
with God. For this reason even an evil will is a
strong proof of a good nature at the start. But just
as God is superlatively good as creator of good
natures, so he is superlatively just as regulator of
evil wills. The result is that when evil wills make ill
use of good natures, he himself makes a good use
even of evil wills. In this way he brought it about
that the devil, who was good by God's creative act
but became evil by his own will, was reduced to an
inferior status and derided by God's angels. In other
words, God sees to it that the temptations through
which the devil aims to injure the saints redound instead to their profit. And since God in creating him
was certainly not unaware of the hostility to good that
would characterize him and foresaw the good that
he himself was to bring about by using the devil's

ipse facturus, propterea psalmus ait: *Draco hic, quem finxisti ad inludendum ei*, ut in eo ipso quod eum finxit, licet per suam bonitatem bonum, iam per suam praescientiam praeparasse intellegatur quo modo illo uteretur et malo.

XVIII

De pulchritudine universitatis, quae per ordinationem Dei etiam ex contrariorum fit oppositione luculentior.

Neque enim Deus ullum, non dico angelorum, sed vel hominum crearet, quem malum futurum esse praescisset, nisi pariter nosset quibus eos bonorum usibus commodaret atque ita ordinem saeculorum tamquam pulcherrimum carmen etiam ex quibusdam quasi antithetis honestaret. Antitheta enim quae appellantur in ornamentis elocutionis sunt decentissima, quae Latine ut appellentur opposita, vel, quod expressius dicitur, contraposita, non est apud nos huius vocabuli consuetudo, cum tamen eisdem ornamentis locutionis etiam sermo Latinus utatur, immo linguae omnium gentium. His antithetis et Paulus apostolus in secunda ad Corinthios epistula illum locum suaviter explicat, ubi dicit: *Per arma iustitiae dextra et sinistra: per gloriam et ignobilitatem, per infamiam et bonam famam; ut seductores et veraces, ut qui ignoramur et cognoscimur; quasi morientes, et ecce*

---

[1] Psalm 104.26. (Cf. Septuagint Psalm 103.26.)
[2] Cf. Cicero, *Orator* 49.166; Quintilian 9.3.81.

wickedness, it is to this that the psalmist refers when he says: "This serpent which thou didst form to be a laughing-stock."[1] He wanted us to know that at the very moment when God created the devil, although in his own goodness he created him good, he had already through his own foreknowledge prepared a way to use him even after he became bad.

XVIII

The beauty of the universe which, as God has arranged it, becomes even more brilliant by the contrast of opposites.

Now God would never create any man, much less any angel, if he already knew that he was destined to be evil, were he not equally aware how he was to turn them to account in the interest of the good and thereby add lustre to the succession of the ages as if it were an exquisite poem enhanced by what might be called antitheses.[2] Antitheses, as they are termed, are among the most elegant ornaments of style. In Latin they might be called *opposita* or, more accurately, *contraposita*. We are not in the habit of using this term, although Latin and indeed the languages of all nations employ the same ornaments of style. These antitheses are gracefully demonstrated by the apostle Paul too, in his second letter to the Corinthians, where he says: "With the weapons of righteousness for the right hand and for the left; in honour and dishonour, in ill repute and in good repute; treated as imposters, and yet truthful; as unknown, and yet well known; as dying,

495

vivimus, ut coherciti et non mortificati; ut tristes, semper autem gaudentes, sicut egeni, multos autem ditantes, tamquam nihil habentes et omnia possidentes. Sicut ergo ista contraria contrariis opposita sermonis pulchritudinem reddunt, ita quadam non verborum, sed rerum eloquentia contrariorum oppositione saeculi pulchritudo componitur. Apertissime hoc positum est in libro ecclesiastico isto modo: *Contra malum bonum est et contra mortem vita; sic contra pium peccator. Et sic intuere in omnia opera Altissimi, bina bina, unum contra unum.*

XIX

Quid sentiendum videatur de eo quod scriptum est: Divisit Deus inter lucem et tenebras.

QUAMVIS itaque divini sermonis obscuritas etiam ad hoc sit utilis, quod plures sententias veritatis parit et in lucem notitiae producit, dum alius eum sic, alius sic intellegit—ita tamen ut quod in obscuro loco intellegitur, vel adtestatione rerum manifestarum vel aliis locis minime dubiis asseratur; sive, cum multa tractantur, ad id quoque perveniatur quod sensit ille qui scripsit, sive id lateat, sed ex occasione tractandae profundae obscuritatis alia quaedam vera dicantur—, non mihi videtur ab operi-

---

[1] 2 Corinthians 6.7–10.
[2] Ecclesiasticus 33.14–15.

496

and behold we live; as punished, and yet not killed; as sorrowful, and yet always rejoicing; as poor, yet making many rich; as having nothing, and yet possessing everything." [1] So, just as beauty of language is achieved by a contrast of opposites in this way, the beauty of the course of this world is built up by a kind of rhetoric, not of words but of things, which employs this contrast of opposites. This is very clearly stated in the book of Ecclesiasticus as follows: " Good is the opposite of evil, and life the opposite of death; so the sinner is the opposite of the godly. And so you are to regard all the works of the Most High: two by two, one the opposite of the other." [2]

XIX

What we are to think of the words:
" God separated the light from
the darkness."

WE see that the obscurity of the divine Word actually has the advantage of engendering more than one interpretation of the truth and of bringing these interpretations into the bright light of general knowledge, as different readers understand a passage differently. Nevertheless any interpretation of an obscure passage should be supported by the evidence of manifest facts or that of other passages where the meaning is not at all open to doubt. In this way we shall by the examination of several views either arrive finally at the meaning of the author himself or, if there is no light on that, the discussion of a profoundly

bus Dei absurda sententia si, cum lux prima illa
facta est, angeli creati intelleguntur, inter sanctos
angelos et inmundos fuisse discretum, ubi dictum
est: *Et divisit Deus inter lucem et tenebras; et vocavit
Deus lucem diem et tenebras vocavit noctem.* Solus
quippe ille ista discernere potuit, qui potuit etiam
priusquam caderent praescire casuros et privatos
lumine veritatis in tenebrosa superbia remansuros.
Nam inter istum nobis notissimum diem et noctem, id
est inter hanc lucem et has tenebras, vulgatissima
sensibus nostris luminaria caeli ut dividerent im-
peravit: *Fiant*, inquit, *luminaria in firmamento caeli,
ut luceant super terram et dividant inter diem et noctem;*
et paulo post: *Et fecit*, inquit, *Deus duo luminaria
magna, luminare maius in principia diei, et luminare
minus in principia noctis, et stellas; et posuit illa Deus in
firmamento caeli lucere super terram et praeesse diei et
nocti et dividere inter lucem et tenebras.* Inter illam
vero lucem quae sancta societas angelorum est in-
lustratione veritatis intellegibiliter fulgens, et ei
contrarias tenebras, id est malorum angelorum
aversorum a luce iustitiae taeterrimas mentes, ipse
dividere potuit cui etiam futurum non naturae, sed

---

[1] Genesis 1.4–6. Augustine throws some doubt on the
validity of this interpretation in Chapter XXXIII below.
[2] Genesis 1.14–15.
[3] Genesis 1.16–18.

obscure passage will provide occasion for the statement of a number of other truths. Here my conclusion seems to introduce no discord into the account
of God's works, when I suggest that in the making of
that first light we are meant to see the creation of the
angels and that a distinction between holy and unclean angels is implied by the words: "And God
separated the light from the darkness; and God called
the light day, and the darkness he called night." [1]
Only he, of course, could discriminate in this way,
for only he could foresee which of them would fall
even before they fell and, having lost the light of
truth, would never escape from the dark world of
pride. Now he commanded the heavenly luminaries,
so commonly present to our senses, to mark the
separation between the day and the night that we are
familiar with, that is between our light and our darkness. "Let there be luminaries," he said, "in the
firmament of heaven to give light upon the earth
and to separate the day from the night." [2] A little
later it is stated: "And God made the two great
luminaries, the greater luminary to rule the day, and
the lesser luminary to rule the night; he made the
stars also. And God set them in the firmament of
heaven to give light upon the earth, to rule over the
day and over the night, and to separate the light
from the darkness." [3] But the separation between
that other light, which is the holy fellowship of angels
spiritually radiant with the illumination of truth, and
the darkness which is its opposite and resides in the
foul, loathsome hearts of the bad angels who have
turned their backs on the light of righteousness, was
one that he alone could make, for their coming

voluntatis malum occultum aut incertum esse non
potuit.

XX

De eo quod post discretionem lucis atque
tenebrarum dictum est:
Et vidit Deus lucem quia bona est.

DENIQUE nec illud est praetereundum silentio
quod, ubi dixit Deus: *Fiat lux, et facta est lux*, continuo subiunctum est: *Et vidit Deus lucem quia bona*
est; non postea quam separavit inter lucem et tenebras et vocavit lucem diem et tenebras noctem, ne
simul cum luce etiam talibus tenebris testimonium
placiti sui perhibuisse videretur. Nam ubi tenebrae
inculpabiles sunt, inter quas et lucem istam his oculis
conspicuam luminaria caeli dividunt, non ante, sed
post infertur: *Et vidit Deus quia bonum est. Posuit*
illa, inquit, *in firmamento caeli lucere super terram et*
praeesse diei et nocti et separare inter lucem et tenebras.
Et vidit Deus quia bonum est. Utrumque placuit,
quia utrumque sine peccato est. Ubi autem dixit
Deus: *Fiat lux, et facta est lux. Et vidit Deus lucem*
quia bona est; et postmodum infertur: *Et separavit*

---

[1] Genesis 1.3–4.
[2] Genesis 1.17–18.

perversity, which was a defect not of their nature but of their will, could not be hidden from him or in doubt.

XX

*The remark that comes after the separation
of the light from the darkness:
" And God saw that the light was good."*

FURTHERMORE, we must not pass over in silence the fact that when God said: " ' Let there be light,' and there was light," a comment is immediately added: " And God saw that the light was good." [1] This is not put after his separating light from darkness and his naming the light day and the darkness night, for fear of giving the impression that he also stated his approval of such darkness along with his approval of the light. Note that when the darkness mentioned is free from guilt, namely the darkness that is separated by the heavenly luminaries from the light that is clearly visible to our own eyes, then the words " And God saw that it was good," are introduced not before the separation but after it. The text runs: " He set them in the firmament of heaven to give light upon the earth, to rule over the day and over the night, and to separate the light from the darkness. And God saw that it was good." [2] He approved of both, because both are without sin. But when God said: " ' Let there be light '; and there was light; and God saw that the light was good "; and then we read later: " And God separated the light from the darkness, and God called the light day and the dark-

*Deus inter lucem et tenebras; et vocavit Deus lucem diem
et tenebras vocavit noctem*, non hoc loco additum est:
Et vidit Deus quia bonum est, ne utrumque appellaretur
bonum, cum esset horum alterum malum, vitio pro-
prio, non natura. Et ideo sola ibi lux placuit Conditori; tenebrae autem angelicae, etsi fuerant
ordinandae, non tamen fuerant adprobandae.

XXI

*De aeterna et incommutabili scientia Dei ac voluntate,
qua semper illi universa quae fecit sic placuerunt
facienda, quem ad modum facta.*

QUID est enim aliud intellegendum in eo quod per
omnia dicitur: *Vidit Deus quia bonum est*, nisi operis
adprobatio secundum artem facti, quae sapientia
Dei est? Deus autem usque adeo non, cum factum
est, tunc didicit bonum ut nihil eorum fieret, si ei
fuisset incognitum. Dum ergo videt quia bonum
est quod, nisi vidisset antequam fieret, non utique
fieret, docet bonum esse, non discit. Et Plato
quidem plus ausus est dicere, elatum esse scilicet
Deum gaudio mundi universitate perfecta. Ubi et

---

[1] Genesis 1.4, 10, 12, 18, 21, 25, 30.
[2] Augustine here argues against the Manichaean view. Cf.
De Genesi contra Manichaeos 1.8.13.
[3] *Timaeus* 37 C.

ness he called night," at this point the additional
phrase: "And God saw that it was good" does not
occur, lest both should be described as good although
one of them was bad, not as created but by its own
fault. Here we have the explanation why only the
light found favour with its Maker in this case.
Though the darkness of angelic hearts was to be included in the divine plan, it was not to be included in
the divine approval.

XXI

The eternal and unchangeable knowledge of God,
and the will of God, which is such that
everything created by him always won
his approval to the same degree
before its creation as after.

WHAT other meaning can be assigned to the words
that appear everywhere: "God saw that it was
good"[1] than approval of a finished product skilfully
wrought, that is, wrought with a skill that is the wisdom of God? But God was not previously so ignorant
that he could only discover that his work was good
when it was complete. Far from it. Nothing that
he created would have been created, if he had not
known it well beforehand.[2] Therefore when he sees
that a thing is good, a thing that he would not have
made at all, had he not seen that it was good before
he made it, he is teaching us, and not learning for
himself, that it is good. Even Plato, to be sure, dared
to go farther and say that God was transported with
joy when the universal world attained completion.[3]

ipse non usque adeo desipiebat ut putaret Deum sui
operis novitate factum beatiorem; sed sic ostendere
voluit artifici suo placuisse iam factum, quod placuerat
in arte faciendum; non quod ullo modo Dei scientia
varietur, ut aliud in ea facient quae nondum sunt,
aliud quae iam sunt, aliud quae fuerunt; non enim
more nostro ille vel quod futurum est prospicit, vel
quod praesens est aspicit, vel quod praeteritum est
respicit; sed alio modo quodam a nostrarum cogitationum consuetudine longe alteque diverso. Ille
quippe non ex hoc in illud cogitatione mutata, sed
omnino incommutabiliter videt; ita ut illa quidem
quae temporaliter fiunt, et futura nondum sint et
praesentia iam sint et praeterita iam non sint, ipse
vero haec omnia stabili ac sempiterna praesentia con-
prehendat; nec aliter oculis, aliter mente; non
enim ex animo constat et corpore; nec aliter nunc
et aliter antea et aliter postea; quoniam non sicut
nostra, ita eius quoque scientia trium temporum,
praesentis videlicet et praeteriti vel futuri, varietate
mutatur, *apud quem non est inmutatio nec momenti
obumbratio.*

Neque enim eius intentio de cogitatione in cogita-
tionem transit, in cuius incorporeo contuitu simul adsunt cuncta quae novit; quoniam tempora ita novit

---

[1] James 1.17.

And Plato too was not, when he said this, so foolish
as to suppose that God's happiness was made greater
by surprise at his new creation; he merely wished to
show by his words that the work won the approval
of the artist as much when finished as when it was
but a design for skilful execution. It is not that
there is any difference in God's knowledge according
as it is produced by things not yet in existence, by
things now or by things that are no more. Unlike us,
he does not look ahead to the future, see the present
before him, and look back to the past. Rather he
sees events in another way, far and profoundly different from any experience that is familiar to our minds.
For he does not variably turn his attention from one
thing to another. No, there is no alteration whatsoever in his contemplation. Hence all events in time,
events that will be and are not yet, and those that
are now, being present, and those that have passed
and are no more, all of them are apprehended by him
in a motionless and everlasting present moment.
Nor does he see them in one way with his eyes and in
another way with his mind, for he is not a compound
of mind and body. Nor does it make any difference
whether he looks at them from present, past or
future, since his knowledge, unlike ours, of the three
kinds of time, namely present, past and future, does
not change as time changes, " for with him there is
no variation or shadow of any movement." [1]

Neither does his attention stray from one subject of
thought to another, for his incorporeal, inclusive
vision simultaneously embraces everything that he
knows. For he knows events in time without any
temporal acts of knowing of his own, just as he sets

nullis suis temporalibus notionibus, quem ad modum temporalia movet nullis suis temporalibus motibus. Ibi ergo vidit bonum esse quod fecit, ubi bonum esse vidit ut faceret; nec quia factum vidit scientiam duplicavit vel ex aliqua parte auxit, tamquam minoris scientiae fuerit priusquam faceret quod videret, qui tam perfecte non operaretur nisi tam perfecta scientia cui nihil ex eius operibus adderetur.

Quapropter, si tantummodo nobis insinuandum esset quis fecerit lucem, sufficeret dicere, fecit Deus lucem; si autem non solum quis fecerit, verum etiam per quid fecerit, satis esset ita enuntiari: *Et dixit Deus: Fiat lux, et facta est lux*; ut non tantum Deum, sed etiam per Verbum lucem fecisse nossemus. Quia vero tria quaedam maxime scienda de creatura nobis oportuit intimari, quis eam fecerit, per quid fecerit, quare fecerit: *Dixit Deus*, inquit: *Fiat lux, et facta est lux. Et vidit Deus lucem quia bona est.* Si ergo quaerimus, quis fecerit: *Deus est*; si per quid fecerit: *Dixit: Fiat, et facta est;* si quare fecerit: *Quia bona est.*

Nec auctor est excellentior Deo, nec ars efficacior Dei verbo, nec causa melior quam ut bonum crearetur a Deo bono. Hanc etiam Plato causam con-

---

[1] Genesis 1.3.

temporal things in motion without any temporal movements of his own. Consequently there was no distinction between his seeing that what he made was good and his seeing that it was good for him to make it. His act of seeing it when made did not double or in any degree increase his knowledge, as if his knowledge was less before he made something to see. He would not be the perfect craftsman he is, if his knowledge were not so complete that it can receive no increase from his works.

Therefore, if it had been necessary to impart to us only the knowledge who made the light, it would be enough to say: "God made the light." Again, if it had been right that we should know, not only who made it, but also by what means he made it, it would be enough to report: "And God said, 'Let there be light'; and there was light," [1] in order to inform us, not only that it was God who made the light, but also that he made it by his Word. But in fact there were three chief matters concerning a work of creation that had to be reported to us and that it behoved us to know, namely who made it, by what means, and why. So what Scripture says is: "God said, 'Let there be light'; and there was light. And God saw that the light was good." So if we ask: "Who made it?" the answer is: "It was God." If we ask: "By what means?" the answer is: "God said, 'Let it be'; and it was." If we ask: "Why?" the answer is: "Because it is good."

Nor is there any originator more excellent than God, any skill more effective than God's word, any purpose better than that something good should be created by a good God. Plato too gives this as the

dendi mundi iustissimam dicit, ut a bono Deo bona
opera fierent; sive ista legerit, sive ab his qui
legerant forte cognoverit; sive acerrimo ingenio
invisibilia Dei per ea quae facta sunt intellecta con-
spexerit, sive ab his qui ista conspexerant et ipse
didicerit.

XXII

*De his quibus in universitate rerum a bono
Creatore bene conditarum quaedam
displicent, et putant nonnullam
malam esse naturam.*

Hanc tamen causam, id est ad bona creanda bonitatem Dei, hanc, inquam, causam tam iustam atque
idoneam, quae diligenter considerata et pie cogitata
omnes controversias quaerentium mundi originem
terminat, quidam haeretici non viderunt, quia egenam
carnis huius fragilemque mortalitatem iam de iusto
supplicio venientem, dum ei non conveniunt, plurima offendunt, sicut ignis aut frigus aut fera bestia
aut quid eius modi; nec adtendunt quam vel in suis
locis naturisque vigeant pulchroque ordine dis-

---

[1] *Timaeus* 28 A; see Cicero, *Timaeus* 3.9.
[2] Cf. Romans 1.20.
[3] The Manichaeans.
[4] The reference is to the curse of Adam after his fall.

proper reason, beyond all other reasons, for the world's creation, namely that good works might be created by a good God.[1] He may have read our passage, or may have got knowledge of it from those who had read it, or else by his superlatively keen insight he gained vision of the unseen truths of God through understanding God's creation,[2] or he too may have learned of these truths from such men as had gained vision of them.

XXII

On those who find fault with certain features of the whole scheme of things well created by a good creator, and who believe that there is some substantive evil in nature.

THIS reason, however, for creating good things, namely the goodness of God, though it is, I repeat, most right and fitting, and if it is carefully weighed and seen with a religious eye it puts an end to all controversy among those who inquire into the origin of the universe, yet certain heretics[3] have not recognized it. They see that our mortal state, which cannot do without the flesh and is a brittle thing, since it reaches us now after punishment justly inflicted,[4] suffers hurt from very many things, such as fire, cold, wild beasts or anything that, like these, does not conform to its requirements. These heretics do not take note how vigorous such agents are in their natural character and proper situation, in what a beautiful scale of being they are distributed, how

ponantur, quantumque universitati rerum pro suis portionibus decoris tamquam in communem rem publicam conferant vel nobis ipsis, si eis congruenter atque scienter utamur, commoditatis adtribuant, ita ut venena ipsa, quae per inconvenientiam perniciosa sunt, convenienter adhibita in salubria medicamenta vertantur; quamque a contrario etiam haec quibus delectantur, sicut cibus et potus et ista lux, inmoderato et inopportuno usu noxia sentiantur. Unde nos admonet divina providentia non res insipienter vituperare, sed utilitatem rerum diligenter inquirere, et ubi nostrum ingenium vel infirmitas deficit, ita credere occultam, sicut erant quaedam quae vix potuimus invenire; quia et ipsa utilitatis occultatio aut humilitatis exercitatio est aut elationis adtritio; cum omnino natura nulla sit malum nomenque hoc non sit nisi privationis boni.

Sed a terrenis usque ad caelestia et a visibilibus usque ad invisibilia sunt aliis alia bona meliora, ad hoc inaequalia, ut essent omnia; Deus autem ita est artifex magnus in magnis ut minor non sit in parvis; quae parva non sua granditate—nam nulla est—,

---

[1] Compare the Stoic view as described by Cicero, *De Natura Deorum* 2.47–53.

much they contribute, in proportion to their share of beauty, to the universe as if to their common polity,[1] or how they serve our needs as well, if we employ them with a knowledge of their appropriate uses. Thus even poisons, which are deadly if we use them in the wrong way, are turned into wholesome remedies when suitably applied. Nor do they notice how, the other way around, even things that are pleasant, like food, drink and sunlight, are found to be harmful if used to excess or unsuitably. By such lessons divine providence warns us not to denounce things foolishly, but to engage in studious research how to profit by them. In cases where our wit, or, if you please, our weakness, is at fault, we must believe that the profit to be got from them is there, though concealed in the same way as were some other useful discoveries that we have barely succeeded in making. The very fact that the good to be got from them is concealed is of service to us either as an exercise in humility or a means of abrading our conceit; for no substance or being whatsoever in nature is an evil; indeed the word has reference only to the absence of a good.

Still, as we range from things earthly to things heavenly, from things visible to things invisible, some good things there are that are better than others. Their inequality it was that made it possible for them all to exist. Moreover, God is a great craftsman when he makes great things, but without any implication that he is an inferior craftsman when he makes small things. Such small things are to be rated, not by their own greatness, for they have none, but by the skill of the artist who made them. Sup-

sed artificis sapientia metienda sunt; sicut in specie visibilis hominis, si unum radatur supercilium, quam propemodum nihil corpori, et quam multum detrahitur pulchritudini, quoniam non mole constat, sed parilitate ac dimensione membrorum!

Nec sane multum mirandum est quod hi qui nonnullam malam putant esse naturam suo quodam contrario exortam propagatamque principio, nolunt accipere istam causam creationis rerum, ut bonus Deus conderet bona, credentes eum potius ad haec mundana molimina rebellantis adversum se mali repellendi extrema necessitate perductum suamque naturam bonam malo cohercendo superandoque miscuisse, quam turpissime pollutam et crudelissime captivatam et oppressam labore magno vix mundet ac liberet; non tamen totam, sed quod eius non potuerit ab illa inquinatione purgari, tegmen ac vinculum futurum hostis victi et inclusi. Sic autem Manichaei non desiperent vel potius insanirent, si Dei naturam, sicuti est, incommutabilem atque omnino incorruptibilem crederent, cui nocere nulla res possit; animam vero, quae voluntate mutari in deterius et peccato corrumpi potuit atque ita incommutabilis veritatis luce privari, non Dei partem nec

pose we shave off one eye-brow from the face of a
man whom we can see, how nearly nothing does it
subtract from the body itself, yet how much it sub-
tracts from the beauty of that body! For beauty
depends not on bulk, but on the symmetry and proportion of the parts.

And surely it is no great matter for astonishment
that those who suppose some substantial elements
in nature to be evil, originating in and fostered
by some contrary principle of its own, refuse
to accept the reason I have given for the world's
creation, namely, that a good God might create good
things. They rather believe that God was ultimately
driven to construct this massive universe by a dire
need to beat off the evil that was in revolt against
him. To restrain and overcome this evil, he mingled
with it his own natural goodness, and when this divine
goodness is most shamefully defiled and most cruelly
imprisoned and oppressed, then by a great effort he
barely succeeds in restoring it to purity and freedom;
yet not all of it is so restored; such part of it as could
not be cleansed from its defilement is to serve as a
wrapping and a chain to hold fast the conquered and
imprisoned enemy. The Manichaeans would not
be as nonsensical as this or rather so completely
mad, if they could believe the essential nature of
God to be, as it is, unchangeable and altogether incorruptible, and that no evil influence has the power
to harm it; nor would they if they held in Christian
sanity to the belief that the soul on its part, since it
was capable of changing for the worse of its own
choice and of being debased by sin and in this way
made blind to the light of unchangeable truth, is no

eius naturae quae Dei est, sed ab illo conditam longe inparem Conditori Christiana sanitate sentirent.

XXIII

De errore in quo Origenis doctrina culpatur.

SED multo est mirandum amplius quod etiam quidam qui unum nobiscum credunt omnium rerum esse principium, ullamque naturam quae non est quod Deus est nisi ab illo conditore esse non posse, noluerunt tamen istam causam fabricandi mundi tam bonam ac simplicem bene ac simpliciter credere, ut Deus bonus conderet bona et essent post Deum quae non essent quod est Deus, bona tamen, quae non faceret nisi bonus Deus; sed animas dicunt, non quidem partes Dei, sed factas a Deo, peccasse a Conditore recedendo et diversis progressibus pro diversitate peccatorum a caelis usque ad terras diversa corpora quasi vincula meruisse, et hunc esse mundum eamque causam mundi fuisse faciendi, non ut conderentur bona, sed ut mala cohiberentur. Hinc Origenes iure culpatur. In libris enim quos appellat περὶ ἀρχῶν, id est de principiis, hoc sensit,

---

[1] Origen, *De Principiis* 1.4.1 (Koetschau, p. 64).

fragment of God nor of the same substance as God, but is a thing created by him and vastly inferior to its creator.

XXIII

On the error for which Origen's doctrine is condemned.

But what is much more surprising is that even among those who believe with us that there is a single origin of all things and that it is impossible for any natural substance or being that is not identical with God to have any existence except from God as its creator, some have still refused to accept in good and simple faith so good and simple a purpose for the making of the world as this, that a good God might create good things and that things might exist that are not of God's substance and are inferior to him, though they are still good things that only a good God would create. But they say that souls, though not, it is true, fragments of God, but created by God, sinned by departing from the Creator and, after moving on to distances between heaven and earth varying according to the gravity of their sins, were condemned to a variety of bodies, which served as bonds. The result is our universe, they say, and this is the reason why the universe was created, not to provide a place for good things to be conserved, but for evil things to be confined. On this point Origen is rightly censured. For in the books which he calls *Peri Archōn*, that is *On First Principles*, this is the view that he adopted, this he set down.[1] And here I am

hoc scripsit. Ubi plus quam dici potest miror hominem in ecclesiasticis litteris tam doctum et exer-
citatum non adtendisse, primum quam hoc esset
contrarium scripturae huius tantae auctoritatis in-
tentioni, quae per omnia opera Dei subiungens: *Et
vidit Deus quia bonum est*, completisque omnibus
inferens: *Et vidit Deus omnia quae fecit, et ecce bona
valde*, nullam aliam causam faciendi mundi intellegi
voluit nisi ut bona fierent a bono Deo.

Ubi si nemo peccasset, tantummodo naturis bonis
esset mundus ornatus et plenus; et quia peccatum
est, non ideo cuncta sunt impleta peccatis, cum
bonorum longe maior numerus in caelestibus suae
naturae ordinem servet; nec mala voluntas, quia
naturae ordinem servare noluit, ideo iusti Dei leges
omnia bene ordinantis effugit; quoniam sicut pictura
cum colore nigro loco suo posito, ita universitas
rerum, si quis possit intueri, etiam cum peccatoribus
pulchra est, quamvis per se ipsos consideratos sua
deformitas turpet.

Deinde videre debuit Origenes et quicumque ista
sapiunt, si haec opinio vera esset, mundum ideo
factum ut animae pro meritis peccatorum suorum
tamquam ergastula quibus poenaliter includerentur

---

[1] Genesis 1.31.

more surprised than I can say that a man so erudite
and so well versed in ecclesiastical literature should
have failed to notice, first how far his view conflicted
with the purport of our Scriptural passage, whose
authority is so high. When after its description of
all the works of God the sentence was added in each
case: " And God saw that it was good," and after
the whole account was complete, the words were
brought in: " And God saw everything that he made,
and behold, it was very good,"[1] we were meant to
understand that the world was created solely for the
purpose of providing for the creation of good things
by a good God.

If no one in this world had sinned, the world
would have been adorned and filled exclusively with
beings naturally good. And, though sin came in, it
does not follow that the whole universe is filled with
sin on that account, for the far greater number, who
are good, among the heavenly angels keep to the right
pattern with which they were created. Nor did the
evil will, evil because it did not choose to keep the
right pattern of its nature, thereby escape the laws
of a just God who orders all things well. For a beautiful picture is improved by dark colours if they are
fitly placed, and just so the universe of real things, if
it could be so contemplated, is beautiful, sinners and
all. To be sure, if you consider sinners as they are in
themselves, their ugliness is a disfiguring blemish.

Moreover, Origen and his followers should have
seen that, if their opinion were true, and the world
was so designed that souls should receive bodies
graded according to the degree of their sins, houses
of correction, as it were, in which they should be held

corpora acciperent, superiora et leviora quae minus, inferiora vero et graviora quae amplius peccaverunt, daemones, quibus deterius nihil est, terrena corpora, quibus inferius et gravius nihil est, potius quam homines etiam bonos[1] habere debuisse. Nunc vero, ut intellegeremus animarum merita non qualitatibus corporum esse pensanda, aerium pessimus daemon, homo autem, et nunc licet malus longe minoris mitiorisque malitiae, et certe ante peccatum, tamen luteum corpus accepit.

Quid autem stultius dici potest quam istum solem, ut in uno mundo unus esset, non decori pulchritudinis vel etiam saluti rerum corporalium consuluisse artificem Deum, sed hoc potius evenisse quia una anima sic peccaverat ut tali corpore mereretur includi? Ac per hoc si contigisset ut non una, sed duae; immo non duae, sed decem vel centum similiter aequaliterque peccassent, centum soles haberet hic mundus? Quod ut non fieret, non opificis provisione mirabili ad rerum corporalium salutem decoremque consultum est, sed contigit potius tanta unius animae progressione peccantis ut sola corpus tale mereretur. Non plane animarum, de quibus nesciunt quid loquantur, sed eorum ipsorum qui talia sapiunt

[1] malos *Migne*.

---

[1] Origen, *De Principiis* 1, Praefatio 8 (Koetschau, p. 15).

for punishment, in that case, there would be higher and lighter bodies for the lesser sinners and lower and heavier bodies for those whose sins were greater. Demons, rather than men, good men among them, should have earthen bodies, than which nothing is lower and heavier, for nothing is more wicked than demons. Actually, however, in order to make us see that souls are not to be rated good or bad by the kinds of bodies that they have, the worst demon has an aerial body, whereas a man has a body of clay,[1] although man, wicked as he is, is even now far from equal to the demon in the amount and virulence of his will to evil; before he sinned there could be no doubt of this.

But what could be more foolish than to say that the sun is the only sun in the only world, not because God the artificer took thought to adorn his world with beauty or even to further the well-being of the physical world, but rather that it came out so just because one and only one soul had sinned to such a degree that it deserved to be imprisoned in such a body as this? According to this theory, if it had happened that not one but two, nay, not two but ten or a hundred souls, had sinned in the same way and to the same degree, our world would possess one hundred suns. That this did not take place was due, they think, not to the amazing foresight of a Creator who was intent on the health and adornment of physical beings and things, but to the mere chance that one sinning soul arrived at precisely such distance that it alone was duly awarded such a body. Surely it is not the straying of souls, of which they speak without knowing what they are speaking

519

multum longe a veritate, merito est cohercenda progressio.

Haec ergo tria quae superius commendavi, cum in unaquaque creatura requirantur, quis eam fecerit, per quid fecerit, quare fecerit, ut respondeatur "Deus, per Verbum, quia bona est," utrum altitudine mystica nobis ipsa trinitas intimetur, hoc est Pater et Filius et Spiritus sanctus, an aliquid occurrat quod hoc loco scripturarum id accipiendum esse prohibeat, multi sermonis est quaestio, nec omnia uno volumine ut explicemus urgendum est.

XXIV

De trinitate divina, quae per omnia opera sua signi-
ficationis suae sparsit indicia.

CREDIMUS et tenemus et fideliter praedicamus quod Pater genuerit Verbum, hoc est sapientiam, per quam facta sunt omnia, unigenitum Filium, unus unum, aeternus coaeternum, summe bonus aequaliter bonum; et quod Spiritus sanctus simul et Patris et Filii sit Spiritus et ipse consubstantialis et coaeternus ambobus; atque hoc totum et trinitas sit propter proprietatem personarum et unus Deus propter in-

about, but their own straying, who are in their thinking so far from the truth, that deserves to be checked and restrained.

So when those three questions which I suggested above are asked in the case of any creature whatever: " Who made it? By what means did he make it? Why did he make it? " in the answer that we give: " God; by means of the Word; because it is good," we may have in some profound mystic way an intimation of the Trinity, that is, Father, Son and Holy Spirit. Whether this is so or whether some objection may intervene to prevent the acceptance of such an interpretation of this text of Scripture is a matter that would require a great deal of discussion; and we must not be pressed to explain everything in one book.

XXIV

*On the divine Trinity, which has scattered
everywhere in its works symbolic
references to itself.*

WE believe, we maintain and we faithfully preach that the Father begot the Word, that is wisdom, by which all things were made, his only-begotten Son, one as the Father is one, eternal as the Father is eternal, supremely good as the Father is equally good; that the Holy Spirit is at the same time the Spirit of both the Father and the Son, and is itself consubstantial and coeternal with both; and that the whole is a Trinity because of the individuality of its persons, and at the same time a single God by

separabilem divinitatem, sicut unus Omnipotens propter inseparabilem omnipotentiam; ita tamen ut etiam cum de singulis quaeritur unusquisque eorum et Deus et omnipotens esse respondeatur; cum vero de omnibus simul, non tres dii vel tres omnipotentes, sed unus Deus omnipotens; tanta ibi est in tribus inseparabilis unitas, quae sic se voluit praedicari.

Utrum autem boni Patris et boni Filii Spiritus sanctus, quia communis ambobus est, recte bonitas dici possit amborum, non audeo temerariam praecipitare sententiam; verum tamen amborum eum dicere sanctitatem facilius ausus fuero, non amborum quasi qualitatem, sed ipsum quoque substantiam in trinitate personam. Ad hoc enim me probabilius ducit quod, cum sit et Pater spiritus et Filius spiritus, et Pater sanctus et Filius sanctus, proprie tamen ipse vocatur Spiritus sanctus tamquam sanctitas substantialis et consubstantialis amborum.

Sed si nihil est aliud bonitas divina quam sanctitas, profecto et illa diligentia rationis est, non praesumptionis audacia, ut in operibus Dei secreto quodam loquendi modo, quo nostra exerceatur intentio, eadem nobis insinuata intellegatur trinitas, unam-

reason of their indivisible divinity, just as there is
one single Almighty by reason of their indivisible
omnipotence. Yet when a question is asked con-
concerning its individual members, the reply must
be that each of them is God and each is Almighty;
but when the query concerns all of them together,
the answer is that they are not three Gods or three
Almighties, but one God Almighty, so great is the
inseparable oneness there in the three, and this is
how their oneness has chosen to have itself proclaimed.

But whether the Holy Spirit of the good Father
and the good Son may properly be called the goodness of both because he is common to both, I do not
venture to hazard a rash and overbold opinion.
Nevertheless I shall not find it so hard to say boldly
that he is the holiness of both, not in the sense that
he is a quality belonging to both, but that he is himself a substantial being and the third person in the
Trinity. I am led to accept this view with the more
conviction in that, though the Father is a spirit and
the Son is a spirit, and the Father is holy and the Son
is holy, yet he individually has the name of Holy
Spirit as being a substantial holiness consubstantial
with the other two.

But if divine goodness is nothing else than holiness,
then certainly it is a studious use of reason rather than
a rash jump to conclusions that makes us see a hint
of this same Trinity in the account of God's works
of creation. It is a hint expressed in a kind of crypto-
gram in order to develop our acumen, as we ask concerning everything created by him whatsoever:
" Who made it ? By what means did he make it ?

quamque creaturam quis fecerit, per quid fecerit, propter quid fecerit. Pater quippe intellegitur Verbi, qui dixit ut fiat; quod autem illo dicente factum est, procul dubio per Verbum factum est; in eo vero quod dicitur: *Vidit Deus quia bonum est*, satis significatur Deum nulla necessitate, nulla suae cuiusquam utilitatis indigentia, sed sola bonitate fecisse quod factum est, id est, quia bonum est; quod ideo postea quam factum est dicitur, ut res quae facta est congruere bonitati propter quam facta est indicetur. Quae bonitas si Spiritus sanctus recte intellegitur, universa nobis trinitas in suis operibus intimatur. Inde est civitatis sanctae quae in sanctis angelis sursum est, et origo et informatio et beatitudo. Nam si quaeratur unde sit: Deus eam condidit; si unde sit sapiens: A Deo inluminatur; si unde sit felix: Deo fruitur; subsistens modificatur, contemplans inlustratur, inhaerens iucundatur; est, videt, amat; in aeternitate Dei viget, in veritate Dei lucet, in bonitate Dei gaudet.

---

[1] Cf. Galatians 4.26.
[2] Cf. Revelation 22.5.

Why did he make it?" The answer, that is, is
discovered to be that it was the Father of the Word
who said: "Let it be made," and that what was
created when he spoke was undoubtedly created
through the Word. Again in the statement: "God
saw that it was good," it is made abundantly clear
that it was not from any compulsion, nor from the
least need of any personal advantage, that God made
what was made, but solely from his goodness, that is,
he made it because it is good. And it is so described
after it was made, in order to show that the thing
that was made corresponds exactly to the goodness
that was the purpose of its creation. And if we are
right in recognizing that this goodness is the Holy
Spirit, then the whole Trinity is inwardly presented
to us in its works of creation. In this Trinity is the
origin, the instruction and the blessedness of the
holy city which is above [1] among the holy angels.
For if we ask: "Whence comes it?" the answer is:
"God established it"; if "Whence comes its wisdom?" the reply is "God gives it light"; [2] and if
"Whence comes its happiness?" the explanation is:
"It enjoys God." By abiding in him it receives its
pattern, by contemplating him it receives its light,
by clinging to him it receives its joy. It is, it sees, it
loves; in God's eternity is its strength, in God's
truth its light, and in God's goodness is its joy.

XXV

De tripertita totius philosophiae disciplina.

QUANTUM intellegi datur, hinc philosophi sapientiae disciplinam tripertitam esse voluerunt, immo tripertitam esse animadvertere potuerunt—neque enim ipsi instituerunt ut ita esset, sed ita esse potius invenerunt—, cuius una pars appellaretur physica, altera logica, tertia ethica—quarum nomina Latina iam multorum litteris frequentata sunt, ut naturalis, rationalis moralisque vocarentur; quas etiam in octavo libro breviter strinximus—; non quo sit consequens ut isti in his tribus aliquid secundum Deum de trinitate cogitaverint, quamvis Plato primus istam distributionem repperisse et commendasse dicatur, cui neque naturarum omnium auctor nisi Deus visus est neque intellegentiae dator neque amoris quo bene beateque vivitur inspirator. Sed certe cum et de natura rerum et de ratione indagandae veritatis et de boni fine ad quem cuncta quae agimus referre debemus, diversi diversa sentiant, in his tamen tribus magnis et generalibus quaestionibus omnis eorum versatur intentio. Ita cum in unaquaque earum quid quisque sectetur multiplex discrepantia sit

---

[1] See above, Book 8.4–8.

XXV

On the division of all philosophic training into three parts.

As far as it is given to me to see, philosophers took their lead from this very truth when they decreed that the study of philosophy should be subsumed under three heads, or rather they succeeded in observing that it came under three heads, for they did not themselves create this classification but rather discovered that the truth of the matter is so. One head or division was called physics, the second logic, and the third ethics. The corresponding Latin terms have become common in the writings of many authors as " natural," " rational " and " moral " philosophy; and on these I touched in the eighth book as well.[1] We need not conclude from this that these philosophers in making this threefold division had any thought of a Trinity as it is found in God, although Plato, who is said to have been the first to discover and sponsor this division, was convinced that none other than God must be the creator of all natural beings, the giver of understanding, and the inspirer of the love which leads to a good and happy life. But it is certain that philosophers, though they may hold different views about nature, about method in the search for truth, and about the supremely good goal towards which we ought to direct all our actions, still agree in devoting all their study to these three important general fields of research. Thus, although there is a discordant variety of opinion on the question which sect each man should follow in any

opinionum, esse tamen aliquam naturae causam, scientiae formam, vitae summam nemo cunctatur.

Tria etiam sunt quae in unoquoque homine artifice spectantur, ut aliquid efficiat: natura, doctrina, usus; natura ingenio, doctrina scientia, usus fructu diiudicandus est. Nec ignoro quod proprie fructus fruentis, usus utentis sit, atque hoc interesse videatur, quod ea re frui dicimur quae nos non ad aliud referenda per se ipsa delectat; uti vero ea re quam propter aliud quaerimus—unde temporalibus magis utendum est quam fruendum, ut frui mereamur aeternis; non sicut perversi qui frui volunt nummo, uti autem Deo; quoniam non nummum propter Deum inpendunt, sed Deum propter nummum colunt—; verum tamen eo loquendi modo quem plus obtinuit consuetudo, et fructibus utimur et usibus fruimur; nam et fructus iam proprie dicuntur agrorum, quibus utique omnes temporaliter utimur.

Hoc itaque more usum dixerim in his tribus quae in homine spectanda commonui, quae sunt natura, doctrina, usus. Ex his propter obtinendam beatam vitam tripertita, ut dixi, a philosophis inventa est

given field, no one doubts that there is some cause that explains nature, some formal system of knowledge, and a highest motive in life.

There are also three important things to be considered in regarding any artist who hopes to complete a work of art: natural endowment, instruction and practice. The criterion by which we must judge natural endowment is native talent, that of instruction is knowledge, and that of practice is enjoyment. I am not forgetting that *fructus* ' enjoyment ' is properly the act of someone who enjoys, and *usus* ' practice ' of one who uses. The difference between the words seems to be that we are said to enjoy something that gives us pleasure in itself without reference to anything else, but to use something we need for the sake of something else. So with temporal things, we ought to use rather than enjoy them in order that we may be rewarded by the enjoyment of things eternal. We must not be like those perverse men who want to enjoy money, but to make use of God, for they do not spend money for the sake of God but worship God for the sake of money. However, in the current expression which has obtained the sanction of custom, we use what we enjoy and enjoy what we use. For in common parlance we speak of enjoying harvests from the land, and these of course we all use for food in our present life.

It was in this customary sense, then, that I would use the term *usus* ' practice ' among the three things to be considered in judging a man, namely natural endowment, instruction and practice. These three are the basis on which, in order to attain a happy life, the philosophers, as I said, devised their threefold

disciplina, naturalis propter naturam, rationalis propter doctrinam, moralis propter usum. Si ergo natura nostra esset a nobis, profecto et nostram nos genuissemus sapientiam nec eam doctrina, id est aliunde discendo, percipere curaremus; et noster amor a nobis profectus et ad nos relatus et ad beate vivendum sufficeret nec bono alio quo frueremur ullo indigeret; nunc vero quia natura nostra ut esset Deum habet auctorem, procul dubio ut vera sapiamus ipsum debemus habere doctorem, ipsum etiam ut beati simus suavitatis intimae largitorem.

XXVI

De imagine summae trinitatis quae secundum quendam modum in natura etiam necdum beatificati hominis invenitur.

Et nos quidem in nobis, tametsi non aequalem, immo valde longeque distantem, neque coaeternam et, quo brevius totum dicitur, non eiusdem substantiae cuius Deus est, tamen qua Deo nihil sit in rebus ab eo factis natura propinquius, imaginem Dei, hoc est illius summae trinitatis, agnoscimus, adhuc reformatione perficiendam ut sit etiam similitudine proxima. Nam et sumus et nos esse novimus et id

training in philosophy. Natural philosophy has nature as its object, rational philosophy has instruction as its goal, and moral philosophy aims at practice. Therefore, if our natural being originated in ourselves, it follows that we should have generated our own wisdom too and should not take pains to acquire it by instruction, that is, by learning it from some other source. Our love too, proceeding from ourselves and coming back to ourselves, would not only be sufficient to provide a happy life but would have no need of any other enjoyment. As it is, however, since our natural being has God for author of its existence, undoubtedly we are bound to find in him both our teacher that we may have true wisdom, and our dispenser of the bounty of inner sweetness to make us happy.

XXVI

On the image of the most high Trinity that in a certain fashion is found in human nature even before a man has attained bliss.

We too as a matter of fact recognize in ourselves an image of God, that is of this most high Trinity, even if the image is not equal to Him in worth, but rather very far short of being so. The image is not co-eternal and, to sum the matter up briefly, it is not formed of the same substance as God. Yet it is nearer to him in the scale of nature than any other thing created by him, although it still requires to be reshaped and perfected in order to be nearest to him in its likeness to him also. For we both are and

esse ac nosse diligimus. In his autem tribus quae
dixi, nulla nos falsitas veri similis turbat. Non
enim ea sicut illa quae foris sunt ullo sensu corporis
tangimus, velut colores videndo, sonos audiendo,
odores olfaciendo, sapores gustando, dura et mollia
contrectando sentimus, quorum sensibilium etiam
imagines eis simillimas nec iam corporeas cogitatione versamus, memoria tenemus et per ipsas in
istorum desideria concitamur; sed sine ulla phan-
tasiarum vel phantasmatum imaginatione ludifi-
catoria mihi esse me idque nosse et amare certissimum est.

Nulla in his veris Academicorum argumenta
formido dicentium, Quid si falleris? Si enim
fallor, sum. Nam qui non est, utique nec falli
potest; ac per hoc sum, si fallor. Quia ergo sum
si fallor, quo modo esse me fallor, quando certum est
me esse, si fallor? Quia igitur essem qui fallerer,
etiamsi fallerer, procul dubio in eo quod me novi
esse, non fallor. Consequens est autem ut etiam in
eo quod me novi nosse, non fallar. Sicut enim novi
esse me, ita novi etiam hoc ipsum, nosse me. Eaque
duo cum amo, eundem quoque amorem quiddam

---

[1] For the principles on which the Academicians based their
scepticism, see esp. Cicero, *Academica Priora* 2.13.40-42.

know that we are, and we love our existence and our knowledge of it. Moreover, in these three statements that I have made we are not confused by any mistake masquerading as truth. For we do not get in touch with these realities, as we do with external objects, by means of any bodily sense. We know colours, for instance, by seeing them, sounds by hearing them, odours by smelling them, the taste of things by tasting them, and hard and soft objects by feeling them. We also have images that closely resemble these physical objects, but they are not material. They live in our minds, where we use them in thinking, preserve them in our memory, and are stimulated by them to desire the objects themselves. But it is without any deceptive play of my imagination, with its real or unreal visions, that I am quite certain that I am, that I know that I am, and that I love this being and this knowing.

Where these truths are concerned I need not quail before the Academicians when they say: " What if you should be mistaken ? " [1] Well, if I am mistaken, I exist. For a man who does not exist can surely not be mistaken either, and if I am mistaken, therefore I exist. So, since I am if I am mistaken, how can I be mistaken in believing that I am when it is certain that if I am mistaken I am. Therefore, from the fact that, if I were indeed mistaken, I should have to exist to be mistaken, it follows that I am undoubtedly not mistaken in knowing that I am. It follows also that in saying that I know that I know, I am not mistaken. For just as I know that I am, so it holds too that I know that I know. And when I love these two things, I add this same love as a third particular

tertium nec inparis aestimationis eis quas novi rebus
adiungo. Neque enim fallor amare me, cum in his
quae amo non fallar; quamquam etsi illa falsa essent,
falsa me amare verum esset. Nam quo pacto recte
reprehenderer et recte prohiberer ab amore falsorum,
si me illa amare falsum esset? Cum vero et illa
vera atque certa sint, quis dubitet quod eorum, cum
amantur, et ipse amor verus et certus est? Tam
porro nemo est qui esse se nolit quam nemo est qui
non esse beatus velit. Quo modo enim potest
beatus esse, si nihil sit?

XXVII

De essentia et scientia et utriusque amore.

Ita vero vi quadam naturali ipsum esse iucundum
est ut non ob aliud et hi qui miseri sunt nolint interire
et, cum se miseros esse sentiant, non se ipsos de
rebus, sed miseriam suam potius auferri velint. Illis
etiam qui et sibi miserrimi apparent et plane sunt et
non solum a sapientibus, quoniam stulti, verum et ab
his qui se beatos putant, miseri iudicantur, quia
pauperes atque mendici sunt, si quis inmortalitatem
daret qua nec ipsa miseria moreretur, proposito sibi

---

[1] See *De Moribus Ecclesiae Catholicae* 1.3.4; *De Trinitate*
13.20.25; *Confessions* 10.21.31.

of no smaller value to these things that I know. Nor
is my statement, that I love, a mistake, since I am
not mistaken in the things that I love; yet even if
they were illusions, it would still be true that I love
illusions. For on what grounds could I rightly be
blamed or prevented from loving illusions, if it were
a mistaken belief that I love them? But since these
things are themselves true and certain who can doubt
that, when they are loved, the love itself is also true
and certain? Furthermore, it is as true that there
is no man who does not wish to be as that there is no
man who does not wish to be happy. For how can a
man be happy if he is nothing? [1]

XXVII

On being, knowledge and the love of both.

By some natural drive, just to be is so agreeable that
for no other reason even those who are miserable are
not willing to die. [2] Although they feel that they are
miserable, they do not wish themselves to be removed
from the world, but wish rather that their misery
might be removed from them. Take even those who
appear to themselves to be completely miserable and
clearly are so. They are judged to be miserable,
not only by the wise on the ground that they are
foolish, but also by those who think themselves
happy and judge them unhappy because they are
poor and destitute. If someone were to offer them
an immortality wherein not even their misery would

[2] See Seneca, *Letter* 101.

quod, si in eadem miseria semper esse nollent, nulli
et nusquam essent futuri, sed omni modo perituri,
profecto exultarent laetitia et sic semper eligerent
esse quam omnino non esse. Huius rei testis est
notissimus sensus illorum. Unde enim mori metuunt
et malunt in illa aerumna vivere quam eam morte
finire, nisi quia satis apparet quam refugiat natura
non esse? Atque ideo cum se noverint esse mori-
turos, pro magno beneficio sibi hanc inpendi misericordiam desiderant, ut aliquanto productius in
eadem miseria vivant tardiusque moriantur. Procul
dubio ergo indicant inmortalitatem, saltem talem
quae non habeat finem mendicitatis, quanta gratu-
latione susciperent.

Quid? Animalia omnia etiam inrationalia, quibus
datum non est ista cogitare, ab inmensis draconibus
usque ad exiguos vermiculos nonne se esse velle
atque ob hoc interitum fugere omnibus quibus
possunt motibus indicant? Quid? Arbusta omnesque frutices, quibus nullus est sensus ad vitandam
manifesta motione perniciem, nonne ut in auras
tutum cacuminis germen emittant, aliud[1] terrae
radicis[2] adfigunt quo alimentum trahant atque ita
suum quodam modo esse conservent? Ipsa postremo corpora, quibus non solum sensus, sed nec ulla
saltem seminalis est vita, ita tamen vel exiliunt in
superna vel in ima descendunt vel librantur in mediis

---

[1] altius *two MSS. and Migne.*
[2] radices *six MSS. and Migne.*

die, on the understanding that, if they chose not to remain always in this unhappy state, they would be
non-existent and would have no being anywhere but
would be completely annihilated, they would without
hesitation dance with joy and elect to remain miserable forever rather than not to exist at all. As
proof of this we have the well-known attitude of such
men. For why do they fear to die and prefer to live
their tormented life rather than make an end by
dying, except that we see quite clearly how stoutly
nature reacts against the prospect of not being? This
is the reason, too, why, when they know that they are
doomed to die, they crave as a great boon that they
may be granted the mercy of living a little longer in
the same misery and of dying a little later. Thus
they demonstrate beyond a doubt with what glad
welcome they would accept an offer of immortality,
even such immortality as brought with it no end of
their destitute condition.

What of animals in general, even irrational animals
that have no power to reflect on these things? Do
they not, from huge serpents down to tiny little
worms, show that they want to go on being and, in
order to do so, seek to escape death by every movement at their command? What of trees and shrubs
of every kind that have no sensation to enable them
to avoid destruction by perceptible movement, yet
do they not ensure the growth of their topmost
germinal shoots into the air by fixing another growth,
of root, into the ground so as to draw nourishment
from it and so, in their own fashion, preserve their
existence? Last of all, material masses, which have
neither feeling nor even any seed of life within them,

ut essentiam suam, ubi secundum naturam possunt esse, custodiant.

Iam vero nosse quantum ametur quamque falli nolit humana natura, vel hinc intellegi potest, quod lamentari quisque sana mente mavult quam laetari in amentia. Quae vis magna atque mirabilis mortalibus praeter homini animantibus nulla est, licet eorum quibusdam ad istam lucem contuendam multo quam nobis sit acrior sensus oculorum; sed lucem illam incorpoream contingere nequeunt qua mens nostra quodam modo radiatur ut de his omnibus recte iudicare possimus. Nam in quantum eam capimus, in tantum id possumus.

Verum tamen inest in sensibus inrationalium animantium, etsi scientia nullo modo, at certe quaedam scientiae similitudo; cetera autem rerum corporalium, non quia sentiunt, sed quia sentiuntur, sensibilia nuncupata sunt. Quorum in arbustis hoc simile est sensibus, quod aluntur et gignunt. Verum tamen et haec et omnia corporalia latentes in natura causas habent; sed formas suas, quibus mundi huius visibilis structura formosa est, sentiendas sensibus praebent, ut pro eo quod nosse non possunt quasi innotescere velle videantur. Sed nos ea sensu corporis ita capimus ut de his non sensu corporis iudice-

---

[1] Augustine refers to the doctrine, taken ultimately from Aristotle, that every material body is drawn to its proper place in the universe by its natural weight: fire tends upward, a stone downward, oil poured on water floats. Cf. *Confessions* 13.9.10; *Letters* 55.10.18, 157.9.

nevertheless leap upwards or fall downwards or remain balanced in between so as to keep themselves in
being where nature gives them power to be.[1]

Again, we may appreciate how great is the love of
knowledge implanted in human nature, and how unwilling that nature is to be deceived, by noticing
that everyone prefers to be sad and sane rather than
glad, but at the same time mad. Only in man among
living creatures which are subject to death is this
powerful and marvellous drive towards knowledge
found. Though some animals have a far keener
power of the eye to gaze into the light of ordinary
day, they cannot attain to the incorporeal light whose
rays so enlighten, as it were, our mind that we are
able to judge all these things aright; for our power
to judge is in proportion to the light that we inwardly
receive.

Nevertheless there is in the senses of animals that
cannot reason, if not actual knowledge, at any rate
some semblance of knowledge, whereas other physical things are called sensible, not because they have
sensation, but because they are objects of sense.
In the case of trees, their nourishment and generation is analogous to sensation. Yet, though they
and all physical things have causes that lie hid in
nature, they do display for observation by our senses
their shapes, which give shapeliness to the visible
structure of our world; so that, it would seem, to
make up for their inability to know, they have a will,
as it were, to gain notice and be known. But though
we perceive them by our bodily senses, we do not
pass judgement on them by bodily senses. For we
have another and far nobler sense belonging to the

mus. Habemus enim alium interioris hominis sensum isto longe praestantiorem quo iusta et iniusta sentimus, iusta per intellegibilem speciem, iniusta per eius privationem. Ad huius sensus officium non acies pupulae, non foramen auriculae, non spiramenta narium, non gustus faucium, non ullus corporeus tactus accedit. Ibi me et esse et hoc nosse certus sum, et haec amo atque amare me similiter certus sum.

XXVIII

An etiam ipsum amorem quo et esse et scire diligimus, diligere debeamus, quo magis divinae trinitatis imagini propinquemus.

SED de duobus illis, essentia scilicet et notitia, quantum amentur in nobis, et quem ad modum etiam in ceteris rebus quae infra sunt, eorum reperiatur, etsi differens, quaedam tamen similitudo, quantum suscepti huius operis ratio visa est postulare, satis diximus; de amore autem quo amantur, utrum et ipse amor ametur, non dictum est. Amatur autem; et hinc probamus, quod in hominibus qui rectius amantur,[1] ipse magis amatur. Neque enim vir bonus merito dicitur qui scit quod bonum est, sed qui diligit. Cur ergo et in nobis ipsis non et ipsum amorem nos amare sentimus quo amamus quidquid

---

[1] *The context seems to require* amant *here,* "The more love is rightly directed, the more it is itself loved."

---

[1] *Intellegibilis species* here is the Platonic form, *eidos,* or *idea.* Justice is the intelligible form, *species* or *idea* of justice, and injustice is the absence of this form.

inner man, and by this we perceive both right and
wrong, right by its shape in the mind's eye and wrong
by the lack of any such shapeliness.[1]   This sense is
not served in its operation either by the pupil of the
eye, or by the orifice of the ear, or by the passages in
the nose, or by the taste in the throat, or by any
physical touch.   It is there inwardly that I am certain
that I am and that I know it; and in the same way
I love these certainties and am certain that I love
them.

XXVIII

Should we cherish the very love by which we love
both our being and our knowledge of it, in
order to come closer to the image of the
Holy Trinity?

But we have said enough, as far as the plan of this
work seems to require, about those two things, being
and knowledge and the strength of our love for them,
and the way in which some semblance of them, though
with a difference, is found even throughout the lower
creation.   Yet we have not spoken of the love whereby they are loved, to say whether this love itself is
also loved.   Well, it is loved, and we have proof of
this in that, when men are more justly loved, the love
itself is the more cherished.   Nor in fact does that
man deserve to be described as good who merely
knows what is good; a good man must cherish the
good.   Why then do we not judge in our own case
too that we love the love itself with which we love

boni amamus? Est enim et amor quo amatur et
quod amandum non est, et istum amorem odit in se
qui illum diligit quo id amatur quod amandum est.
Possunt enim ambo esse in uno homine, et hoc
bonum est homini, ut illo proficiente quo bene vivimus iste deficiat quo male vivimus, donec ad perfectum sanetur et in bonum commutetur omne quod
vivimus. Si enim pecora essemus, carnalem vitam et
quod secundum sensum eius est amaremus idque esset
sufficiens bonum nostrum et secundum hoc cum
esset nobis bene, nihil aliud quaereremus. Item si
arbores essemus, nihil quidem sentiente motu amare
possemus, verum tamen id quasi adpetere videremur
quo feracius essemus uberiusque fructuosae. Si
essemus lapides aut fluctus aut ventus aut flamma vel
quid huius modi, sine ullo quidem sensu atque vita,
non tamen nobis deesset quasi quidam nostrorum
locorum atque ordinis adpetitus. Nam velut amores
corporum momenta sunt ponderum, sive deorsum
gravitate sive sursum levitate nitantur. Ita enim
corpus pondere, sicut animus amore fertur quocumque fertur.

Quoniam igitur homines sumus ad nostri creatoris
imaginem creati, cuius est vera aeternitas, aeterna
veritas, aeterna et vera caritas, estque ipse aeterna
et vera et cara trinitas neque confusa neque separata,

---

[1] Cf. *Confessions* 13.9.10. Note that love in the soul corresponds to weight in bodies; love draws the soul towards its
natural resting place.

whatever good we love? For there is also a love by
which that is loved which should not be loved, and
that is a love that a man hates in himself, if he
cherishes the love with which he loves what should
be loved. Indeed both loves can exist in the same
man; and good for man consists in this, that as one
love thrives, the one whereby we live rightly, the
other, whereby we lead an evil life, grows less and
less, until our entire life is completely restored to
health and transformed into a good one. For if we
were beasts, we should love a carnal life and whatever
accords with its sensuality. Such a life would be
sufficient for our well-being, and when all went well
with us carnally, we should look for nothing further.
Likewise if we were trees, though we should be
unable to love anything by any conscious impulse,
nevertheless we might in a way appear to pursue
the aim of becoming more productive and bounti-
fully fruitful. If we were stones, waves, wind, flame
or something of this sort, though without any sensation or life, we still should not be without a kind of
impulse to seek our proper place in the order of
nature. I mean that the force exerted upon bodies
by their weight is a kind of love or attraction making
them strive downwards if they are heavy and upwards
if light. For the body is impelled by weight just as
the soul is impelled by love to move in the direction
that it does.[1]

Since then we are men created in the image of our
Creator whose eternity is true, whose truth is eternal,
and whose cherishing love is eternal and true, and
who is himself the eternal, the true and the dearly
loved Trinity in whom there is neither confusion nor

in his quidem rebus quae infra nos sunt, quoniam et
ipsa nec aliquo modo essent nec aliqua specie contine-
rentur nec aliquem ordinem vel adpeterent vel tene-
rent nisi ab illo facta essent qui summe est, qui
summe sapiens est, qui summe bonus est, tamquam
per omnia quae fecit mirabili stabilitate currentes
quasi quaedam eius alibi magis, alibi minus inpressa
vestigia colligamus; in nobis autem ipsis eius
imaginem contuentes tamquam minor ille evangelicus
filius ad nosmet ipsos reversi surgamus et ad illum
redeamus a quo peccando recesseramus. Ibi esse
nostrum non habebit mortem, ibi nosse nostrum non
habebit errorem, ibi amare nostrum non habebit
offensionem. Nunc autem tria ista nostra quamvis
certa teneamus nec aliis ea credamus testibus, sed
nos ipsi praesentia sentiamus atque interiore vera-
cissimo cernamus aspectu, tamen quamdiu futura vel
utrum numquam defutura et quo si male, quo autem
si bene agantur perventura sint, quoniam per nos
ipsos nosse non possumus, alios hinc testes vel quaerimus vel habemus; de quorum fide cur nulla debeat
esse dubitatio, non est iste, sed posterior erit diligentius disserendi locus.

In hoc autem libro de civitate Dei quae non peregrinatur in huius vitae mortalitate, sed inmortalis

---

[1] See *City of God*, Book 12.2.
[2] Luke 15.18.

separation of the three persons, since, moreover, in the world that exists at a lower level than ourselves, the beings that are there could in no wise exist, nor be classed in a particular species, nor strive towards a certain proper place in nature or keep their place there if they had not been made by him who is supremely existent, supremely wise and supremely good, let us run through all his works which he created miraculously without movement or change on his part, and let us gather up, as it were, the footprints that he left, deeply impressed in one place, more lightly in another.[1] Then, as we contemplate his image in ourselves, may we, like the younger son in the Gospel,[2] come to ourselves and arise and go to our father from whom we had departed through our sin. With him our being will not know death, with him our knowledge will not know error, with him our love will know no obstacle. In our present state, although we have these three certainties and accept them, not on the testimony of others but by our own awareness of their presence and by seeing them with the inward contemplation that is the truest witness, yet we cannot know of ourselves how long they will last, nor whether they will never come to an end, and what their final destiny will be according as they receive good or bad treatment. Hence we seek or already have other witnesses. We must have no doubt of the trust to be put in these, but I will postpone to a later opportunity the fuller discussion of that point—this is not the appropriate place.

This book, then, deals with the City of God in so far as it is not a sojourner in this mortal life, but is forever immortal in the heavens. That is to say, it is

semper in caelis est, id est de angelis sanctis Deo cohaerentibus, qui nec fuerunt umquam nec futuri sunt desertores, inter quos et illos qui aeternam lucem deserentes tenebrae facti sunt Deum primitus divisisse iam diximus, illo adiuvante quod coepimus ut possumus explicemus.

XXIX

*De sanctorum angelorum scientia qua trinitatem in
ipsa eius deitate noverunt et qua operum causas
artificis prius in operantis arte quam in
ipsis operibus intuentur.*

ILLI quippe angeli sancti non per verba sonantia Deum discunt, sed per ipsam praesentiam inmutabilis veritatis, hoc est Verbum eius unigenitum, et ipsum Verbum et Patrem et eorum Spiritum sanctum, eamque esse inseparabilem trinitatem singulasque in ea personas esse substantiam,[1] et tamen omnes non tres deos esse, sed unum Deum, ita noverunt ut eis magis ista quam nos ipsi nobis cogniti simus. Ipsam quoque creaturam melius ibi, hoc est in sapientia Dei, tamquam in arte qua facta est, quam in ea ipsa sciunt; ac per hoc et se

---

[1] esse substantiam *MS. V (saec. V) and others:* unam esse substantiam *three MSS. and Welldon:* esse unam substantiam *three MSS. and Migne.*

---

[1] See above, Book 11.13.

composed of the holy angels who cling to God, who never were nor ever will be apostates. I have already said that God made a distinction in the beginning between them and those who deserted the light ever-lasting and became the realm of darkness.[1] With his help and to the best of my ability let me continue the work of exposition on which I have embarked.

XXIX

On the knowledge whereby the holy angels know the Trinity in its very Godhead and whereby they behold the causes of God's works in the Maker's own design for creation before they behold them in the Artist's actual works.

THE holy angels, be it noted, learn to know God, not by the sound of words, but by the actual presence of unchangeable truth, that is by his only begotten Word; they learn to know him as the Word itself and the Father and their Holy Spirit. They know too that this Trinity is indivisible, that within it each of the Persons is a substantial being and yet that all together they form not three Gods, but one single God. Their knowledge is such that those truths are more surely known to them than we ourselves are known to ourselves. They also know every created being or thing better in the realm of God's wisdom and, as it were, in the design according to which it was made than they know it after it is created; and by this means they even know themselves better in that realm than in themselves; nevertheless they

547

ipsos ibi melius quam in se ipsis, verum tamen et in
se ipsis. Facti sunt enim et aliud sunt quam ille qui
fecit. Ibi ergo tamquam in diurna cognitione, in se
ipsis autem tamquam in vespertina, sicut iam supra
diximus.

Multum enim differt utrum in ea ratione cognosca-
tur aliquid secundum quam factum est, an in se ipso;
sicut aliter scitur rectitudo linearum seu veritas
figurarum cum intellecta conspicitur, aliter cum in
pulvere scribitur; et aliter iustitia in veritate incommutabili, aliter in anima iusti. Sic deinde cetera,
sicut firmamentum inter aquas superiores et inferiores, quod caelum vocatum est; sicut deorsum
aquarum congeries terraeque nudatio et herbarum
institutio atque lignorum; sicut solis ac lunae stel-
larumque conditio; sicut ex aquis animalium, volucrum scilicet atque piscium beluarumque natantium;
sicut quorumque in terra gradientium atque repen-
tium et ipsius hominis, qui cunctis in terra rebus
excelleret. Omnia haec aliter in Verbo Dei cognos-
cuntur ab angelis, ubi habent causas rationesque
suas, id est secundum quas facta sunt, incommutabiliter permanentes, aliter in se ipsis; illa clariore,
hac obscuriore cognitione, velut artis atque operum;
quae tamen opera cum ad ipsius Creatoris laudem

---

[1] See above, Book 11.7.

also know themselves as they are in themselves. For they were created and are of a different substance from their Creator. So in contemplating the Word, they have, as it were, a daylight knowledge, but in observing themselves a kind of twilight knowledge, as we said above.[1]

Indeed, there is a great difference between acquaintance with something as a part of the concept according to which it was made and acquaintance with it by itself, just as straight lines or the true shapes of figures are known on one level when they are present to the mind and on a different level when drawn in the sand. Justice too is known on different levels in the realm of unchangeable truth and in the soul of a just man. So it is finally with everything else, the firmament, called heaven, that is between the waters above and those below, the gathering together of the lower waters with exposure of the dry land and the establishment of plants and trees; so too the putting in place of sun, moon and stars; so too with the animals issuing from the waters, I mean birds and fishes and monsters of the deep; so too with all animals that walk or crawl on the earth, as well as man himself, who was designed to surpass all else on earth. All these are known in one way by the angels in the Word of God, in which lie unchangeable and permanent the purposes and patterns according to which these things were made, and in another way as these things are in themselves. One knowledge is clear, the other clouded, just as the knowledge of the craftsman's design surpasses that which can be gained from the works themselves. And yet when these works are viewed as leading to praise

549

venerationemque referuntur, tamquam mane lucescit
in mentibus contemplantium.

XXX

*De senarii numeri perfectione, qui primus partium
suarum quantitate completur.*

Haec autem propter senarii numeri perfectionem
eodem die sexiens repetito sex diebus perfecta narrantur, non quia Deo fuerit necessaria mora temporum, quasi qui non potuerit creare omnia simul,
quae deinceps congruis motibus peragerent tempora; sed quia per senarium numerum est operum
significata perfectio. Numerus quippe senarius
primus completur suis partibus, id est sexta sui parte
et tertia et dimidia, quae sunt unum et duo et tria,
quae in summam ducta sex fiunt. Partes autem in
hac consideratione numerorum illae intellegendae
sunt quae quotae sint dici potest; sicut dimidia, tertia, quarta et deinceps ab aliquo numero denomina-
tae. Neque enim exempli gratia quia in novenario
numero quattuor pars aliqua eius est, ideo dici potest
quota eius sit; unum autem potest, nam nona eius
est; et tria potest, nam tertia eius est. Coniunctae
vero istae duae partes eius, nona scilicet atque tertia,
id est unum et tria, longe sunt a tota summa eius,
quod est novem. Itemque in denario quaternarius
est aliqua pars eius; sed quota sit dici non potest;
unum autem potest; nam decima pars eius est.

---

¹ See *De Musica* 5.8.16, 5.10.20; *De Genesi ad Litteram*
4.2.2–6; *De Trinitate* 4.4.7–9.

and adoration of the Creator himself, it is like
the break of day in the minds of those who contemplate them.

XXX

*On the perfect number six, the first number
which is the sum of its factors.*

Now the reason why Scripture records that the
creation was made perfect in six days, with the same
day repeated six times, is that six is a perfect number, not that any interval of time was necessary for
God, as if he could not have simultaneously created
all things, which would thenceforth by regular movements mark the successive units of time. No, the
number six is brought in to symbolize the perfection of
his works. Six, be it noted, is the first number that
is the exact sum of its factors, that is to say, its sixth,
its third and its half, that is, of one, two and three,
which when added together make six.[1] In studying
numbers in this way, factors or parts must be understood as aliquot parts like a half, a third, a fourth, and
so on, which have a whole number as denominator.
For example, though four is a part of nine, that does
not mean that we can demonstrate what part of nine
it is. The number one, however, can be so denomi-
nated, for it is a ninth, and so can three, for it is a
third. However, these two aliquot parts, the ninth
and the third, that is one and three, are far from making up when added the complete number nine. In
the same way four is part of ten, but it cannot be
named by its denominator; one however can be so

Habet et quintam, quod sunt duo; habet et dimidiam, quod sunt quinque. Sed hae tres partes eius, decima et quinta et dimidia, id est unum et duo et quinque, simul ductae non complent decem; sunt enim octo. Duodenarii vero numeri partes in summam ductae transeunt eum; habet enim duodecimam, quod est unum; habet sextam, quae sunt duo; habet quartam, quae sunt tria; habet tertiam, quae sunt quattuor; habet et dimidiam, quae sunt sex; unum autem et duo et tria et quattuor et sex non duodecim, sed amplius, id est sedecim, fiunt. Hoc breviter commemorandum putavi ad commendandam senarii numeri perfectionem, qui primus, ut dixi, partibus suis in summam redactis ipse perficitur; in quo perfecit Deus opera sua. Unde ratio numeri contemnenda non est, quae in multis sanctarum scripturarum locis quam magni aestimanda sit elucet diligenter intuentibus. Nec frustra in laudibus Dei dictum est: *Omnia in mensura et numero et pondere disposuisti.*[1]

XXXI

De die septimo, in quo plenitudo et requies commendatur.

In septimo autem die, id est eodem die septiens repetito, qui numerus etiam ipse alia ratione perfectus est, Dei requies commendatur, in qua primum sanctificatio sonat. Ita Deus noluit istum diem in

---

[1] Wisdom 11.20.
[2] Genesis 2.2–3.

named, for it is a tenth. Ten has also a fifth which is two, and a half which is five. But these three aliquot parts, the tenth, the fifth and the half, that is one, two and five, when added make not ten but eight. On the other hand the aliquot parts of twelve add up to more than twelve, for it has a twelfth which is one, a sixth which is two, a fourth which is three, a third which is four and a half which is six; but one, two, three, four and six add up, not to twelve, but to sixteen, which is too much. I have thought fit to make this brief survey in order to demonstrate the perfection of the number six, which is the first, as I have said, to be perfectly brought about by the sum of its aliquot parts. And six is the number of days in which God perfectly brought about his works. So we see that we should not belittle the theory of numbers, for its great value is eminently clear to the attentive student in many passages of the holy Scriptures. The praises of God do not for nothing include this statement: " Thou hast ordered all things by measure and number and weight."[1]

XXXI

Concerning the seventh day, whereon completeness and rest are introduced.

On the seventh day, that is on the seventh repetition of the same day—seven being a number which is itself perfect by another method of reckoning— the rest that God took is introduced,[2] and this rest is the first thing we hear of that is hallowed. We see that God did not choose to hallow this day by any

ullis suis operibus sanctificare, sed in requie sua, quae non habet vesperam; neque enim ulla creatura est, ut etiam ipsa aliter in Dei Verbo, aliter in se cognita faciat aliam velut diurnam, aliam velut vespertinam notitiam.

De septenarii porro numeri perfectione dici quidem plura possunt; sed et liber iste iam prolixus est, et vereor ne occasione comperta scientiolam nostram leviter magis quam utiliter iactare velle videamur. Habenda est itaque ratio moderationis atque gravitatis ne forte, cum de numero multum loquimur, mensuram et pondus neglegere iudicemur. Hoc itaque satis sit admonere, quod totus inpar primus numerus ternarius est, totus par quaternarius; ex quibus duobus septenarius constat. Ideo pro universo saepe ponitur, sicuti est: *Septiens cadet iustus, et resurget*; id est: Quotienscumque ceciderit, non peribit; quod non de iniquitatibus, sed de tribulationibus ad humilitatem perducentibus intellegi voluit; et: *Septiens in die laudabo te*; quod alibi alio modo dictum est: *Semper laus eius in ore meo*; et multa huius modi in divinis auctoritatibus reperiuntur, in quibus septenarius numerus, ut dixi, pro cuiusque rei universitate poni solet. Propter hoc eodem saepe numero significatur Spiritus sanctus, de quo Dominus ait: *Docebit vos omnem veritatem*. Ibi requies Dei, qua requiescitur in Deo. In toto quippe, id est in plena perfectione, requies; in parte

---

[1] Proverbs 24.16.
[2] Psalm 119.164.   Cf. *De Doctrina Christiana* 35.51.
[3] Psalm 34.1.
[4] John 16.13.   Cf. Augustine, *Sermon* 8.13.

of his works, but by his rest, which has no evening since it is not a created thing; not being known, like created things, one way in the Word of God and another way in itself, it does not give rise to a two-fold knowledge, one a daylight knowledge, as it were, the other a twilight knowledge.

Assuredly more could be said about the perfection of the number seven, but this book is already prolix and I am also in danger of appearing to take advantage of the opportunity to parade my scrap of knowledge with more vanity than profit. So I must observe moderation and gravity lest, in dwelling at length on number, I be convicted of neglecting measure and weight. Accordingly let it suffice to observe that the first odd integer is three, that four is the first even integer, and that the sum of these is seven. For this reason seven is often used to indicate universality, as in: " A righteous man will fall seven times, and will rise again," [1] meaning: However many times he may fall, he will not perish—a passage that was not meant to be taken as referring to sins, but to the kind of trouble that inculcates humility. So it is also in " Seven times a day will I praise thee," [2] which appears elsewhere in the form: " His praise shall be continually in my mouth." [3] Many such passages are found in the sacred writers, where the number seven, as I have said, is customarily employed to express universality or completeness in every sphere. For this reason the same number is often used to indicate the Holy Spirit, of whom the Lord said: " He will teach you the whole truth." [4] In this number is God's rest, the rest that we find in him. Rest, it is understood, is in a whole, that is in com-

autem labor. Ideo laboramus quamdiu ex parte
scimus, *sed cum venerit quod perfectum est, quod ex
parte est evacuabitur.* Hinc est quod etiam scripturas istas cum labore rimamur. Sancti vero angeli
quorum societati et congregationi in hac peregrinatione laboriosissima suspiramus, sicut habent per-
manendi aeternitatem, ita cognoscendi facilitatem
et requiesecndi felicitatem. Sine difficultate quippe
nos adiuvant, quoniam spiritalibus motibus puris et
liberis non laborant.

XXXII

De opinione eorum qui angelorum creationem anterio-
rem volunt esse quam mundi.

Ne quis autem contendat et dicat non sanctos angelos esse significatos in eo quod scriptum est: *Fiat lux,
et facta est lux,* sed quamlibet lucem tunc primum
factam esse corpoream aut opinetur aut doceat;
angelos autem prius esse factos non tantum ante
firmamentum quod inter aquas et aquas factum
appellatum est caelum, sed ante illud de quo dictum
est: *In principio fecit Deus caelum et terram*; atque
illud quod dictum est: *In principio,* non ita dictum
tamquam primum hoc factum sit, cum ante fecerit
angelos, sed quia omnia in sapientia fecit, quod est
Verbum eius et ipsum scriptura principium nominavit

---

[1] 1 Corinthians 13.10.
[2] Genesis 1.3.   [3] Genesis 1.1.

plete perfection; but labour is in a part. This is why we toil as long as we know only in part, "but when the perfect comes, the imperfect will pass away."[1] This is why we even labour when we search the Scriptures. But the holy angels, to whose fellowship and assemblage we aspire through this most laborious pilgrimage of ours, possess facility of knowledge and felicity of rest, along with never-ending security. Note also that they help us without themselves labouring, since their spiritual activities, being pure and free, are not laborious.

XXXII

On the opinion of those who hold that the angels were created at an earlier time than the world.

Perhaps, however, someone may object and say that the holy angels are not meant in the Scriptural words: "'Let there be light'; and there was light."[2] He may believe or teach that some material light was created then for the first time, but that the angels were made, not only before the firmament was created between the waters and called heaven, but even before what is described in the words: "In the beginning God created the heaven and the earth."[3] He may think that the words "in the beginning" are not used to mean that this was the first creation, since God had already made the angels, but to mean that he made everything by his Wisdom, which is his Word and is itself described in the Scripture as the Beginning, where he himself replied, as the Gospel

—sicut ipse in evangelio Iudaeis quaerentibus quis esset respondit se esse principium—, non e contrario referam contentionem, maxime quia hoc me delectat plurimum, quod etiam in summo exordio sancti libri geneseos trinitas commendatur. Cum enim ita dicitur: *In principio fecit Deus caelum et terram*, ut Pater fecisse intellegatur in Filio, sicut adtestatur psalmus, ubi legitur: *Quam magnificata sunt opera tua Domine! Omnia in sapientia fecisti*: convenientissime paulo post commemoratur etiam Spiritus sanctus. Cum enim dictum esset qualem terram Deus primitus fecerit, vel quam molem materiamve futurae constructionis mundi caeli et terrae nomine nuncupaverit subiciendo et addendo: *Terra autem erat invisibilis et incomposita et tenebrae erant super abyssum*, mox ut trinitatis commemoratio compleretur: *Et spiritus*, inquit, *Dei superferebatur super aquam.*

Proinde ut volet quisque accipiat, quod ita profundum est ut ad exercitationem legentium a fidei regula non abhorrentes plures possit generare sententias, dum tamen angelos sanctos in sublimibus sedibus non quidem Deo coaeternos, sed tamen de sua sempiterna et vera felicitate securos et certos

---

[1] See John 8.25 and cf. above, Book 10.24.

[2] On the possibility of eliciting more than one legitimate interpretation from a passage of Scripture, see in particular *De Doctrina Christiana* 3.27.38, *Confessions* 12.18.27, and above, Book 11.19.

[3] Psalm 104.24. Note that Augustine's interpretation of these passages is based on his belief that the preposition *in*

tells us, to the Jews, when they asked who he was, by saying that he was the Beginning.[1] I shall not challenge this view, chiefly because I am overjoyed to find the Trinity introduced at the very beginning of the holy book of Genesis.[2] The point is that Scripture says, " In the beginning God created the heaven and the earth," so that we may understand that the Father made them through the Son, as the psalm testifies when it says: " How magnificent are thy works, O Lord! In wisdom hast thou made them all." [3] Then the Holy Spirit is also most suitably mentioned a little later. For when Scripture had described what the earth was like as originally made, that is, what the mass of raw material was like which God named heaven and earth and provided for the coming construction of the world—and this description is given in the appended words, " the earth moreover was invisible and inchoate, and darkness was over the deep "—, then, in order to complete the account of the Trinity, it says: " And the Spirit of God was moving above the water." [4]

Therefore let each interpret these words as he will. They are so profound that, being designed for the purpose of training readers to use their wits, they can give birth to several different views that are not inconsistent with the rule of faith. There is one proviso, that no one must put the fact in doubt that the holy angels, though not coeternal with God in their heavenly abodes, are yet assured and certain

is to be taken in the sense of " through " or " by means of." The Latin translations of the Bible do, in fact, frequently use *in* with this sense. The usage is Hebrew in origin.
  [4] Genesis 1.1–2. Cf. *De Genesi ad Litteram* 1.6.12.

esse nemo ambigat. Ad quorum societatem pertinere parvulos suos Dominus docens non solum
illud ait: *Erunt aequales angelis Dei;* verum ipsi
quoque angeli qua contemplatione fruantur ostendit
ubi ait: *Videte ne contemnatis unum ex pusillis istis;*
dico enim vobis quia angeli eorum in caelis semper vident
faciem Patris mei qui in caelis est.

XXXIII

De duabus angelorum societatibus diversis atque dis-
paribus, quae non incongrue intelleguntur lucis et
tenebrarum nominibus nuncupatae.

PECCASSE autem quosdam angelos et in huius
mundi ima detrusos, qui eis velut carcer est usque ad
futuram in die iudicii ultimam damnationem, apostolus Petrus apertissime ostendit dicens quod Deus
angelis peccantibus non pepercerit, sed carceribus
caliginis inferi retrudens tradiderit in iudicio puniendos reservari. Inter hos ergo et illos Deum vel
praescientia vel opere divisisse quis dubitet? Illos-
que lucem merito appellari quis contradicat? Quando quidem nos adhuc in fide viventes et eorum
aequalitatem adhuc sperantes, utique nondum
tenentes iam lux dicti ab apostolo sumus: *Fuistis*
enim, inquit, *aliquando tenebrae, nunc autem lux in*

---

[1] Matthew 22.30.
[2] Matthew 18.10.
[3] 2 Peter 2.4.

of their real and everlasting felicity. When the Lord instructs us that his little ones belong to their company he not only says: " They shall be equal to the angels of God," [1] but he also reveals to us what sort of contemplation is enjoyed by the angels themselves with the words: " See to it that you do not despise one of these little ones; for I tell you that in heaven their angels always behold the face of my Father who is in heaven." [2]

XXXIII

On the two distinct and opposing angelic communities,
which are not inappropriately understood as
meant by the terms light and darkness.

THAT certain angels did sin and were thrust to the lowest depths of this world, which serves as their prison until the final damnation that awaits them on the day of judgement, is made clear in the plainest terms by the apostle Peter when he says that God did not spare the angels when they sinned, but thrust them away into dungeons of nether gloom and committed them to be kept for punishment until the judgement.[3] Consequently who can doubt that God, both by foreknowledge and by action, made a distinction between them and the holy angels? And who would dispute that the latter are deservedly designated light? For even we who still live by faith and are still only hoping for equality with them, and certainly do not as yet possess it, are already called light by the Apostle. " For," he says, " once you were darkness, but now you are light in the

Domino. Istos vero desertores tenebras aptissime nuncupari profecto advertunt qui peiores esse hominibus infidelibus sive intellegunt sive credunt.

Quapropter, etsi alia lux in isto huius libri loco intellegenda est ubi legimus: *Dixit Deus: Fiat lux, et facta est lux,* et aliae tenebrae significatae sunt in eo quod scriptum est: *Divisit Deus inter lucem et tenebras,* nos tamen has duas angelicas societates, unam fruentem Deo, alteram tumentem typho; unam cui dicitur: *Adorate eum omnes angeli eius,* aliam cuius princeps dicit: *Haec omnia tibi dabo, si prostratus adoraveris me;* unam Dei sancto amore flagrantem, alteram propriae celsitudinis inmundo amore fumantem; et quoniam, sicut scriptum est, *Deus superbis resistit, humilibus autem dat gratiam,* illam in caelis caelorum habitantem, istam inde deiectam in hoc infimo aerio caelo tumultuantem; illam luminosa pietate tranquillam, istam tenebrosis cupiditatibus turbulentam; illam Dei nutu clementer subvenientem, iuste ulciscentem, istam suo fastu subdendi et nocendi libidine exaestuantem; illam, ut quantum vult consulat, Dei bonitati ministram, istam, ne quantum vult noceat, Dei potestate frenatam; illam huic inludentem, ut nolens prosit persecutionibus suis, hanc illi invidentem, cum peregrinos colligit

---

[1] Ephesians 5.8.   [2] Genesis 1.3–4.
[3] Psalm 148.2.   [4] Matthew 4.9.
[5] James 4.6; 1 Peter 5.5.
[6] On the air as the region assigned to demons for their dwelling place, see above, Book 8.14.

Lord." [1] But as for the apostate angels, such men as either know or believe that those angels are worse than unbelievers assuredly take note that they are most fittingly called by the name of darkness.

For this reason, even if another kind of light is to be understood in the passage of this book where we read: " God said, ' Let there be light '; and there was light," and another kind of darkness is meant in the passage: " God separated the light from the darkness," [2] still for us there are these two communities of angels, one enjoying God, the other puffed up with pride. To the one it is said: " Praise him, all his angels," [3] while the prince of the other says: " All these will I give you, if you will fall down and worship me." [4] One is on fire with a holy love for God, the other reeks with the filthy love of its own exaltation. And since, as it is written, " God opposes the proud, but gives grace to the humble," [5] one dwells in the heaven of heavens, the other cast down from thence, lives amidst riot and disorder in this lowest heaven of ours, a heaven of air; [6] one is calm in the brightness of piety, the other is a seething mass of dark passions; one at a sign from God brings merciful help or just vengeance, the other in its arrogance rages and boils over with a passion for dominating and hurting; one, in order to give as much guidance as it has the will to give, puts itself at the service of God's goodness, the other is restrained by the bridle of God's power from doing as much harm as it has the will to do. The former makes sport of the latter so that, in spite of itself, it confers benefit by its persecutions, the latter is envious of the former when it gathers in its pilgrims. Of these

suos,—nos ergo has duas societates angelicas inter
se dispares atque contrarias, unam et natura bonam
et voluntate rectam, aliam vero natura bonam, sed
voluntate perversam, aliis manifestioribus divinarum
scripturarum testimoniis declaratas quod etiam in
hoc libro cui nomen est genesis, lucis tenebrarumque
vocabulis significatas existimavimus, etiamsi aliud
hoc loco sensit forte qui scripsit, non est inutiliter
obscuritas huius pertractata sententiae quia, etsi
voluntatem auctoris libri huius indagare nequivimus,
a regula tamen fidei, quae per alias eiusdem auctoritatis sacras litteras satis fidelibus nota est, non
abhorruimus.

Etsi enim corporalia hic commemorata sunt opera
Dei, habent procul dubio nonnullam similitudinem
spiritalium, secundum quam dicit apostolus: *Omnes
enim vos filii lucis estis et filii diei, non sumus noctis neque
tenebrarum.* Si autem hoc sensit etiam ille qui scripsit, ad perfectiorem disputationis finem nostra pervenit intentio, ut homo Dei tam eximiae divinaeque
sapientiae, immo per eum Spiritus Dei in comme-
morandis operibus Dei, quae omnia sexto die dicit
esse perfecta, nullo modo angelos praetermisisse
credatur, sive *in principio* quia primo fecit, sive, quod
convenientius intellegitur, *in principio* quia in Verbo
unigenito fecit, scriptum sit: *In principio fecit Deus*

---

[1] 1 Thessalonians 5.5.
[2] Genesis 1.1.

two dissimilar and opposite communities of angels, one is both naturally good and willingly upright, while the other is naturally good, it is true, but wilfully perverse. They are so described by the testimony of other and plainer passages of divine Scriptures, and I have adopted the view that they are also referred to symbolically in the book of Genesis under the names light and darkness. It is possible that the author had some other thought in mind in this passage, yet even so it has been worth while to deal at some length with the problem raised by this view, for though we may have failed to penetrate the intention of the writer of this book, still it has not caused us to dissent from the rule of faith, which is quite well known to the faithful from other sacred writings of comparable authority.

It is true that the works of God here mentioned are material, but they undoubtedly bear some resemblance to spiritual things, as suggested by the words of the Apostle: " For you are all sons of light and sons of the day; we are not of the night nor of darkness." [1] Now if this was also the opinion of the writer of Genesis, my effort in this debate has reached a more satisfactory result, to render it absolutely incredible that a man of God, of such exceptional and divine wisdom—nay more, that the Spirit of God working through him—in recording the works of God, all of which he says were completed on the sixth day, should have omitted the angels, whether in the words: " In the beginning God created the heaven and the earth " [2] the expression " in the beginning " is used because he made these first or—a more suitable interpretation—" by the beginning " be-

565

caelum et terram; quibus nominibus universalis est
significata creatura, vel spiritalis et corporalis, quod
est credibilius, vel magnae duae mundi partes quibus
omnia quae creata sunt continentur, ut primitus eam
totam proponeret ac deinde partes eius secundum
mysticum dierum numerum exsequeretur.

XXXIV

*De eo quod quidam putant in conditione firmamenti
aquarum discretarum nomine angelos significatos,
et quod quidam aquas aestimant non creatas.*

Quamquam nonnulli putaverint aquarum nomine
significatos quodam modo populos angelorum et hoc
esse quod dictum est: *Fiat firmamentum inter aquam
et aquam*, ut supra firmamentum angeli intellegantur,
infra vero vel aquae istae visibiles vel malorum
angelorum multitudo vel omnium hominum gentes.
Quod si ita est, non illic apparet ubi facti sint angeli,
sed ubi discreti; quamvis et aquas, quod perversissi-
mae atque impiae vanitatis est, negent quidam factas
a Deo, quoniam nusquam scriptum est: Dixit Deus:
Fiant aquae. Quod possunt simili vanitate etiam
de terra dicere; nusquam enim legitur: Dixit Deus:

---

[1] Genesis 1.6. This interpretation is attributed to Origen
by Epiphanius of Salamis in his letter to John of Jerusalem.
See St. Jerome's translation of this letter, Letter 51.5 in the
corpus of Jerome's correspondence. Augustine himself implies his acceptance of this interpretation in *Confessions*
13.15.18 and 13.32.47. But he later reconsidered and withdrew this acceptance. See *Retractations* 2.6.2.

cause he made them through his only begotten Word. These terms heaven and earth refer to the whole creation, whether they designate the spiritual and material creation, and this is preferable, or the two great divisions of the universe in which are situated all created things. On this interpretation, the writer first exhibits the whole and then enumerates the parts in detail, assigning them to the mystical number of days.

XXXIV

On two opinions, first that the language used of the waters sundered when the firmament was established refers to the angels, second that the waters were not created.

Some have thought that the word waters somehow described the angelic hosts and that this is the meaning of the sentence: " Let there be a firmament be-between water and water." [1] On this interpretation the angels are supposed to be above the firmament, and below it either the visible waters, or the multitude of bad angels, or the nations of all mankind. If this is so, it is not revealed here at what point the angels were created, but at what point they became divided. There are some, however, who deny with a folly that is most perverse and irreligious that the waters were also made by God, on the grounds that it is nowhere written: " God said, ' Let there be waters.' " They could make the same remark with equal folly about the earth, for nowhere do we read: " God said, ' Let there be earth.' " " But," say

Fiat terra. Sed, inquiunt, scriptum est: *In principio fecit Deus caelum et terram.* Illic ergo et aqua
intellegenda est; uno enim nomine utrumque con-
prehensum est. Nam *ipsius et mare,* sicut in psalmo
legitur, *et ipse fecit illud, et aridam terram manus eius
finxerunt.*

Sed hi qui in nomine aquarum quae super caelos
sunt, angelos intellegi volunt, ponderibus elementorum moventur et ideo non putant aquarum fluvi-
dam gravemque naturam in superioribus mundi locis
potuisse constitui; qui secundum rationes suas, si
ipsi hominem facere possent, non ei pituitam, quod
Graece φλέγμα dicitur et tamquam in elementis corporis nostri aquarum vicem obtinet, in capite pone-
rent. Ibi enim sedes est phlegmatis, secundum Dei
opus utique aptissime, secundum istorum autem con-
iecturam tam absurde ut, si hoc nesciremus et in hoc
libro similiter scriptum esset quod Deus umorem
fluvidum et frigidum ac per hoc gravem in superiore
omnibus ceteris humani corporis parte posuerit, isti
trutinatores elementorum nequaquam crederent, et
si auctoritati eiusdem scripturae subditi essent, aliquid aliud ex hoc intellegendum esse censerent.

Sed quoniam, si diligenter singula scrutemur atque
tractemus quae in illo divino libro de constitutione
mundi scripta sunt, et multa dicenda et a proposito
instituti operis longe digrediendum est, iamque de
duabus istis diversis inter se atque contrariis

---

[1] Psalm 95.5.

they, " it is written, ' In the beginning God created the heaven and the earth.' " Well then, the water must also be understood in this place, for both land and water are included in the word earth. For " the sea is his," as the psalm says, " and he made it; and his hands formed the dry land." [1]

But those who by the words " waters that are above the heavens " want us to understand " angels " are disturbed by the relative weights of the elements and therefore do not think that water, which is naturally fluid and heavy, could have been planted in the higher regions of the universe. According to their reasoning, if they themselves could make a man, they would not place in his head the pituitary secretion which the Greeks call *phlegma* and which corresponds to water among the constituent elements of our body. For the head is the seat of phlegm, and most fittingly chosen without a doubt, for that is implied in a work of God; but so absurdly chosen, their view implies, that if we were ignorant of the fact and if there were a corresponding statement in this book that God placed a cold and consequently heavy fluid in the part of the human body that is higher than all the others, these balancers of elemental weights would absolutely refuse to believe it, or if they were overcome by the authority of the aforesaid Scripture, they would maintain that the meaning must be something else.

But if we were to search into and examine with care word by word everything written in that divine book on the formation of the world, not only would there be much to say, but it would be necessary to make a long digression from the original plan of my

societatibus angelorum, in quibus sunt quaedam exordia duarum etiam in rebus humanis civitatum, de quibus deinceps dicere institui, quantum satis esse visum est disputavimus, hunc quoque librum aliquando claudamus.

work. I have already devoted as much discussion as I saw fit to these two communities of angels which differ from each other and are opposites. In them we see a kind of prologue to the two cities that are also found in the history of man, a subject that I mean to discuss next; and now at last let us bring this book too to a close.

Printed in Great Britain by
Richard Clay (The Chaucer Press), Ltd.,
Bungay, Suffolk

THE LOEB CLASSICAL LIBRARY

VOLUMES ALREADY PUBLISHED

Latin Authors

AMMIANUS MARECLLINUS. Translated by J. C. Rolfe. 3 Vols.

APULEIUS: THE GOLDEN ASS (METAMORPHOSES). W. Adlington (1566). Revised by S. Gaselee.

ST. AUGUSTINE: CITY OF GOD. 7 Vols. Vol. I. G. E. McCracken Vol. II. W. M. Green. Vol. III. D. Wiesen. Vol. IV. P. Levine. Vol. V. E. M. Sanford and W. M. Green. Vol. VI. W. C. Greene.

ST. AUGUSTINE, CONFESSIONS OF. W. Watts (1631). 2 Vols.

ST. AUGUSTINE, SELECT LETTERS. J. H. Baxter.

AUSONIUS. H. G. Evelyn White. 2 Vols.

BEDE. J. E. King. 2 Vols.

BOETHIUS: TRACTS and DE CONSOLATIONE PHILOSOPHIAE. Rev. H. F. Stewart and E. K. Rand.

CAESAR: ALEXANDRIAN, AFRICAN and SPANISH WARS. A. G. Way.

CAESAR: CIVIL WARS. A. G. Peskett.

CAESAR: GALLIC WAR. H. J. Edwards.

CATO: DE RE RUSTICA; VARRO: DE RE RUSTICA. H. B. Ash and W. D. Hooper.

CATULLUS. F. W. Cornish; TIBULLUS. J. B. Postgate; PERVIGILIUM VENERIS. J. W. Mackail.

CELSUS: DE MEDICINA. W. G. Spencer. 3 Vols.

CICERO: BRUTUS, and ORATOR. G. L. Hendrickson and H. M. Hubbell.

[CICERO]: AD HERENNIUM. H. Caplan.

CICERO: DE ORATORE, etc. 2 Vols. Vol. I. DE ORATORE, Books I. and II. E. W. Sutton and H. Rackham. Vol. II. DE ORATORE, Book III. De Fato; Paradoxa Stoicorum; De Partitione Oratoria. H. Rackham.

CICERO: DE FINIBUS. H. Rackham.

CICERO: DE INVENTIONE, etc. H. M. Hubbell.

CICERO: DE NATURA DEORUM and ACADEMICA. H. Rackham.

CICERO: DE OFFICIIS. Walter Miller.

CICERO: DE REPUBLICA and DE LEGIBUS; SOMNIUM SCIPIONIS. Clinton W. Keyes.

CICERO: DE SENECTUTE, DE AMICITIA, DE DIVINATIONE. W. A. Falconer.

CICERO: IN CATILINAM, PRO FLACCO, PRO MURENA, PRO SULLA. Louis E. Lord.

CICERO: LETTERS to ATTICUS. E. O. Winstedt. 3 Vols.

CICERO: LETTERS TO HIS FRIENDS. W. Glynn Williams. 3 Vols.

CICERO: PHILIPPICS. W. C. A. Ker.

CICERO: PRO ARCHIA POST REDITUM, DE DOMO, DE HARUSPICUM RESPONSIS, PRO PLANCIO. N. H. Watts.

CICERO: PRO CAECINA, PRO LEGE MANILIA, PRO CLUENTIO, PRO RABIRIO. H. Grose Hodge.

CICERO: PRO CAELIO, DE PROVINCIIS CONSULARIBUS, PRO BALBO. R. Gardner.

CICERO: PRO MILONE, IN PISONEM, PRO SCAURO, PRO FONTEIO, PRO RABIRIO POSTUMO, PRO MARCELLO, PRO LIGARIO, PRO REGE DEIOTARO. N. H. Watts.

CICERO: PRO QUINCTIO, PRO ROSCIO AMERINO, PRO ROSCIO COMOEDO, CONTRA RULLUM. J. H. Freese.

CICERO: PRO SESTIO, IN VATINIUM. R. Gardner.

CICERO: TUSCULAN DISPUTATIONS. J. E. King.

CICERO: VERRINE ORATIONS. L. H. G. Greenwood. 2 Vols.

CLAUDIAN. M. Platnauer. 2 Vols.

COLUMELLA: DE RE RUSTICA. DE ARBORIBUS. H. B. Ash, E. S. Forster and E. Heffner. 3 Vols.

CURTIUS, Q.: HISTORY OF ALEXANDER. J. C. Rolfe. 2 Vols.

FLORUS. E. S. Forster; and CORNELIUS NEPOS. J. C. Rolfe.

FRONTINUS: STRATAGEMS and AQUEDUCTS. C. E. Bennett and M. B. McElwain.

FRONTO: CORRESPONDENCE. C. R. Haines. 2 Vols.

GELLIUS, J. C. Rolfe. 3 Vols.

HORACE: ODES AND EPODES. C. E. Bennett.

HORACE: SATIRES, EPISTLES, ARS POETICA. H. R. Fairclough.

JEROME: SELECTED LETTERS. F. A. Wright.

JUVENAL and PERSIUS. G. G. Ramsay.

LIVY. B. O. Foster, F. G. Moore, Evan T. Sage, and A. C. Schlesinger and R. M. Geer (General Index). 14 Vols.

LUCAN. J. D. Duff.

LUCRETIUS. W. H. D. Rouse.

MARTIAL. W. C. A. Ker. 2 Vols.

MINOR LATIN POETS: from PUBLILIUS SYRUS to RUTILIUS NAMATIANUS, including GRATTIUS, CALPURNIUS SICULUS, NEMESIANUS, AVIANUS, and others with " Aetna " and the " Phoenix." J. Wight Duff and Arnold M. Duff.

OVID: THE ART OF LOVE and OTHER POEMS. J. H. Mozley.

OVID: FASTI. Sir James G. Frazer.

OVID: HEROIDES and AMORES. Grant Showerman.

OVID: METAMORPHOSES. F. J. Miller. 2 Vols.

OVID: TRISTIA and EX PONTO. A. L. Wheeler.

PERSIUS. Cf. JUVENAL.

PETRONIUS. M. Heseltine; SENECA; APOCOLOCYNTOSIS.
W. H. D. Rouse.

PHAEDRUS AND BABRIUS (Greek). B. E. Perry.

PLAUTUS. Paul Nixon. 5 Vols.

PLINY: LETTERS. Melmoth's Translation revised by W. M. L.
Hutchinson. 2 Vols.

PLINY: NATURAL HISTORY.
10 Vols. Vols. I.–V. and IX. H. Rackham. Vols. VI.–
VIII. W. H. S. Jones. Vol. X. D. E. Eichholz.

PROPERTIUS. H. E. Butler.

PRUDENTIUS. H. J. Thomson. 2 Vols.

QUINTILIAN. H. E. Butler. 4 Vols.

REMAINS OF OLD LATIN. E. H. Warmington. 4 Vols. Vol. I.
(ENNIUS AND CAECILIUS.) Vol. II. (LIVIUS, NAEVIUS,
PACUVIUS, ACCIUS.) Vol. III. (LUCILIUS and LAWS OF XII
TABLES.) Vol. IV. (ARCHAIC INSCRIPTIONS.)

SALLUST. J. C. Rolfe.

SCRIPTORES HISTORIAE AUGUSTAE. D. Magie. 3 Vols.

SENECA: APOCOLOCYNTOSIS. Cf. PETRONIUS.

SENECA: EPISTULAE MORALES. R. M. Gummere. 3 Vols.

SENECA: MORAL ESSAYS. J. W. Basore. 3 Vols.

SENECA: TRAGEDIES. F. J. Miller. 2 Vols.

SIDONIUS: POEMS and LETTERS. W. B. ANDERSON. 2 Vols.

SILIUS ITALICUS. J. D. Duff. 2 Vols.

STATIUS. J. H. Mozley. 2 Vols.

SUETONIUS. J. C. Rolfe. 2 Vols.

TACITUS: DIALOGUES. Sir Wm. Peterson. AGRICOLA and
GERMANIA. Maurice Hutton.

TACITUS: HISTORIES AND ANNALS. C. H. Moore and J. Jackson.
4 Vols.

TERENCE. John Sargeaunt. 2 Vols.

TERTULLIAN: APOLOGIA and DE SPECTACULIS. T. R. Glover.
MINUCIUS FELIX. G. H. Rendall.

VALERIUS FLACCUS. J. H. Mozley.

VARRO: DE LINGUA LATINA. R. G. Kent. 2 Vols.

VELLEIUS PATERCULUS and RES GESTAE DIVI AUGUSTI. F. W.
Shipley.

VIRGIL. H. R. Fairclough. 2 Vols.

VITRUVIUS: DE ARCHITECTURA. F. Granger. 2 Vols.

Greek Authors

ACHILLES TATIUS. S. Gaselee.

AELIAN: ON THE NATURE OF ANIMALS. A. F. Scholfield. 3 Vols.

AENEAS TACTICUS, ASCLEPIODOTUS and ONASANDER. The Illinois Greek Club.

AESCHINES. C. D. Adams.

AESCHYLUS. H. Weir Smyth. 2 Vols.

ALCIPHRON, AELIAN, PHILOSTRATUS: LETTERS. A. R. Benner and F. H. Fobes.

ANDOCIDES, ANTIPHON, Cf. MINOR ATTIC ORATORS.

APOLLODORUS. Sir James G. Frazer. 2 Vols.

APOLLONIUS RHODIUS. R. C. Seaton.

THE APOSTOLIC FATHERS. Kirsopp Lake. 2 Vols.

APPIAN: ROMAN HISTORY. Horace White. 4 Vols.

ARATUS. Cf. CALLIMACHUS.

ARISTOPHANES. Benjamin Bickley Rogers. 3 Vols. Verse trans.

ARISTOTLE: ART OF RHETORIC. J. H. Freese.

ARISTOTLE: ATHENIAN CONSTITUTION, EUDEMIAN ETHICS, VICES AND VIRTUES. H. Rackham.

ARISTOTLE: GENERATION OF ANIMALS. A. L. Peck.

ARISTOTLE: HISTORIA ANIMALIUM. A. L. Peck. Vol. I.

ARISTOTLE: METAPHYSICS. H. Tredennick. 2 Vols.

ARISTOTLE: METEOROLOGICA. H. D. P. Lee.

ARISTOTLE: MINOR WORKS. W. S. Hett. On Colours, On Things Heard, On Physiognomies, On Plants, On Marvellous Things Heard, Mechanical Problems, On Indivisible Lines, On Situations and Names of Winds, On Melissus, Xenophanes, and Gorgias.

ARISTOTLE: NICOMACHEAN ETHICS. H. Rackham.

ARISTOTLE: OECONOMICA and MAGNA MORALIA. G. C. Armstrong; (with Metaphysics, Vol. II.).

ARISTOTLE: ON THE HEAVENS. W. K. C. Guthrie.

ARISTOTLE: ON THE SOUL. PARVA NATURALIA. ON BREATH. W. S. Hett.

ARISTOTLE: CATEGORIES, ON INTERPRETATION, PRIOR ANALYTICS. H. P. Cooke and H. Tredennick.

ARISTOTLE: POSTERIOR ANALYTICS, TOPICS. H. Tredennick and E. S. Forster.

ARISTOTLE: ON SOPHISTICAL REFUTATIONS.
On Coming to be and Passing Away, On the Cosmos. E. S. Forster and D. J. Furley.

ARISTOTLE: PARTS OF ANIMALS. A. L. Peck; MOTION AND PROGRESSION OF ANIMALS. E. S. Forster.

4

ARISTOTLE: PHYSICS. Rev. P. Wicksteed and F. M. Cornford. 2 Vols.

ARISTOTLE: POETICS and LONGINUS. W. Hamilton Fyfe; DEMETRIUS ON STYLE. W. Rhys Roberts.

ARISTOTLE: POLITICS. H. Rackham.

ARISTOTLE: PROBLEMS. W. S. Hett. 2 Vols.

ARISTOTLE: RHETORICA AD ALEXANDRUM (with PROBLEMS. Vol. 11.) H. Rackham.

ARRIAN: HISTORY OF ALEXANDER and INDICA. Rev. E. Iliffe Robson. 2 Vols.

ATHENAEUS: DEIPNOSOPHISTAE. C. B. GULICK. 7 Vols.

BABRIUS AND PHAEDRUS (Latin). B. E. Perry.

ST. BASIL: LETTERS. R. J. Deferrari. 4 Vols.

CALLIMACHUS: FRAGMENTS. C. A. Trypanis.

CALLIMACHUS, Hymns and Epigrams, and LYCOPHRON. A. W. Mair; ARATUS. G. R. MAIR.

CLEMENT of ALEXANDRIA. Rev. G. W. Butterworth.

COLLUTHUS. Cf. OPPIAN.

DAPHNIS AND CHLOE. Thornley's Translation revised by J. M. Edmonds; and PARTHENIUS. S. Gaselee.

DEMOSTHENES I.: OLYNTHIACS, PHILIPPICS and MINOR ORATIONS. I.-XVII. AND XX. J. H. Vince.

DEMOSTHENES II.: DE CORONA and DE FALSA LEGATIONE. C. A. Vince and J. H. Vince.

DEMOSTHENES III.: MEIDIAS, ANDROTION, ARISTOCRATES, TIMOCRATES and ARISTOGEITON, I. AND II. J. H. Vince.

DEMOSTHENES IV.-VI.: PRIVATE ORATIONS and IN NEAERAM. A. T. Murray.

DEMOSTHENES VII.: FUNERAL SPEECH, EROTIC ESSAY, EXORDIA and LETTERS. N. W. and N. J. DeWitt.

DIO CASSIUS: ROMAN HISTORY. E. Cary. 9 Vols.

DIO CHRYSOSTOM. J. W. Cohoon and H. Lamar Crosby. 5 Vols.

DIODORUS SICULUS. 12 Vols. Vols. I.-VI. C. H. Oldfather. Vol. VII. C. L. Sherman. Vol. VIII. C. B. Welles. Vols. IX. and X. R. M. Geer. Vols. XI.-XII. F. Walton, General Index, R. M. Geer.

DIOGENES LAERTIUS. R. D. Hicks. 2 Vols.

DIONYSIUS OF HALICARNASSUS: ROMAN ANTIQUITIES. Spelman's translation revised by E. Cary. 7 Vols.

EPICTETUS. W. A. Oldfather. 2 Vols.

EURIPIDES. A. S. Way. 4 Vols. Verse trans.

EUSEBIUS: ECCLESIASTICAL HISTORY. Kirsopp Lake and J. E. L. Oulton. 2 Vols.

GALEN: ON THE NATURAL FACULTIES. A. J. Brock.

THE GREEK ANTHOLOGY. W. R. Paton. 5 Vols.

GREEK ELEGY AND IAMBUS with the ANACREONTEA. J. M. Edmonds. 2 Vols.

THE GREEK BUCOLIC POETS (THEOCRITUS, BION, MOSCHUS). J. M. Edmonds.

GREEK MATHEMATICAL WORKS. Ivor Thomas. 2 Vols.

HERODES. Cf. THEOPHRASTUS: CHARACTERS.

HERODOTUS. A. D. Godley. 4 Vols.

HESIOD AND THE HOMERIC HYMNS. H. G. Evelyn White.

HIPPOCRATES and the FRAGMENTS OF HERACLEITUS. W. H. S. Jones and E. T. Withington. 4 Vols.

HOMER: ILIAD. A. T. Murray. 2 Vols.

HOMER: ODYSSEY. A. T. Murray. 2 Vols.

ISAEUS. E. W. Forster.

ISOCRATES. George Norlin and LaRue Van Hook. 3 Vols.

ST. JOHN DAMASCENE: BARLAAM AND IOASAPH. Rev. G. R. Woodward, Harold Mattingly and D. M. Lang.

JOSEPHUS. 9 Vols. Vols. I.-IV.; H. Thackeray. Vol. V.; H. Thackeray and R. Marcus. Vols. VI.-VII.; R. Marcus. Vol. VIII.; R. Marcus and Allen Wikgren. Vol. IX. L. H. Feldman.

JULIAN. Wilmer Cave Wright. 3 Vols.

LUCIAN. 8 Vols. Vols. I.-V. A. M. Harmon. Vol. VI. K. Kilburn. Vols. VII.-VIII. M. D. Macleod.

LYCOPHRON. Cf. CALLIMACHUS.

LYRA GRAECA. J. M. Edmonds. 3 Vols.

LYSIAS. W. R. M. Lamb.

MANETHO. W. G. Waddell: PTOLEMY: TETRABIBLOS. F. E. Robbins.

MARCUS AURELIUS. C. R. Haines.

MENANDER. F. G. Allinson.

MINOR ATTIC ORATORS (ANTIPHON, ANDOCIDES, LYCURGUS, DEMADES, DINARCHUS, HYPERIDES). K. J. Maidment and J. O. Burtt. 2 Vols.

NONNOS: DIONYSIACA. W. H. D. Rouse. 3 Vols.

OPPIAN, COLLUTHUS, TRYPHIODORUS. A. W. Mair.

PAPYRI. NON-LITERARY SELECTIONS. A. S. Hunt and C. C. Edgar. 2 Vols. LITERARY SELECTIONS (Poetry). D. L. Page.

PARTHENIUS. Cf. DAPHNIS and CHLOE.

PAUSANIAS: DESCRIPTION OF GREECE. W. H. S. Jones. 4 Vols. and Companion Vol. arranged by R. E. Wycherley.

PHILO. 10 Vols. Vols. I.-V.; F. H. Colson and Rev. G. H. Whitaker. Vols. VI.-IX.; F. H. Colson. Vol. X. F. H. Colson and the Rev. J. W. Earp.

PHILO: two supplementary Vols. (*Translation only.*) Ralph Marcus.

PHILOSTRATUS: THE LIFE OF APOLLONIUS OF TYANA. F. C. Conybeare. 2 Vols.

PHILOSTRATUS: IMAGINES; CALLISTRATUS: DESCRIPTIONS. A. Fairbanks.

PHILOSTRATUS and EUNAPIUS: LIVES OF THE SOPHISTS. Wilmer Cave Wright.

PINDAR. Sir J. E. Sandys.

PLATO: CHARMIDES, ALCIBIADES, HIPPARCHUS, THE LOVERS, THEAGES, MINOS and EPINOMIS. W. R. M. Lamb.

PLATO: CRATYLUS, PARMENIDES, GREATER HIPPIAS, LESSER HIPPIAS. H. N. Fowler.

PLATO: EUTHYPHRO, APOLOGY, CRITO, PHAEDO, PHAEDRUS. H. N. Fowler.

PLATO: LACHES, PROTAGORAS, MENO, EUTHYDEMUS. W. R. M. Lamb.

PLATO: LAWS. Rev. R. G. Bury. 2 Vols.

PLATO: LYSIS, SYMPOSIUM, GORGIAS. W. R. M. Lamb.

PLATO: REPUBLIC. Paul Shorey. 2 Vols.

PLATO: STATESMAN, PHILEBUS. H. N. Fowler; ION. W. R. M. Lamb.

PLATO: THEAETETUS and SOPHIST. H. N. Fowler.

PLATO: TIMAEUS, CRITIAS, CLITOPHO, MENEXENUS, EPISTULAE. Rev. R. G. Bury.

PLOTINUS: A. H. Armstrong. Vols. I.–III.

PLUTARCH: MORALIA. 15 Vols. Vols. I.–V. F. C. Babbitt. Vol. VI. W. C. Helmbold. Vols. VII. and XIV. P. H. De Lacy and B. Einarson. Vol. IX. E. L. Minar, Jr., F. H. Sandbach, W. C. Helmbold. Vol. X. H. N. Fowler. Vol. XI. L. Pearson and F. H. Sandbach. Vol. XII. H. Cherniss and W. C. Helmbold.

PLUTARCH: THE PARALLEL LIVES. B. Perrin. 11 Vols.

POLYBIUS. W. R. Paton. 6 Vols.

PROCOPIUS: HISTORY OF THE WARS. H. B. Dewing. 7 Vols.

PTOLEMY: TETRABIBLOS. Cf. MANETHO.

QUINTUS SMYRNAEUS. A. S. Way. Verse trans.

SEXTUS EMPIRICUS. Rev. R. G. Bury. 4 Vols.

SOPHOCLES. F. Storr. 2 Vols. Verse trans.

STRABO: GEOGRAPHY. Horace L. Jones. 8 Vols.

THEOPHRASTUS: CHARACTERS. J. M. Edmonds. HERODES, etc. A. D. Knox.

THEOPHRASTUS: ENQUIRY INTO PLANTS. Sir Arthur Hort, Bart. 2 Vols.

THUCYDIDES. C. F. Smith. 4 Vols.

TRYPHIODORUS. Cf. OPPIAN.

XENOPHON: CYROPAEDIA. Walter Miller. 2 Vols.

XENOPHON: HELLENICA, ANABASIS, APOLOGY, and SYMPOSIUM. C. L. Brownson and O. J. Todd. 3 Vols.

XENOPHON: MEMORABILIA and OECONOMICUS. E. C. Marchant.

XENOPHON: SCRIPTA MINORA. E. C. Marchant and G. W. Bowersock.

DESCRIPTIVE PROSPECTUS ON APPLICATION

London   WILLIAM HEINEMANN LTD
Cambridge, Mass.   HARVARD UNIVERSITY PRESS